甘々と稲妻

4

Sweetness & Lightning
Gido Amagakure

雨隠ギド

contents

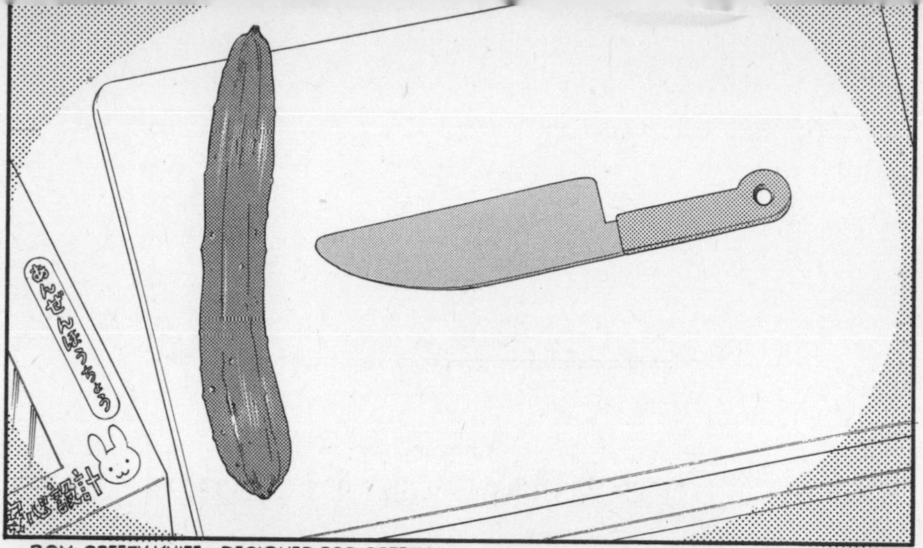
あんぜんほうちょう
心設計
BOX: SAFETY KNIFE - DESIGNED FOR SAFETY

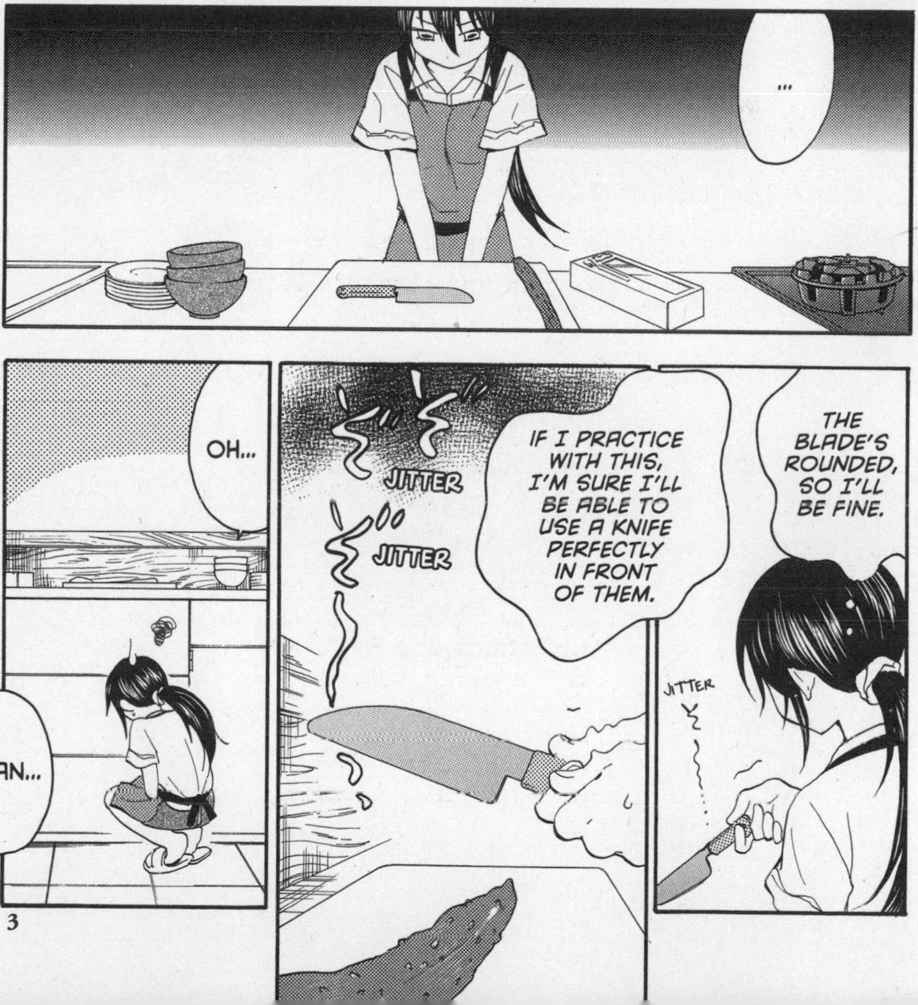
...
THE BLADE'S ROUNDED, SO I'LL BE FINE.
JITTER
IF I PRACTICE WITH THIS, I'M SURE I'LL BE ABLE TO USE A KNIFE PERFECTLY IN FRONT OF THEM.
JITTER
JITTER
OH...
...MAN...

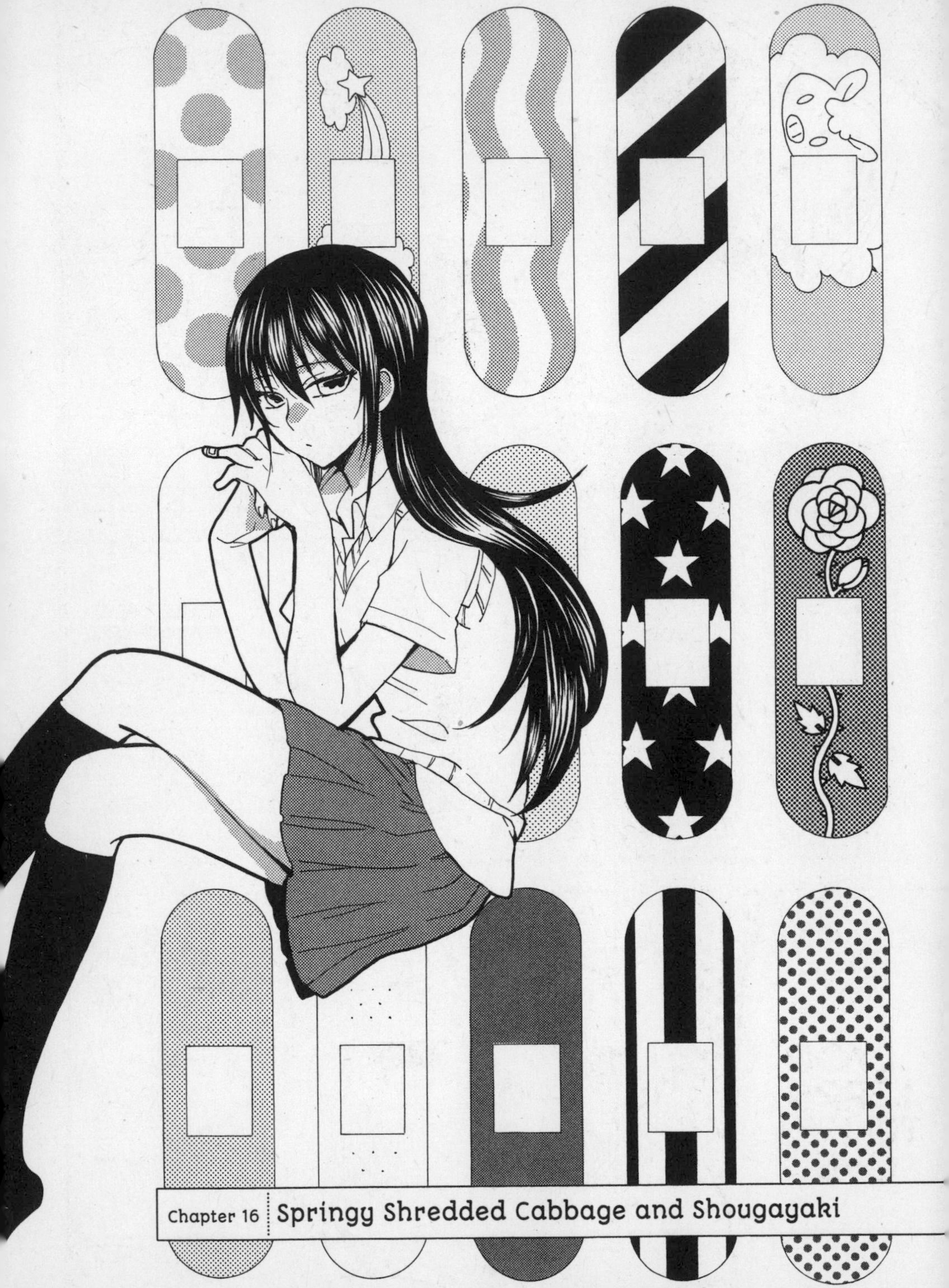

Chapter 16 Springy Shredded Cabbage and Shougayaki

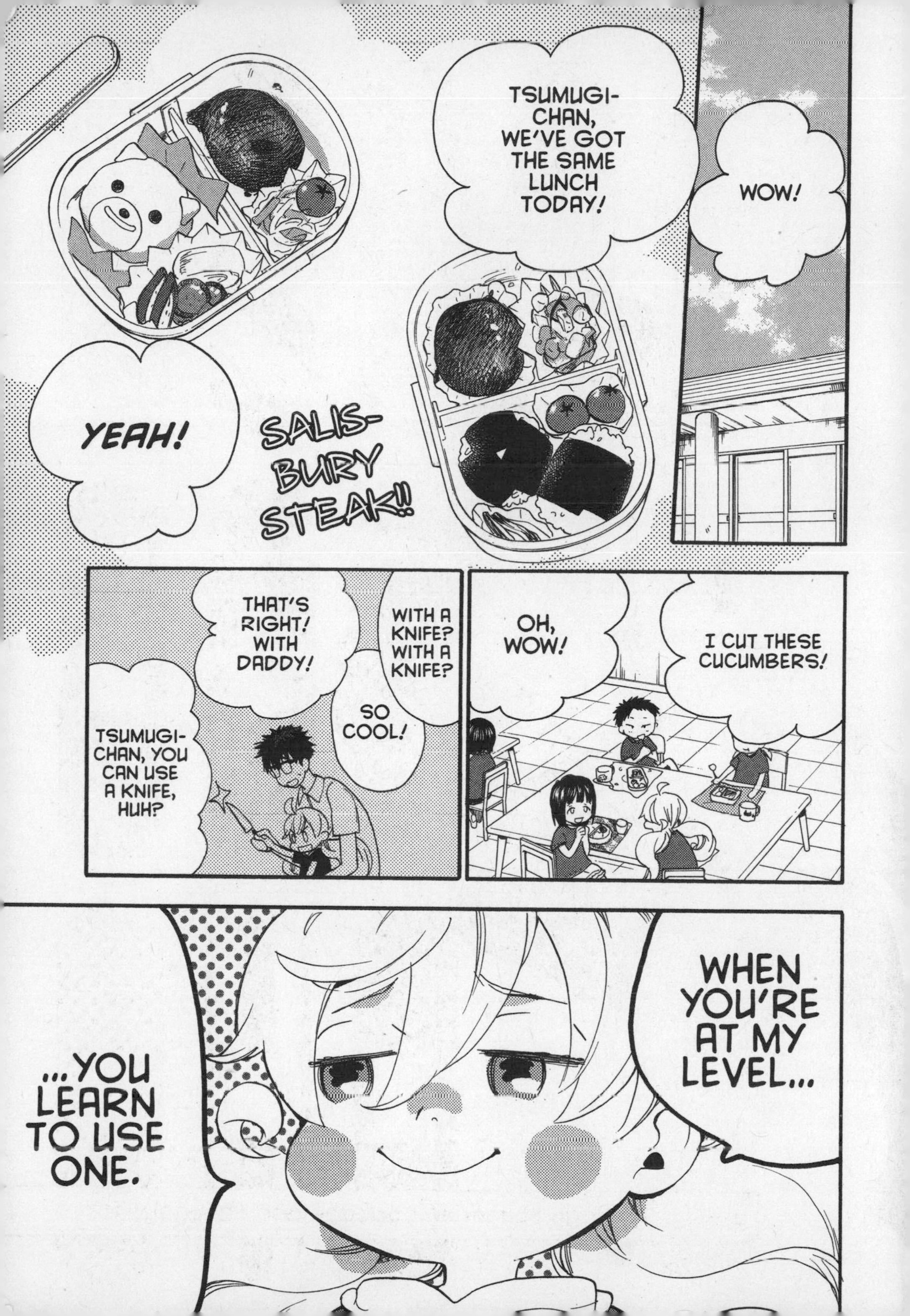
WOW!
TSUMUGI-CHAN, WE'VE GOT THE SAME LUNCH TODAY!
SALIS-BURY STEAK!!
YEAH!
I CUT THESE CUCUMBERS!
OH, WOW!
WITH A KNIFE? WITH A KNIFE?
THAT'S RIGHT! WITH DADDY!
SO COOL!
TSUMUGI-CHAN, YOU CAN USE A KNIFE, HUH?
WHEN YOU'RE AT MY LEVEL...
...YOU LEARN TO USE ONE.

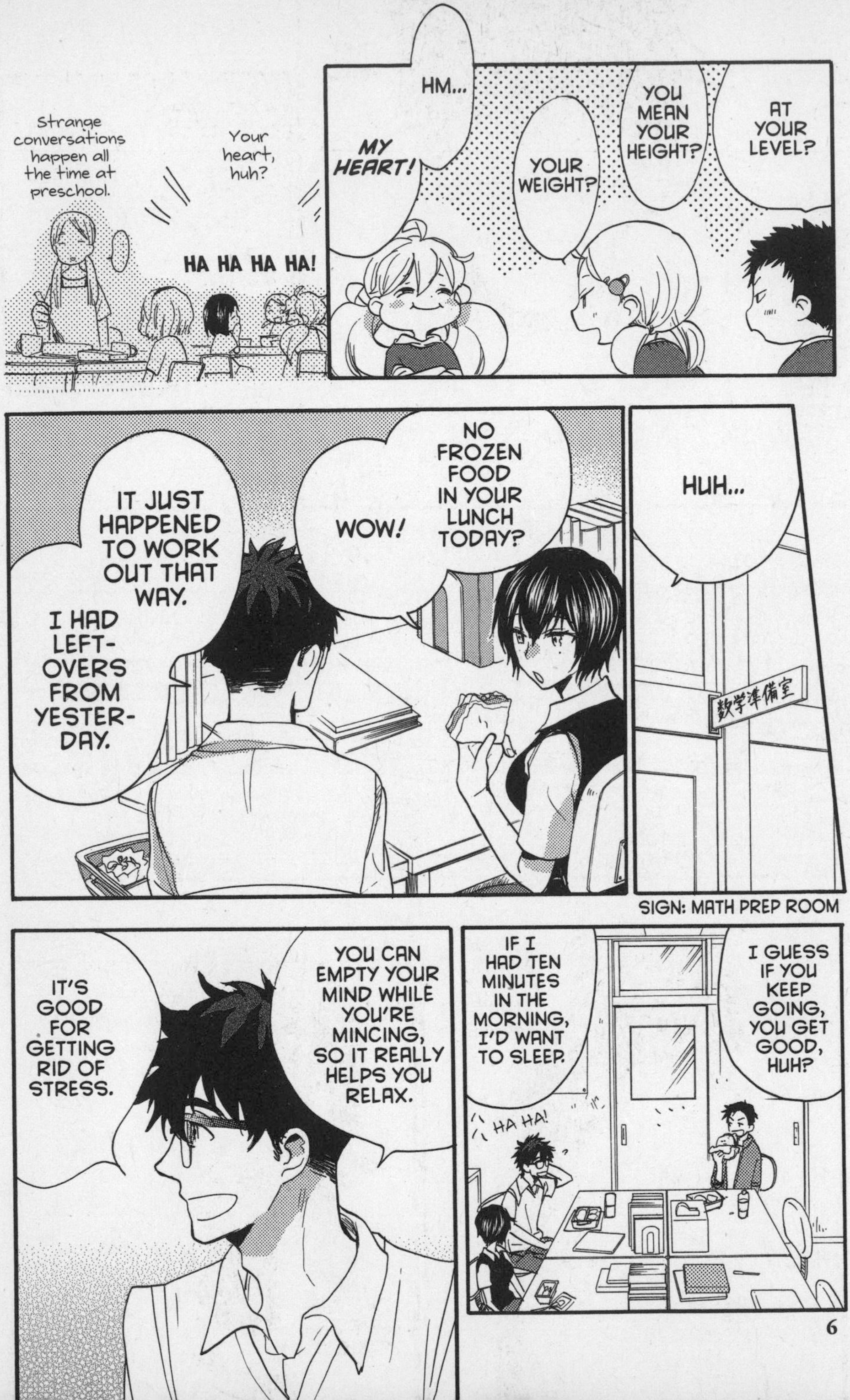
AT YOUR LEVEL?
YOU MEAN YOUR HEIGHT?
YOUR WEIGHT?
HM...
MY HEART!
Your heart, huh?
Strange conversations happen all the time at preschool.
HA HA HA HA!
HUH...
数学準備室
SIGN: MATH PREP ROOM
NO FROZEN FOOD IN YOUR LUNCH TODAY?
WOW!
IT JUST HAPPENED TO WORK OUT THAT WAY.
I HAD LEFT-OVERS FROM YESTER-DAY.
I GUESS IF YOU KEEP GOING, YOU GET GOOD, HUH?
IF I HAD TEN MINUTES IN THE MORNING, I'D WANT TO SLEEP.
HA HA!
YOU CAN EMPTY YOUR MIND WHILE YOU'RE MINCING, SO IT REALLY HELPS YOU RELAX.
IT'S GOOD FOR GETTING RID OF STRESS.

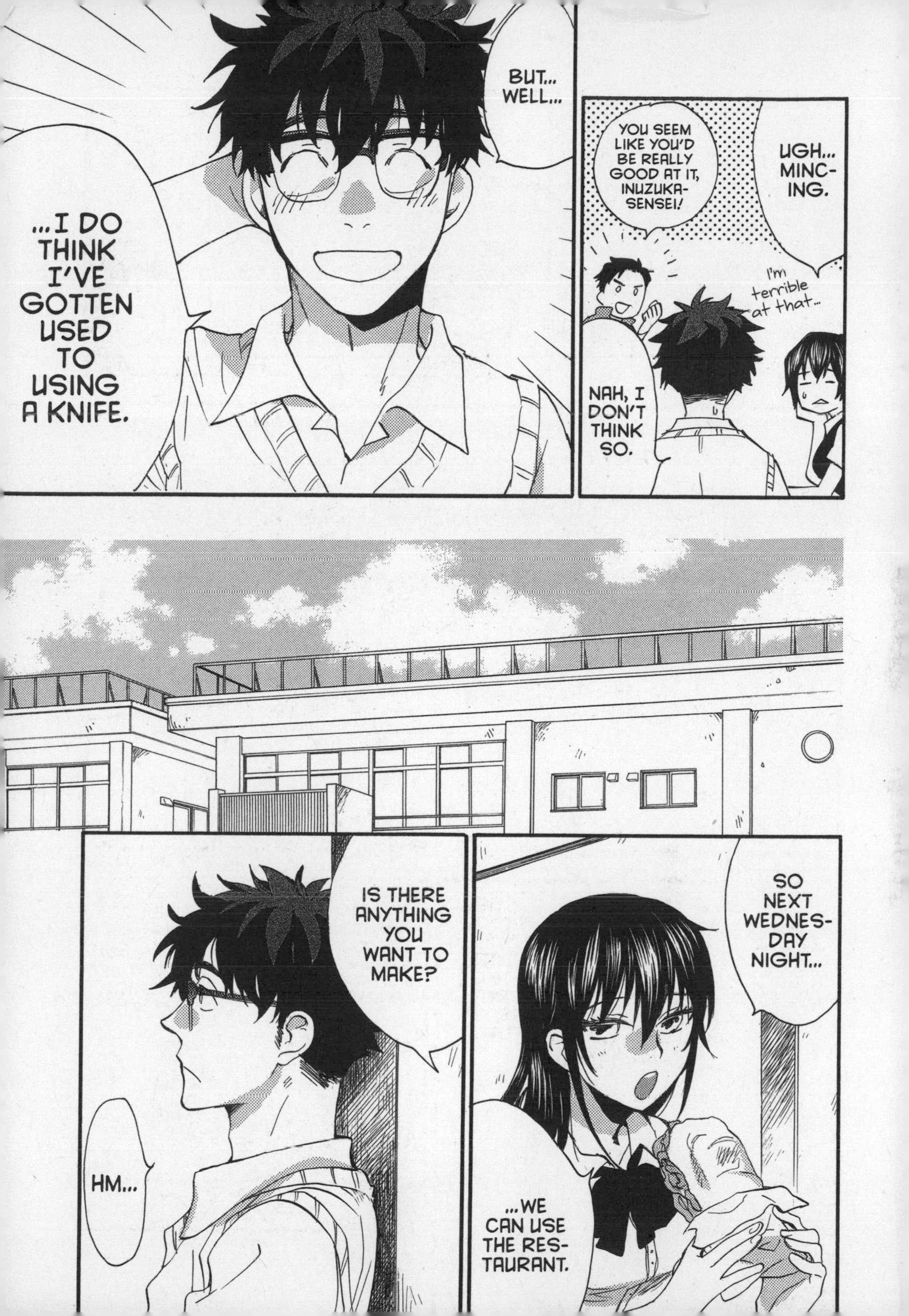
UGH... MINCING.
YOU SEEM LIKE YOU'D BE REALLY GOOD AT IT, INUZUKA-SENSEI!
I'm terrible at that...
NAH, I DON'T THINK SO.
BUT... WELL...
...I DO THINK I'VE GOTTEN USED TO USING A KNIFE.
SO NEXT WEDNESDAY NIGHT...
...WE CAN USE THE RESTAURANT.
IS THERE ANYTHING YOU WANT TO MAKE?
HM...

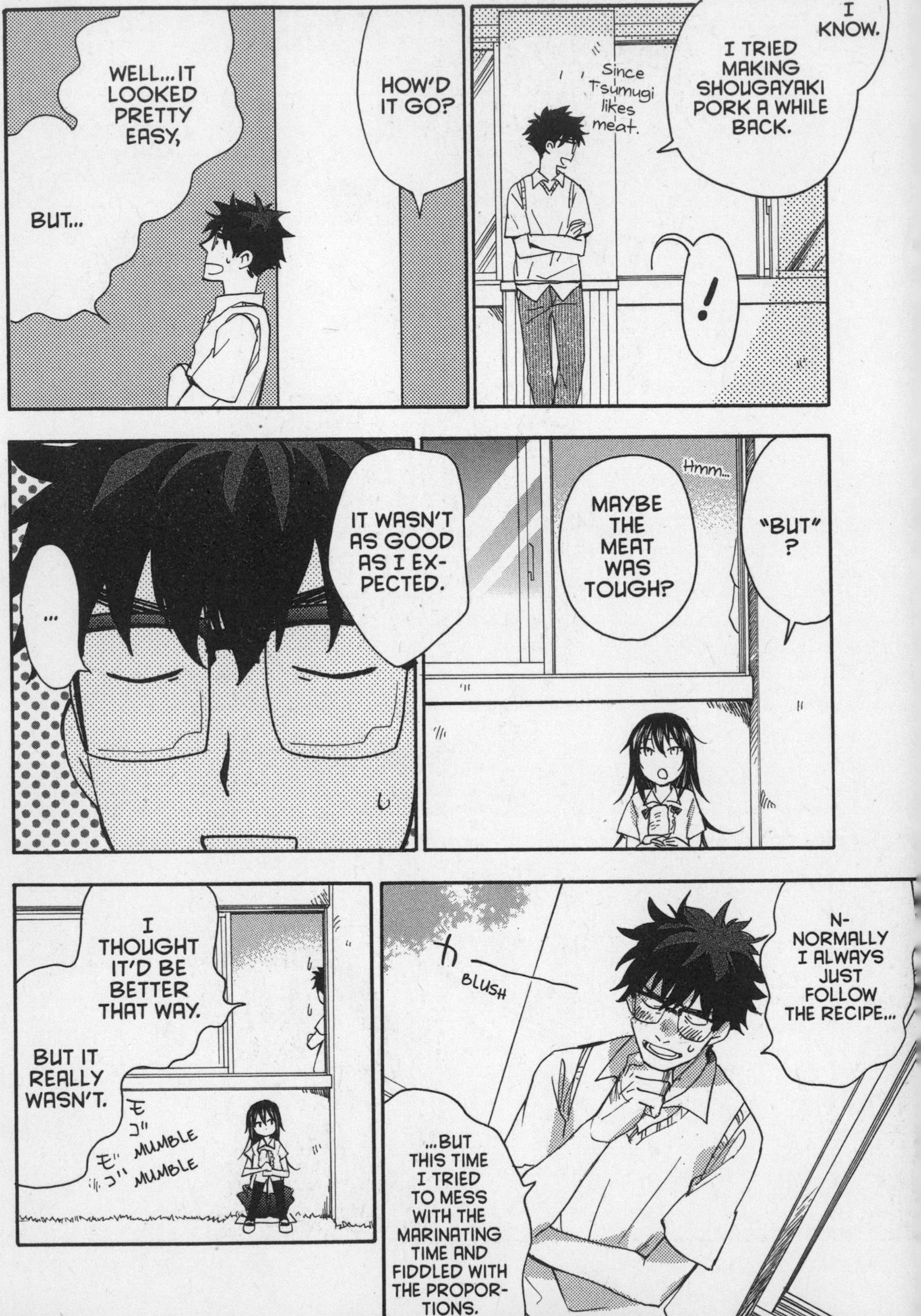
I KNOW.
I TRIED MAKING SHOUGAYAKI PORK A WHILE BACK.
Since Tsumugi likes meat.
!
HOW'D IT GO?
WELL...IT LOOKED PRETTY EASY,
BUT...
"BUT"?
Hmm...
MAYBE THE MEAT WAS TOUGH?
IT WASN'T AS GOOD AS I EXPECTED.
...
N-NORMALLY I ALWAYS JUST FOLLOW THE RECIPE...
BLUSH
...BUT THIS TIME I TRIED TO MESS WITH THE MARINATING TIME AND FIDDLED WITH THE PROPORTIONS.
I THOUGHT IT'D BE BETTER THAT WAY.
BUT IT REALLY WASN'T.
モゴ MUMBLE
モゴ MUMBLE

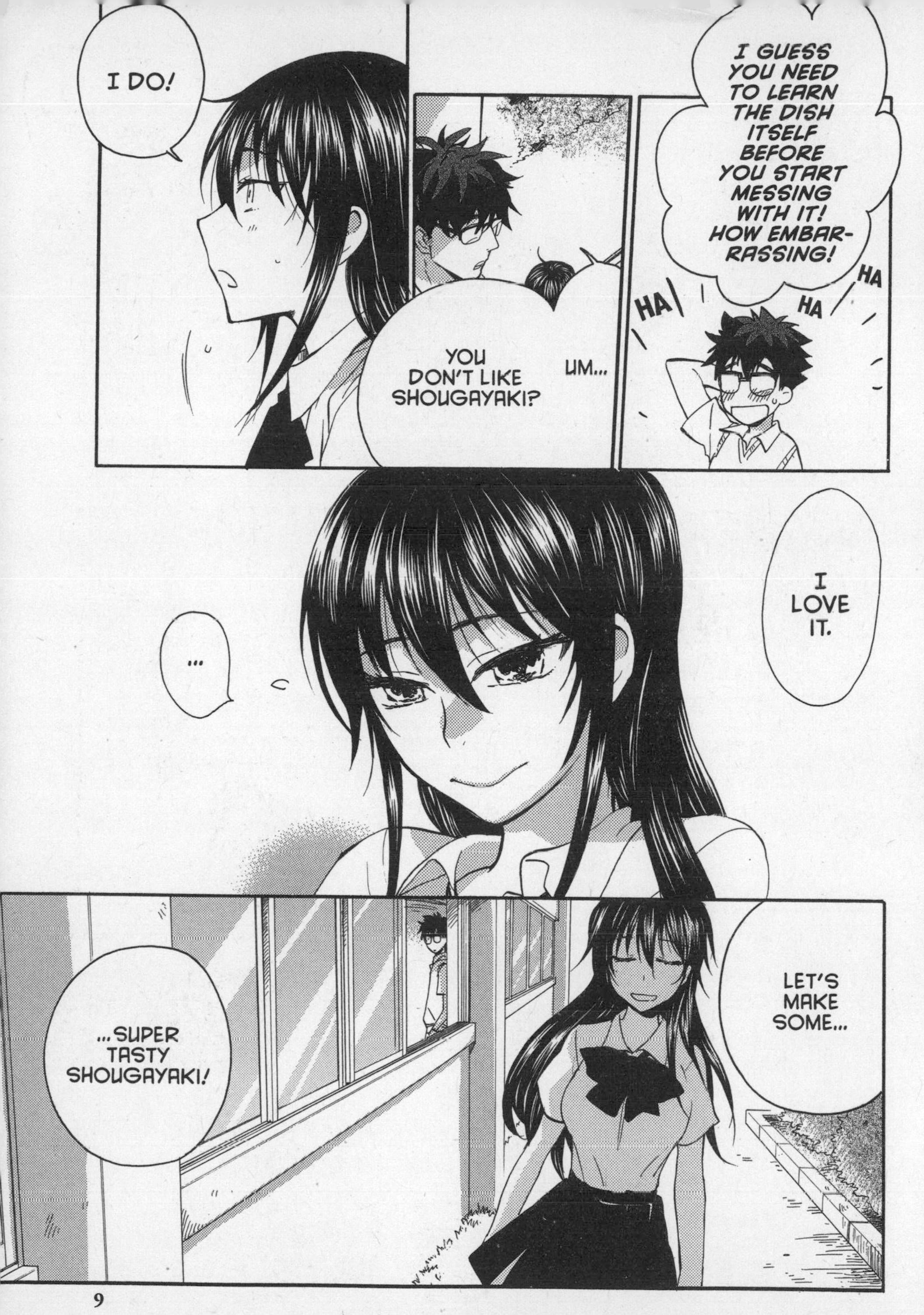
I GUESS YOU NEED TO LEARN THE DISH ITSELF BEFORE YOU START MESSING WITH IT! HOW EMBARRASSING!
HA
HA
HA
UM...
YOU DON'T LIKE SHOUGAYAKI?
I DO!
I LOVE IT.
...
LET'S MAKE SOME...
...SUPER TASTY SHOUGAYAKI!

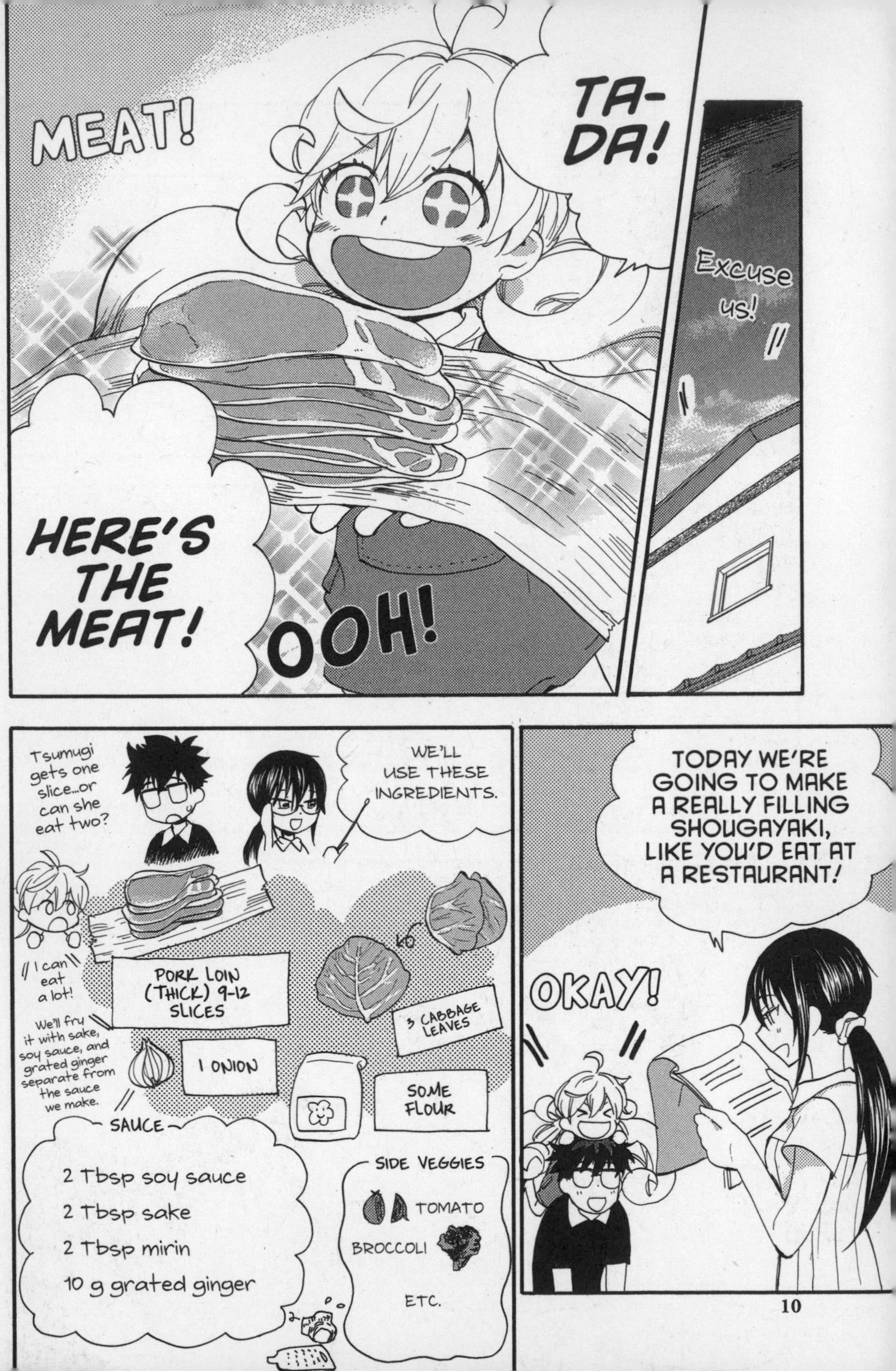
Excuse us!
TA-DA!
MEAT!
HERE'S THE MEAT!
OOH!
TODAY WE'RE GOING TO MAKE A REALLY FILLING SHOUGAYAKI, LIKE YOU'D EAT AT A RESTAURANT!
OKAY!
WE'LL USE THESE INGREDIENTS.
Tsumugi gets one slice...or can she eat two?
I can eat a lot!
PORK LOIN (THICK) 9-12 SLICES
3 CABBAGE LEAVES
We'll fry it with sake, soy sauce, and grated ginger separate from the sauce we make.
1 ONION
SOME FLOUR
SAUCE
2 Tbsp soy sauce
2 Tbsp sake
2 Tbsp mirin
10 g grated ginger
SIDE VEGGIES
TOMATO
BROCCOLI
ETC.

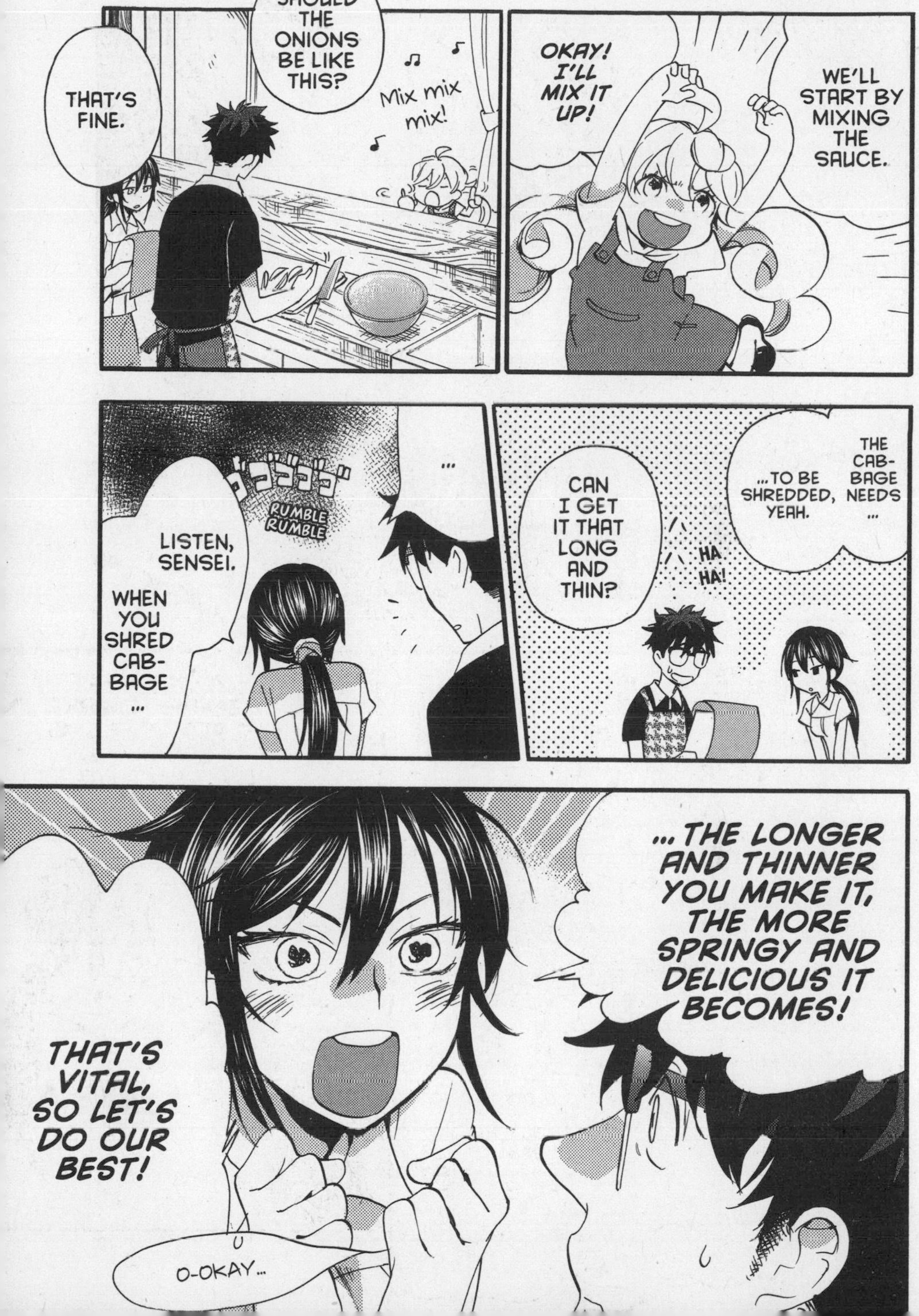
WE'LL START BY MIXING THE SAUCE.
OKAY! I'LL MIX IT UP!
SHOULD THE ONIONS BE LIKE THIS?
Mix mix mix!
THAT'S FINE.
THE CAB-BAGE NEEDS ...
...TO BE SHREDDED, YEAH.
HA HA!
CAN I GET IT THAT LONG AND THIN?
...
ゴゴゴゴ
RUMBLE RUMBLE
LISTEN, SENSEI.
WHEN YOU SHRED CAB-BAGE ...
...THE LONGER AND THINNER YOU MAKE IT, THE MORE SPRINGY AND DELICIOUS IT BECOMES!
THAT'S VITAL, SO LET'S DO OUR BEST!
O-OKAY...

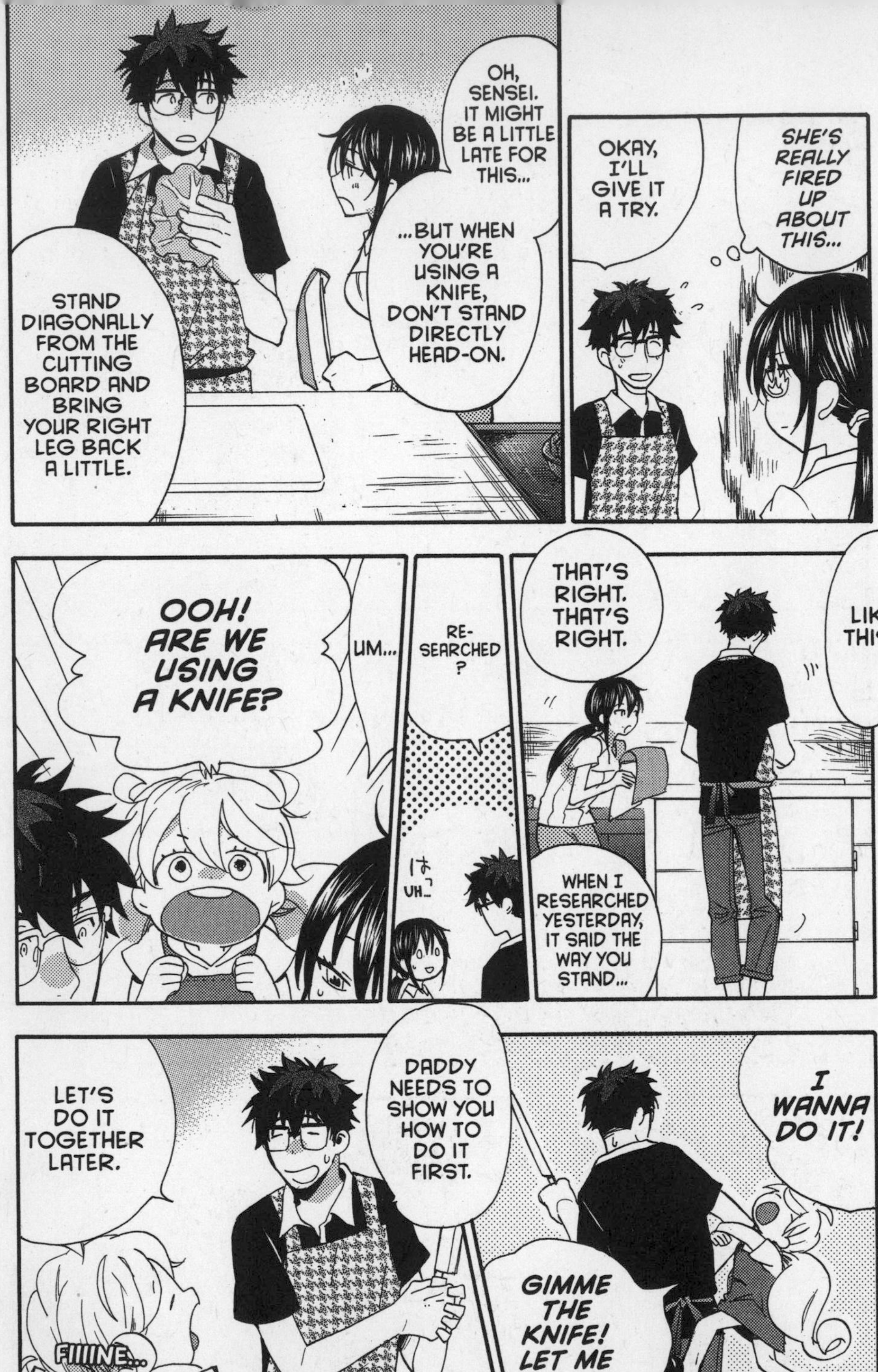
SHE'S REALLY FIRED UP ABOUT THIS...
OKAY, I'LL GIVE IT A TRY.
OH, SENSEI. IT MIGHT BE A LITTLE LATE FOR THIS...
...BUT WHEN YOU'RE USING A KNIFE, DON'T STAND DIRECTLY HEAD-ON.
STAND DIAGONALLY FROM THE CUTTING BOARD AND BRING YOUR RIGHT LEG BACK A LITTLE.
LIKE THIS?
THAT'S RIGHT. THAT'S RIGHT.
WHEN I RESEARCHED YESTERDAY, IT SAID THE WAY YOU STAND...
RE-SEARCHED?
は
UH...
UM...
OOH! ARE WE USING A KNIFE?
I WANNA DO IT!
GIMME THE KNIFE! LET ME DO IT!
DADDY NEEDS TO SHOW YOU HOW TO DO IT FIRST.
LET'S DO IT TOGETHER LATER.
FIIIINE...

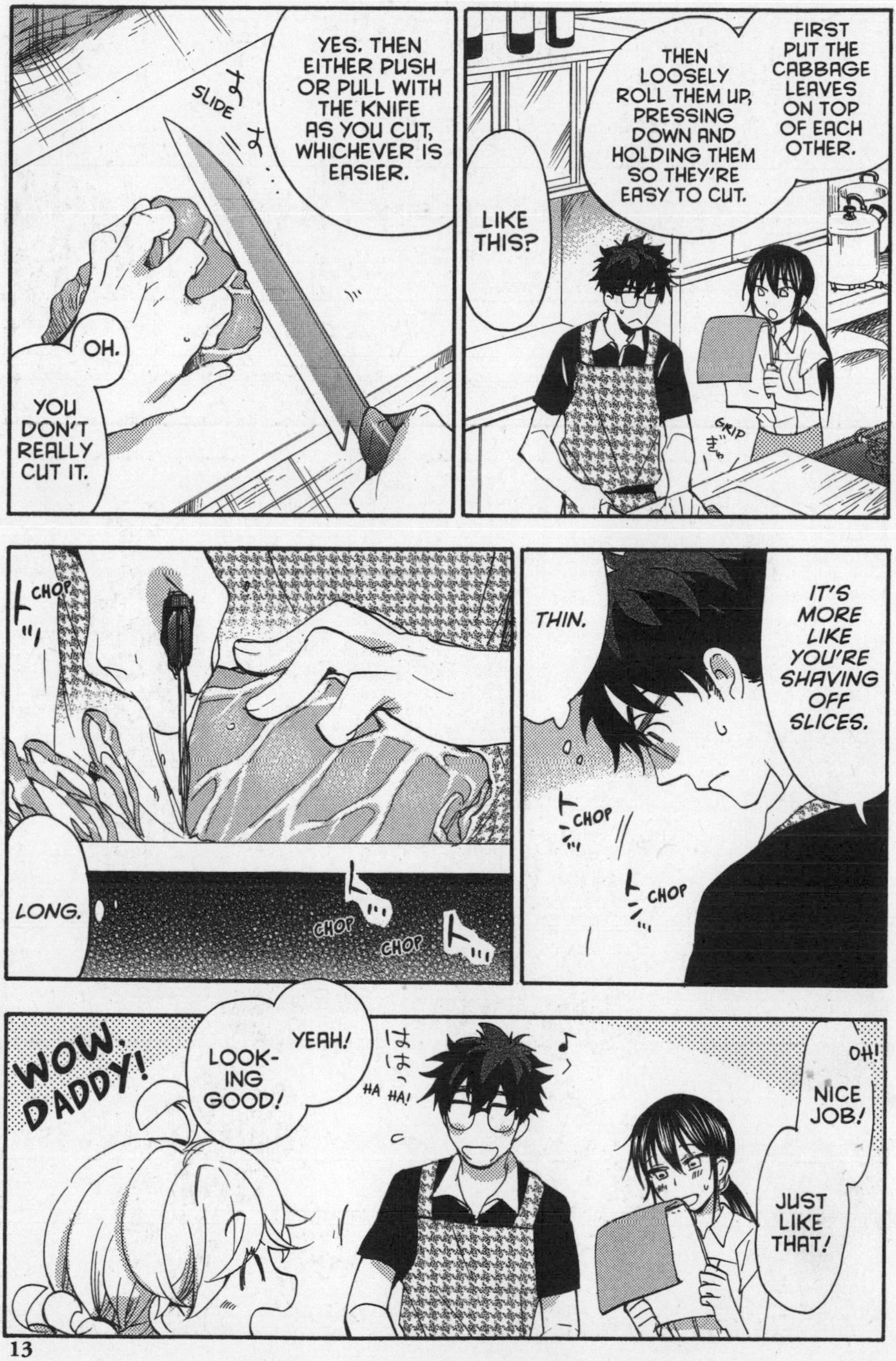

FIRST PUT THE CABBAGE LEAVES ON TOP OF EACH OTHER.
THEN LOOSELY ROLL THEM UP, PRESSING DOWN AND HOLDING THEM SO THEY'RE EASY TO CUT.
LIKE THIS?
GRIP
ぎゅ
YES. THEN EITHER PUSH OR PULL WITH THE KNIFE AS YOU CUT, WHICHEVER IS EASIER.
SLIDE
OH.
YOU DON'T REALLY CUT IT.
IT'S MORE LIKE YOU'RE SHAVING OFF SLICES.
THIN.
CHOP
CHOP
CHOP
LONG.
CHOP
CHOP
OH!
NICE JOB!
JUST LIKE THAT!
YEAH!
LOOK-ING GOOD!
ははっ
HA HA!
WOW, DADDY!

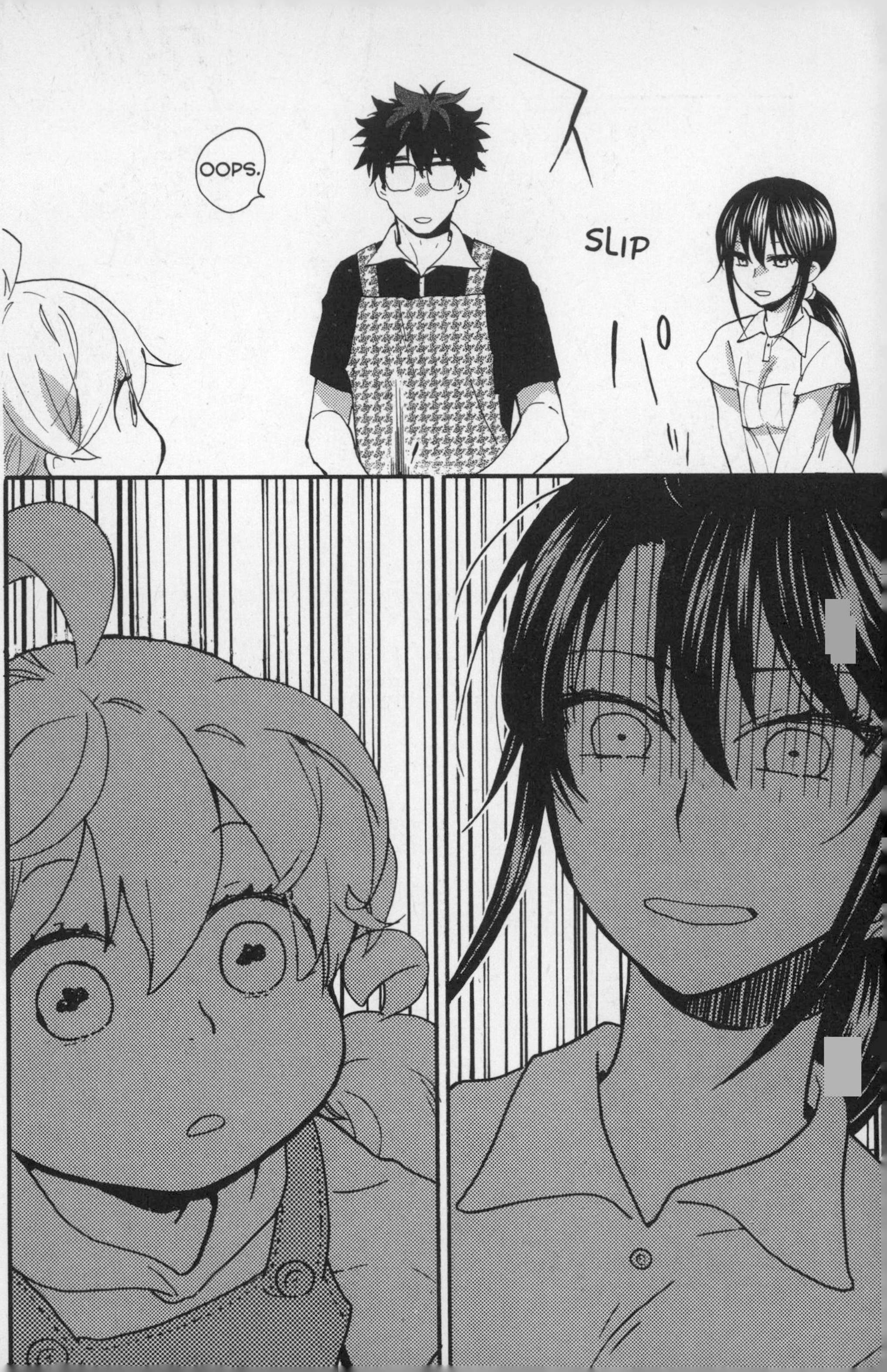
SLIP
OOPS.

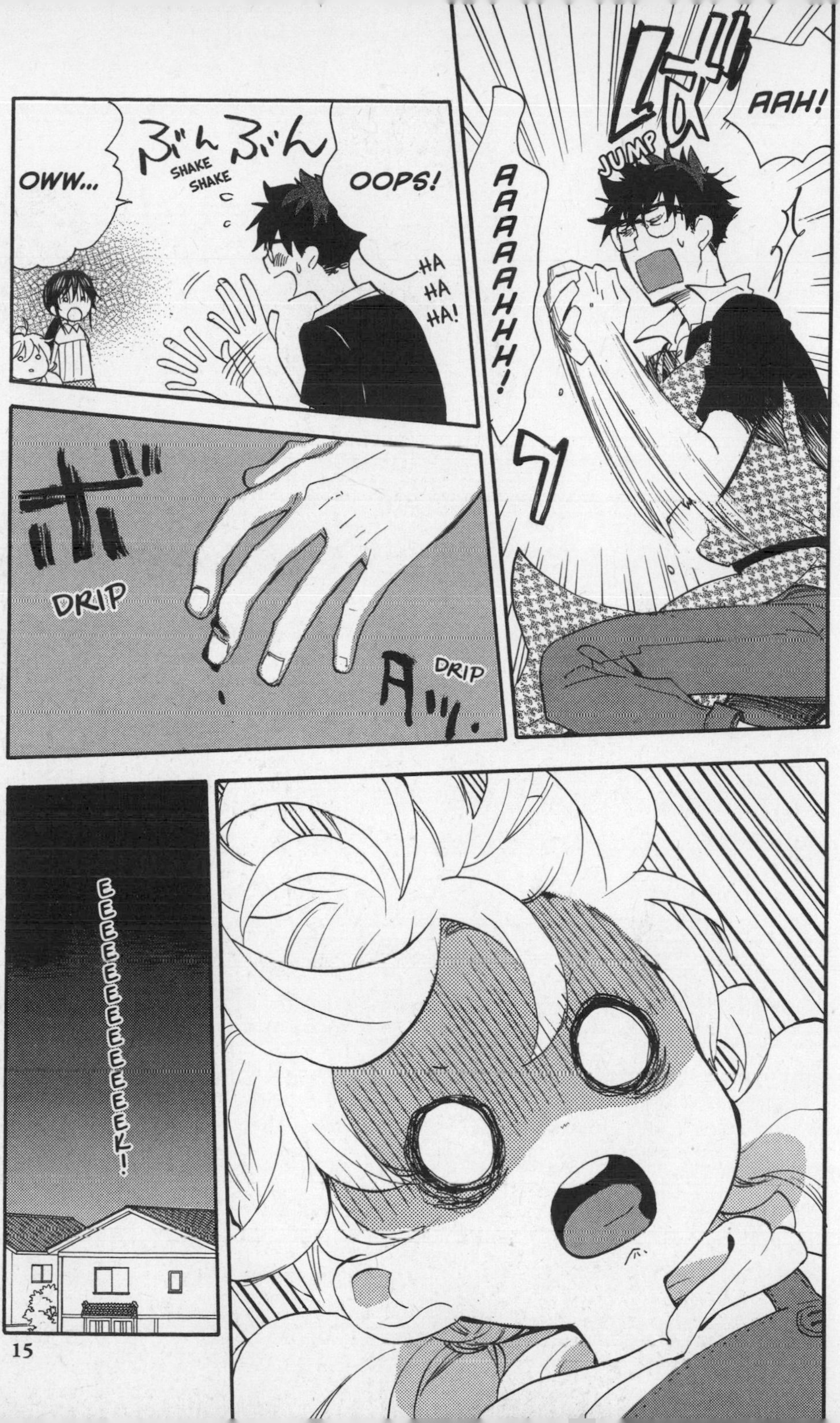
AAH!
JUMP
AAAAAHHH!
OOPS!
HA HA HA!
ぶんぶん
SHAKE SHAKE
OWW...
DRIP
DRIP
EEEEEEEEEEEEK!

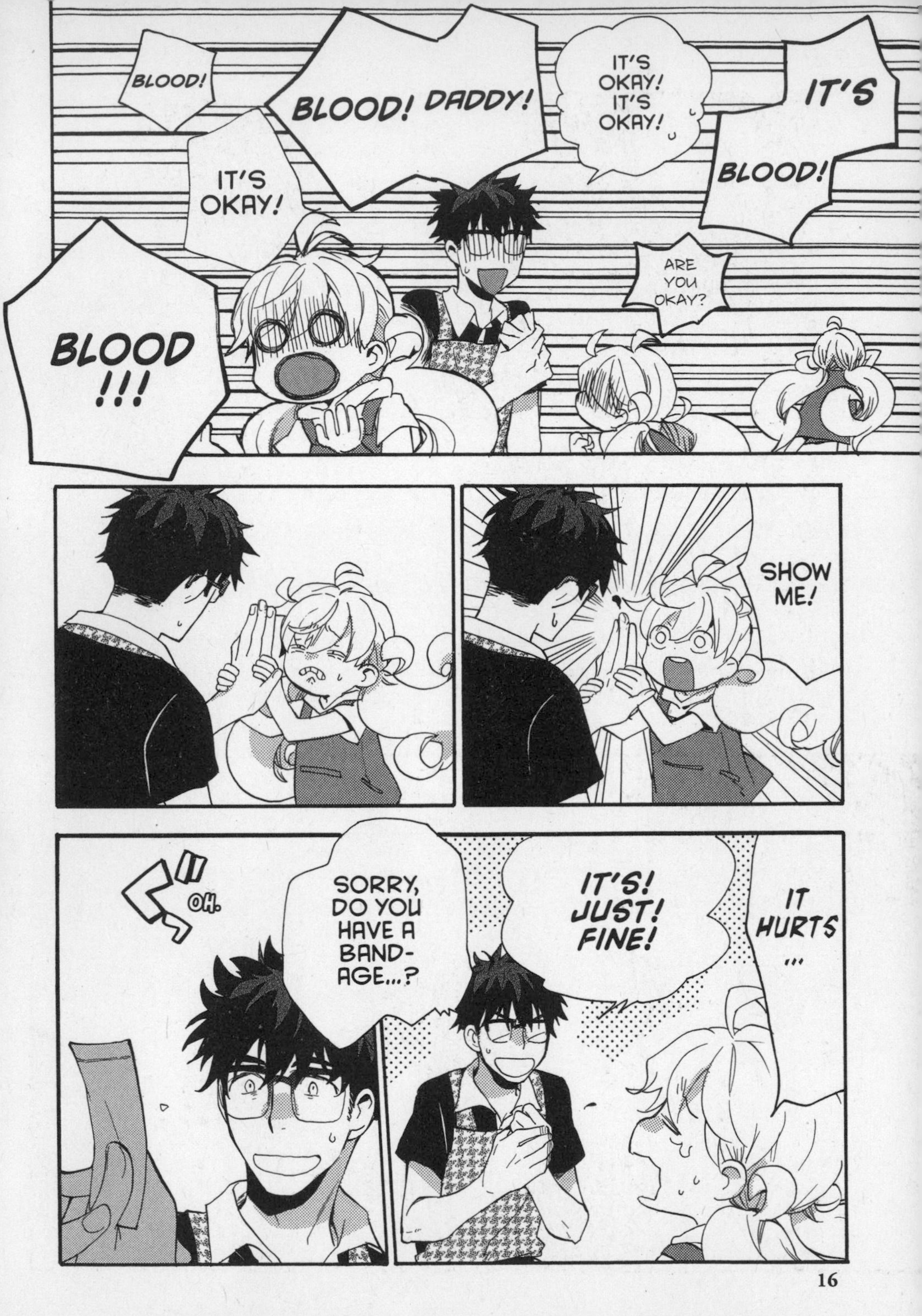
IT'S BLOOD!
ARE YOU OKAY?
IT'S OKAY! IT'S OKAY!
BLOOD! DADDY!
BLOOD!
IT'S OKAY!
BLOOD !!!
SHOW ME!
IT HURTS ...
IT'S! JUST! FINE!
SORRY, DO YOU HAVE A BAND-AGE...?
OH.

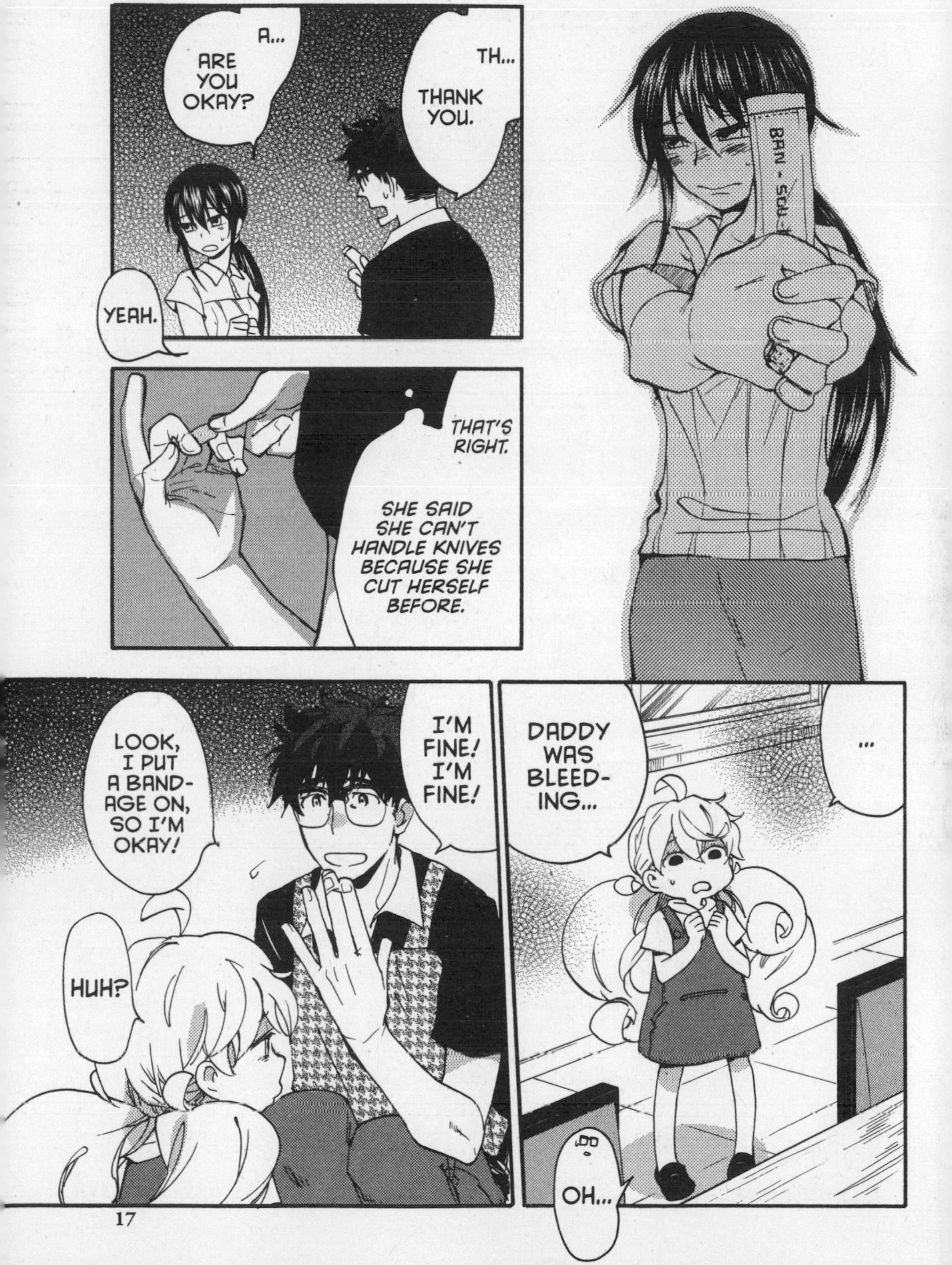
BAN - SOU
TH... THANK YOU.
A... ARE YOU OKAY?
YEAH.
THAT'S RIGHT.
SHE SAID SHE CAN'T HANDLE KNIVES BECAUSE SHE CUT HERSELF BEFORE.
...
DADDY WAS BLEED-ING...
OH...
I'M FINE! I'M FINE!
LOOK, I PUT A BAND-AGE ON, SO I'M OKAY!
HUH?

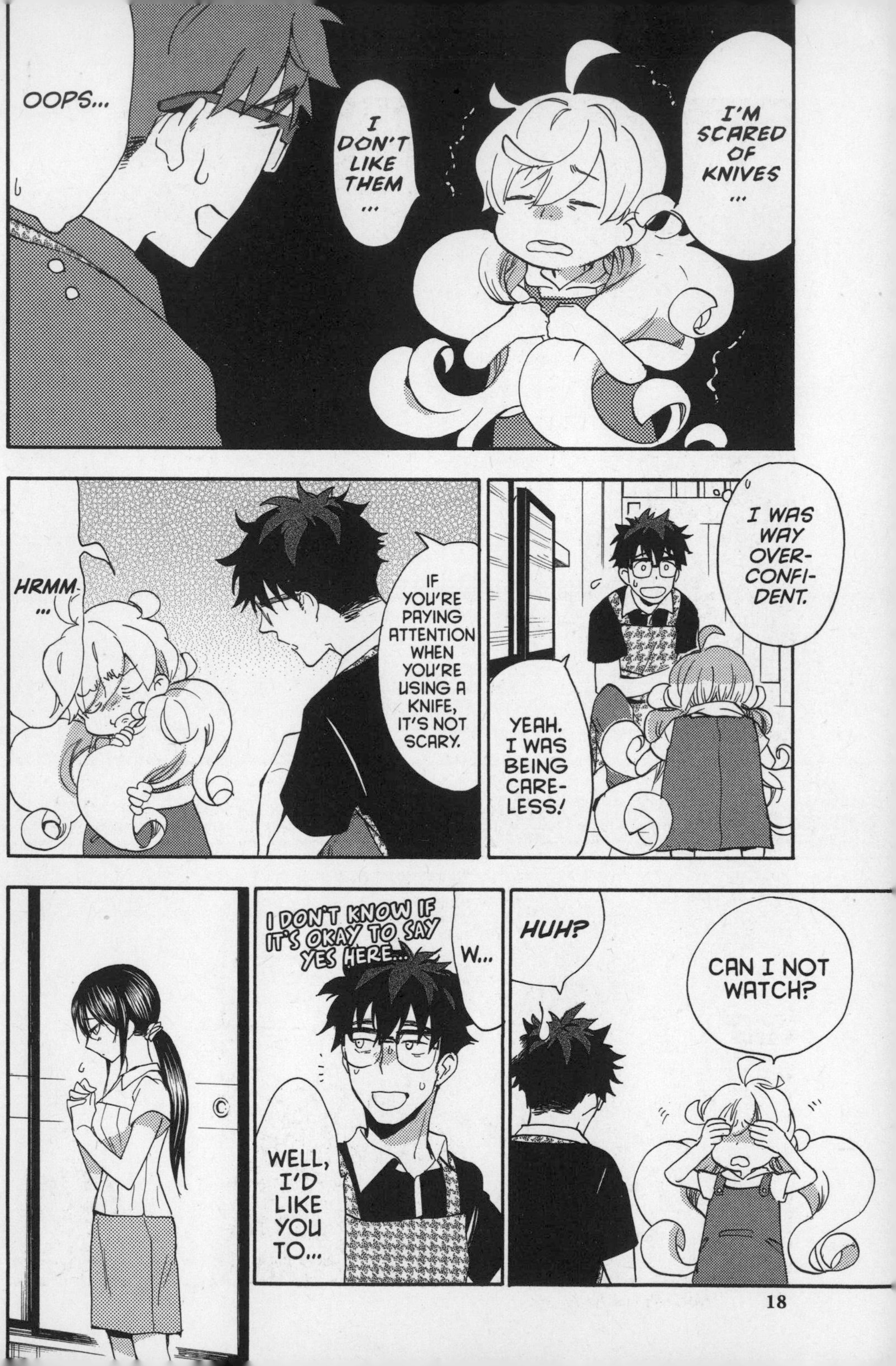
I'M SCARED OF KNIVES ...
I DON'T LIKE THEM ...
OOPS...
I WAS WAY OVER-CONFIDENT.
YEAH. I WAS BEING CARE-LESS!
IF YOU'RE PAYING ATTENTION WHEN YOU'RE USING A KNIFE, IT'S NOT SCARY.
HRMM-...
CAN I NOT WATCH?
HUH?
W...
I DON'T KNOW IF IT'S OKAY TO SAY YES HERE...
WELL, I'D LIKE YOU TO...

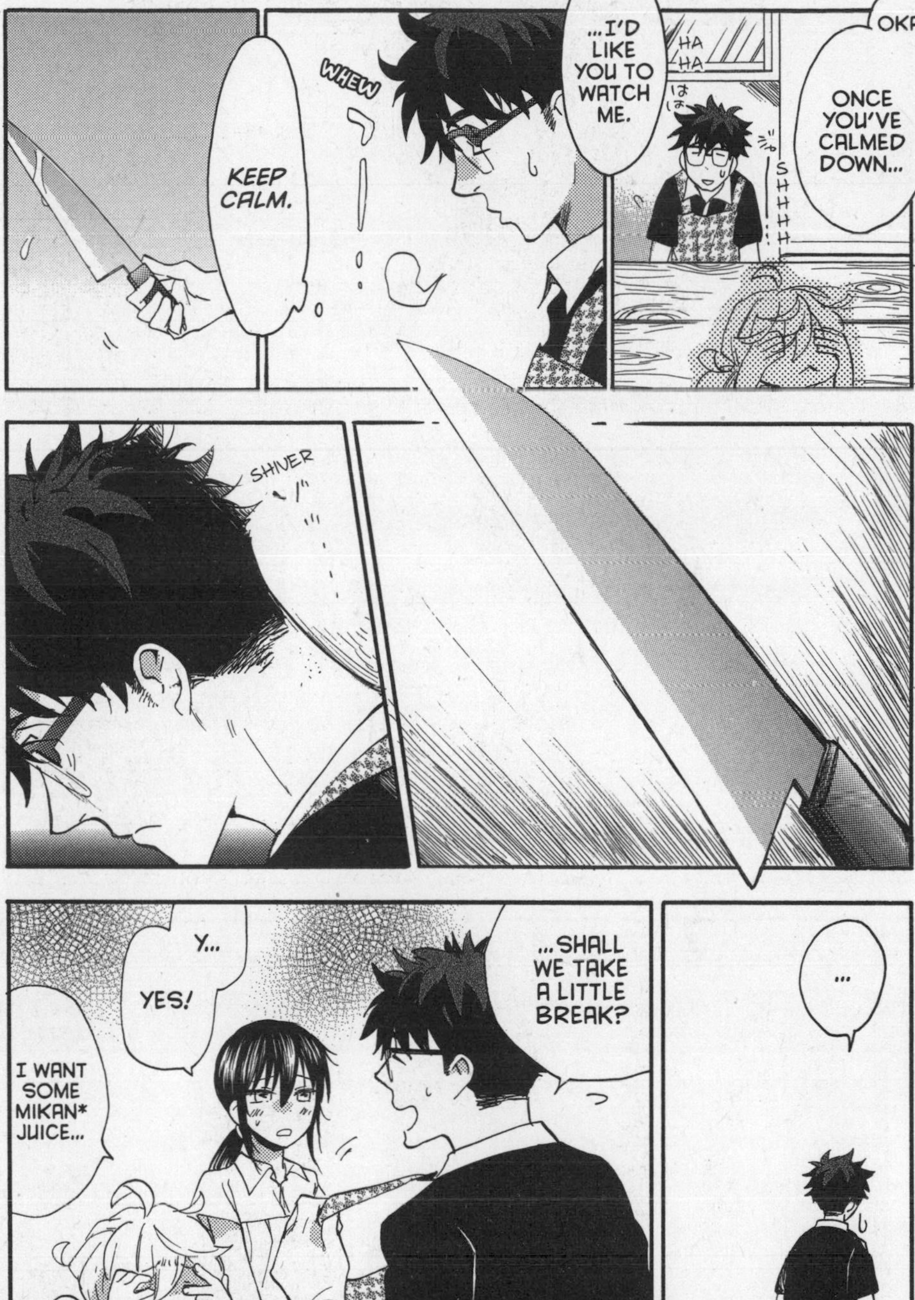
OKAY.
ONCE YOU'VE CALMED DOWN...
HA HA
はは
SHHHH
...I'D LIKE YOU TO WATCH ME.
WHEW
KEEP CALM.
SHIVER
...
...SHALL WE TAKE A LITTLE BREAK?
Y...
YES!
I WANT SOME MIKAN* JUICE...

*MANDARIN ORANGE

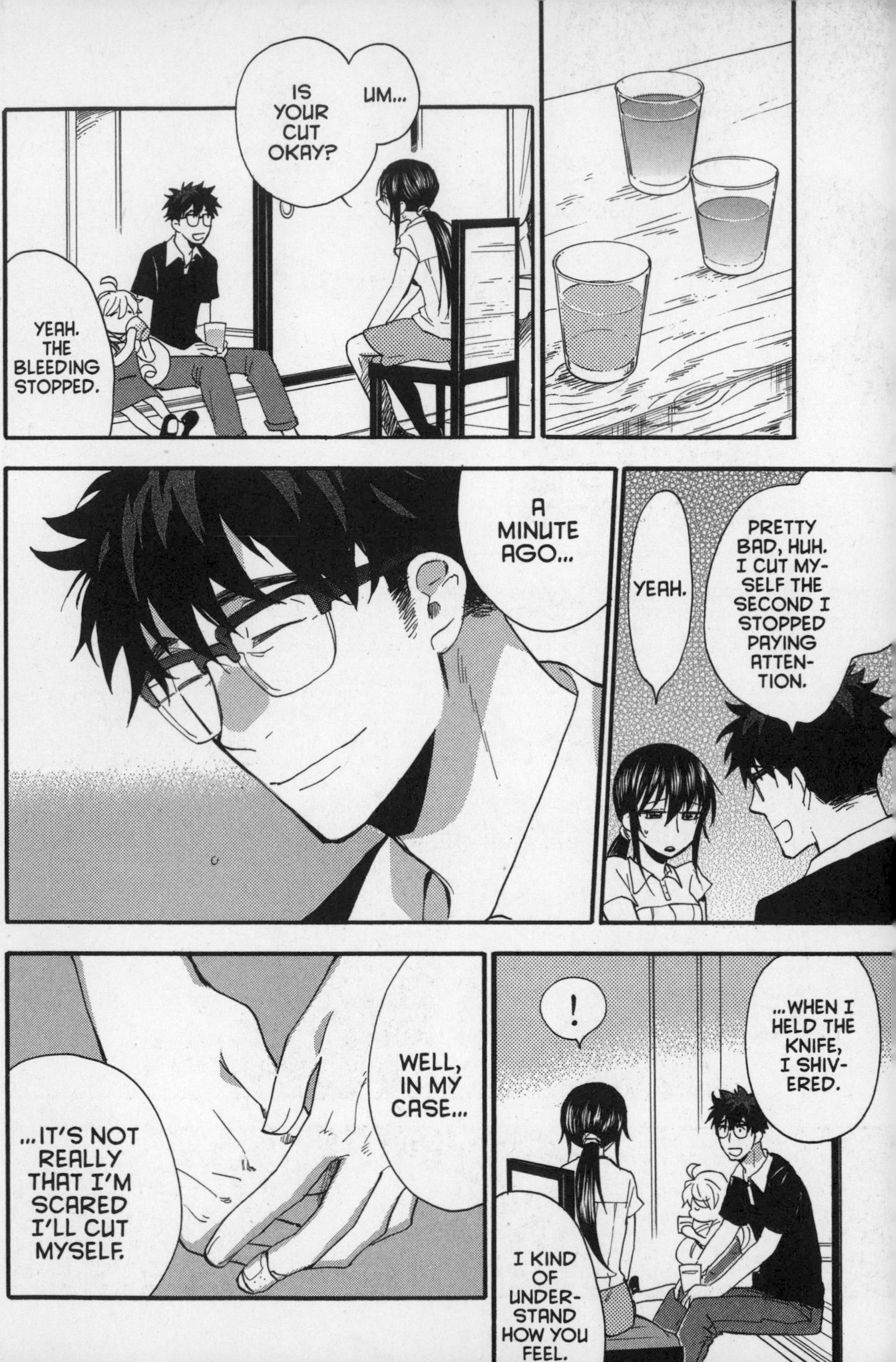
UM... IS YOUR CUT OKAY?
YEAH. THE BLEEDING STOPPED.
PRETTY BAD, HUH. I CUT MY-SELF THE SECOND I STOPPED PAYING ATTEN-TION.
YEAH.
A MINUTE AGO...
...WHEN I HELD THE KNIFE, I SHIV-ERED.
!
I KIND OF UNDER-STAND HOW YOU FEEL.
WELL, IN MY CASE...
...IT'S NOT REALLY THAT I'M SCARED I'LL CUT MYSELF.

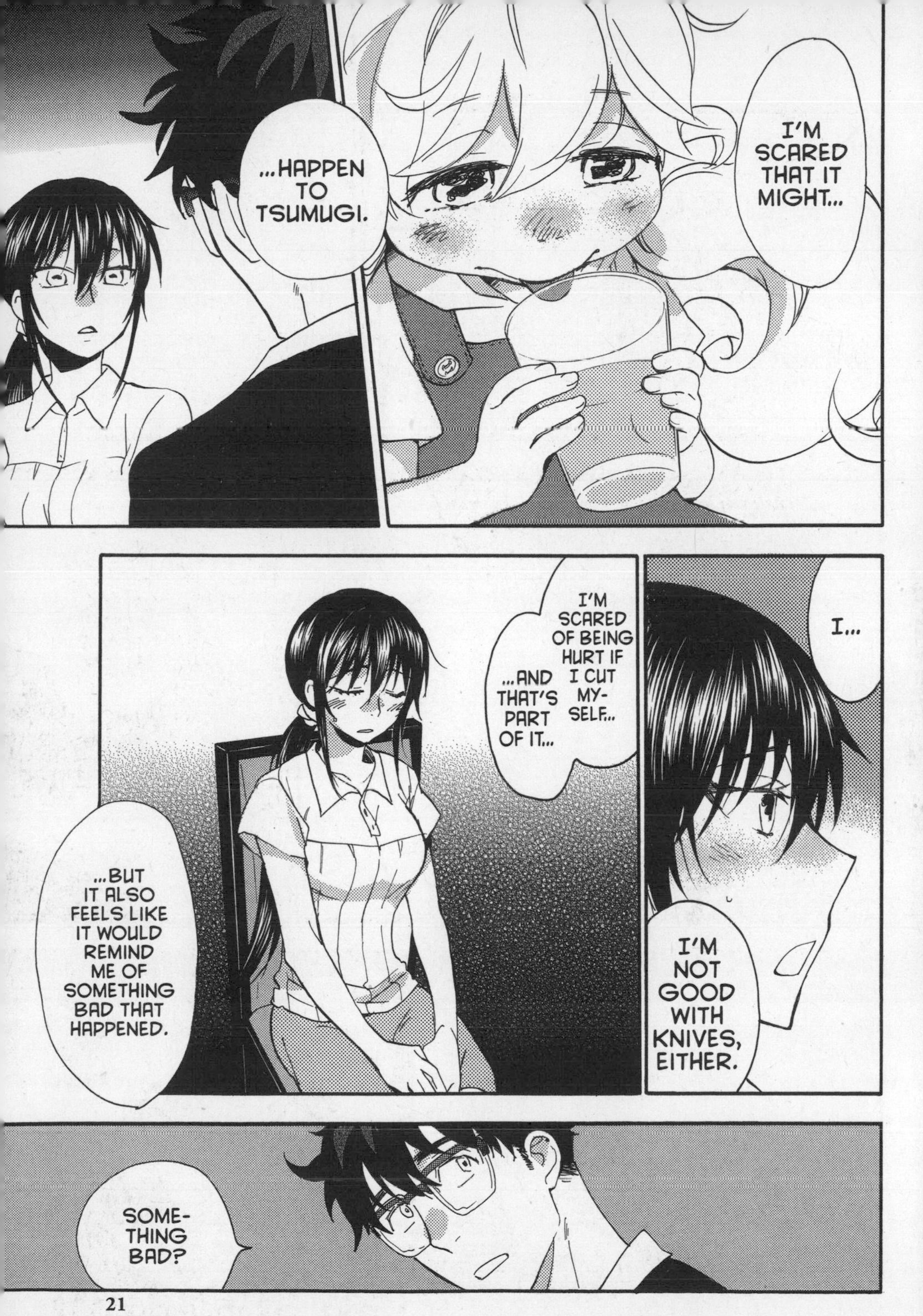
I'M SCARED THAT IT MIGHT...
...HAPPEN TO TSUMUGI.
I...
I'M NOT GOOD WITH KNIVES, EITHER.
I'M SCARED OF BEING HURT IF I CUT MY-SELF...
...AND THAT'S PART OF IT...
...BUT IT ALSO FEELS LIKE IT WOULD REMIND ME OF SOMETHING BAD THAT HAPPENED.
SOME-THING BAD?

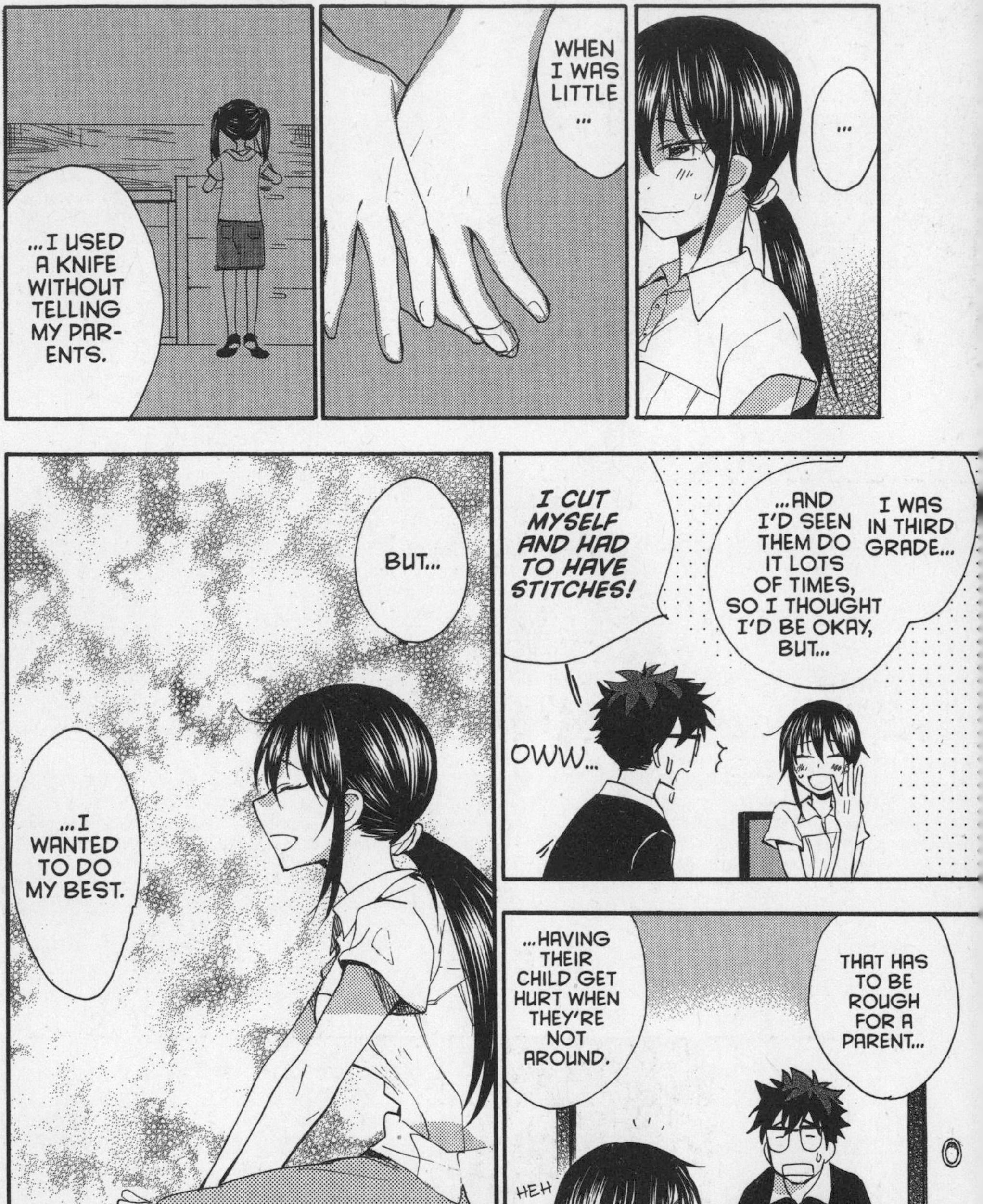
...
WHEN I WAS LITTLE ...
...I USED A KNIFE WITHOUT TELLING MY PARENTS.
I WAS IN THIRD GRADE...
...AND I'D SEEN THEM DO IT LOTS OF TIMES, SO I THOUGHT I'D BE OKAY, BUT...
I CUT MYSELF AND HAD TO HAVE STITCHES!
OWW...
THAT HAS TO BE ROUGH FOR A PARENT...
...HAVING THEIR CHILD GET HURT WHEN THEY'RE NOT AROUND.
HEH
BUT...
...I WANTED TO DO MY BEST.

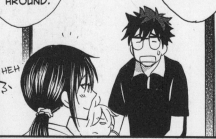

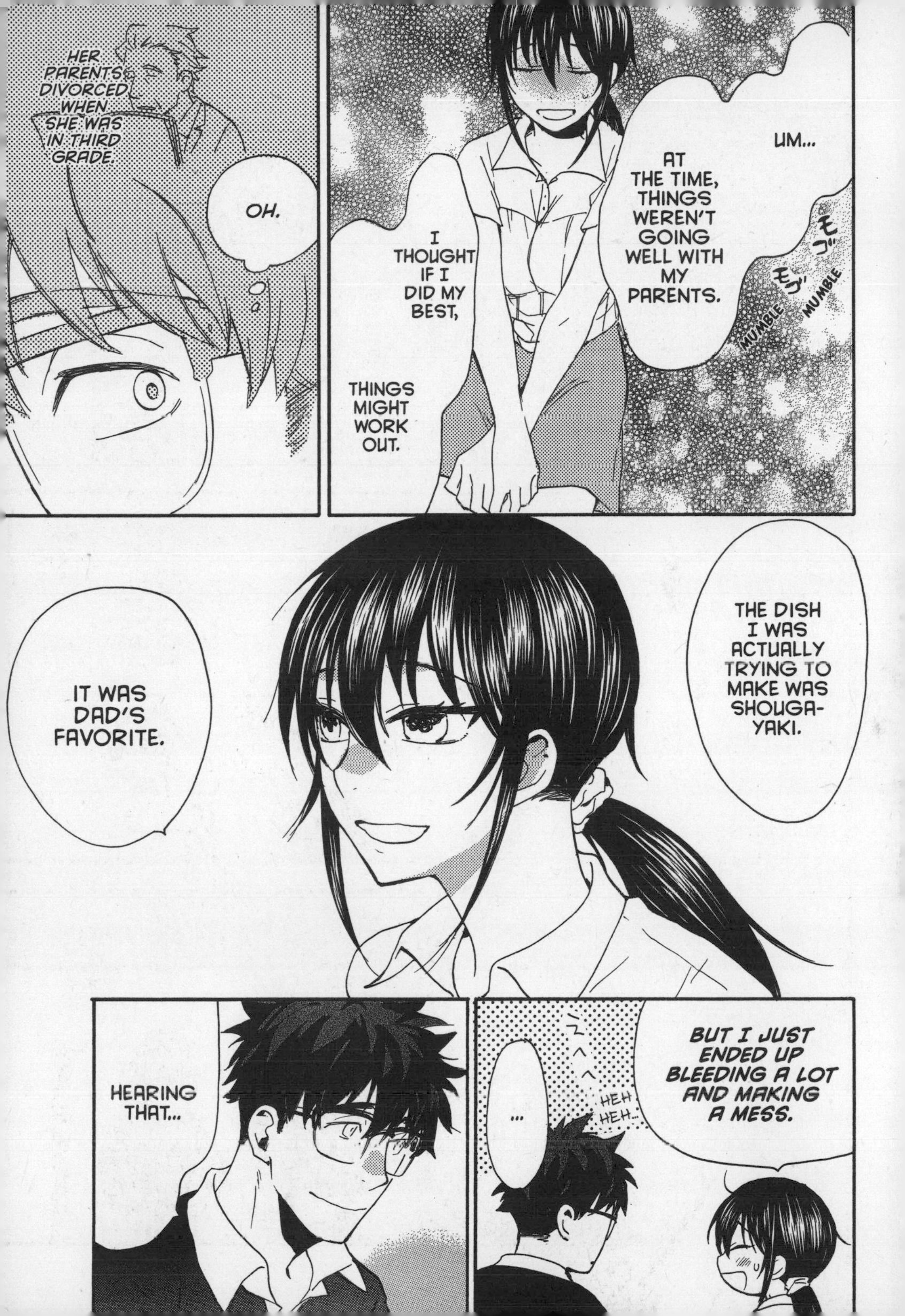
UM...
AT THE TIME, THINGS WEREN'T GOING WELL WITH MY PARENTS.
I THOUGHT IF I DID MY BEST,
THINGS MIGHT WORK OUT.
MUMBLE MUMBLE
HER PARENTS DIVORCED WHEN SHE WAS IN THIRD GRADE.
OH.
THE DISH I WAS ACTUALLY TRYING TO MAKE WAS SHOUGA-YAKI.
IT WAS DAD'S FAVORITE.
BUT I JUST ENDED UP BLEEDING A LOT AND MAKING A MESS.
HEH HEH...
...
HEARING THAT...

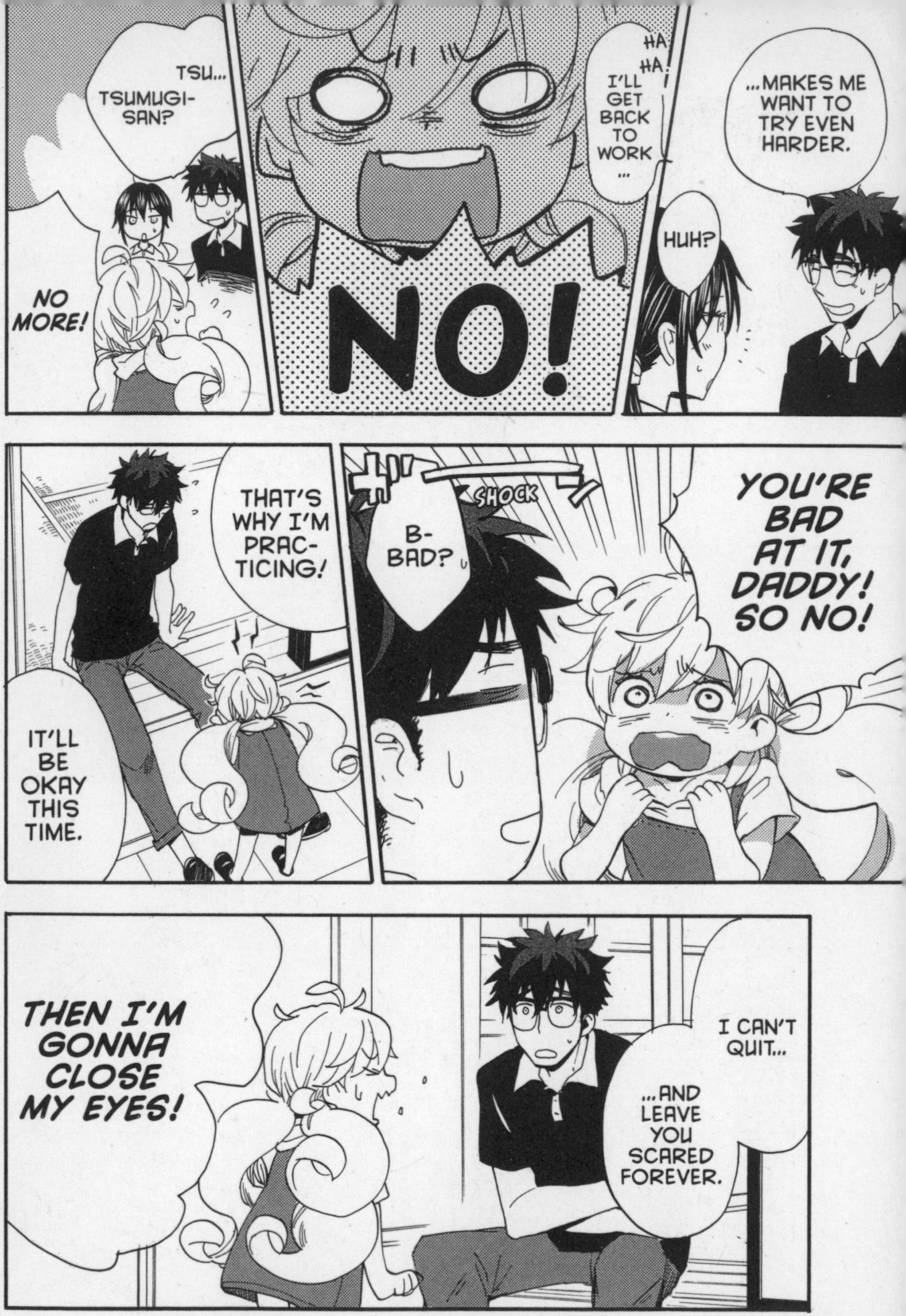
...MAKES ME WANT TO TRY EVEN HARDER.
HA HA! I'LL GET BACK TO WORK...
HUH?
NO!
TSU... TSUMUGI-SAN?
NO MORE!
YOU'RE BAD AT IT, DADDY! SO NO!
SHOCK
B-BAD?
THAT'S WHY I'M PRAC-TICING!
IT'LL BE OKAY THIS TIME.
I CAN'T QUIT...
...AND LEAVE YOU SCARED FOREVER.
THEN I'M GONNA CLOSE MY EYES!

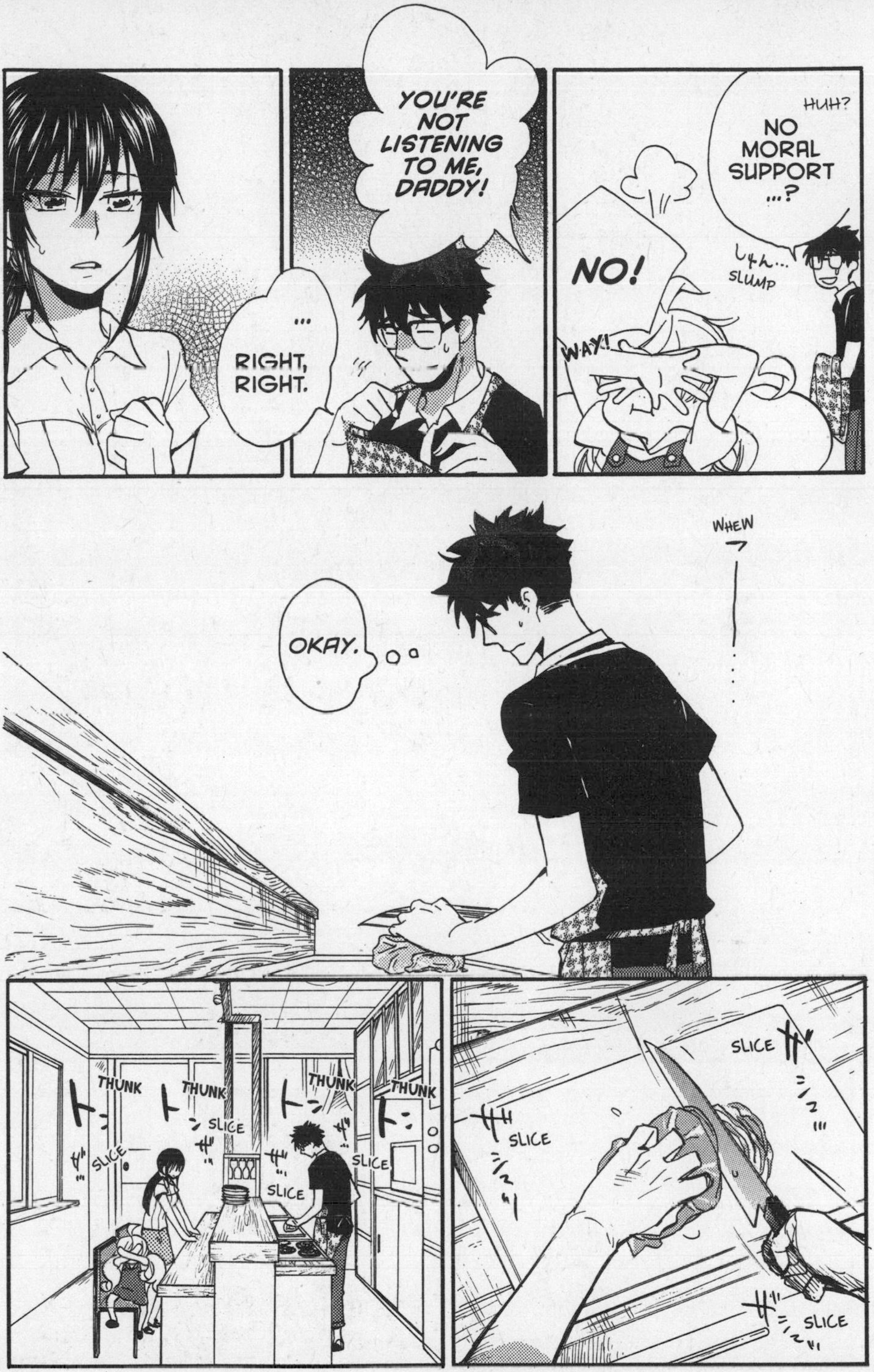
HUH?
NO MORAL SUPPORT ...?
しゅん... SLUMP
NO!
WAY!
YOU'RE NOT LISTENING TO ME, DADDY!
... RIGHT, RIGHT.
WHEW
OKAY.
SLICE
SLICE
SLICE
THUNK
THUNK
THUNK
THUNK
SLICE
SLICE
SLICE
SLICE

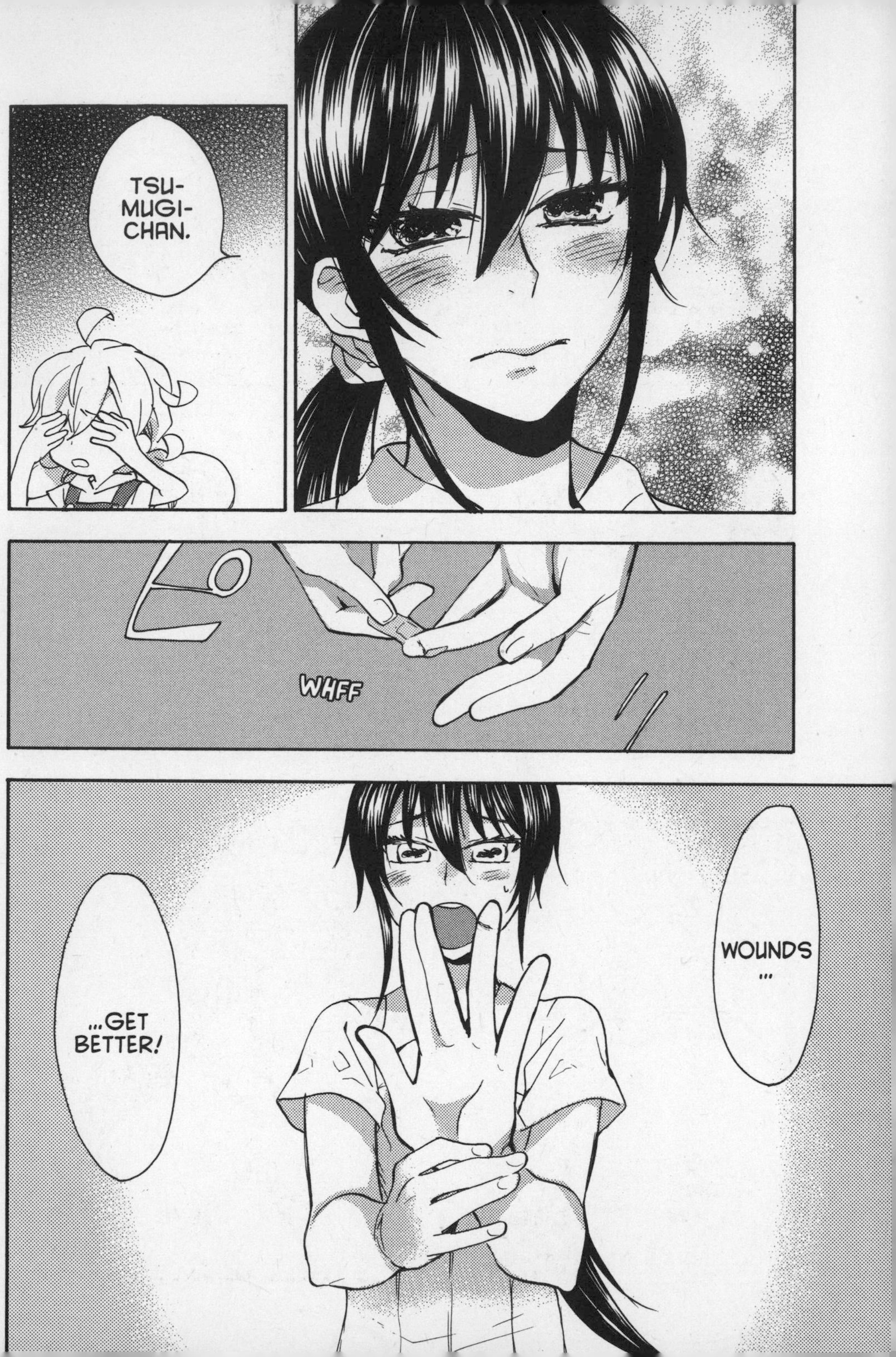
TSU-MUGI-CHAN.
WHFF
WOUNDS ...
...GET BETTER!

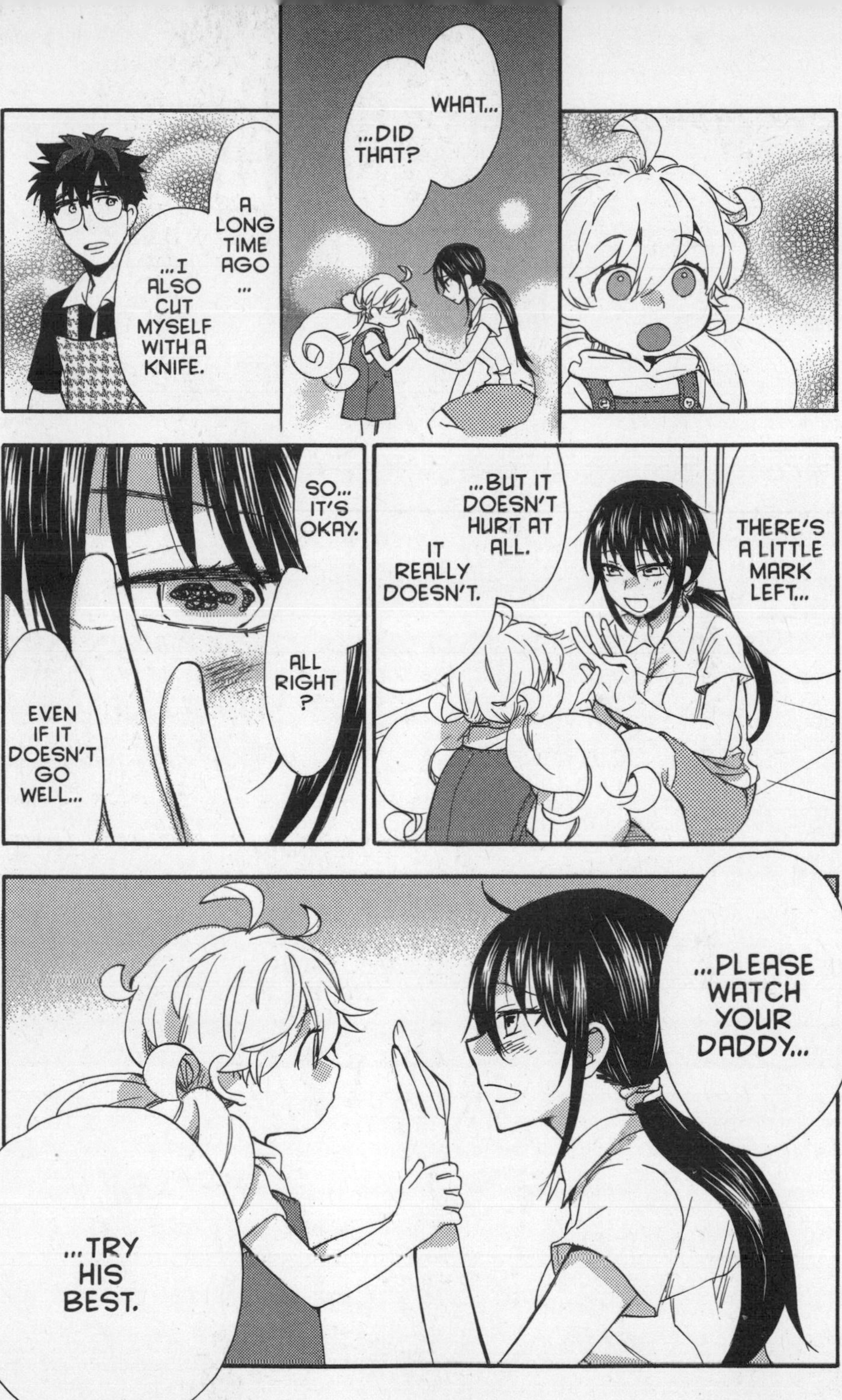
WHAT...
...DID THAT?
A LONG TIME AGO ...
...I ALSO CUT MYSELF WITH A KNIFE.
THERE'S A LITTLE MARK LEFT...
...BUT IT DOESN'T HURT AT ALL.
IT REALLY DOESN'T.
SO... IT'S OKAY.
ALL RIGHT?
EVEN IF IT DOESN'T GO WELL...
...PLEASE WATCH YOUR DADDY...
...TRY HIS BEST.

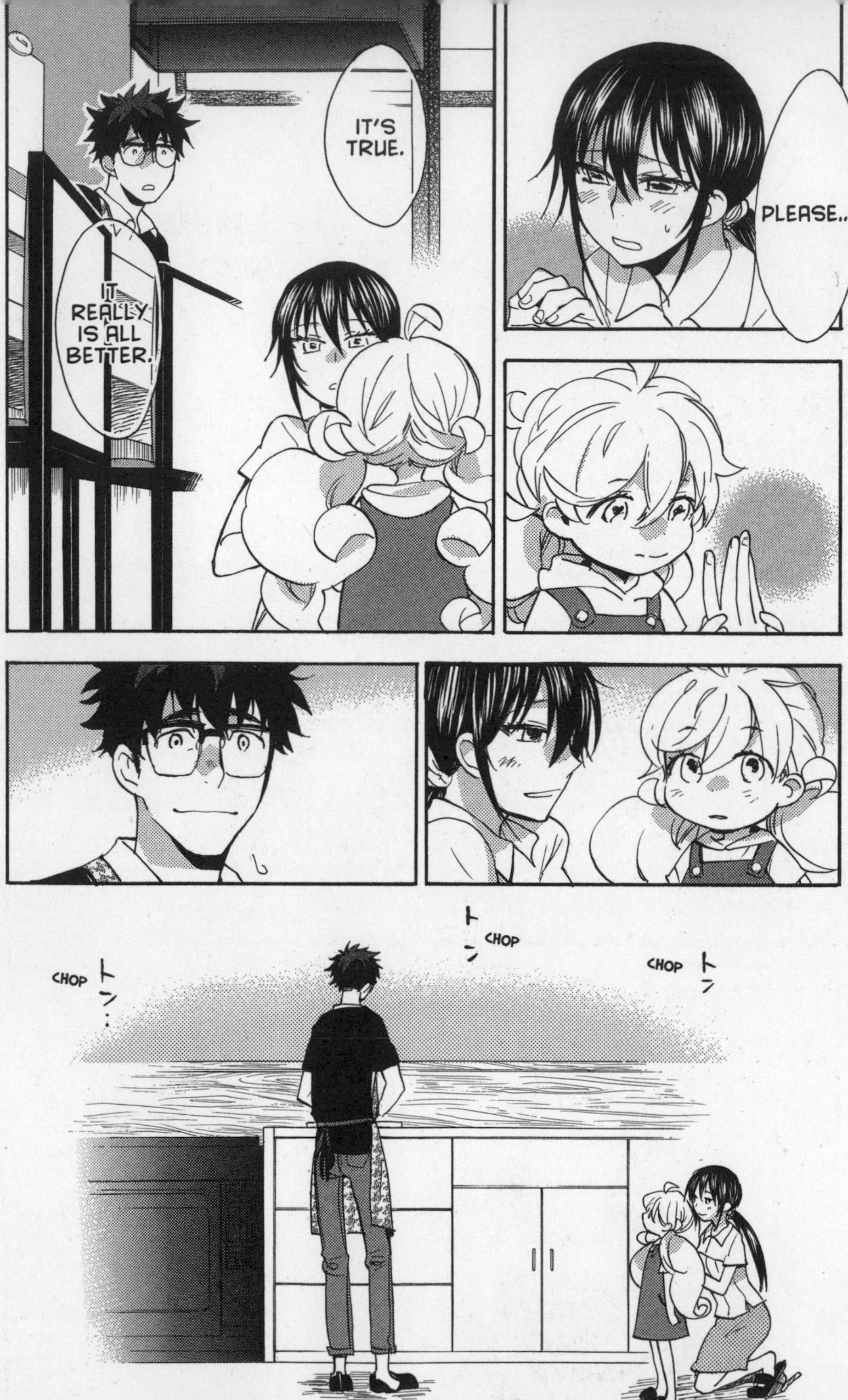
PLEASE...
IT'S TRUE.
IT REALLY IS ALL BETTER.
トン
CHOP
トン
CHOP
トン…
CHOP

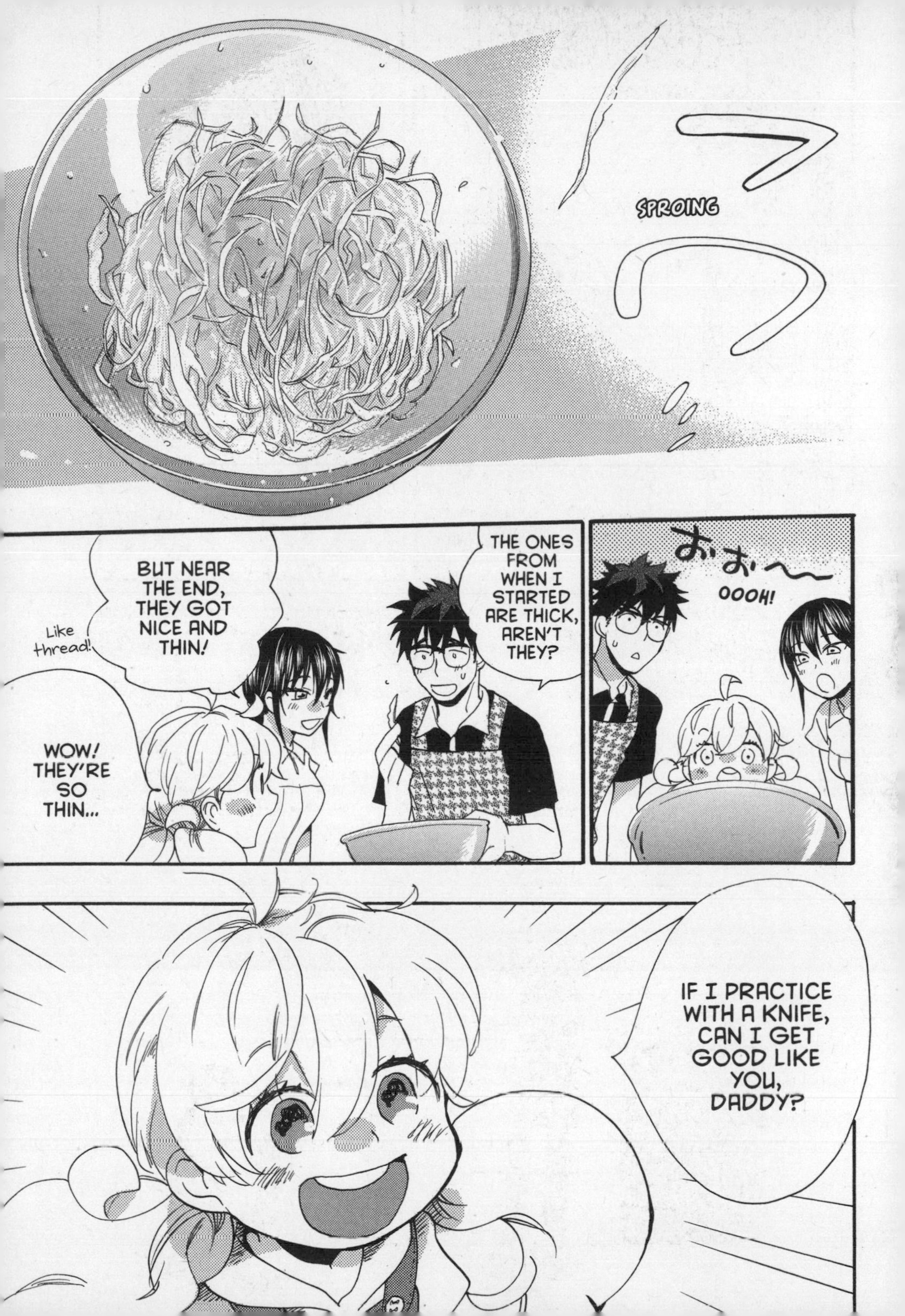
SPROING
おお〜
OOOH!
THE ONES FROM WHEN I STARTED ARE THICK, AREN'T THEY?
BUT NEAR THE END, THEY GOT NICE AND THIN!
Like thread!
WOW! THEY'RE SO THIN...
IF I PRACTICE WITH A KNIFE, CAN I GET GOOD LIKE YOU, DADDY?

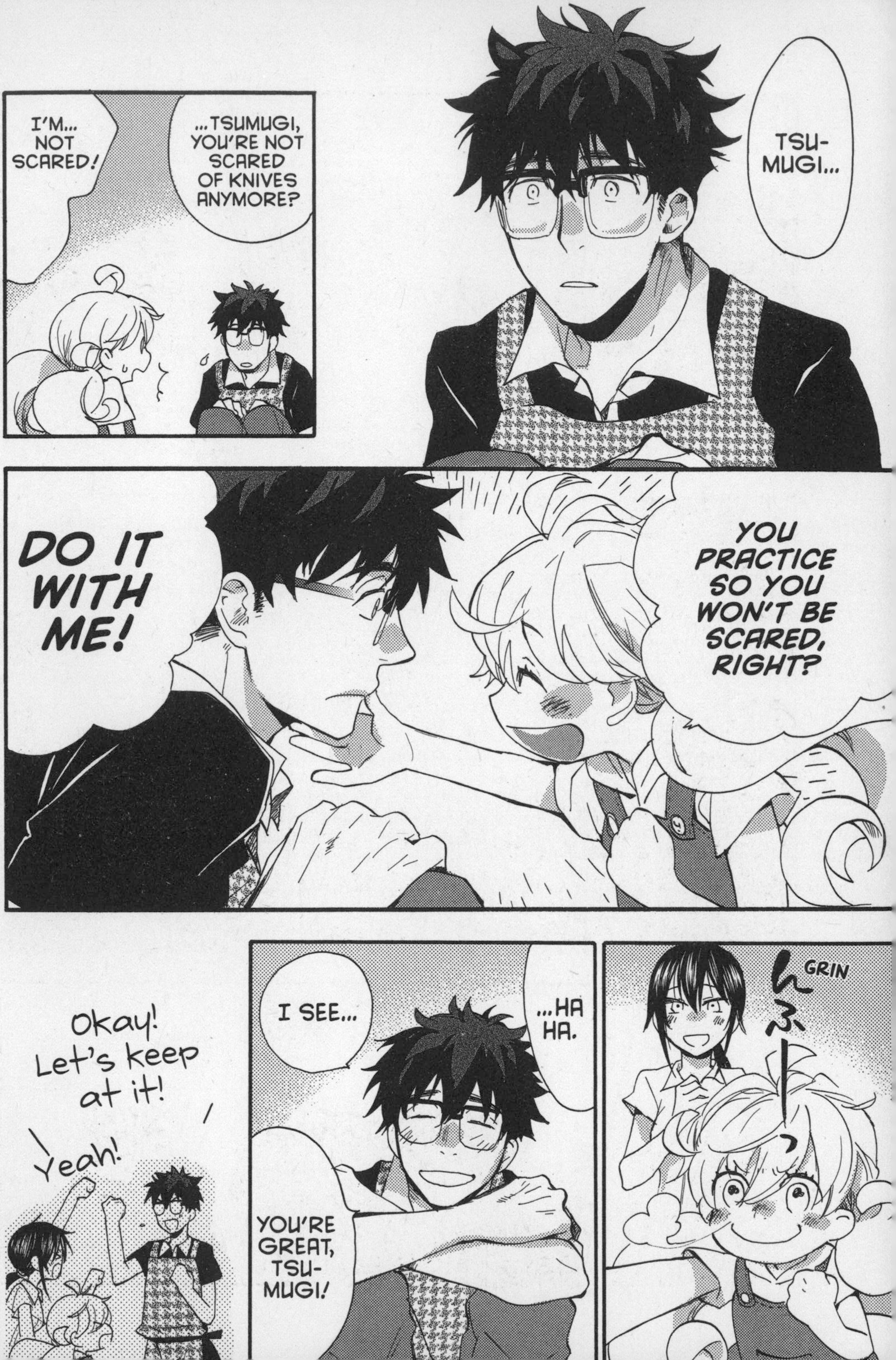
TSU-MUGI...
...TSUMUGI, YOU'RE NOT SCARED OF KNIVES ANYMORE?
I'M... NOT SCARED!
YOU PRACTICE SO YOU WON'T BE SCARED, RIGHT?
DO IT WITH ME!
んふーっ
GRIN
...HA HA.
I SEE...
YOU'RE GREAT, TSU-MUGI!
Okay! Let's keep at it!
Yeah!

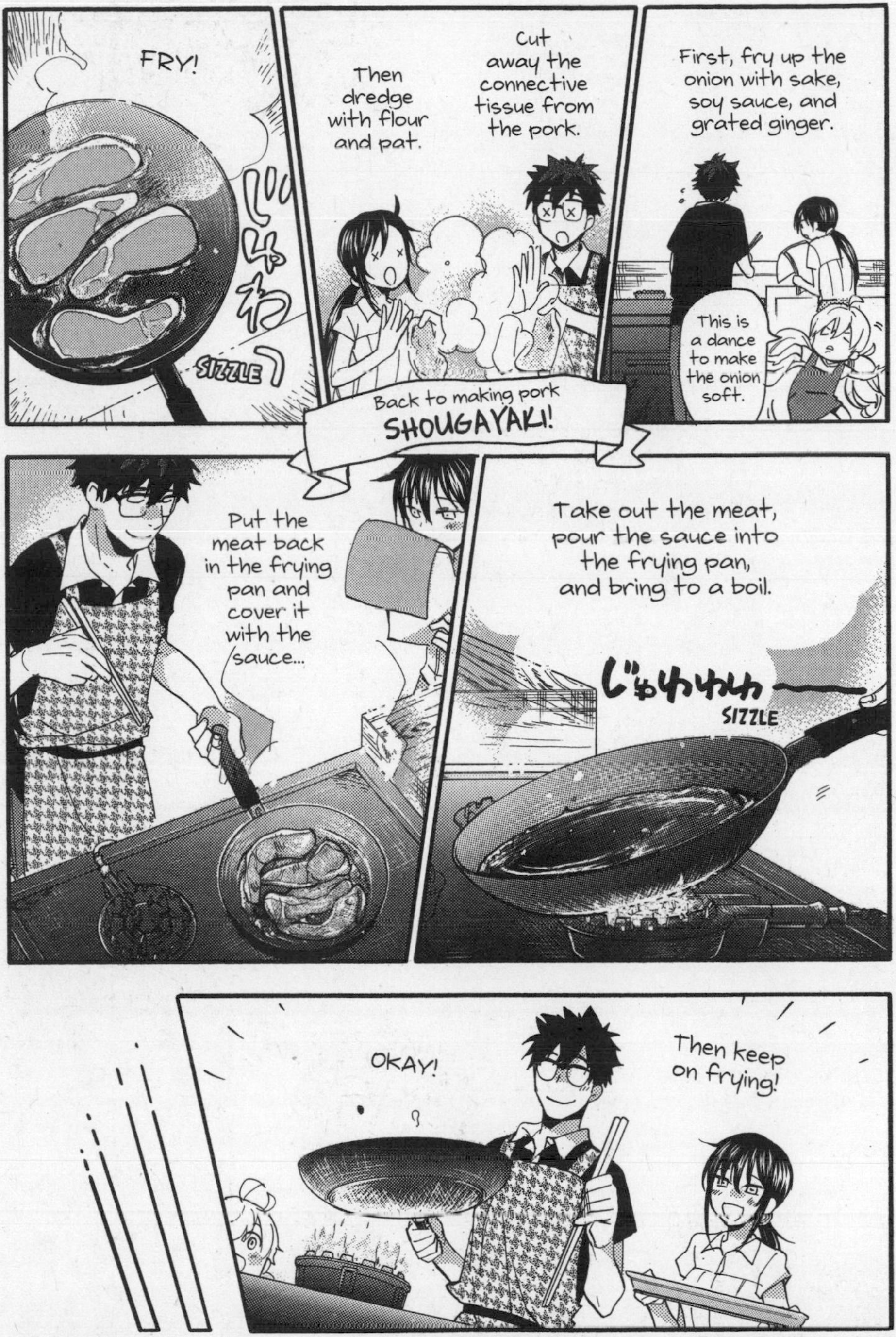

First, fry up the onion with sake, soy sauce, and grated ginger.
This is a dance to make the onion soft.
Cut away the connective tissue from the pork.
Then dredge with flour and pat.
FRY!
じゅわ
SIZZLE
Back to making pork SHOUGAYAKI!
Take out the meat, pour the sauce into the frying pan, and bring to a boil.
じゅわわわー
SIZZLE
Put the meat back in the frying pan and cover it with the sauce...
Then keep on frying!
OKAY!

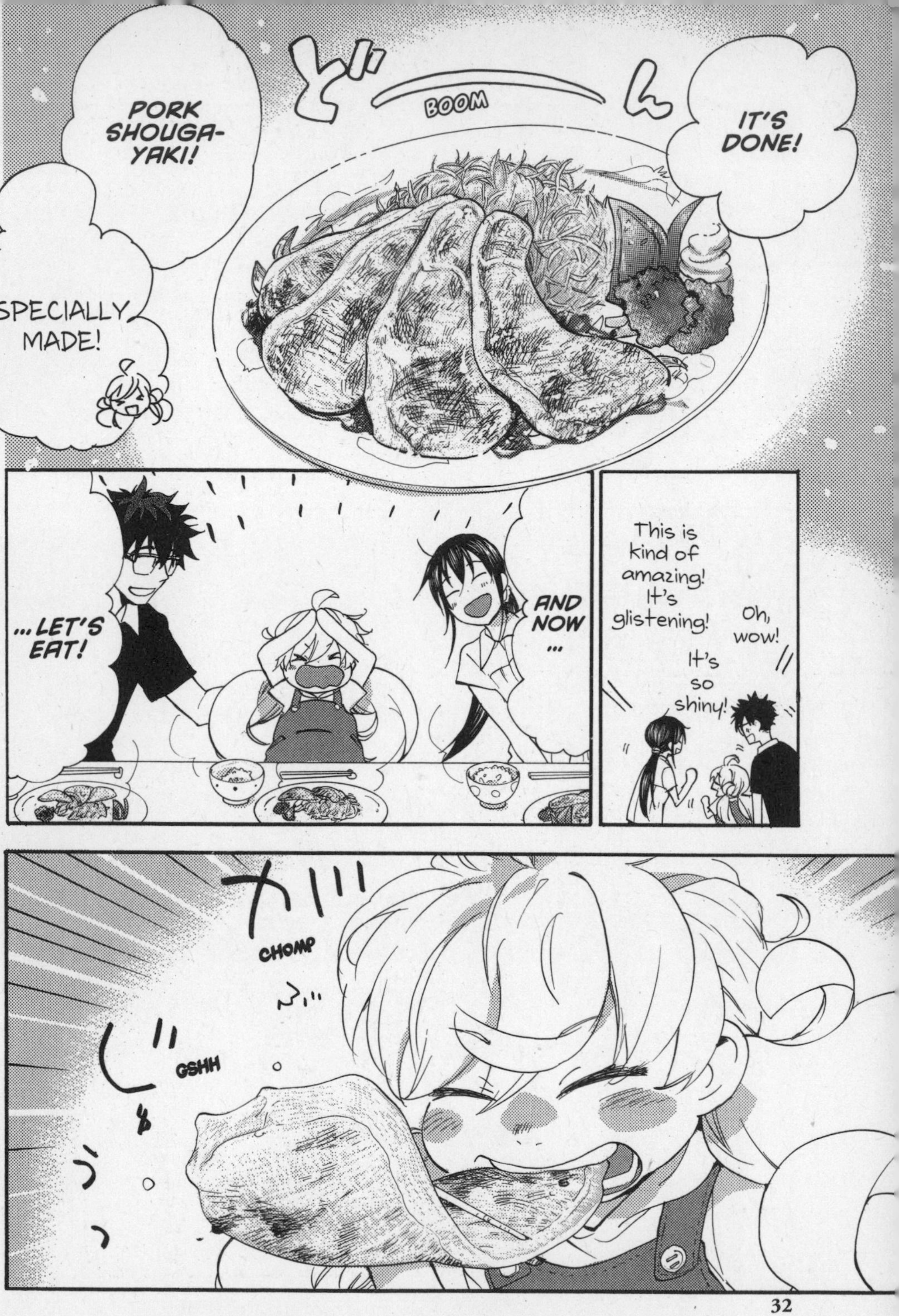
BOOM
IT'S DONE!
PORK SHOUGA-YAKI!
SPECIALLY MADE!
This is kind of amazing! It's glistening!
Oh, wow!
It's so shiny!
AND NOW ...
... LET'S EAT!
CHOMP
GSHH

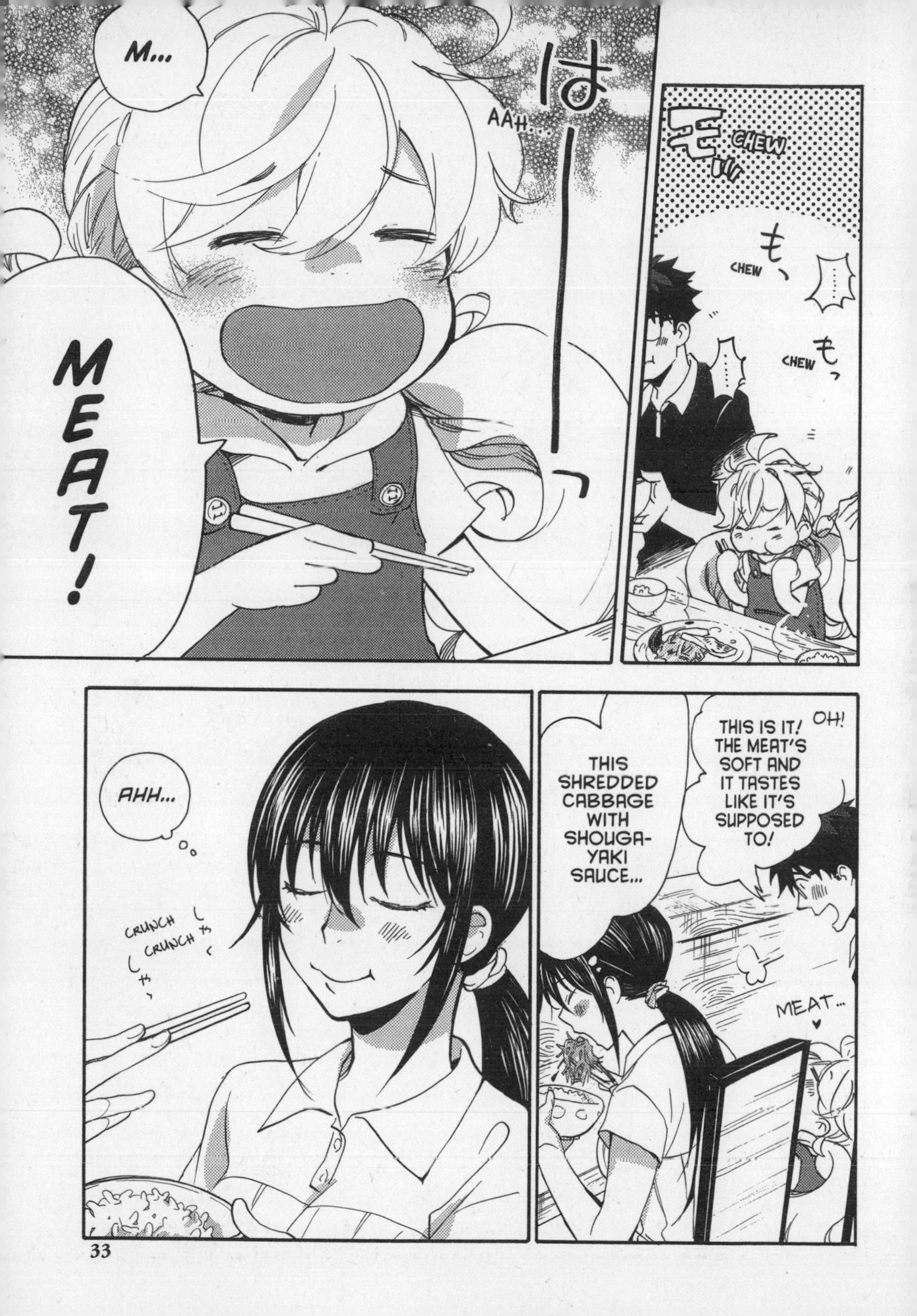
CHEW
CHEW
CHEW
AAH...
M...
MEAT!
OH!
THIS IS IT! THE MEAT'S SOFT AND IT TASTES LIKE IT'S SUPPOSED TO!
THIS SHREDDED CABBAGE WITH SHOUGA-YAKI SAUCE...
MEAT...
AHH...
CRUNCH
CRUNCH

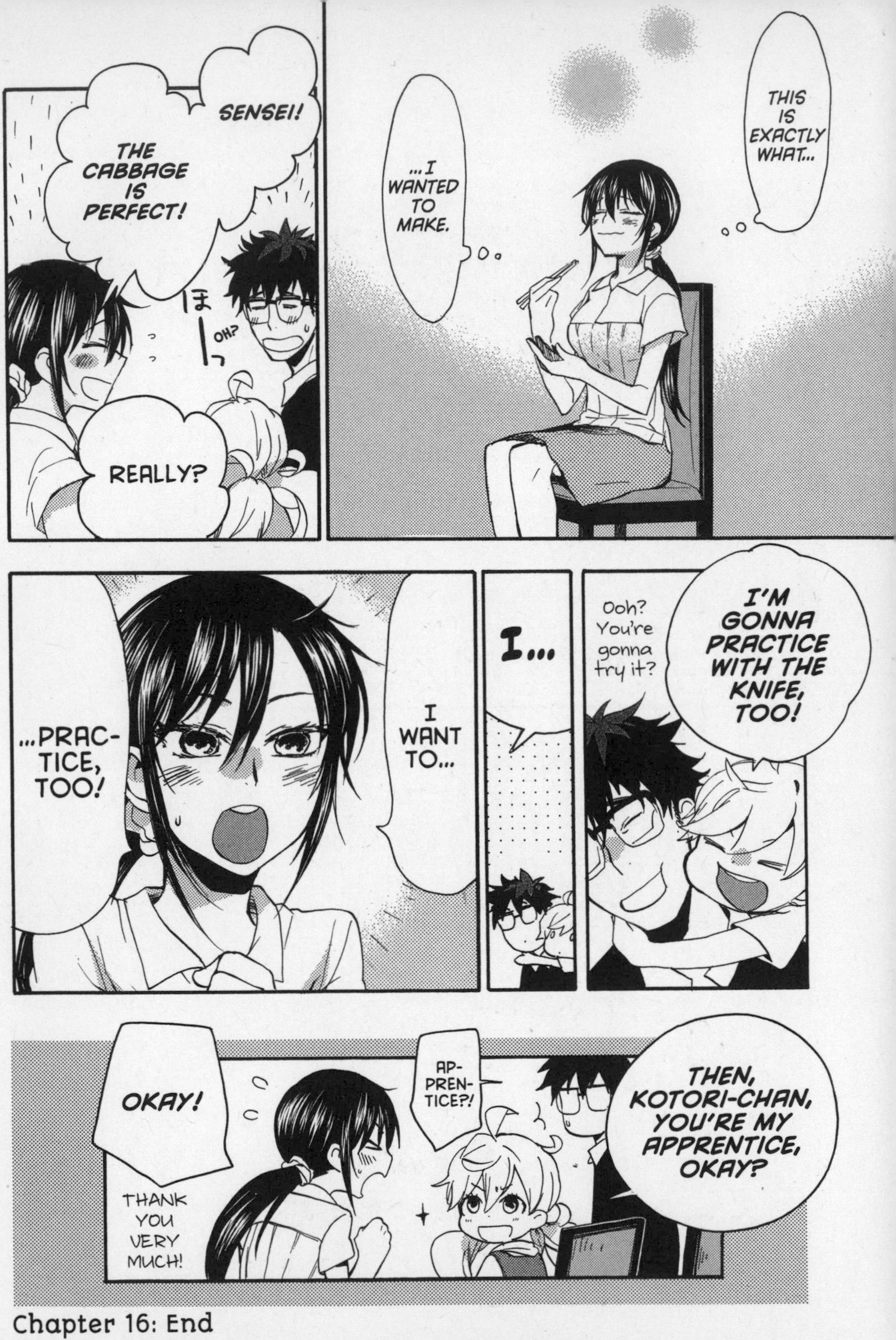
THIS IS EXACTLY WHAT...
...I WANTED TO MAKE.
SENSEI! THE CABBAGE IS PERFECT!
ほーっ
OH?
REALLY?
I'M GONNA PRACTICE WITH THE KNIFE, TOO!
Ooh? You're gonna try it?
I...
I WANT TO...
...PRAC-TICE, TOO!
THEN, KOTORI-CHAN, YOU'RE MY APPRENTICE, OKAY?
AP-PREN-TICE?!
OKAY!
THANK YOU VERY MUCH!

Chapter 16: End

SHOUGAYAKI (GINGER-FRIED PORK)

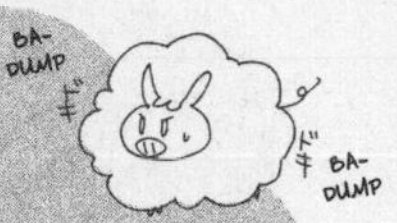

BA-DUMP
BA-DUMP

☆ Ingredients ☆ Serves 3

1 onion
3 cabbage leaves
9-12 slices of pork loin (thick)
Some vegetable oil and flour
Side Vegetables (tomatoes, cucumbers, boiled broccoli, etc.)

Adjust to your liking

(A) 2 Tbsp each of soy sauce, sake, and mirin. 10 g grated ginger
(B) 1/2 Tbsp each of soy sauce and sake, pinch of grated ginger

STEPS

1. Chop the onion into thin slices. Mix Group A thoroughly.
2. Shred the cabbage and soak in ice water for several minutes to make it crisp. Drain.

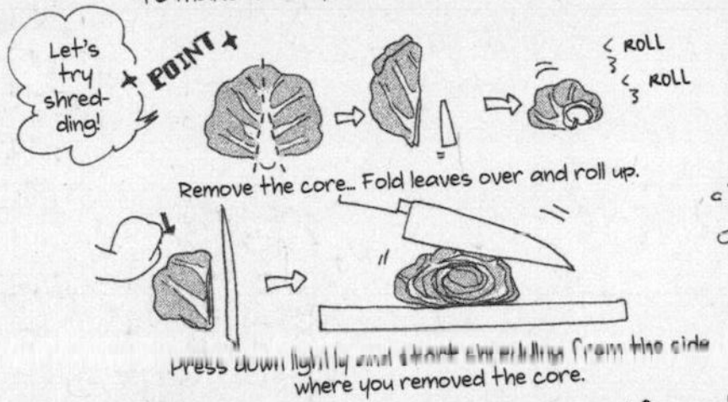

Let's try shredding!
POINT
ROLL
ROLL
Remove the core... Fold leaves over and roll up.
Press down lightly and start shredding from the side where you removed the core.

Be careful not to get hurt!
Pull the knife towards you, or push it away from you as you cut. Try to cut long, thin strips.

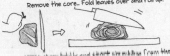

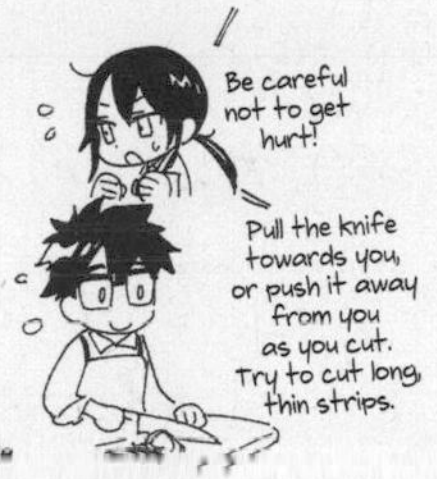

3. Heat vegetable oil in the frying pan and fry up the onion from step 1. Once it softens up, add Group B. Remove the onion when the excess moisture has evaporated.
4. Cut away extra connective tissue from the pork, then dredge with flour and pat. Fry 3-4 pieces of pork at a time, both sides, and then remove when browned.
5. Pour half of the thoroughly mixed Group A into the frying pan from step 4, and bring to a boil. Put half of the pork back in and cover with the sauce. Once it's done, take it out and repeat with the other half.
6. Put the cabbage from step 2 onto a plate, arrange the onions from step 3 in front, and place the pork on top. Add the side vegetables...

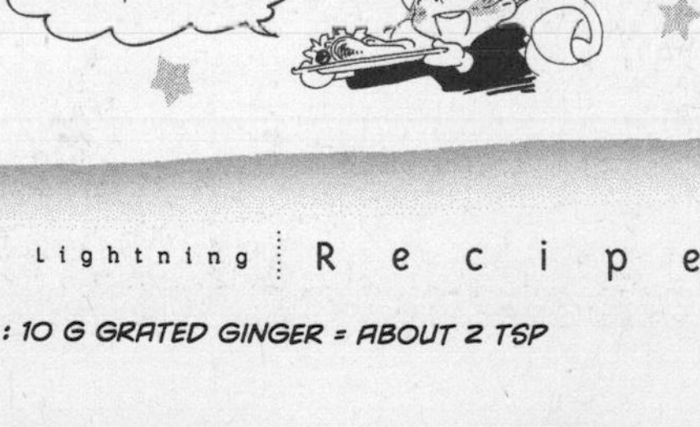

...and you're done!

CONVERSION NOTES : 10 G GRATED GINGER = ABOUT 2 TSP

ほたん
CLICK

SEALED AWAY

Chapter 17 A Play and Sweet Potato Crepes

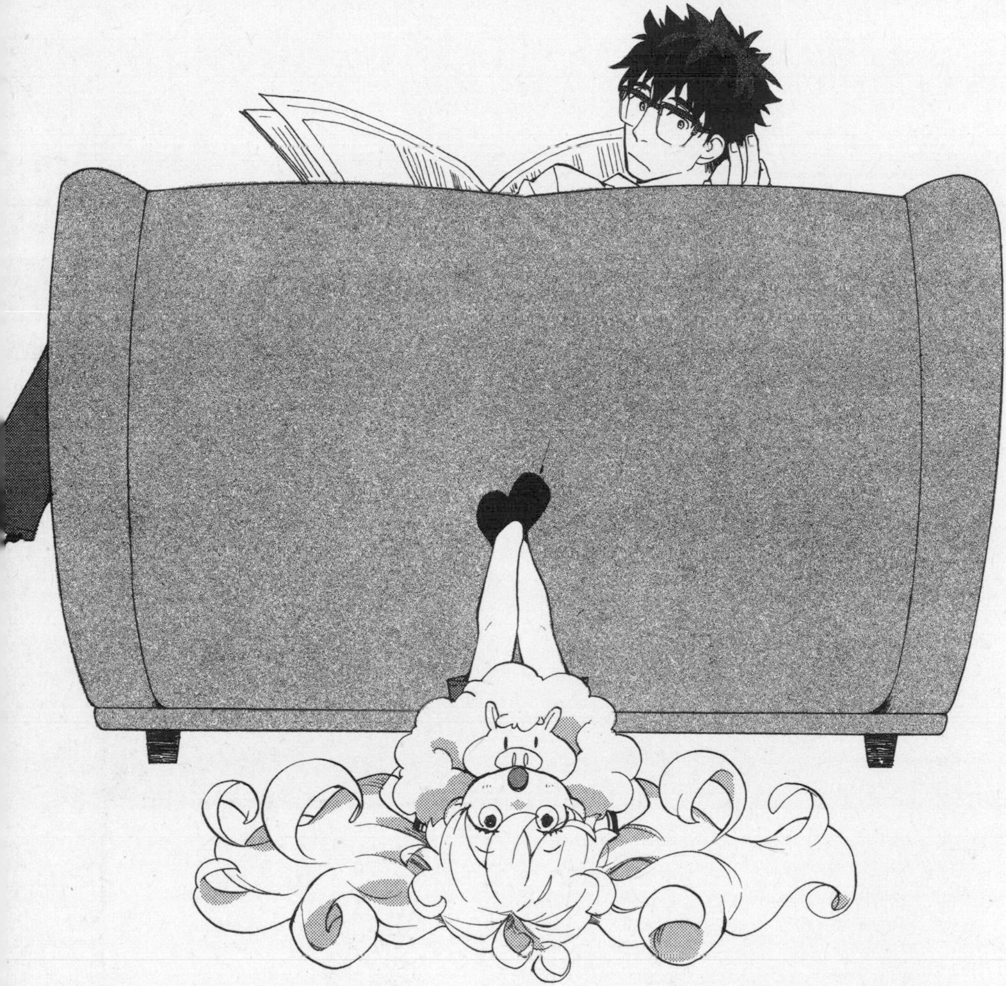

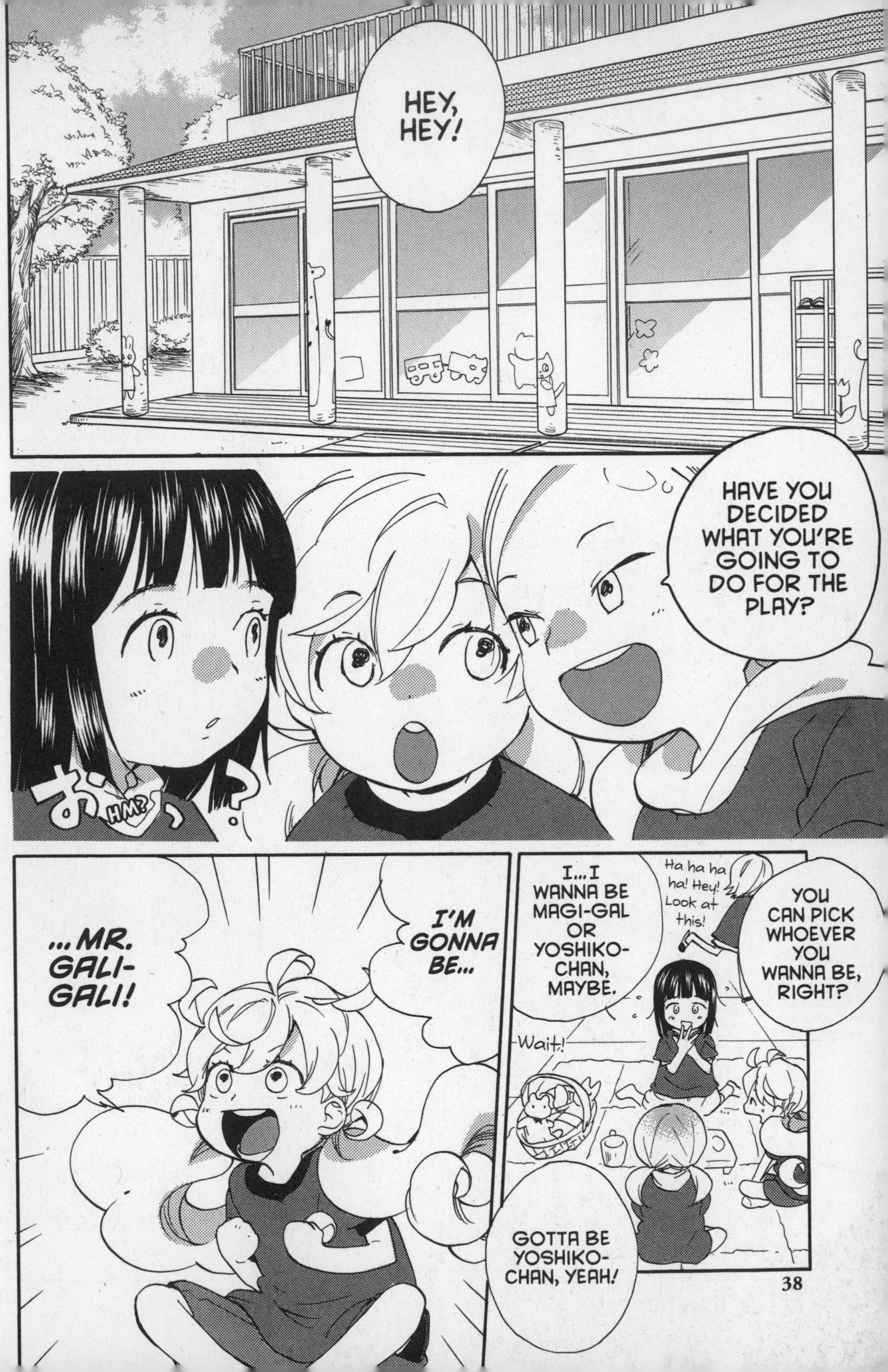
HEY, HEY!
HAVE YOU DECIDED WHAT YOU'RE GOING TO DO FOR THE PLAY?
お
HM?
YOU CAN PICK WHOEVER YOU WANNA BE, RIGHT?
Ha ha ha ha! Hey! Look at this!
I... I WANNA BE MAGI-GAL OR YOSHIKO-CHAN, MAYBE.
-Wait!
GOTTA BE YOSHIKO-CHAN, YEAH!
I'M GONNA BE...
...MR. GALI-GALI!

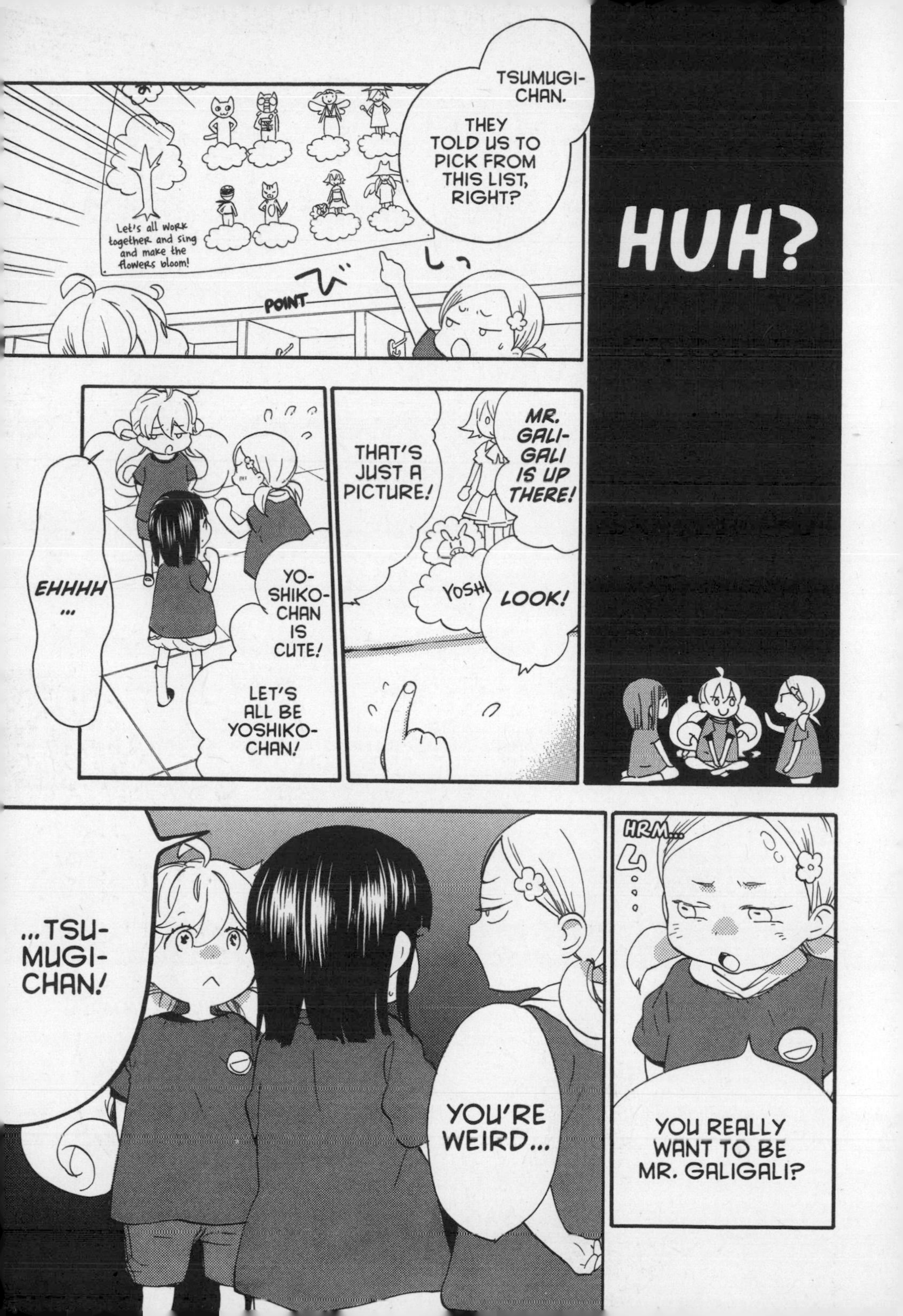
HUH?
Let's all work together and sing and make the flowers bloom!
TSUMUGI-CHAN.
THEY TOLD US TO PICK FROM THIS LIST, RIGHT?
びしっ
POINT
MR. GALI-GALI IS UP THERE!
THAT'S JUST A PICTURE!
LOOK!
YOSH
YO-SHIKO-CHAN IS CUTE!
LET'S ALL BE YOSHIKO-CHAN!
EHHHH ...
HRM...
YOU REALLY WANT TO BE MR. GALIGALI?
YOU'RE WEIRD...
...TSU-MUGI-CHAN!

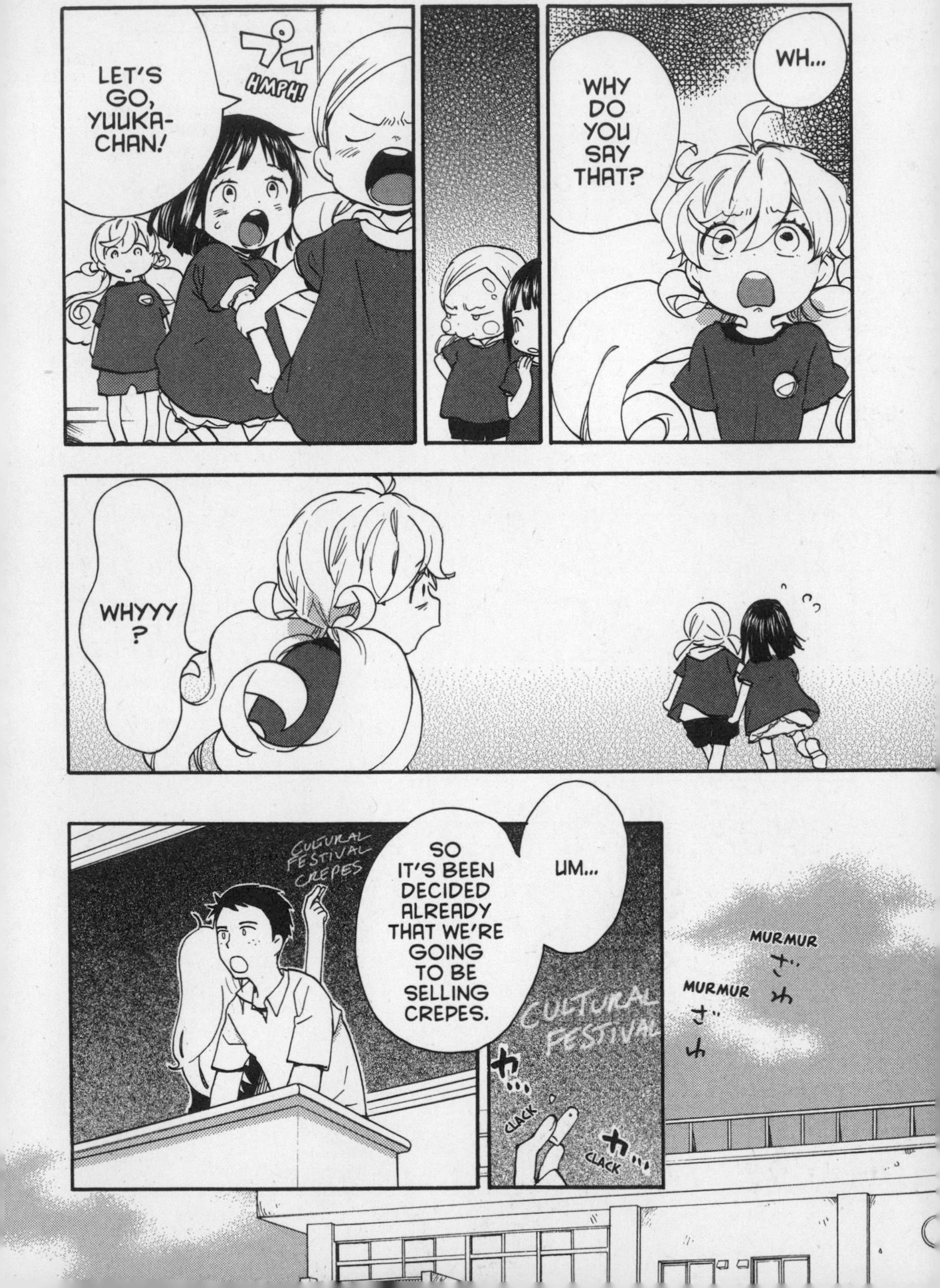
WH...
WHY DO YOU SAY THAT?
プイ
HMPH!
LET'S GO, YUUKA-CHAN!
WHYYY?
MURMUR
MURMUR
ざわ ざわ
UM...
SO IT'S BEEN DECIDED ALREADY THAT WE'RE GOING TO BE SELLING CREPES.
CULTURAL FESTIVAL
CLACK
CLACK
CULTURAL FESTIVAL CREPES

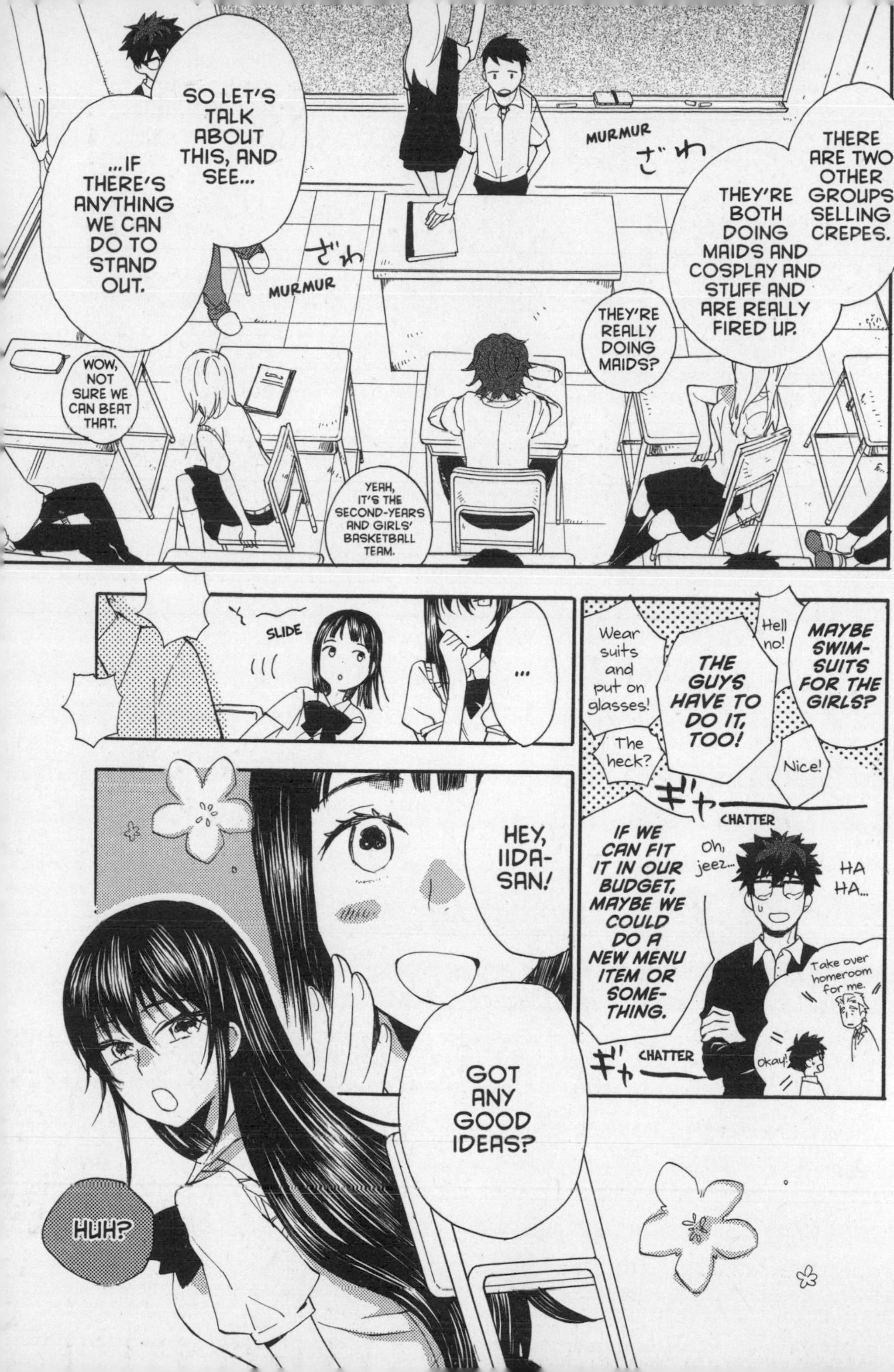
THERE ARE TWO OTHER GROUPS SELLING CREPES.
THEY'RE BOTH DOING MAIDS AND COSPLAY AND STUFF AND ARE REALLY FIRED UP.
MURMUR
SO LET'S TALK ABOUT THIS, AND SEE...
...IF THERE'S ANYTHING WE CAN DO TO STAND OUT.
MURMUR
THEY'RE REALLY DOING MAIDS?
YEAH, IT'S THE SECOND-YEARS AND GIRLS' BASKETBALL TEAM.
WOW, NOT SURE WE CAN BEAT THAT.
MAYBE SWIM-SUITS FOR THE GIRLS?
Hell no!
THE GUYS HAVE TO DO IT, TOO!
Wear suits and put on glasses!
Nice!
The heck?
CHATTER
HA HA...
Oh, jeez...
IF WE CAN FIT IT IN OUR BUDGET, MAYBE WE COULD DO A NEW MENU ITEM OR SOME-THING.
Take over homeroom for me.
Okay!
CHATTER
SLIDE
...
HEY, IIDA-SAN!
GOT ANY GOOD IDEAS?
HUH?

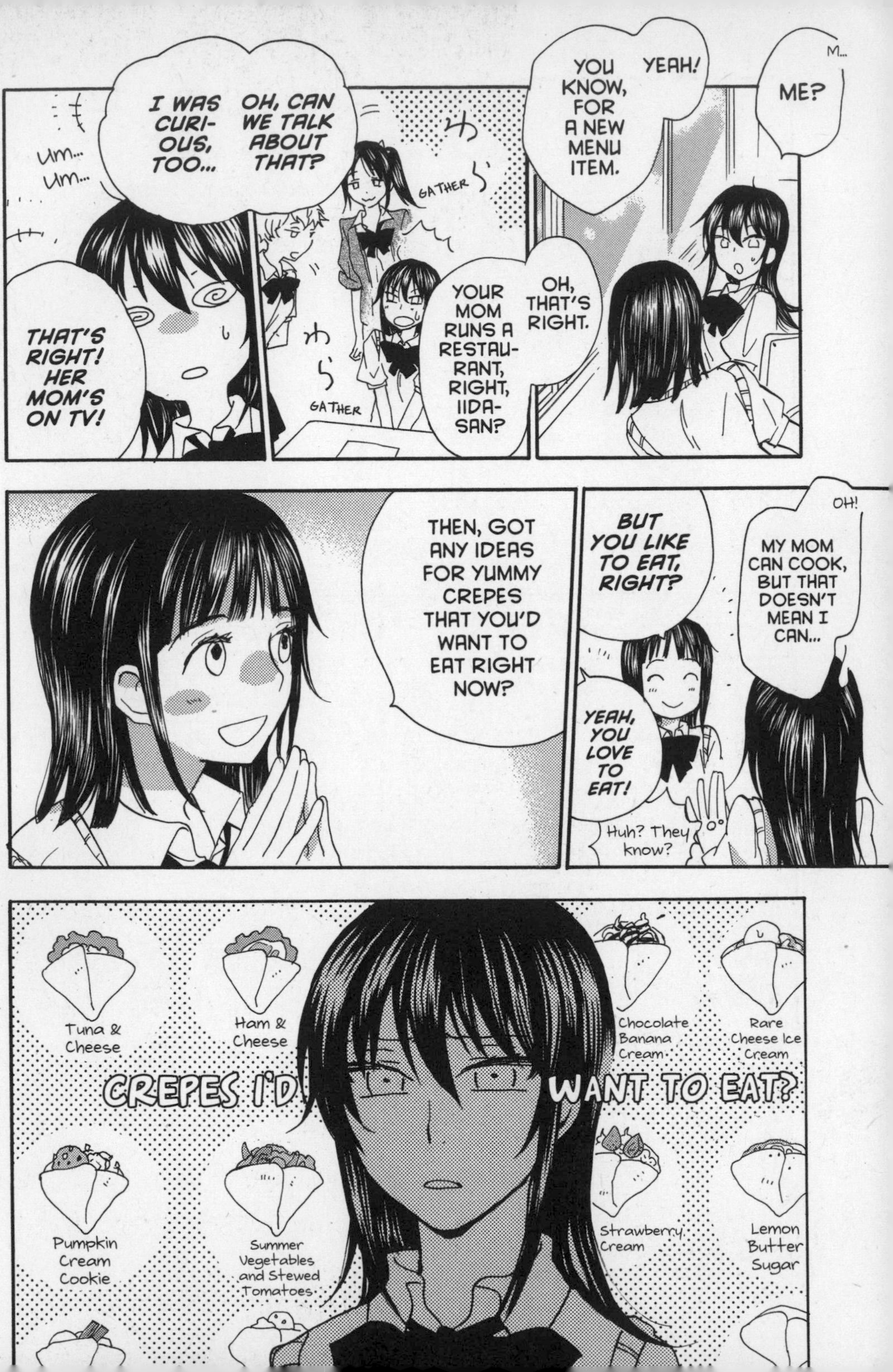
M... ME?
YEAH!
YOU KNOW, FOR A NEW MENU ITEM.
OH, THAT'S RIGHT.
YOUR MOM RUNS A RESTAURANT, RIGHT, IIDA-SAN?
OH, CAN WE TALK ABOUT THAT?
I WAS CURIOUS, TOO...
GATHER
GATHER
Um... Um...
THAT'S RIGHT! HER MOM'S ON TV!
OH!
MY MOM CAN COOK, BUT THAT DOESN'T MEAN I CAN...
BUT YOU LIKE TO EAT, RIGHT?
YEAH, YOU LOVE TO EAT!
Huh? They know?
THEN, GOT ANY IDEAS FOR YUMMY CREPES THAT YOU'D WANT TO EAT RIGHT NOW?
Rare Cheese Ice Cream
Chocolate Banana Cream
Ham & Cheese
Tuna & Cheese
CREPES I'D WANT TO EAT?
Lemon Butter Sugar
Strawberry Cream
Summer Vegetables and Stewed Tomatoes
Pumpkin Cream Cookie

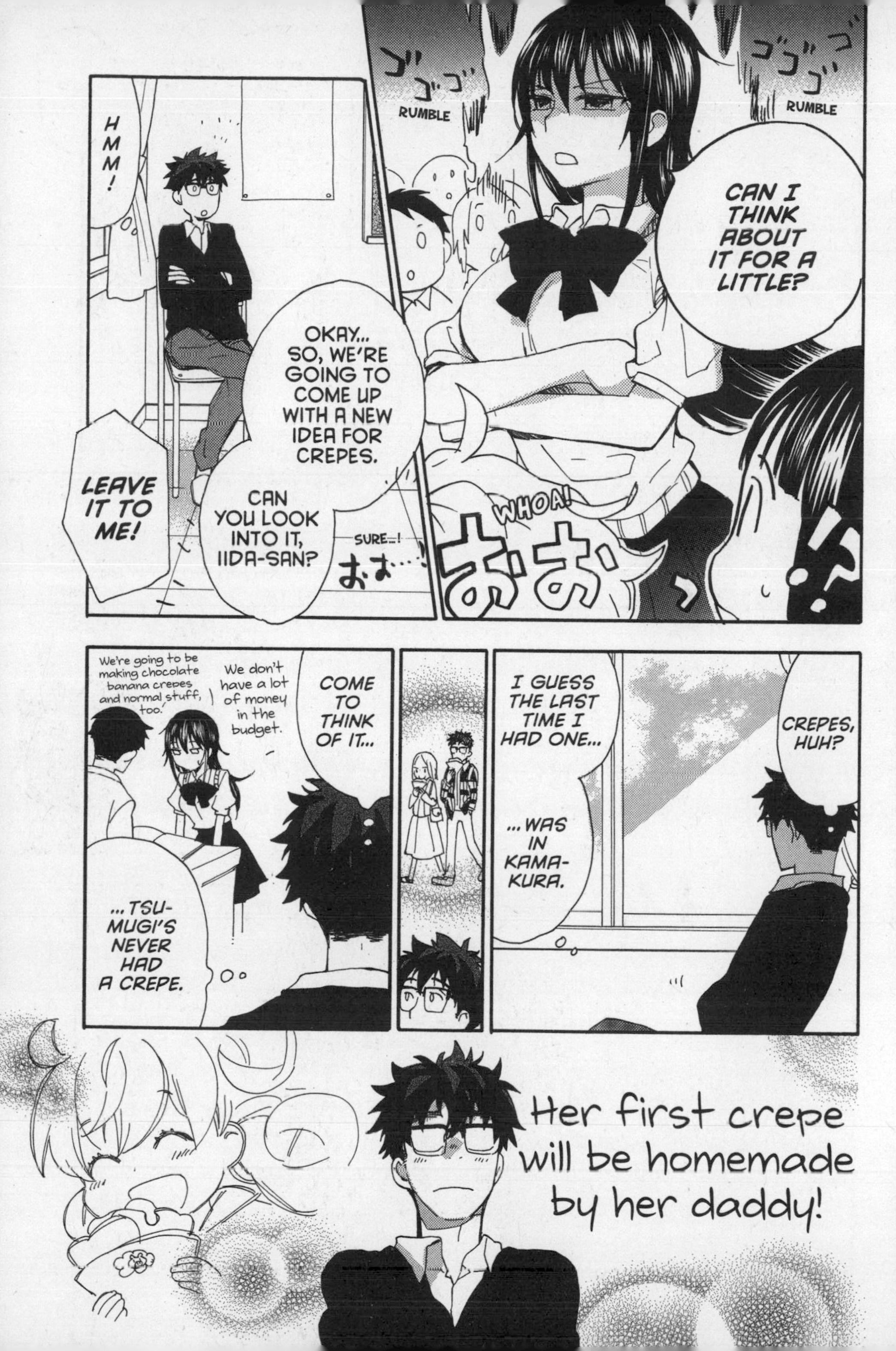
ゴゴゴ
RUMBLE
ゴゴゴ
RUMBLE
CAN I THINK ABOUT IT FOR A LITTLE?
OKAY... SO, WE'RE GOING TO COME UP WITH A NEW IDEA FOR CREPES.
CAN YOU LOOK INTO IT, IIDA-SAN?
WHOA!
おお
!?
HMM!
LEAVE IT TO ME!
SURE...!
CREPES, HUH?
I GUESS THE LAST TIME I HAD ONE...
...WAS IN KAMA-KURA.
COME TO THINK OF IT...
We don't have a lot of money in the budget.
We're going to be making chocolate banana crepes and normal stuff, too.
...TSU-MUGI'S NEVER HAD A CREPE.
Her first crepe will be homemade by her daddy!

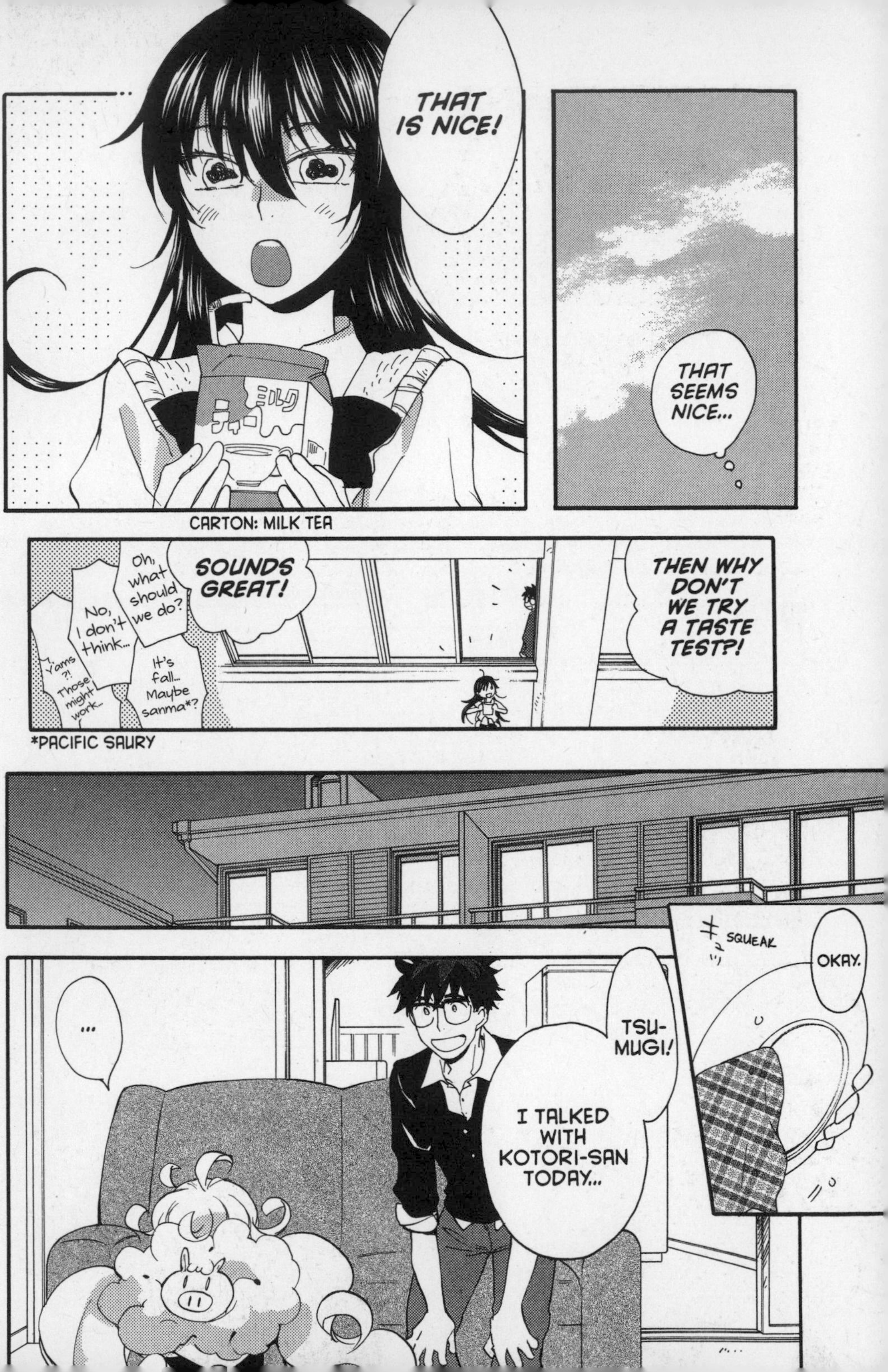
THAT IS NICE!
THAT SEEMS NICE...
CARTON: MILK TEA
THEN WHY DON'T WE TRY A TASTE TEST?!
SOUNDS GREAT!
Oh, what should we do?
No, I don't think...
It's fall... Maybe sanma*?
Yams?! Those might work...
*PACIFIC SAURY
SQUEAK
OKAY.
TSU-MUGI!
I TALKED WITH KOTORI-SAN TODAY...
...

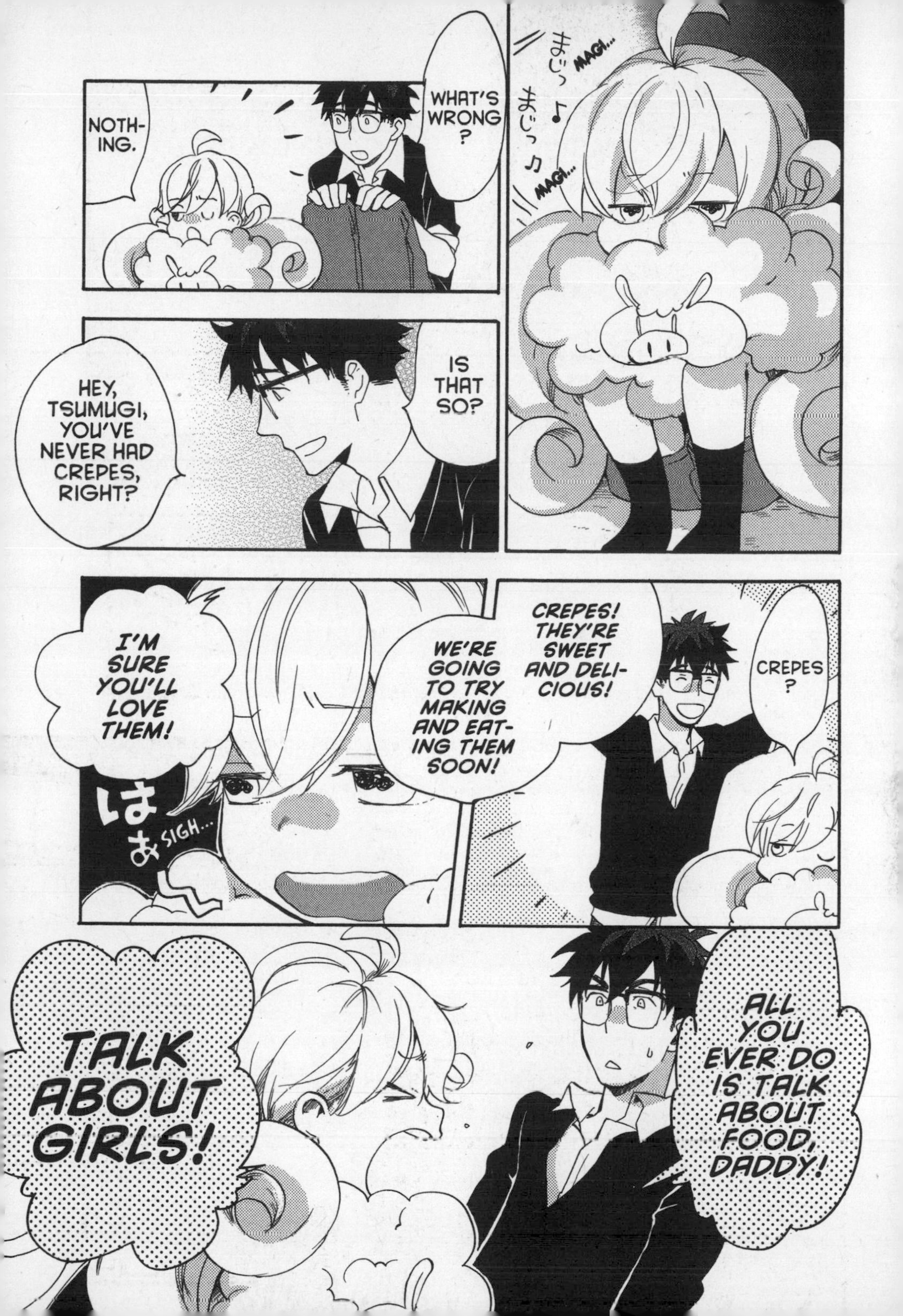
まじっ MAGI...
まじっ ♪
まじっ ♪ MAGI...
WHAT'S WRONG?
NOTHING.
IS THAT SO?
HEY, TSUMUGI, YOU'VE NEVER HAD CREPES, RIGHT?
CREPES?
CREPES! THEY'RE SWEET AND DELICIOUS!
WE'RE GOING TO TRY MAKING AND EATING THEM SOON!
I'M SURE YOU'LL LOVE THEM!
はぁ SIGH...
ALL YOU EVER DO IS TALK ABOUT FOOD, DADDY!
TALK ABOUT GIRLS!

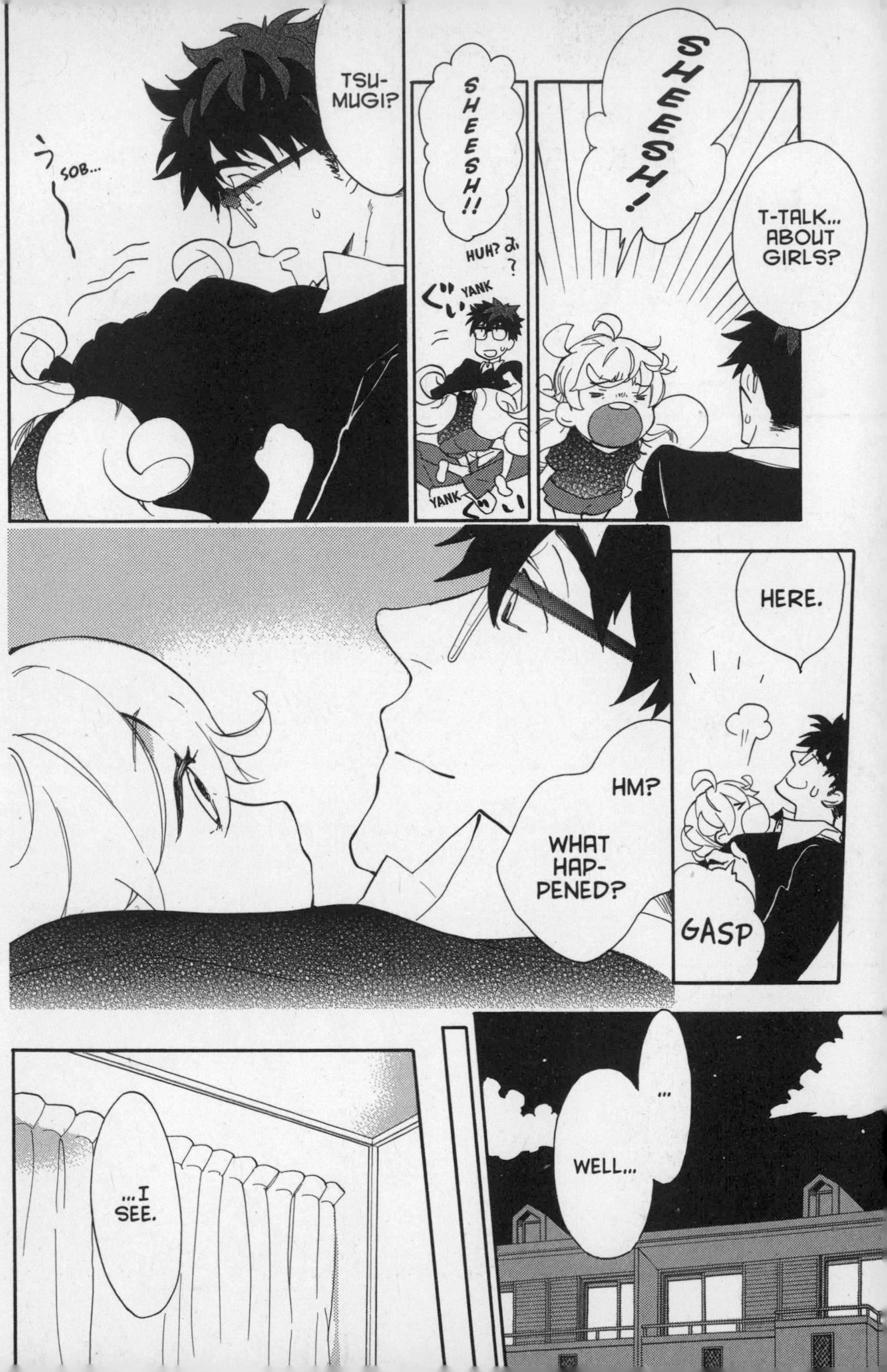
T-TALK... ABOUT GIRLS?
SHEESH!
SHEESH!!
HUH?
YANK
YANK
TSU-MUGI?
SOB...
HERE.
GASP
HM?
WHAT HAP-PENED?
...
WELL...
...I SEE.

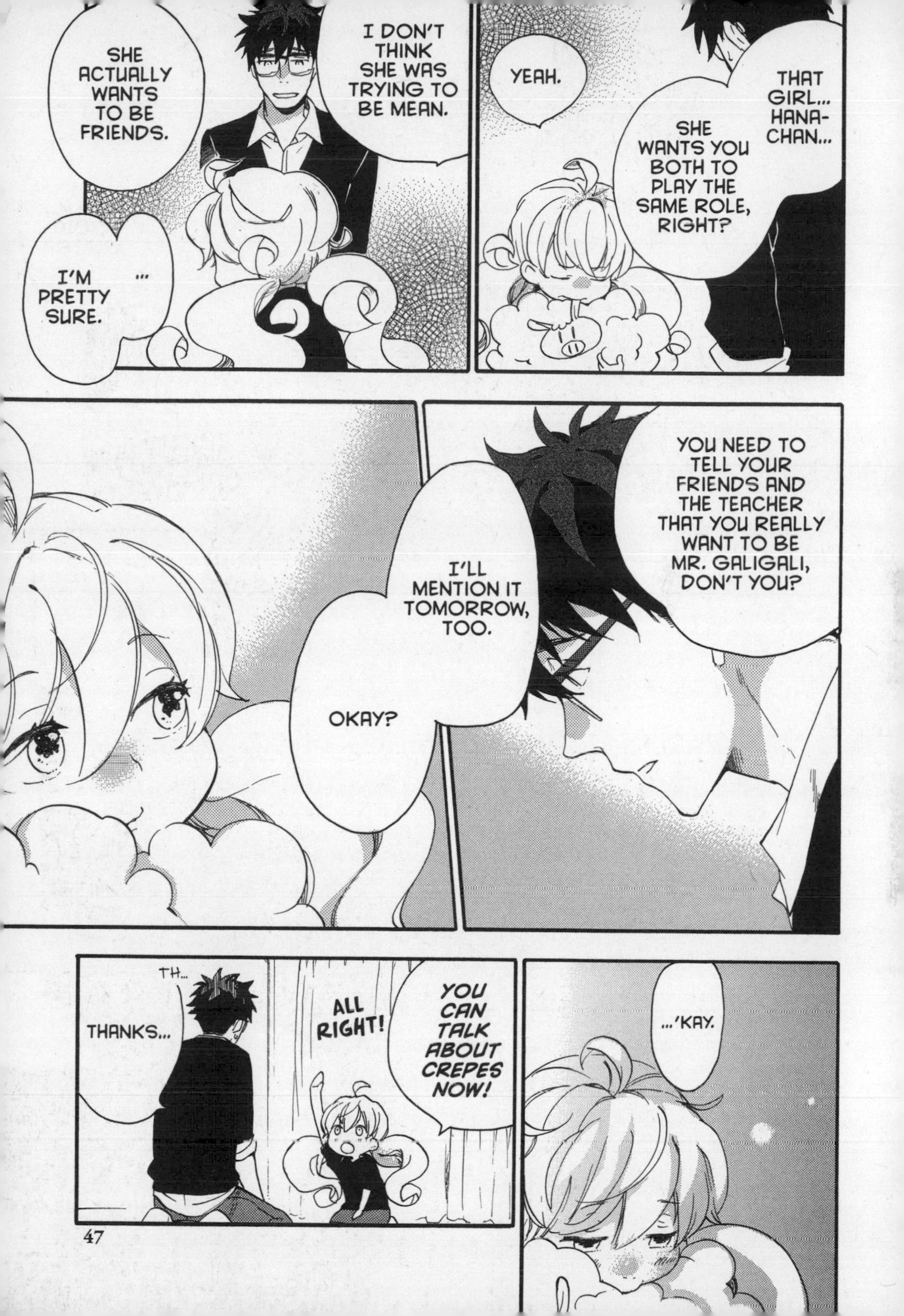
THAT GIRL... HANA-CHAN...
SHE WANTS YOU BOTH TO PLAY THE SAME ROLE, RIGHT?
YEAH.
I DON'T THINK SHE WAS TRYING TO BE MEAN.
SHE ACTUALLY WANTS TO BE FRIENDS.
...
I'M PRETTY SURE.
YOU NEED TO TELL YOUR FRIENDS AND THE TEACHER THAT YOU REALLY WANT TO BE MR. GALIGALI, DON'T YOU?
I'LL MENTION IT TOMORROW, TOO.
OKAY?
...'KAY.
YOU CAN TALK ABOUT CREPES NOW!
ALL RIGHT!
TH...
THANKS...

THE NEXT DAY
OK

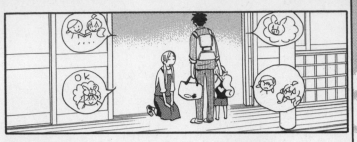

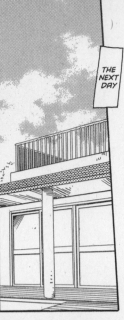

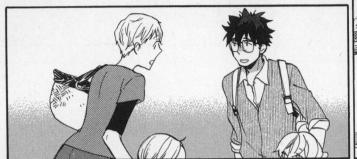

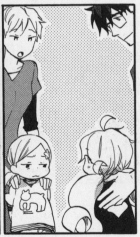

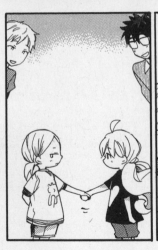

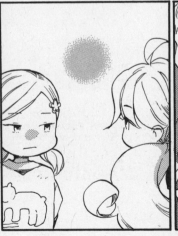

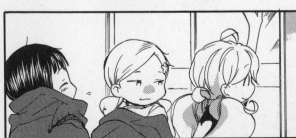

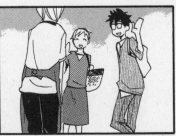

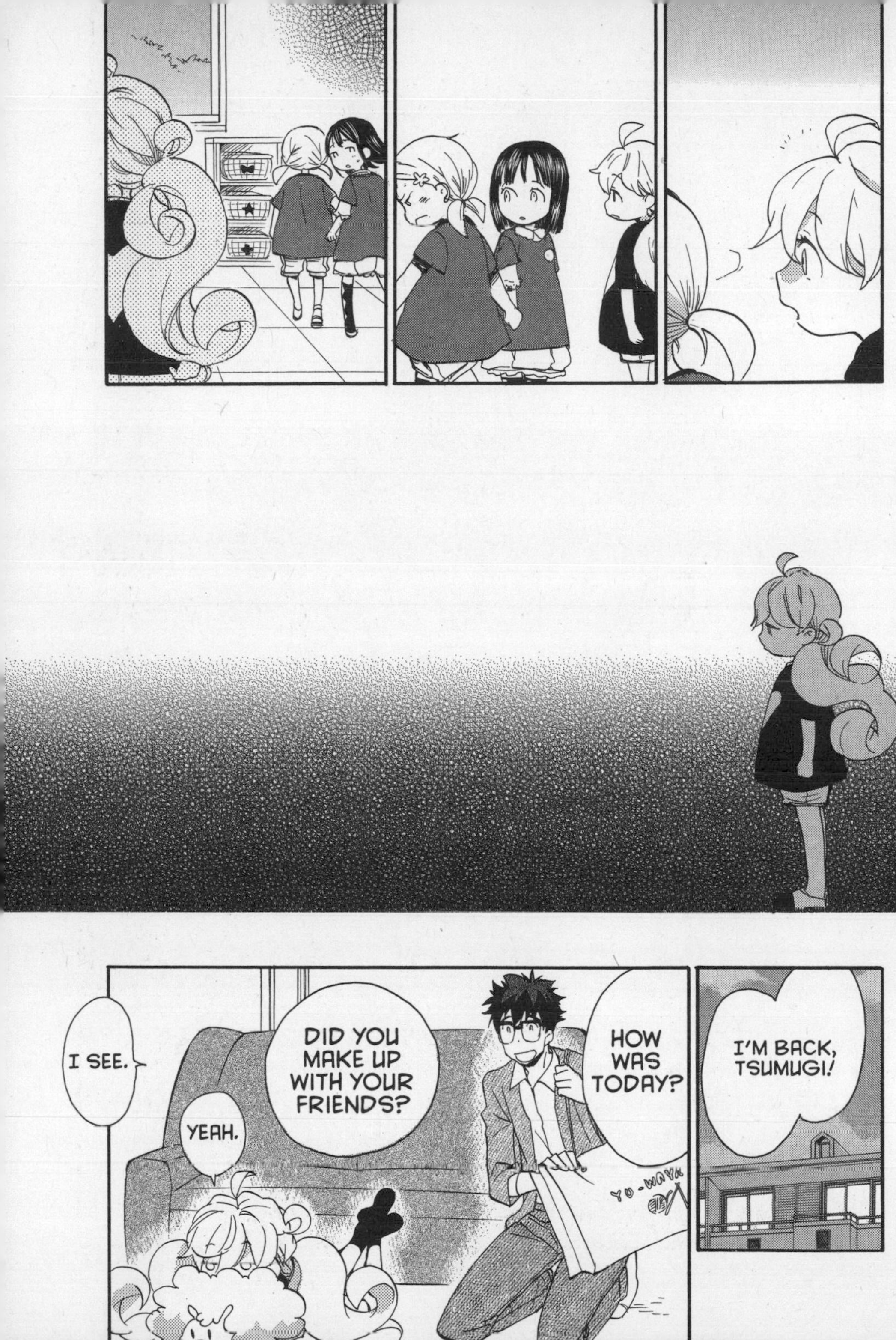

I'M BACK, TSUMUGI!
HOW WAS TODAY?
DID YOU MAKE UP WITH YOUR FRIENDS?
YEAH.
I SEE.

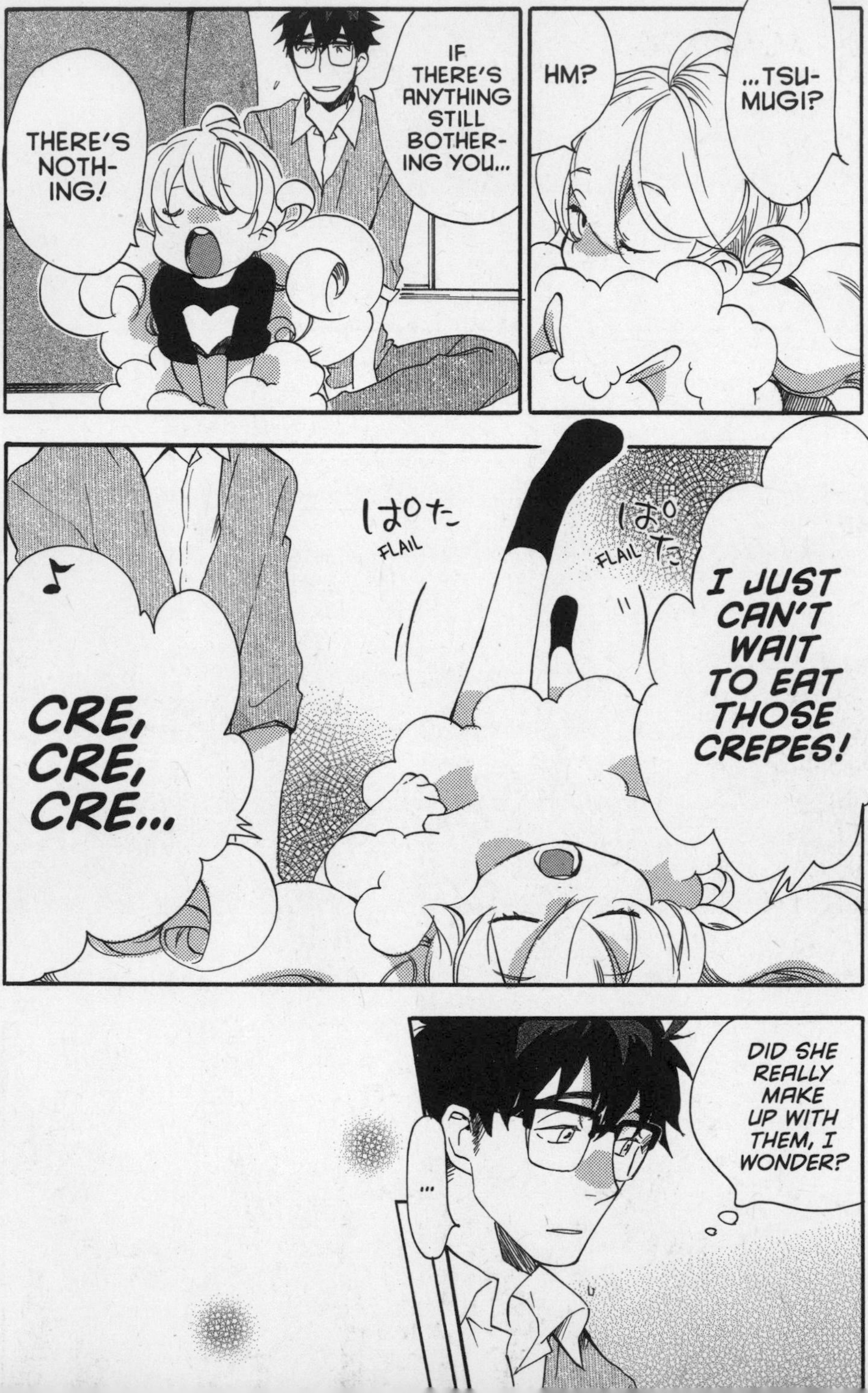
...TSU-MUGI?
HM?
IF THERE'S ANYTHING STILL BOTHERING YOU...
THERE'S NOTHING!
I JUST CAN'T WAIT TO EAT THOSE CREPES!
ぱたぱた
FLAIL
ぱたぱた
FLAIL
♪
CRE, CRE, CRE...
DID SHE REALLY MAKE UP WITH THEM, I WONDER?
...

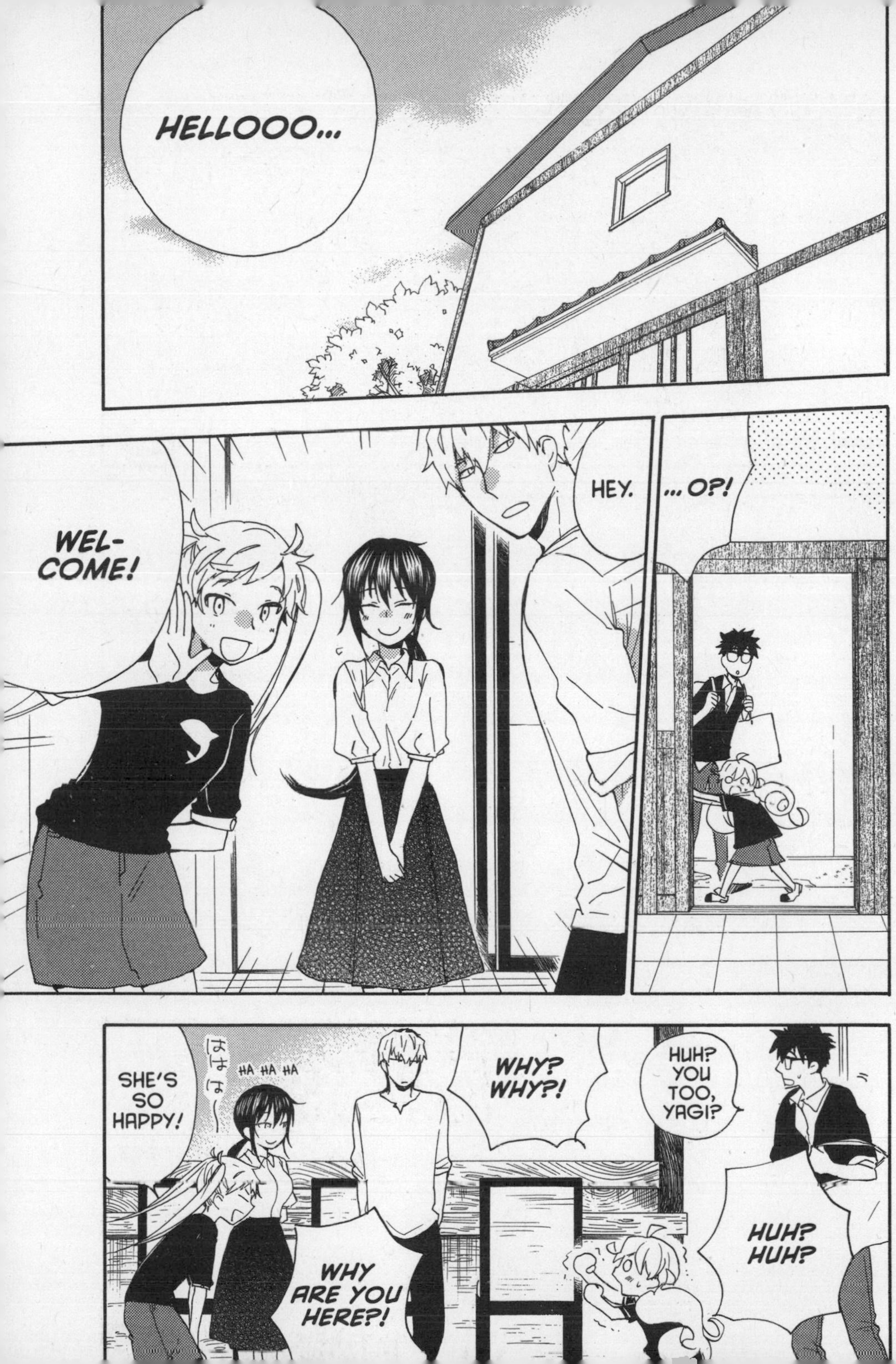
HELLOOO...
...O?!
HEY.
WEL-COME!
HUH? YOU TOO, YAGI?
WHY? WHY?!
ははは
HA HA HA
SHE'S SO HAPPY!
HUH? HUH?
WHY ARE YOU HERE?!

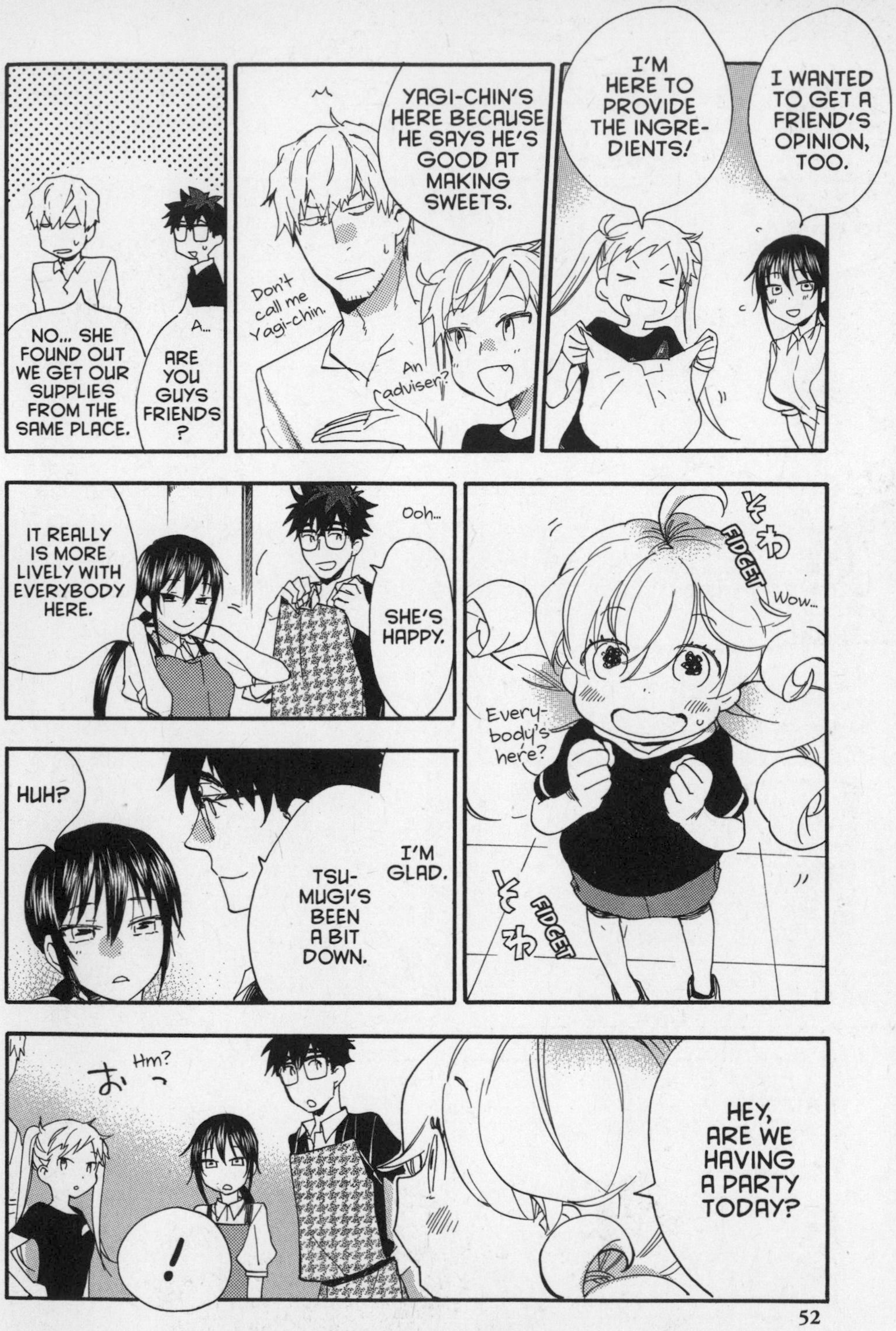
I WANTED TO GET A FRIEND'S OPINION, TOO.
I'M HERE TO PROVIDE THE INGREDIENTS!
YAGI-CHIN'S HERE BECAUSE HE SAYS HE'S GOOD AT MAKING SWEETS.
Don't call me Yagi-chin.
An adviser?
A...
ARE YOU GUYS FRIENDS?
NO... SHE FOUND OUT WE GET OUR SUPPLIES FROM THE SAME PLACE.
FIDGET
Wow...
Every-body's here?
FIDGET
Ooh...
SHE'S HAPPY.
IT REALLY IS MORE LIVELY WITH EVERYBODY HERE.
I'M GLAD.
TSU-MUGI'S BEEN A BIT DOWN.
HUH?
HEY, ARE WE HAVING A PARTY TODAY?
!
Hm?

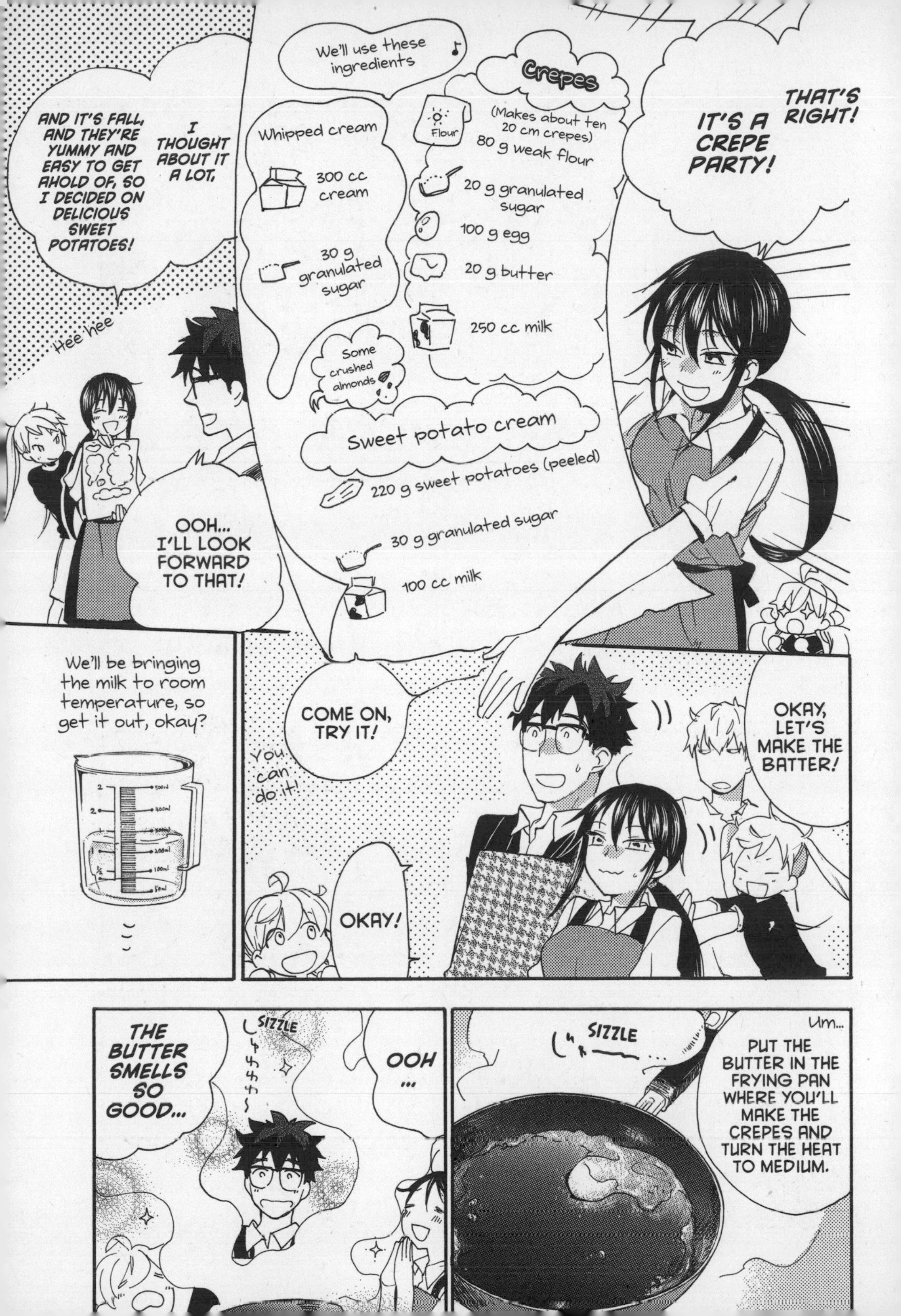
THAT'S RIGHT!
IT'S A CREPE PARTY!
We'll use these ingredients
Crepes
(Makes about ten 20 cm crepes)
Flour
80 g weak flour
20 g granulated sugar
100 g egg
20 g butter
250 cc milk
Whipped cream
300 cc cream
30 g granulated sugar
Some crushed almonds
Sweet potato cream
220 g sweet potatoes (peeled)
30 g granulated sugar
100 cc milk
I THOUGHT ABOUT IT A LOT.
AND IT'S FALL, AND THEY'RE YUMMY AND EASY TO GET AHOLD OF, SO I DECIDED ON DELICIOUS SWEET POTATOES!
Hee hee
OOH... I'LL LOOK FORWARD TO THAT!
OKAY, LET'S MAKE THE BATTER!
COME ON, TRY IT!
You can do it!
OKAY!
We'll be bringing the milk to room temperature, so get it out, okay?
SIZZLE
Um... PUT THE BUTTER IN THE FRYING PAN WHERE YOU'LL MAKE THE CREPES AND TURN THE HEAT TO MEDIUM.
OOH ...
SIZZLE
THE BUTTER SMELLS SO GOOD...

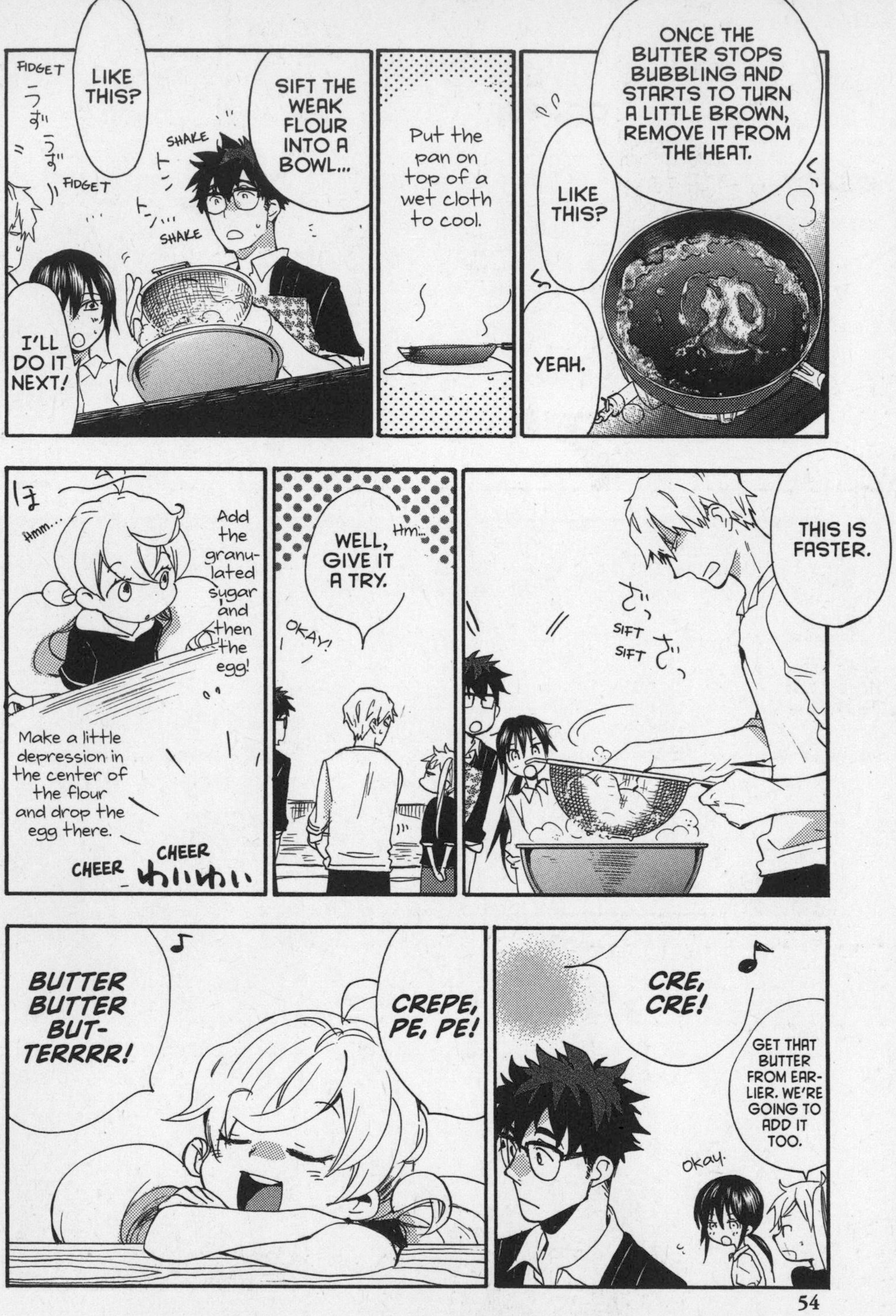
ONCE THE BUTTER STOPS BUBBLING AND STARTS TO TURN A LITTLE BROWN, REMOVE IT FROM THE HEAT.
LIKE THIS?
YEAH.
Put the pan on top of a wet cloth to cool.
SIFT THE WEAK FLOUR INTO A BOWL...
SHAKE
SHAKE
LIKE THIS?
FIDGET
うずうず
FIDGET
I'LL DO IT NEXT!
THIS IS FASTER.
SIFT
SIFT
Hm...
WELL, GIVE IT A TRY.
OKAY!
Hmm...
Add the granulated sugar and then the egg!
Make a little depression in the center of the flour and drop the egg there.
CHEER
CHEER
わいわい
CRE, CRE!
GET THAT BUTTER FROM EARLIER. WE'RE GOING TO ADD IT TOO.
Okay.
CREPE, PE, PE!
BUTTER BUTTER BUT-TERRRR!

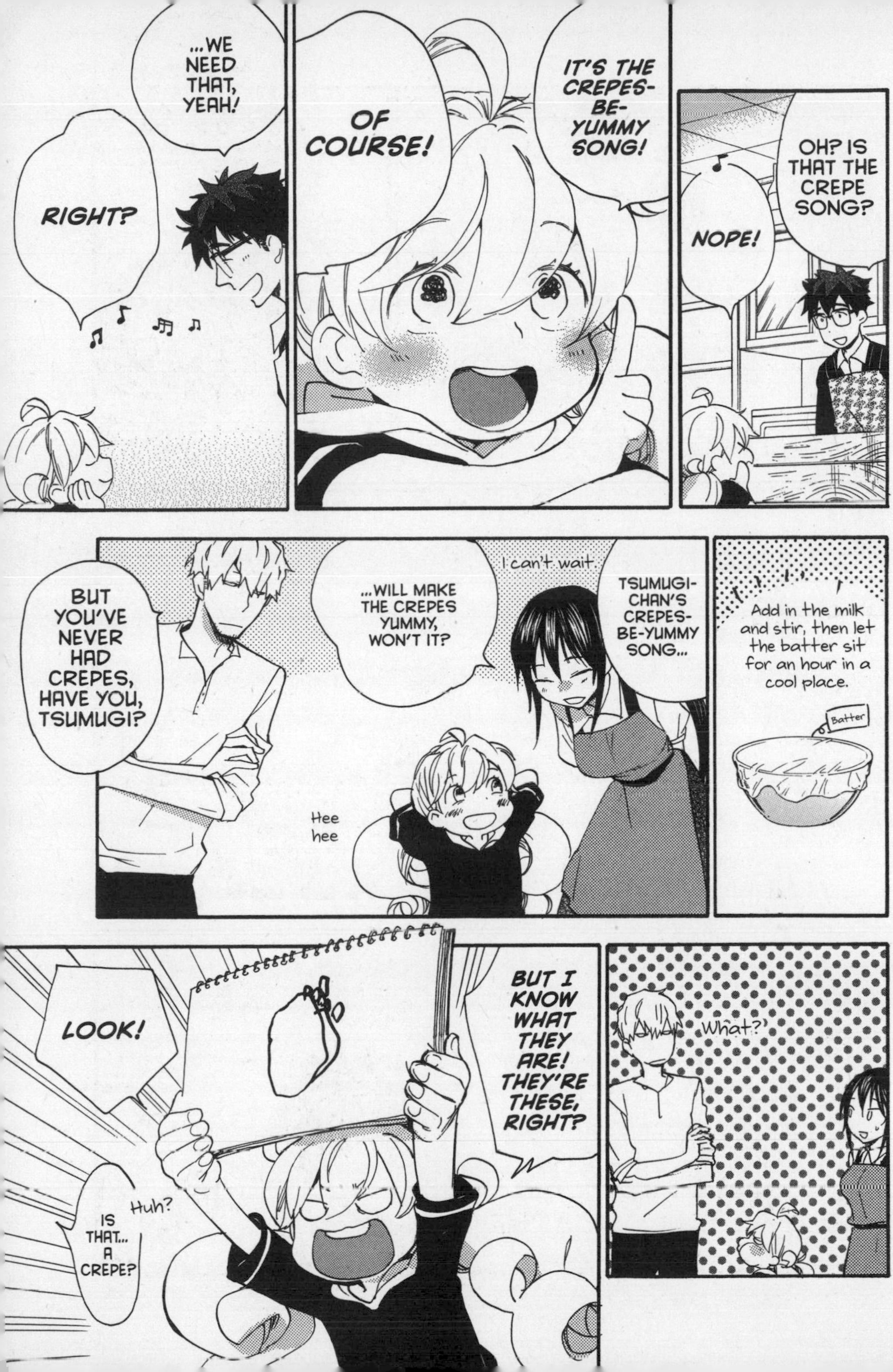
OH? IS THAT THE CREPE SONG?
NOPE!
IT'S THE CREPES-BE-YUMMY SONG!
OF COURSE!
...WE NEED THAT, YEAH!
RIGHT?
Add in the milk and stir, then let the batter sit for an hour in a cool place.
Batter
TSUMUGI-CHAN'S CREPES-BE-YUMMY SONG...
I can't wait.
...WILL MAKE THE CREPES YUMMY, WON'T IT?
BUT YOU'VE NEVER HAD CREPES, HAVE YOU, TSUMUGI?
Hee hee
What?
BUT I KNOW WHAT THEY ARE! THEY'RE THESE, RIGHT?
LOOK!
Huh?
IS THAT... A CREPE?

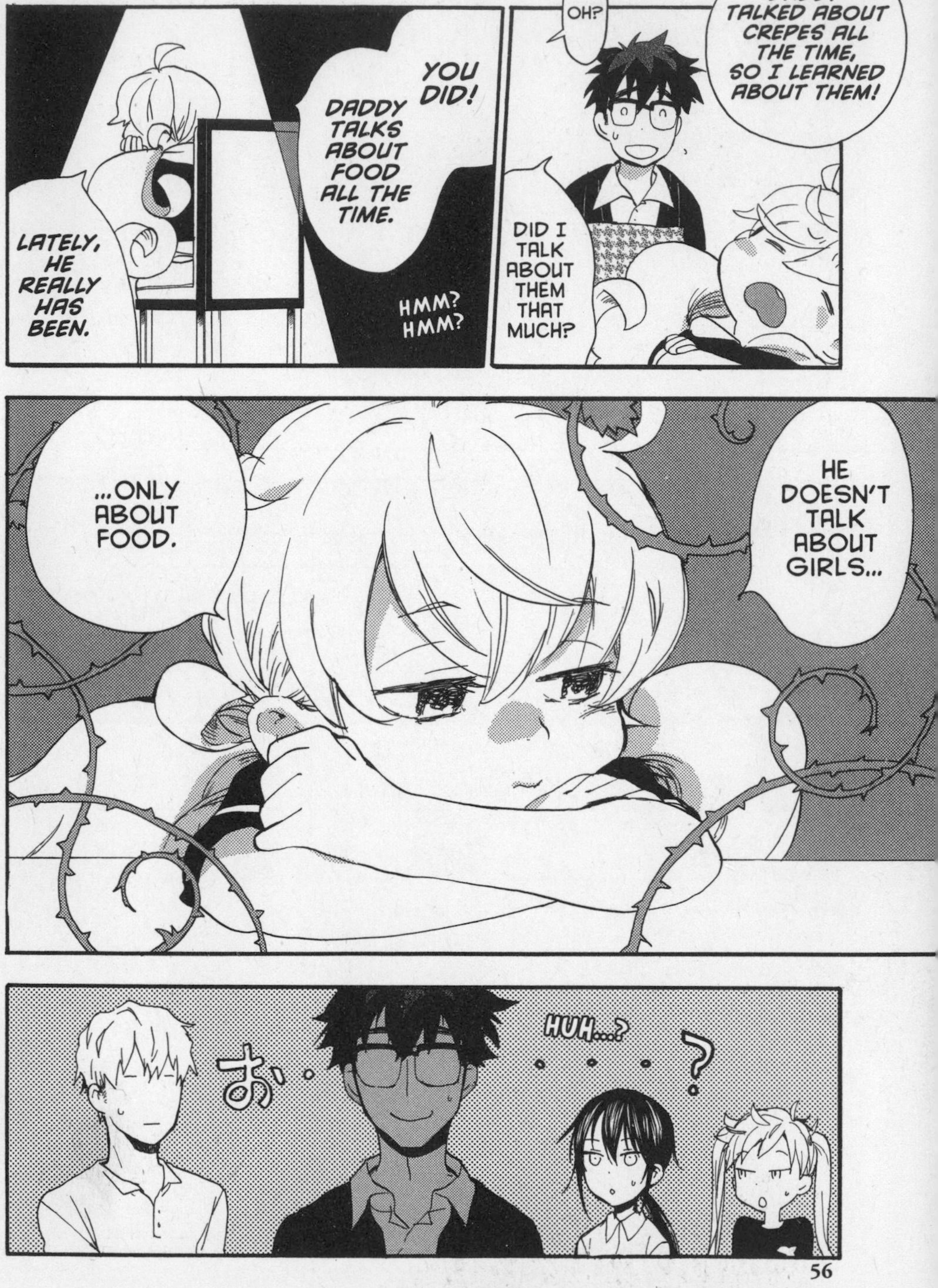
DADDY TALKED ABOUT CREPES ALL THE TIME, SO I LEARNED ABOUT THEM!
OH?
DID I TALK ABOUT THEM THAT MUCH?
YOU DID!
DADDY TALKS ABOUT FOOD ALL THE TIME.
HMM? HMM?
LATELY, HE REALLY HAS BEEN.
HE DOESN'T TALK ABOUT GIRLS...
...ONLY ABOUT FOOD.
HUH...?
お。
...?

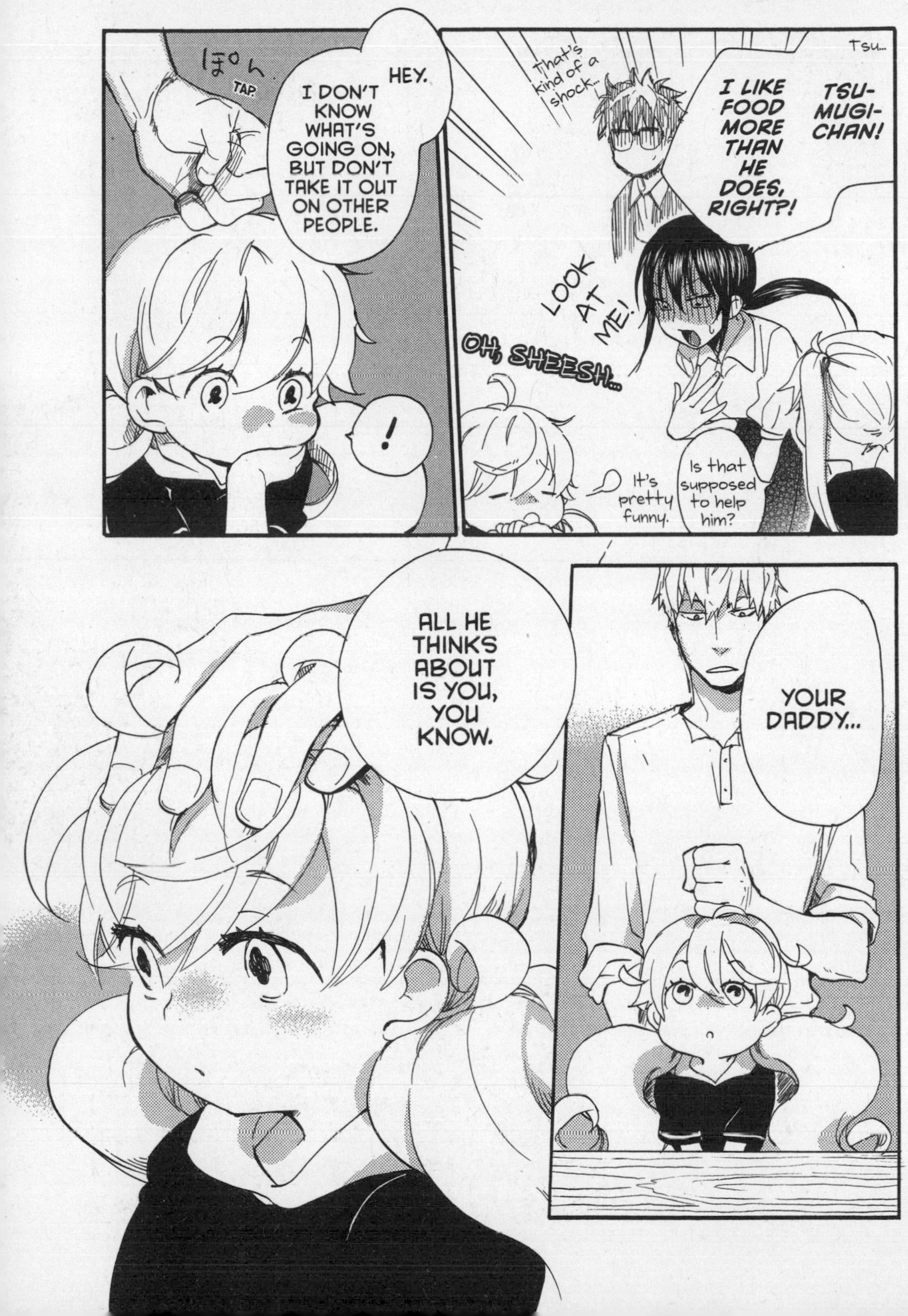
Tsu...
TSU-MUGI-CHAN!
I LIKE FOOD MORE THAN HE DOES, RIGHT?!
That's kind of a shock...
LOOK AT ME!
OH, SHEESH...
Is that supposed to help him?
It's pretty funny.
ぽん
TAP
HEY.
I DON'T KNOW WHAT'S GOING ON, BUT DON'T TAKE IT OUT ON OTHER PEOPLE.
!
YOUR DADDY...
ALL HE THINKS ABOUT IS YOU, YOU KNOW.

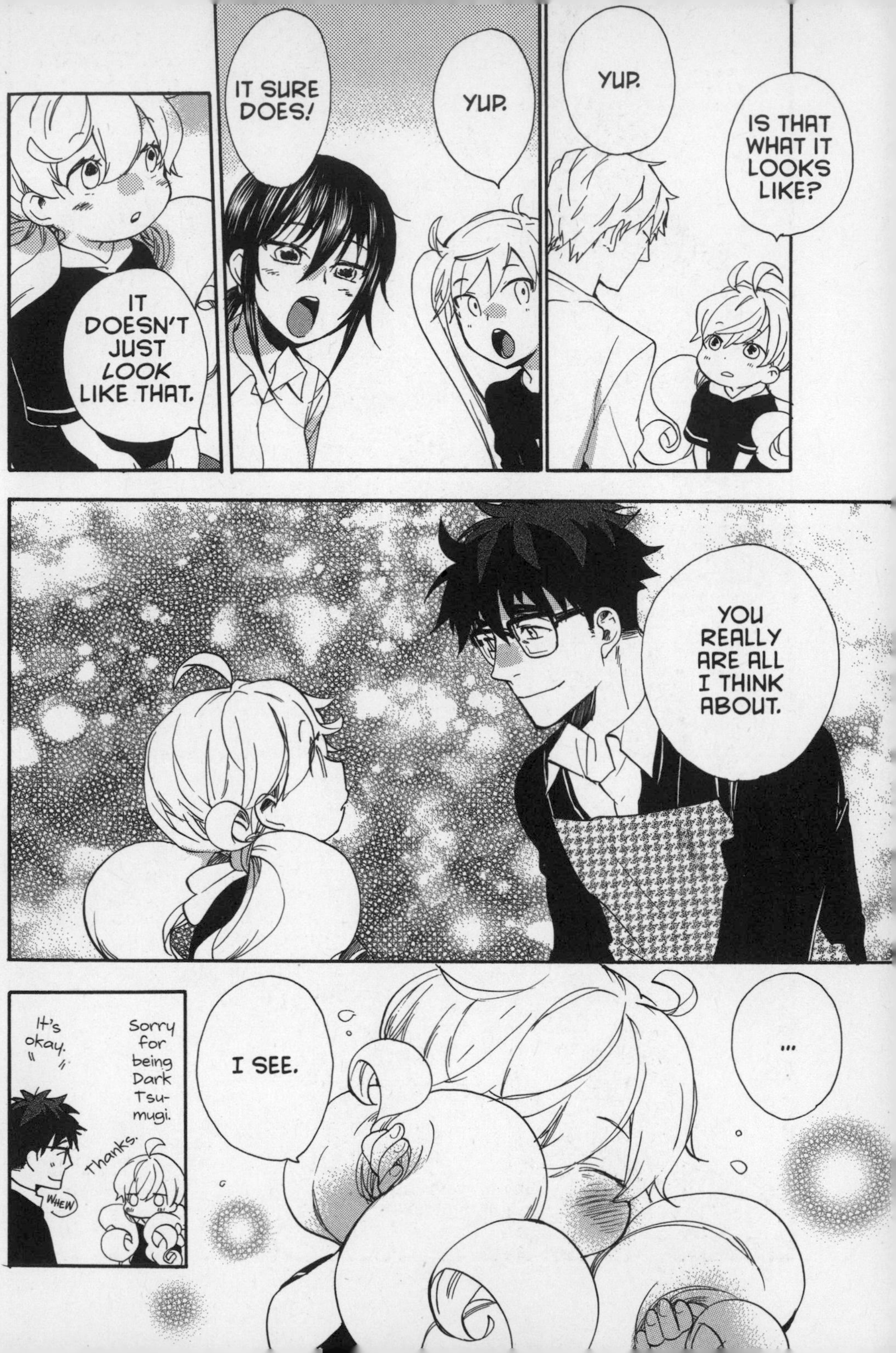
IS THAT WHAT IT LOOKS LIKE?
YUP.
YUP.
IT SURE DOES!
IT DOESN'T JUST *LOOK* LIKE THAT.
YOU REALLY ARE ALL I THINK ABOUT.
...
I SEE.
Sorry for being Dark Tsumugi.
It's okay.
Thanks.
WHEW

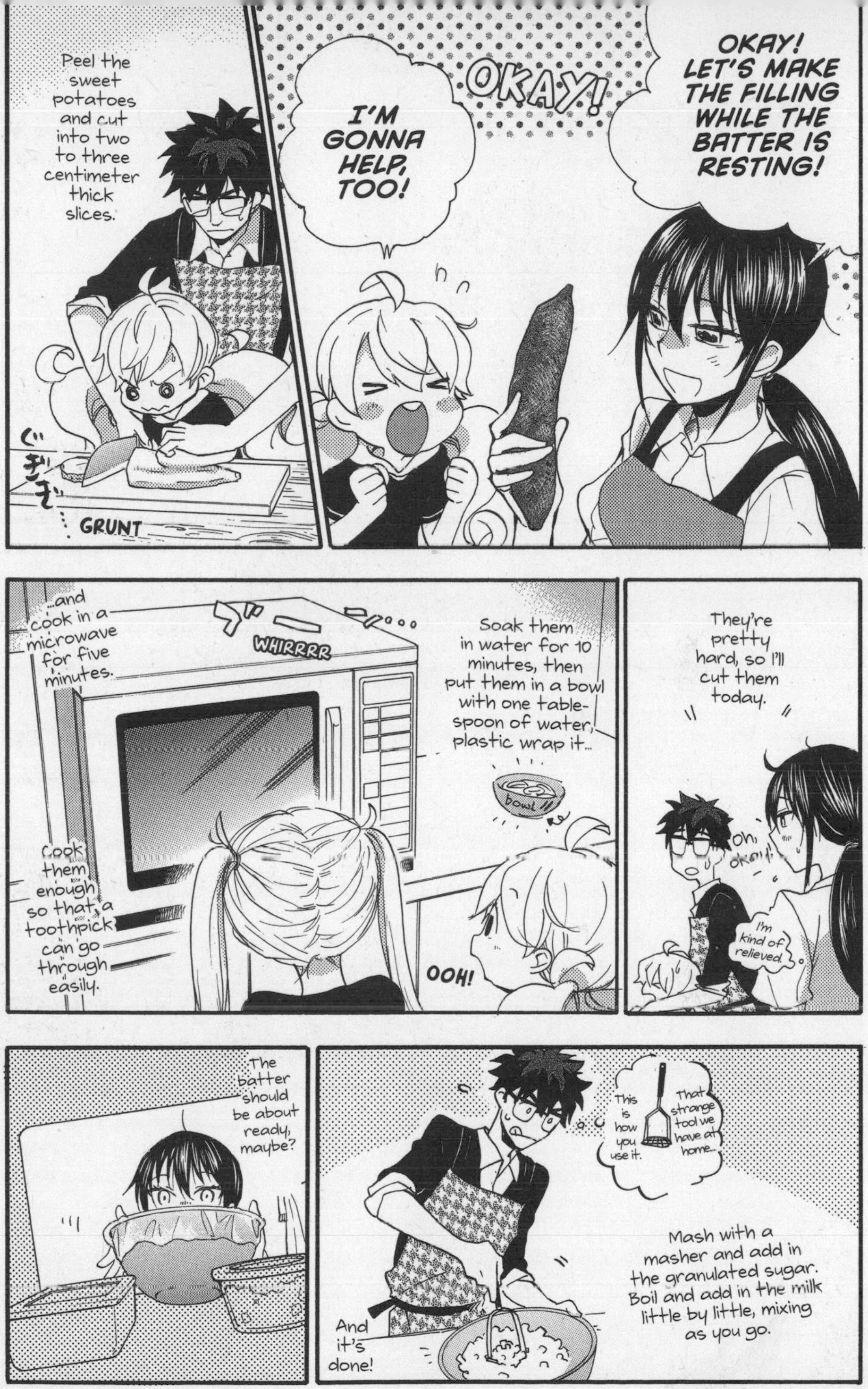
OKAY! LET'S MAKE THE FILLING WHILE THE BATTER IS RESTING!
OKAY!
I'M GONNA HELP, TOO!
Peel the sweet potatoes and cut into two to three centimeter thick slices.
GRUNT
They're pretty hard, so I'll cut them today.
Oh, okay.
I'm kind of relieved.
Soak them in water for 10 minutes, then put them in a bowl with one table-spoon of water, plastic wrap it...
bowl!!
...and cook in a microwave for five minutes.
WHIRRRR
Cook them enough so that a toothpick can go through easily.
OOH!
That strange tool we have at home...
This is how you use it.
Mash with a masher and add in the granulated sugar. Boil and add in the milk little by little, mixing as you go.
And it's done!
The batter should be about ready, maybe?

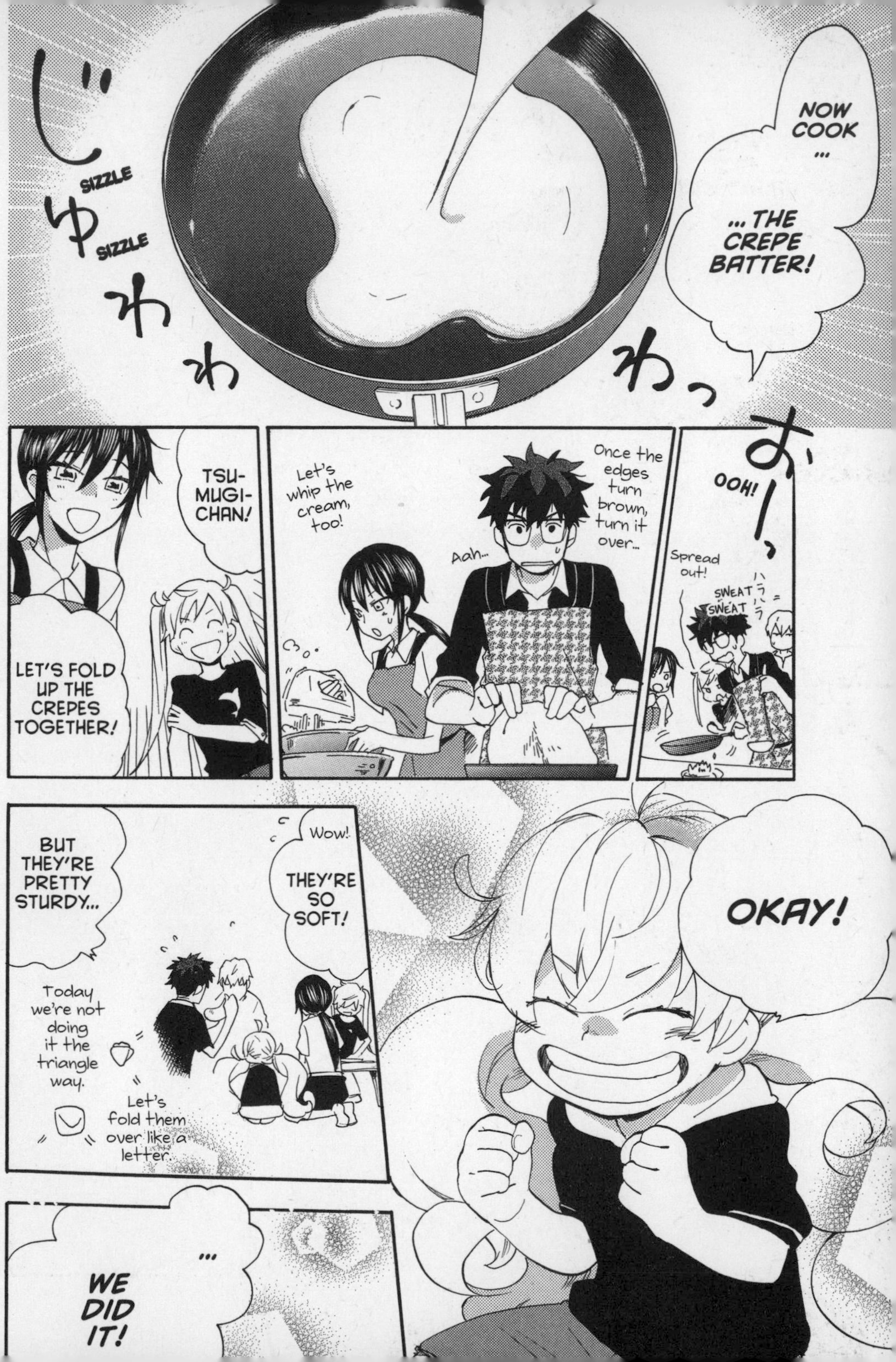
NOW COOK ...
... THE CREPE BATTER!
じゅわわわっ
SIZZLE SIZZLE
おー、
OOH!
Spread out!
ハラハラ
SWEAT SWEAT
Once the edges turn brown, turn it over...
Aah...
Let's whip the cream, too!
TSU-MUGI-CHAN!
LET'S FOLD UP THE CREPES TOGETHER!
OKAY!
Wow!
THEY'RE SO SOFT!
BUT THEY'RE PRETTY STURDY...
Today we're not doing it the triangle way.
Let's fold them over like a letter.
...
WE DID IT!

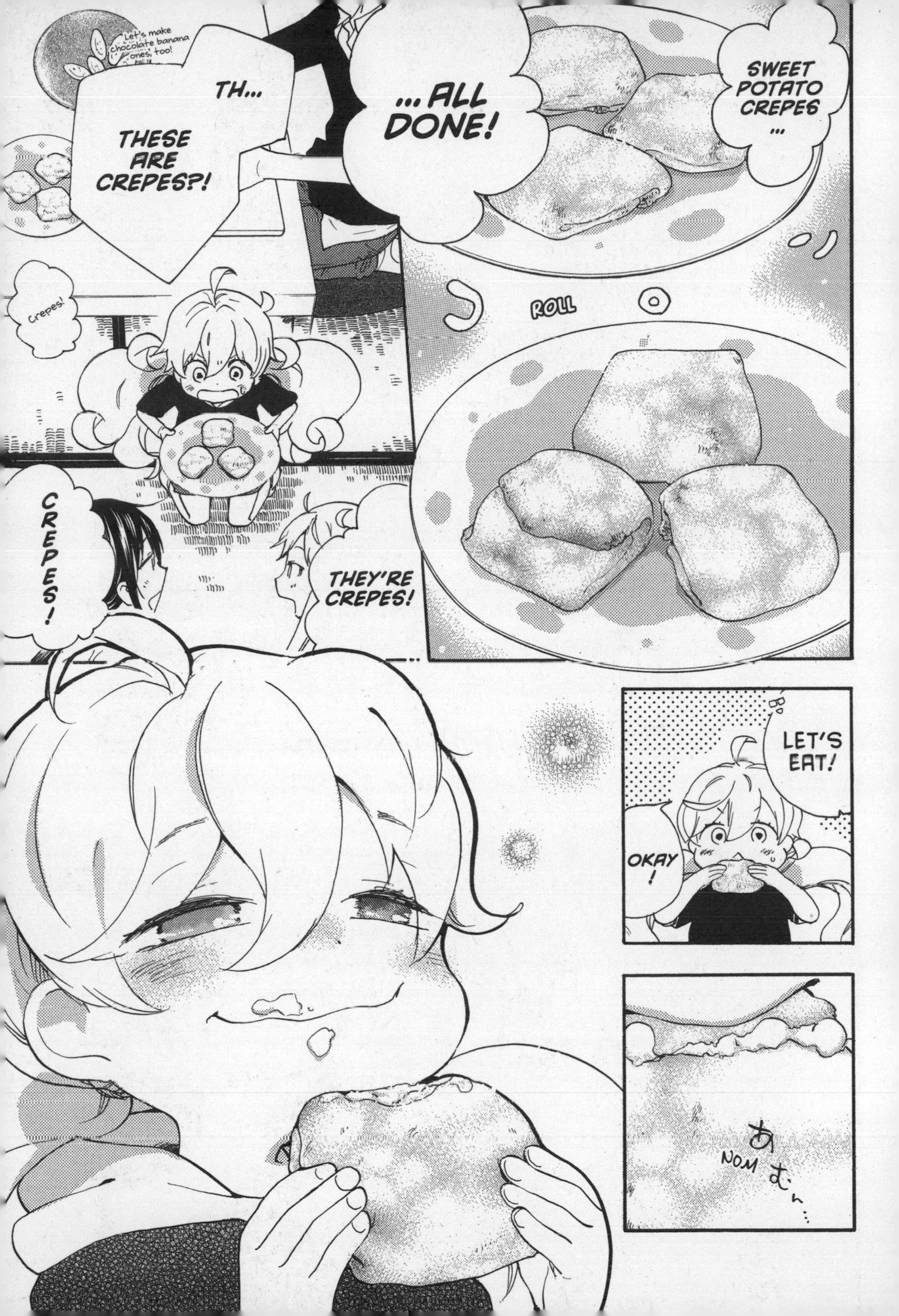
SWEET POTATO CREPES ...
...ALL DONE!
Let's make chocolate banana ones, too!
TH...
THESE ARE CREPES?!
ROLL
Crepes!
THEY'RE CREPES!
CREPES!
LET'S EAT!
OKAY!
あむ…
NOM

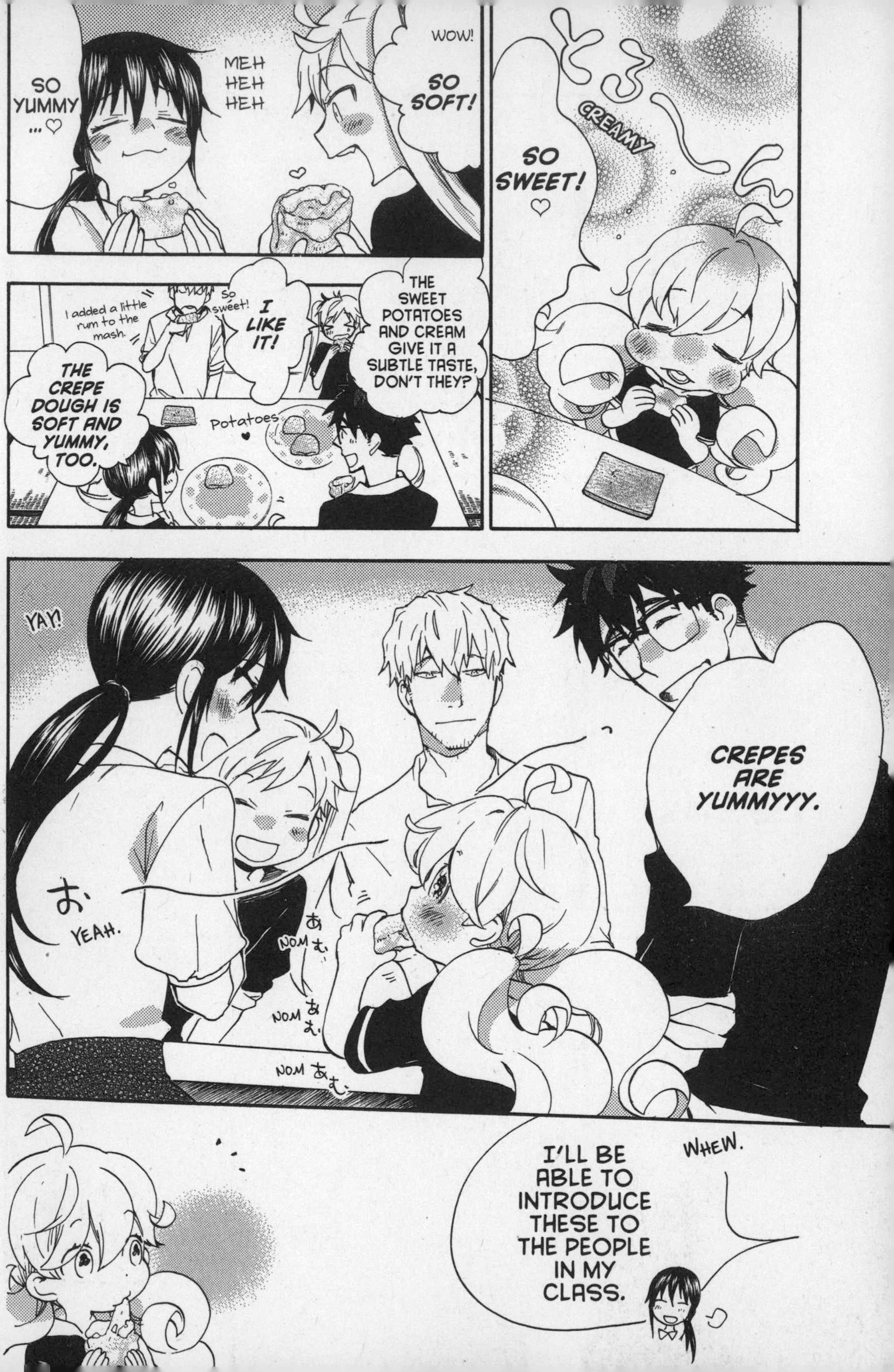
とろーん
CREAMY
SO SWEET! ♡
WOW!
SO SOFT!
MEH HEH HEH
SO YUMMY ...♡
THE SWEET POTATOES AND CREAM GIVE IT A SUBTLE TASTE, DON'T THEY?
I LIKE IT!
So sweet!
I added a little rum to the mash.
THE CREPE DOUGH IS SOFT AND YUMMY, TOO.
Potatoes ♥
CREPES ARE YUMMYYY.
YAY!
あむ NOM
あむ NOM
あむ NOM
お YEAH.
WHEW.
I'LL BE ABLE TO INTRODUCE THESE TO THE PEOPLE IN MY CLASS.

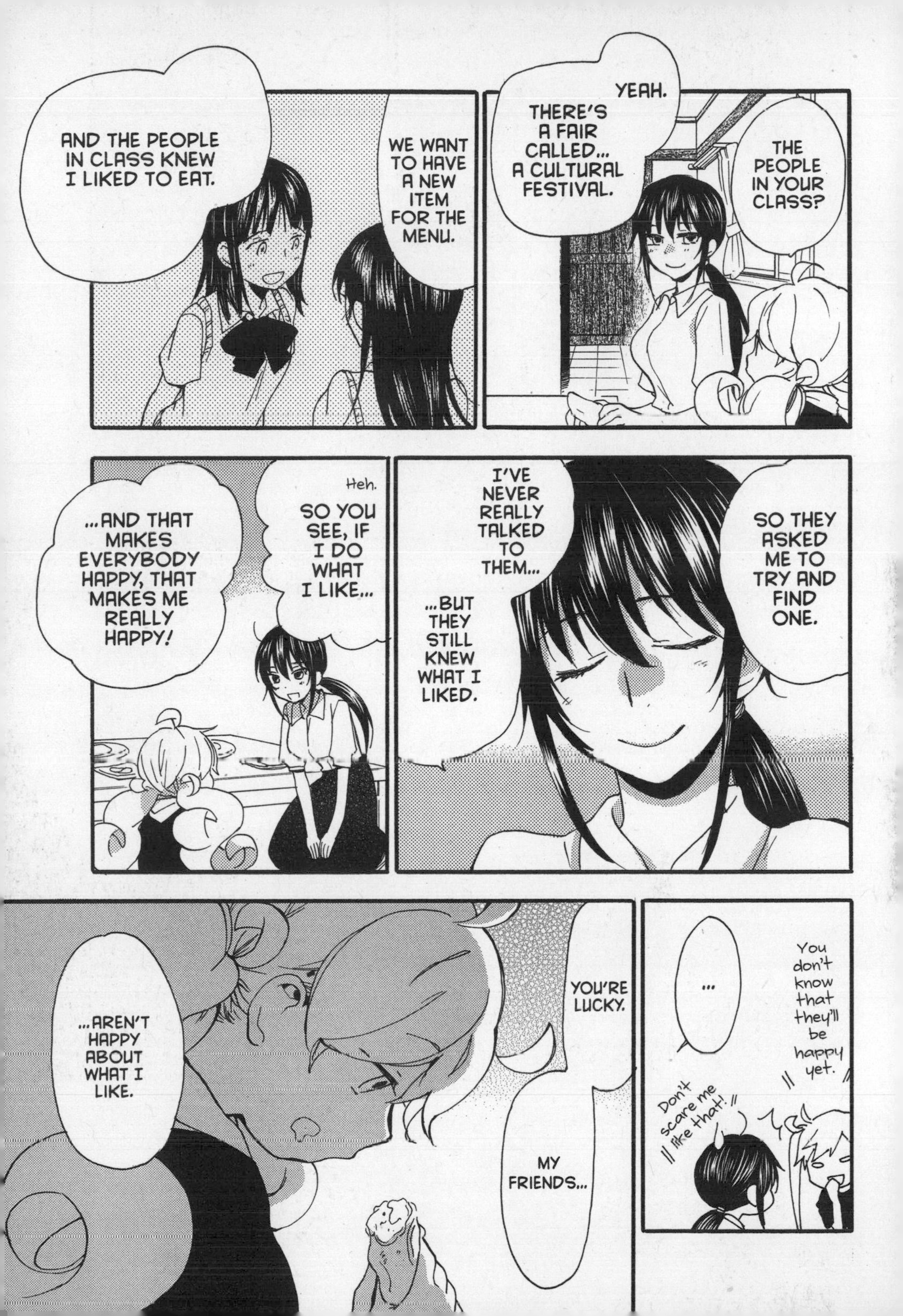
THE PEOPLE IN YOUR CLASS?
YEAH.
THERE'S A FAIR CALLED... A CULTURAL FESTIVAL.
WE WANT TO HAVE A NEW ITEM FOR THE MENU.
AND THE PEOPLE IN CLASS KNEW I LIKED TO EAT.
SO THEY ASKED ME TO TRY AND FIND ONE.
I'VE NEVER REALLY TALKED TO THEM...
...BUT THEY STILL KNEW WHAT I LIKED.
Heh.
SO YOU SEE, IF I DO WHAT I LIKE...
...AND THAT MAKES EVERYBODY HAPPY, THAT MAKES ME REALLY HAPPY!
...
You don't know that they'll be happy yet.
Don't scare me like that!
YOU'RE LUCKY.
MY FRIENDS...
...AREN'T HAPPY ABOUT WHAT I LIKE.

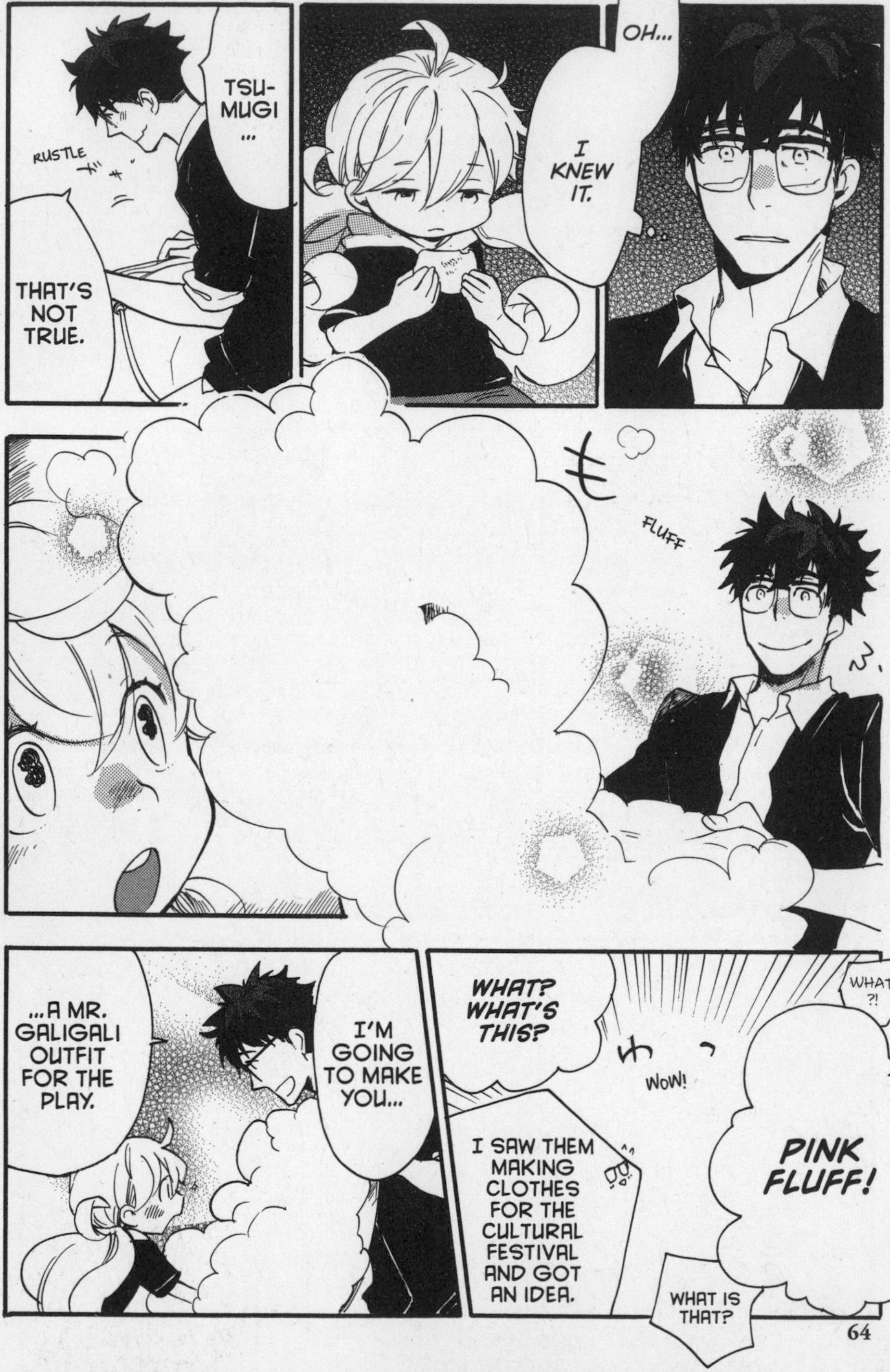
OH...
I KNEW IT.
TSUMUGI...
RUSTLE
THAT'S NOT TRUE.
FLUFF
WHAT ?!
WHAT? WHAT'S THIS?
WOW!
PINK FLUFF!
I SAW THEM MAKING CLOTHES FOR THE CULTURAL FESTIVAL AND GOT AN IDEA.
WHAT IS THAT?
I'M GOING TO MAKE YOU...
...A MR. GALIGALI OUTFIT FOR THE PLAY.

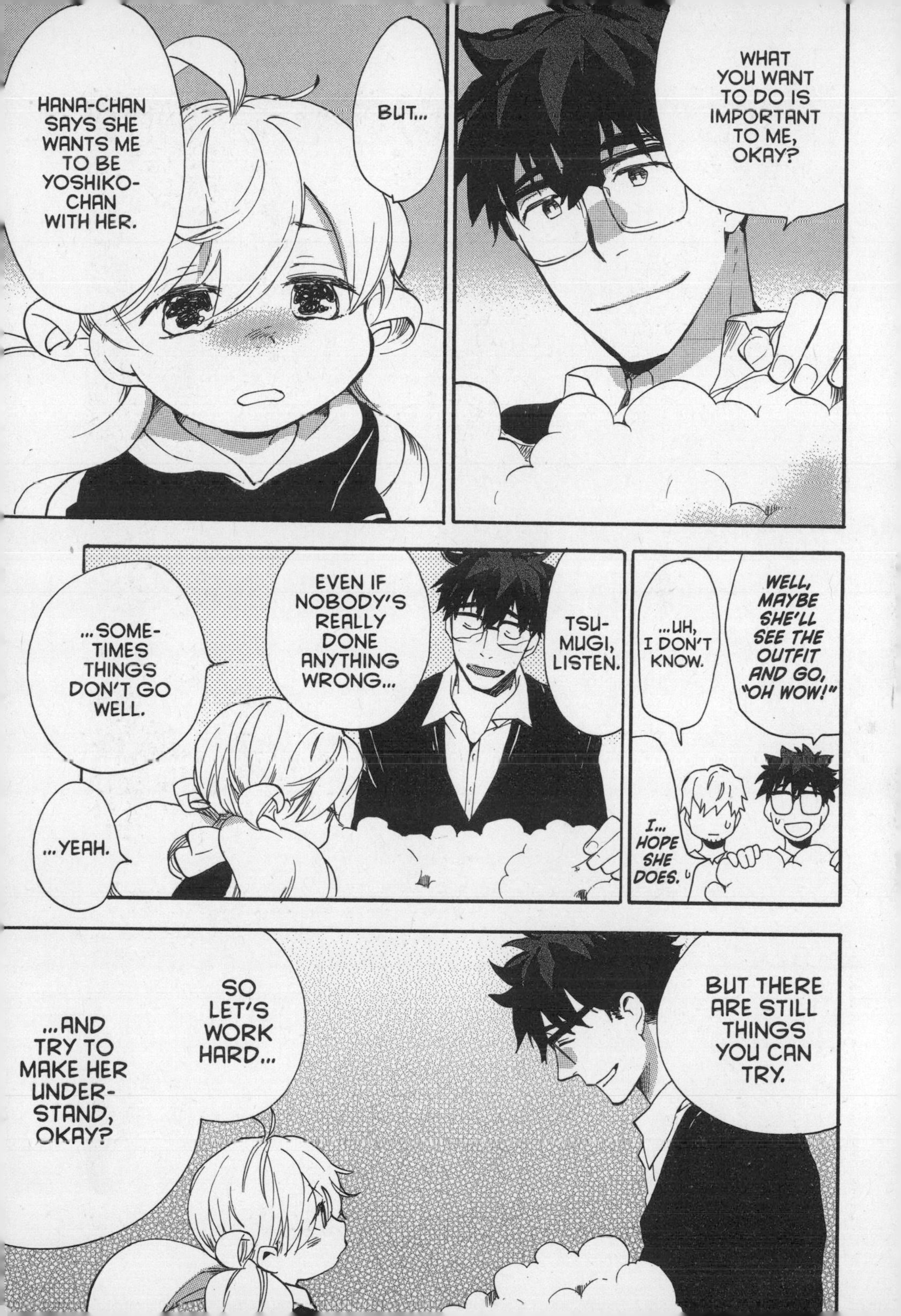
WHAT YOU WANT TO DO IS IMPORTANT TO ME, OKAY?
BUT...
HANA-CHAN SAYS SHE WANTS ME TO BE YOSHIKO-CHAN WITH HER.
WELL, MAYBE SHE'LL SEE THE OUTFIT AND GO, "OH WOW!"
...UH, I DON'T KNOW.
I... HOPE SHE DOES.
TSU-MUGI, LISTEN.
EVEN IF NOBODY'S REALLY DONE ANYTHING WRONG...
...SOME-TIMES THINGS DON'T GO WELL.
...YEAH.
BUT THERE ARE STILL THINGS YOU CAN TRY.
SO LET'S WORK HARD...
...AND TRY TO MAKE HER UNDER-STAND, OKAY?

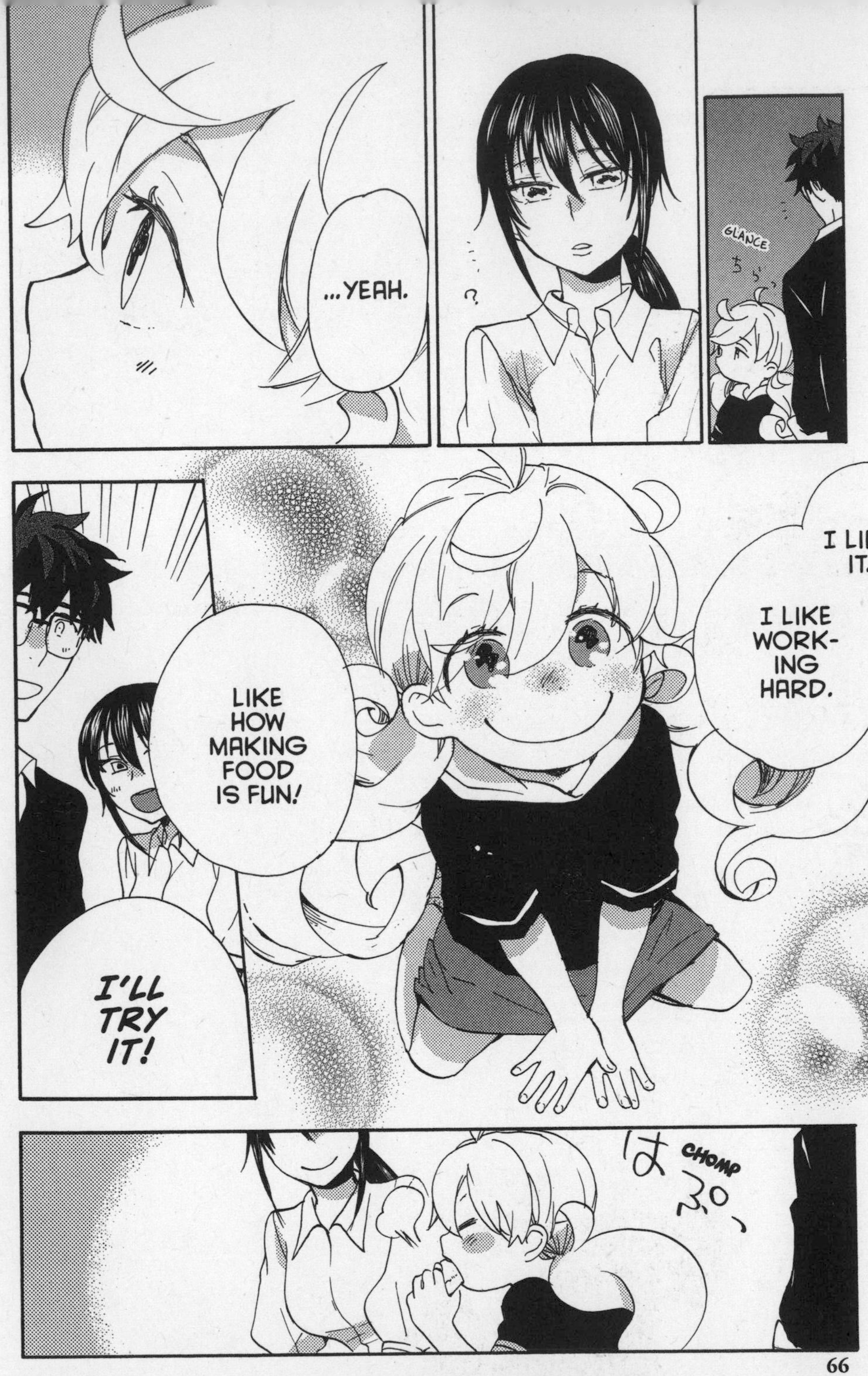
GLANCE
ちらっ
?
...YEAH.
I LIKE IT.
I LIKE WORK-ING HARD.
LIKE HOW MAKING FOOD IS FUN!
I'LL TRY IT!
CHOMP
はぷっ

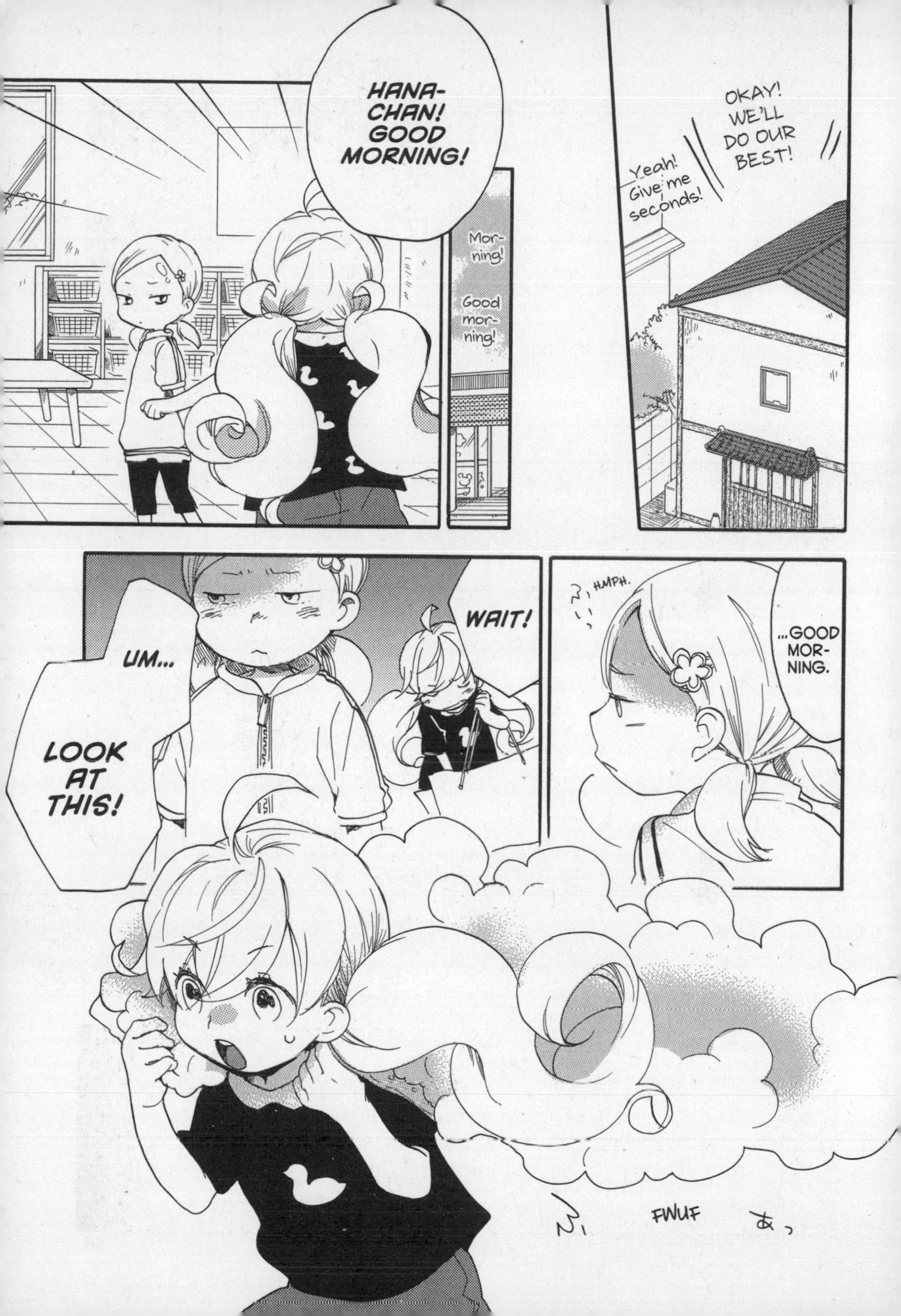
OKAY! WE'LL DO OUR BEST!
Yeah! Give me seconds!
Mor-ning!
Good mor-ning!
HANA-CHAN! GOOD MORNING!
HMPH.
...GOOD MOR-NING.
WAIT!
UM...
LOOK AT THIS!
FWUF
あっ

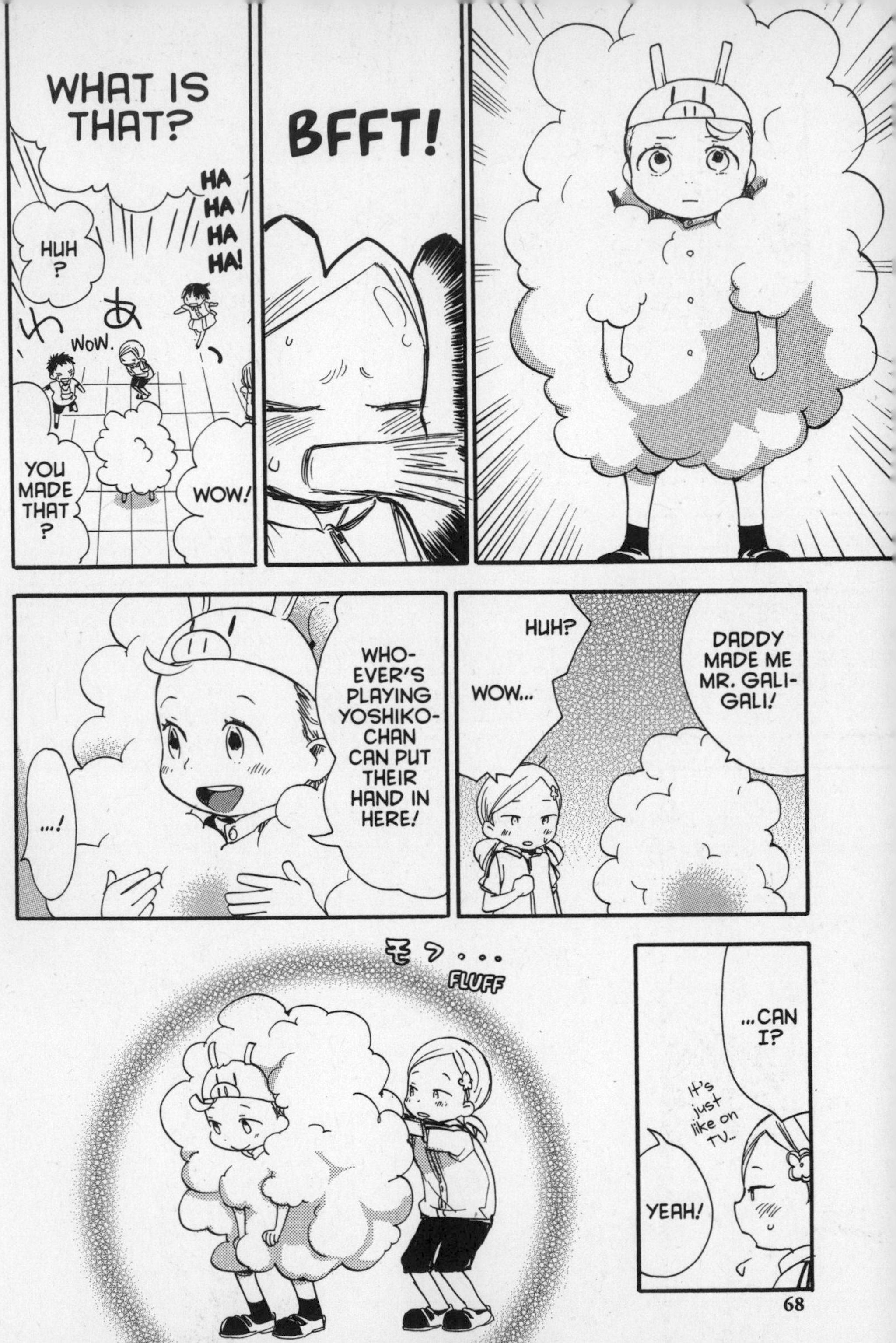
BFFT!
HA HA HA HA!
WHAT IS THAT?
HUH?
わあ
WOW.
WOW!
YOU MADE THAT?
DADDY MADE ME MR. GALI-GALI!
HUH?
WOW...
WHO-EVER'S PLAYING YOSHIKO-CHAN CAN PUT THEIR HAND IN HERE!
...!
...CAN I?
It's just like on TV...
YEAH!
モフ...
FLUFF

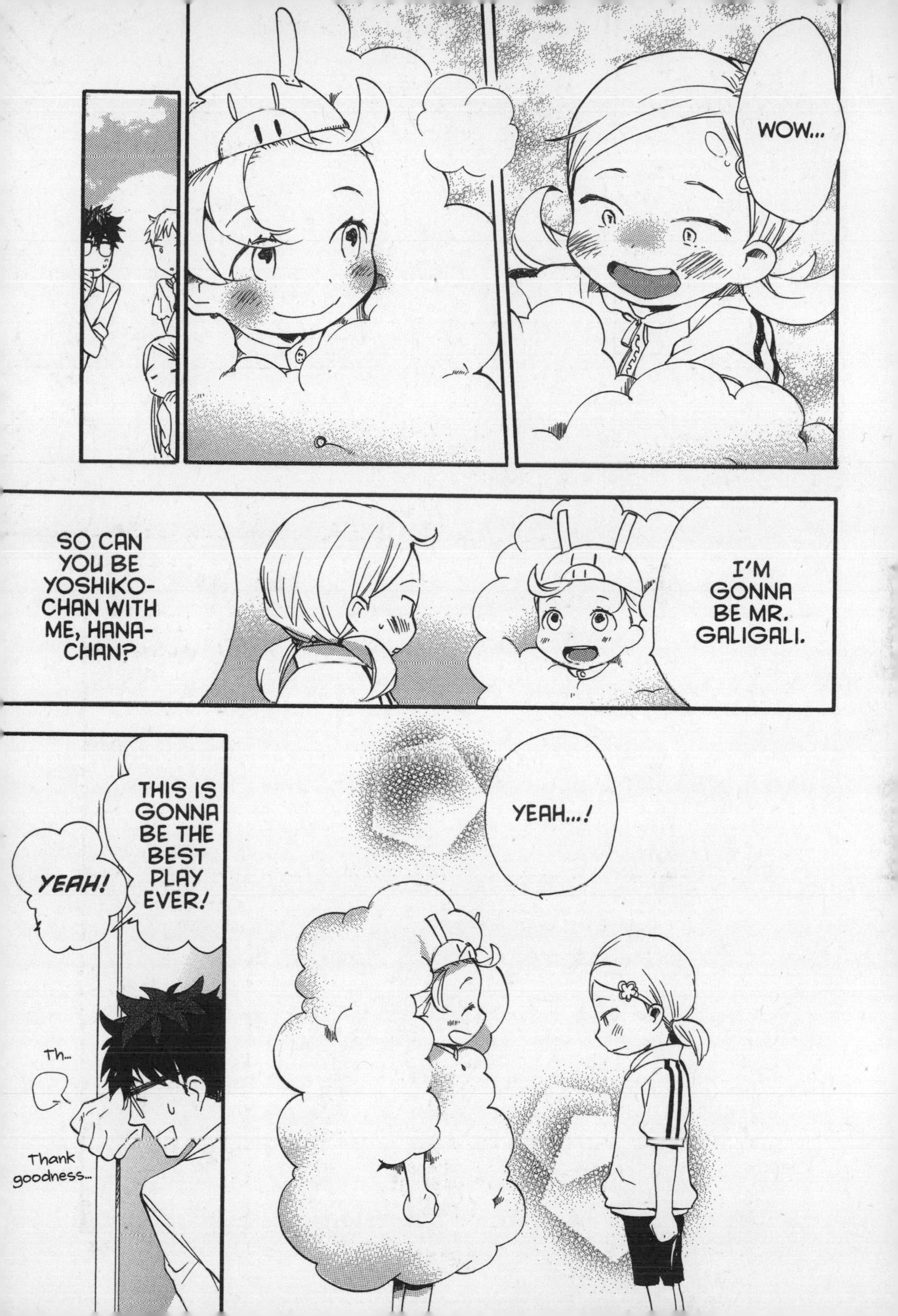
WOW...
I'M GONNA BE MR. GALIGALI.
SO CAN YOU BE YOSHIKO-CHAN WITH ME, HANA-CHAN?
YEAH...!
THIS IS GONNA BE THE BEST PLAY EVER!
YEAH!
Th...
Thank goodness...

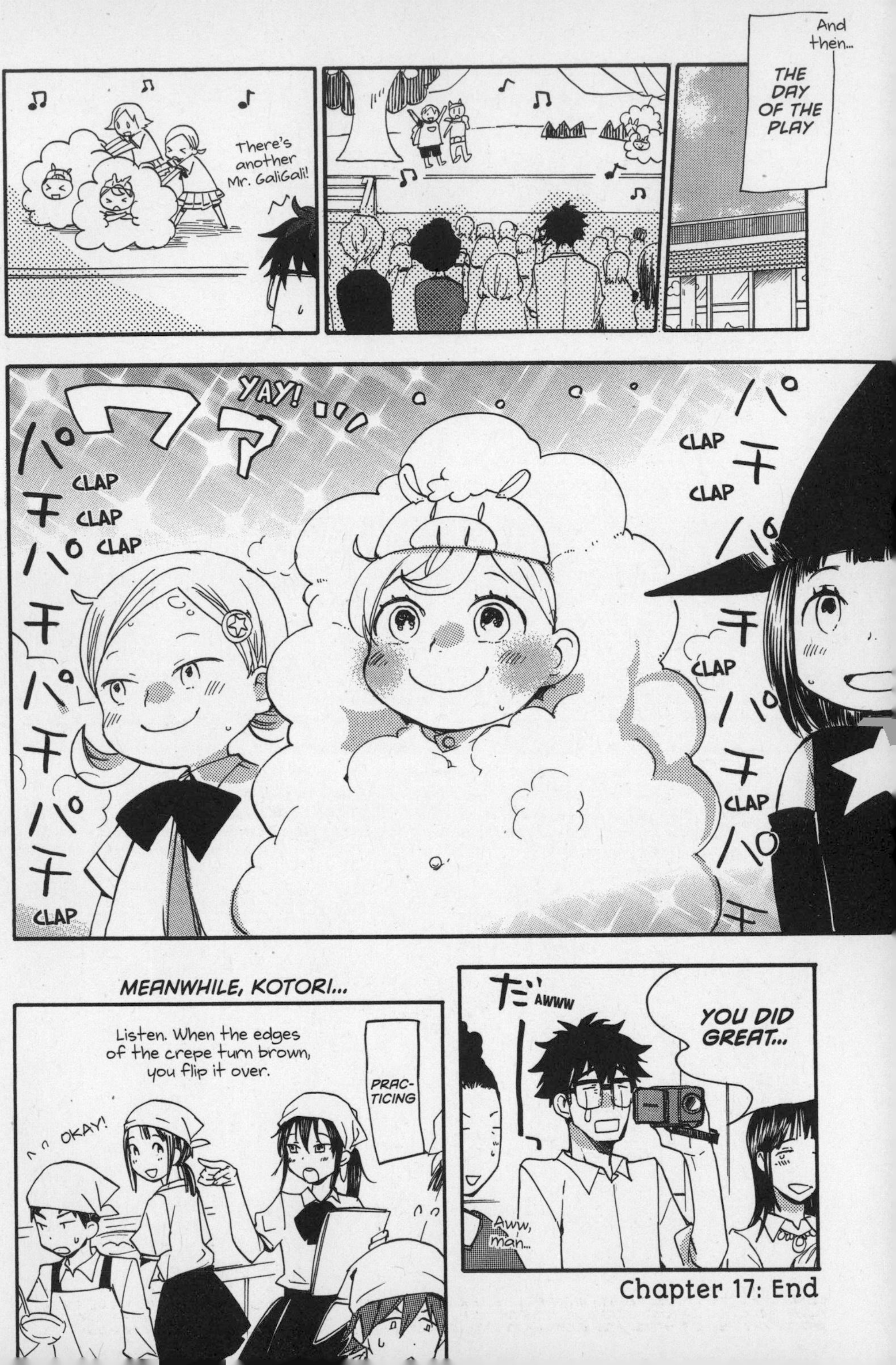
And then...
THE DAY OF THE PLAY
There's another Mr. GaliGali!
パチパチパチパチ
CLAP
CLAP
CLAP
CLAP
YAY!
ワア
CLAP
CLAP
CLAP
パチパチパチパチ
CLAP
だ AWWW
YOU DID GREAT...
Aww, man...
MEANWHILE, KOTORI...
Listen. When the edges of the crepe turn brown, you flip it over.
PRACTICING
OKAY!

Chapter 17: End

SWEET POTATO AND CREAM CREPES

☆ Ingredients ☆ (makes ten 20 cm crepes)

♥ Batter
250 cc milk 20 g butter 80 g weak flour
20 g granulated sugar 100 g eggs

◆ Sweet Potato Cream
220 g sweet potatoes (peeled)
30 g granulated sugar 100 cc milk

● Whipped Cream
Group A: 300 cc cream 30 g granulated sugar
Some Crushed Almonds

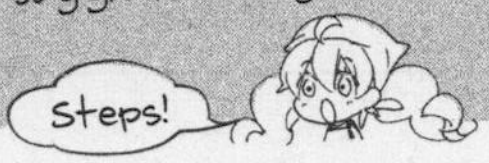
Steps!

1. Make the batter. Bring the milk to room temperature. Put the butter in a frying pan on medium heat. Once the bubbles in the butter disappear and it turns a light brown, take it off the heat and cool on top of a wet cloth.
2. Sift the weak flour into a bowl, add the granulated sugar, and stir well. Make a little depression in the center, add the egg, and mix. Add in the butter from step 1 and mix thoroughly.

POINT: Leave any remaining butter in the frying pan.

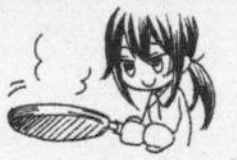

3. Add the milk from step 1 little by little into the ingredients from step 2, stirring as you go. Let the batter sit in a cool place for around an hour.
4. Make the sweet potato cream. Cut the sweet potatoes into 2-3 cm slices, and place them in water to get rid of any bitterness. When about 10 minutes have passed, take them out and put them in a bowl with 1 Tbsp of water. Wrap and microwave for 5 minutes.

POINT: If a toothpick goes clean through, they're ready.

5. Mash the ingredients in step 4 with a masher and mix in the granulated sugar. Boil the milk and stir in little by little.

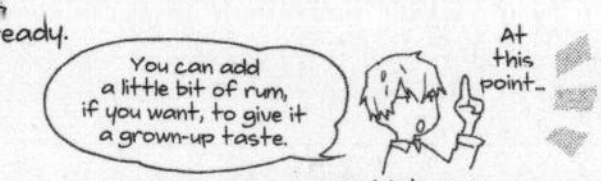
At this point...
You can add a little bit of rum, if you want, to give it a grown-up taste.

6. Place the ingredients from A into a bowl, then place that bowl into a larger bowl which you have filled with ice water. Whip the cream until it's at the point where it forms stiff peaks.
7. Heat the frying pan from step 2 on medium heat and wipe away excess butter with a paper towel.
8. Ladle approximately 40 ccs of the batter into the center of the pan. Spread it out in a circle by tilting the pan. Move the frying pan so that all parts are heated evenly.

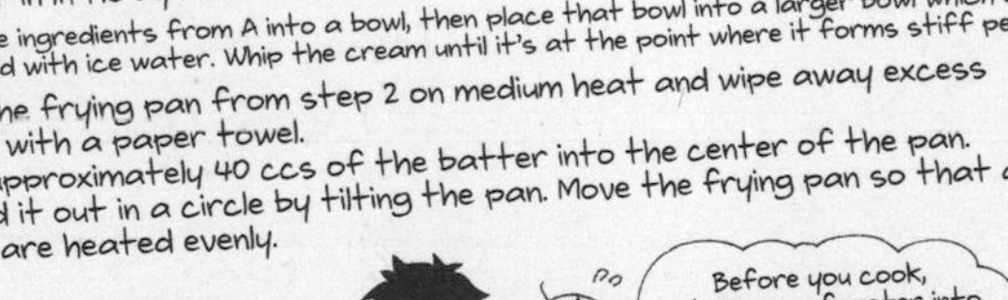
Before you cook, put 40 ccs of water into the ladle to see how much you need. Then you can just eyeball it...
It's a bit of a pain to measure out 40 ccs every time you want to fry one.

9. Once the edges of the crepe start turning brown, take the pan off the heat. Pinch the edges of the crepe, and flip it from back to front. Put the pan back on the fire and in 25 seconds, it'll be done!

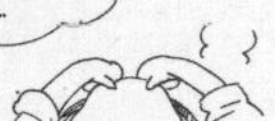
Don't get burned by the frying pan!

10. Repeat steps 8 and 9 to cook the batter. Put about 30 g each (approximately 1/10th of the total) of sweet potato cream and whipped cream on every crepe. Add some crushed almonds, wrap it up, and you're done!

CONVERSION NOTES : 20 CM CREPES = UNDER 8 INCHES, 250 CC MILK = 1 CUP, 20 G BUTTER = JUST UNDER 1 1/2 TBSP, 80 G WEAK FLOUR = ABOUT 2/3 CUPS, 20 G GRANULATED SUGAR = 1 TBSP AND 1 TSP, 100 G EGGS = ABOUT 2/3 CUP, 220 G SWEET POTATOES = ABOUT 1 1/2 CUPS, 30 G GRANULATED SUGAR = 2 TBSP, 100 CC MILK = ABOUT 1/2 CUP, 300 CC CREAM = ABOUT 1 1/4 CUP

AFTER THE PLAY
I'm going to sleep in this tonight!
That looks hard to sleep in...

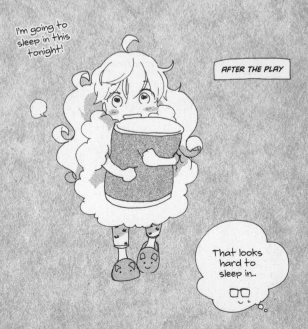

Chapter 18 | Kobachi and Kinpira Gobou

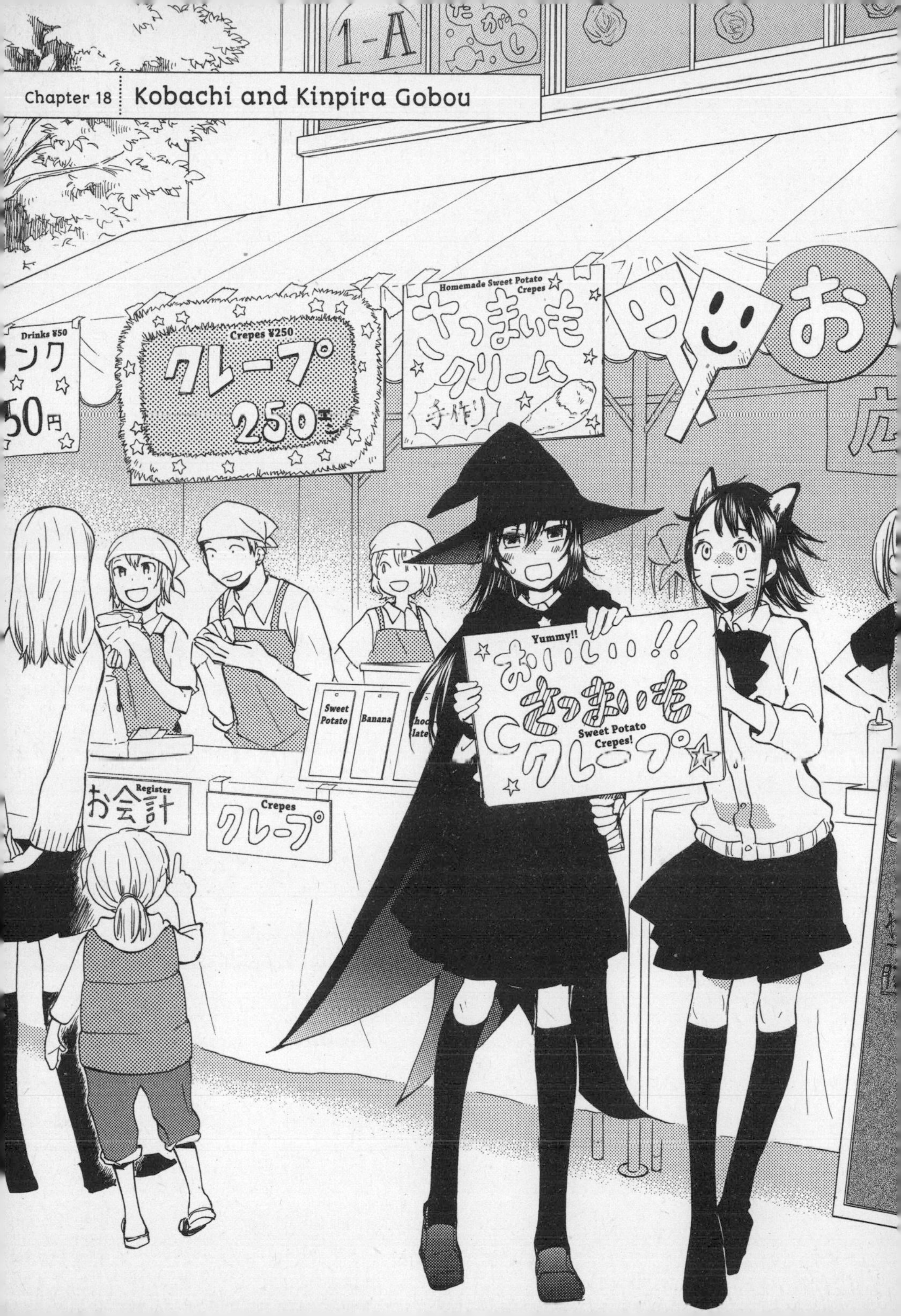
1-A
Homemade Sweet Potato Crepes
さつまいもクリーム
手作り
Crepes ¥250
クレープ
250円
Drinks ¥50
ンク
50円
Yummy!!
おいしい!!
さつまいも
Sweet Potato Crepes!
クレープ
Sweet Potato
Banana
Crepes
クレープ
Register
お会計

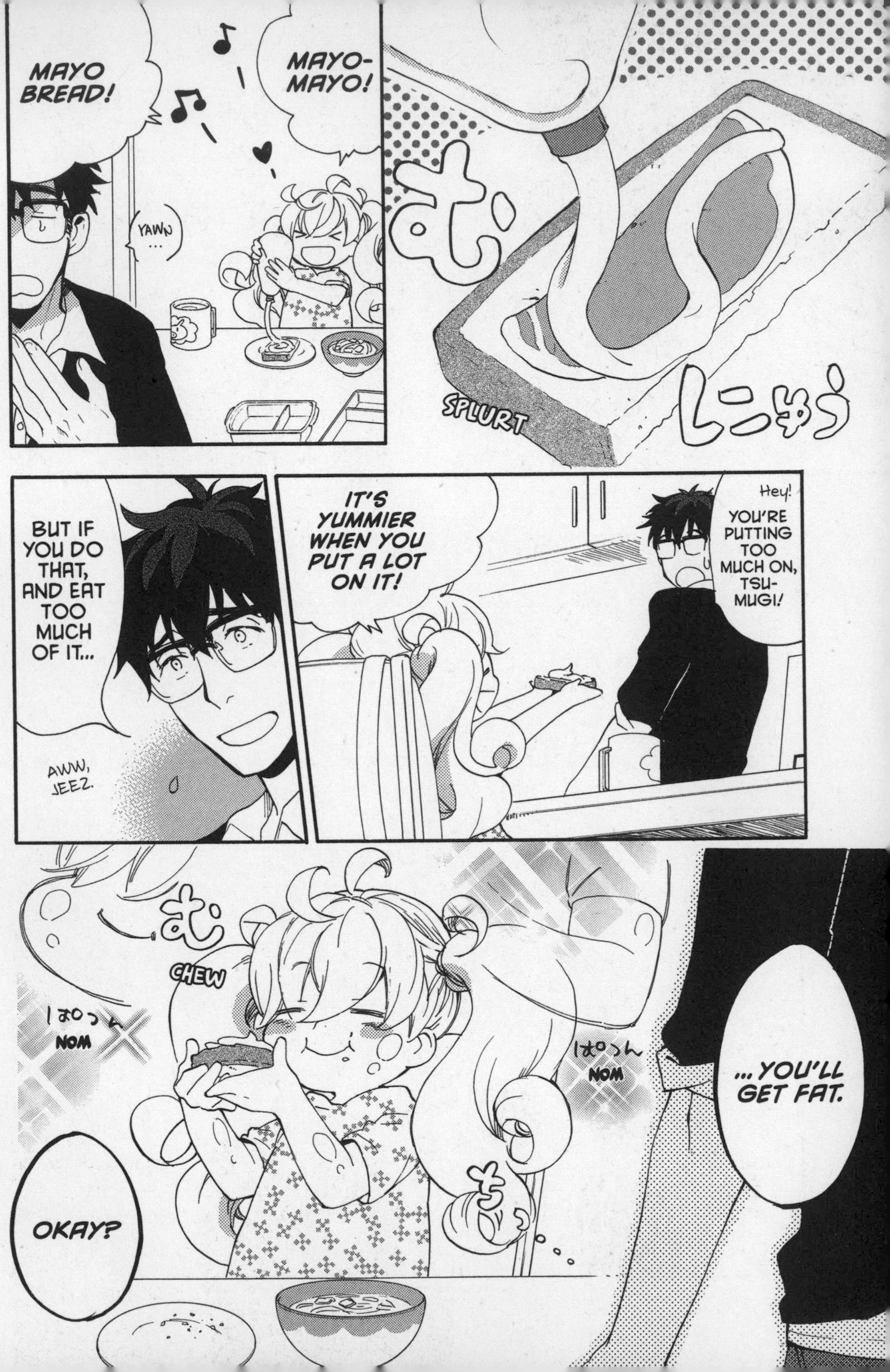
SPLURT
MAYO-MAYO!
MAYO BREAD!
YAWN...
Hey! YOU'RE PUTTING TOO MUCH ON, TSU-MUGI!
IT'S YUMMIER WHEN YOU PUT A LOT ON IT!
BUT IF YOU DO THAT, AND EAT TOO MUCH OF IT...
AWW, JEEZ.
...YOU'LL GET FAT.
NOM
CHEW
NOM
OKAY?

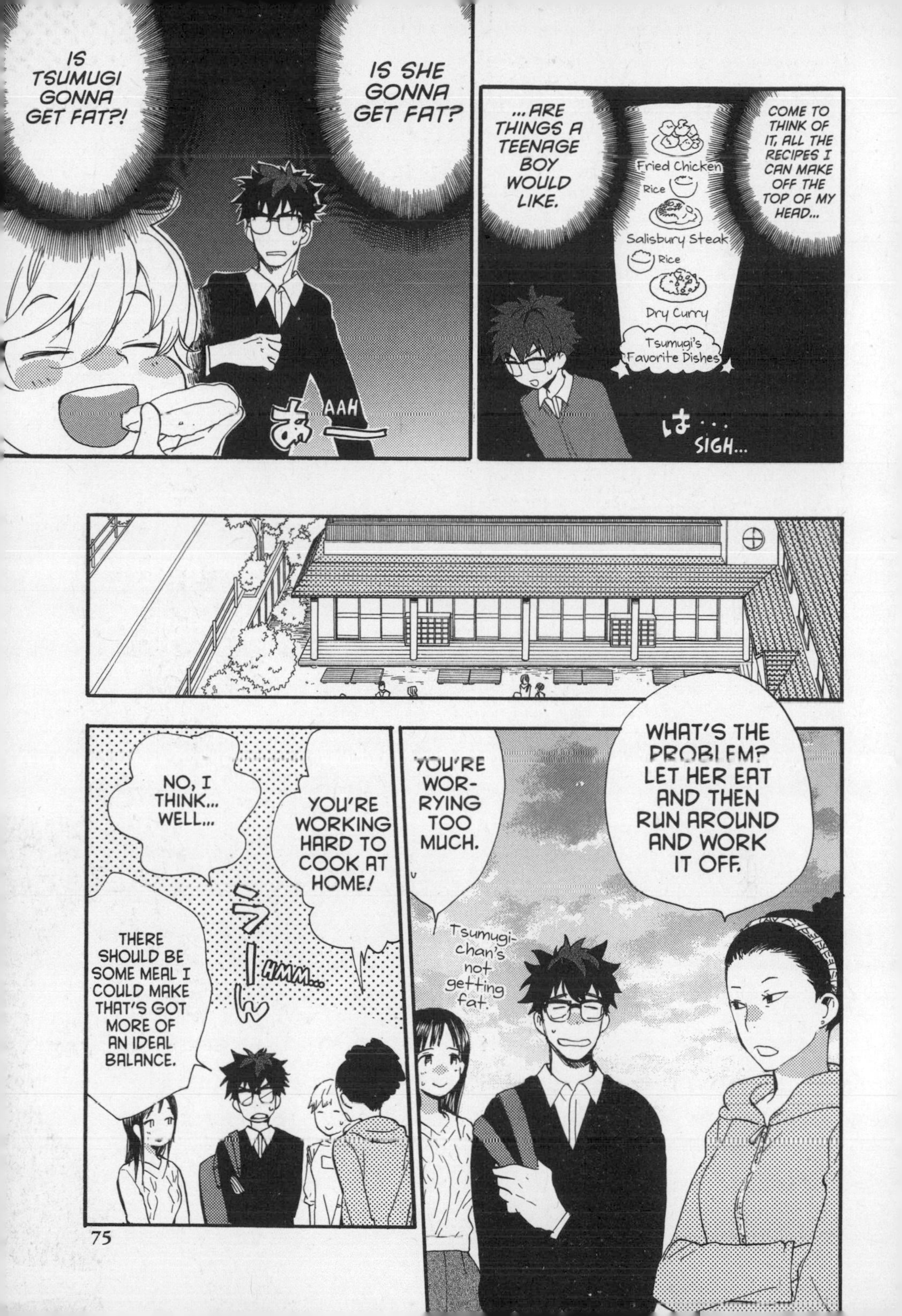
COME TO THINK OF IT, ALL THE RECIPES I CAN MAKE OFF THE TOP OF MY HEAD...
...ARE THINGS A TEENAGE BOY WOULD LIKE.
Fried Chicken
Rice
Salisbury Steak
Rice
Dry Curry
Tsumugi's Favorite Dishes
は...
SIGH...
IS SHE GONNA GET FAT?
IS TSUMUGI GONNA GET FAT?!
あー
AAH
WHAT'S THE PROBLEM? LET HER EAT AND THEN RUN AROUND AND WORK IT OFF.
YOU'RE WOR-RYING TOO MUCH.
Tsumugi-chan's not getting fat.
YOU'RE WORKING HARD TO COOK AT HOME!
うーん
HMM...
NO, I THINK... WELL...
THERE SHOULD BE SOME MEAL I COULD MAKE THAT'S GOT MORE OF AN IDEAL BALANCE.

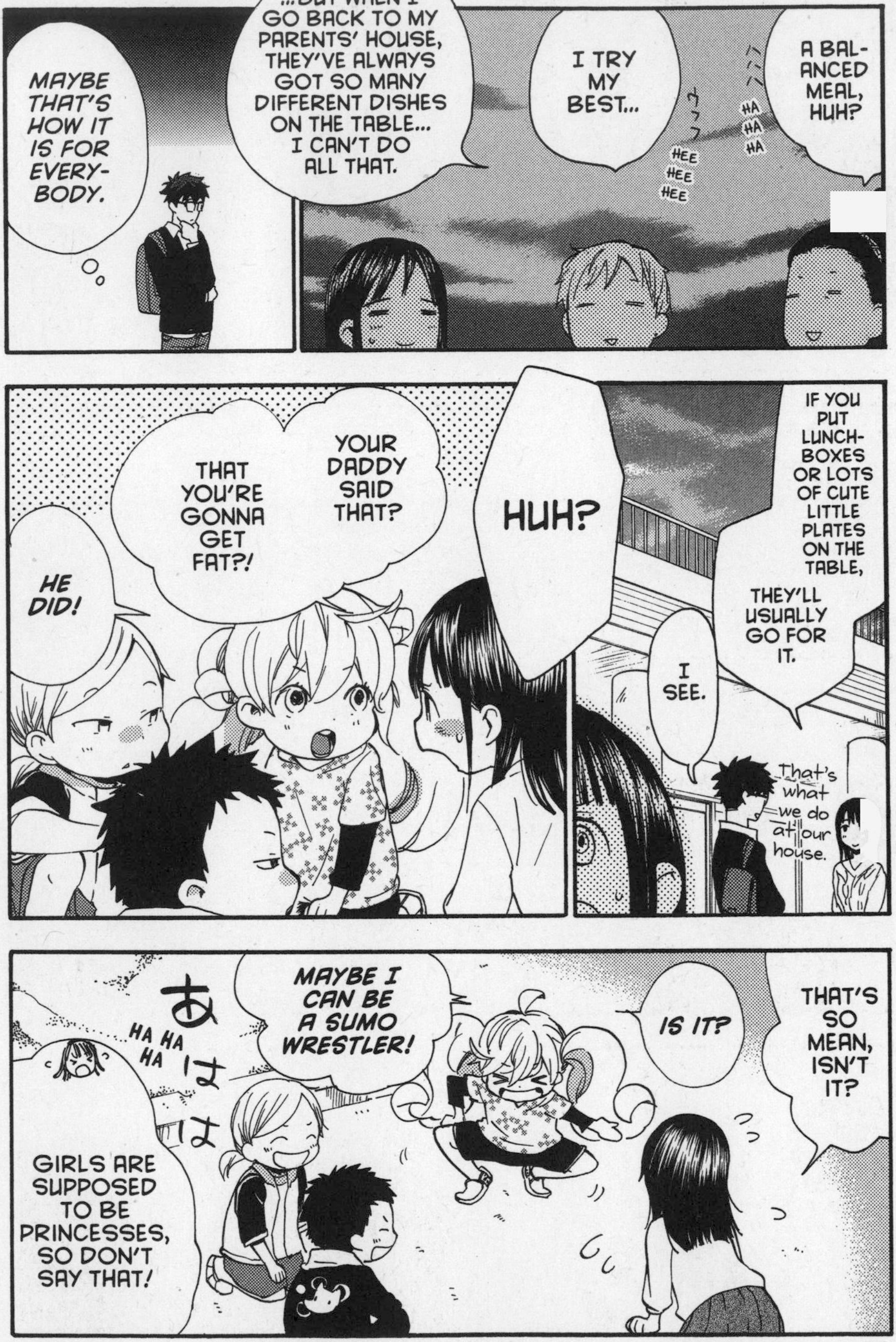
A BAL-ANCED MEAL, HUH?
ハハハ
HA HA HA
I TRY MY BEST...
ウフフ
HEE HEE HEE
...BUT WHEN I GO BACK TO MY PARENTS' HOUSE, THEY'VE ALWAYS GOT SO MANY DIFFERENT DISHES ON THE TABLE... I CAN'T DO ALL THAT.
MAYBE THAT'S HOW IT IS FOR EVERY-BODY.
IF YOU PUT LUNCH-BOXES OR LOTS OF CUTE LITTLE PLATES ON THE TABLE,
THEY'LL USUALLY GO FOR IT.
I SEE.
That's what we do at our house.
HUH?
YOUR DADDY SAID THAT?
THAT YOU'RE GONNA GET FAT?!
HE DID!
THAT'S SO MEAN, ISN'T IT?
IS IT?
MAYBE I CAN BE A SUMO WRESTLER!
あはは
HA HA HA
GIRLS ARE SUPPOSED TO BE PRINCESSES, SO DON'T SAY THAT!

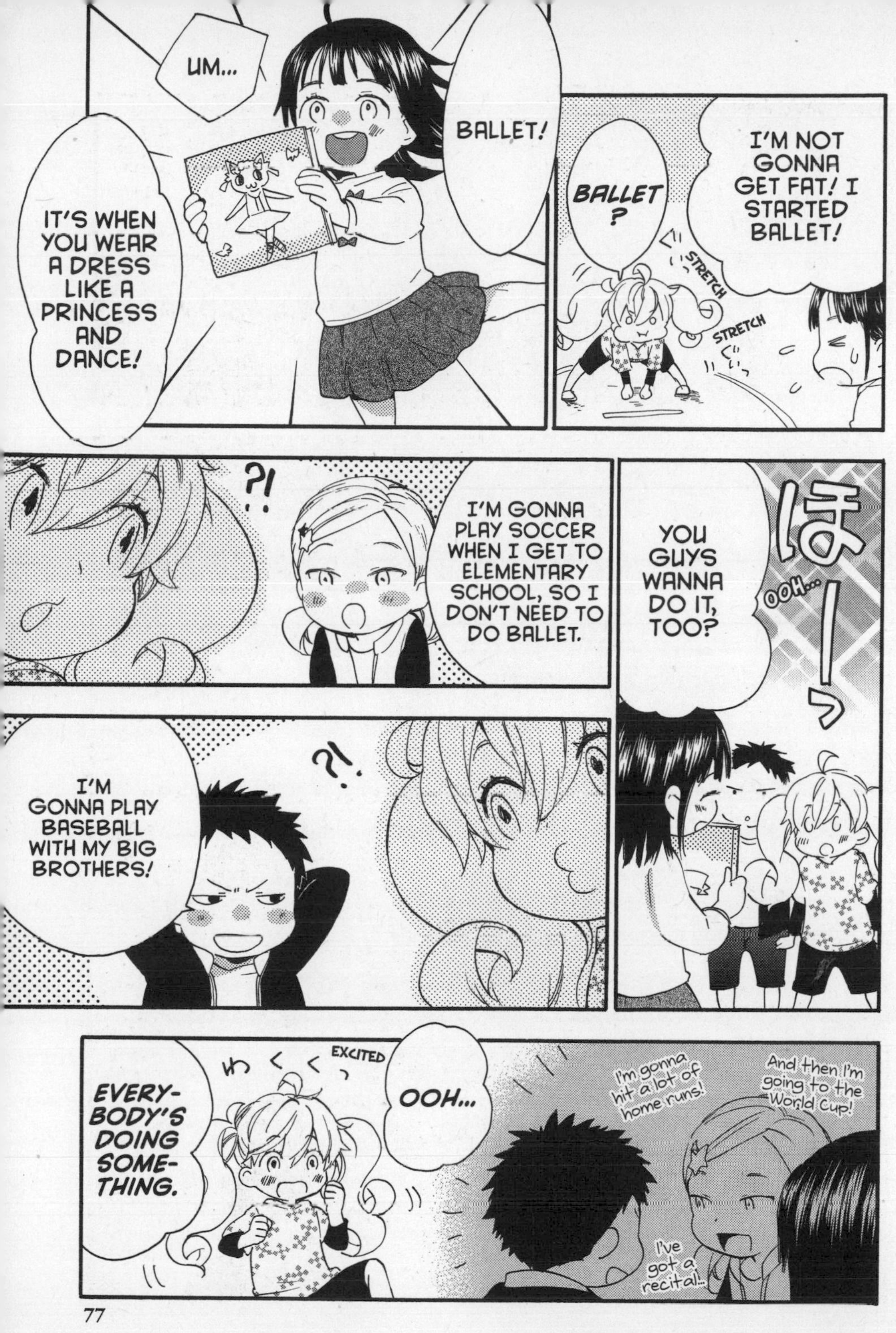
I'M NOT GONNA GET FAT! I STARTED BALLET!
BALLET?
STRETCH
STRETCH
BALLET!
UM...
IT'S WHEN YOU WEAR A DRESS LIKE A PRINCESS AND DANCE!
ほーっ
OOH...
YOU GUYS WANNA DO IT, TOO?
I'M GONNA PLAY SOCCER WHEN I GET TO ELEMENTARY SCHOOL, SO I DON'T NEED TO DO BALLET.
?!
I'M GONNA PLAY BASEBALL WITH MY BIG BROTHERS!
?!
And then I'm going to the World Cup!
I'm gonna hit a lot of home runs!
I've got a recital...
OOH...
わくくっ
EXCITED
EVERY-BODY'S DOING SOME-THING.

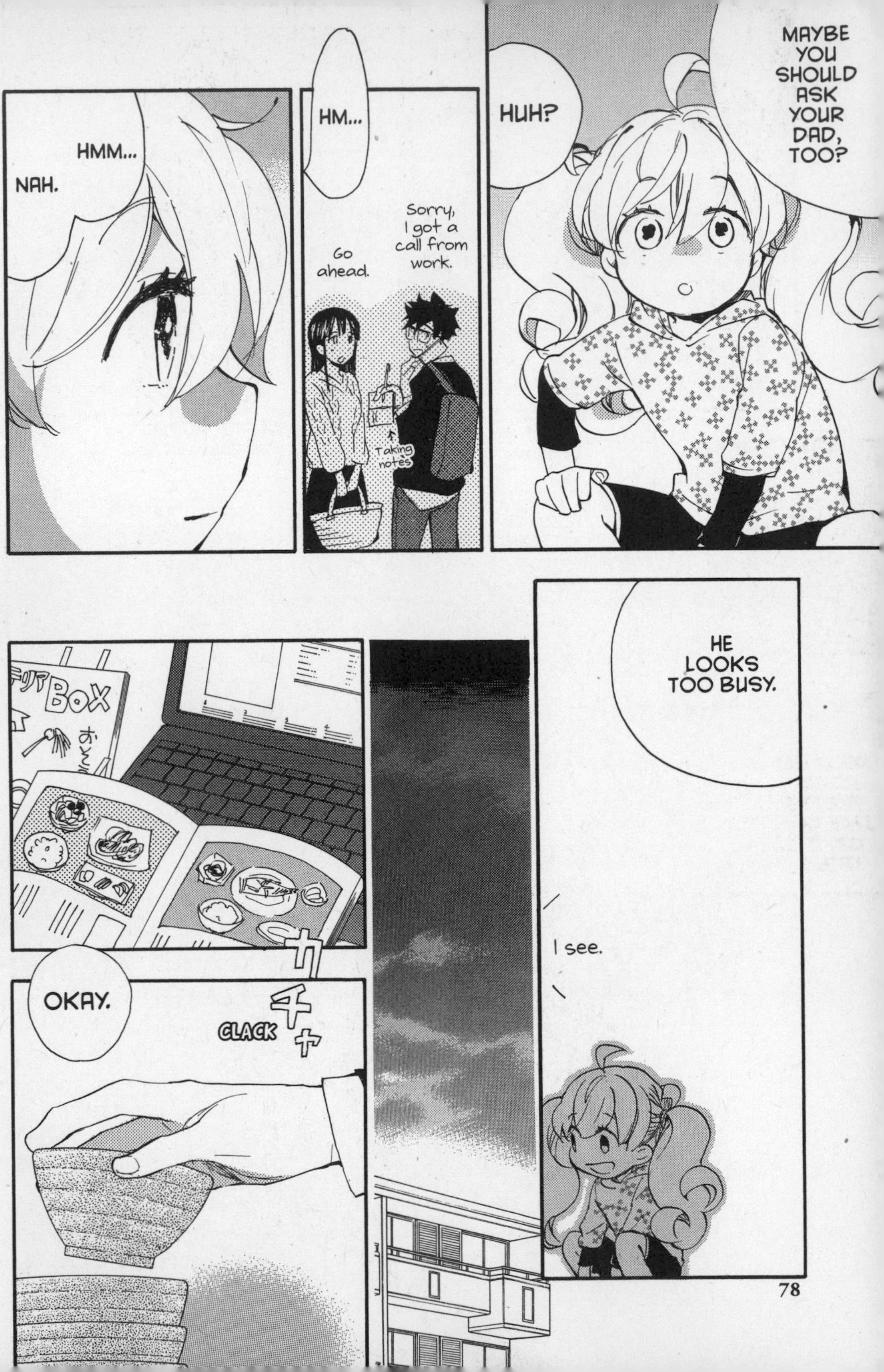
MAYBE YOU SHOULD ASK YOUR DAD, TOO?
HUH?
HM...
Sorry, I got a call from work.
Go ahead.
Taking notes
HMM...
NAH.
HE LOOKS TOO BUSY.
I see.
BOX
OKAY.
カチャ
CLACK

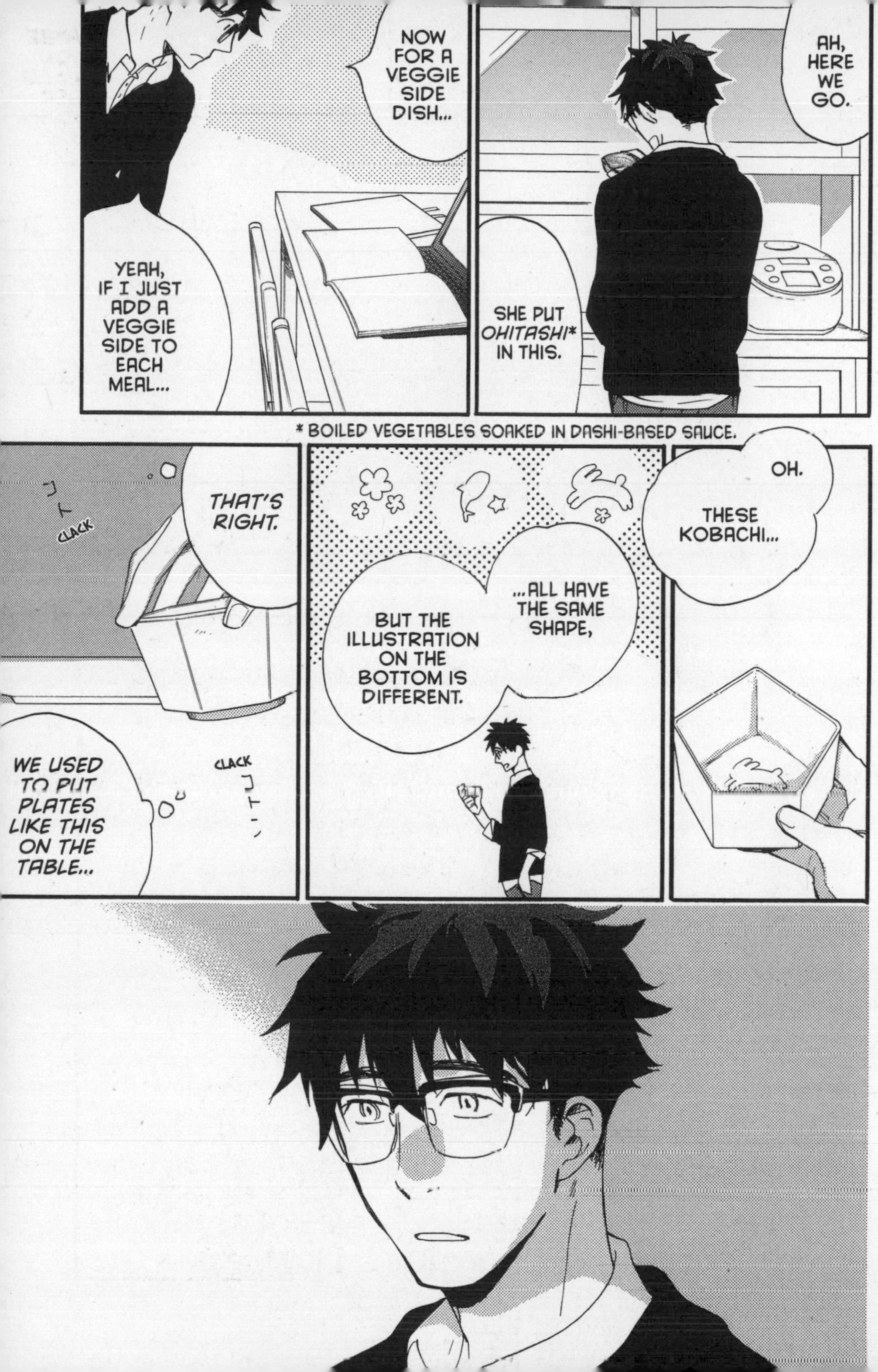
AH, HERE WE GO.
SHE PUT OHITASHI* IN THIS.
NOW FOR A VEGGIE SIDE DISH...
YEAH, IF I JUST ADD A VEGGIE SIDE TO EACH MEAL...
* BOILED VEGETABLES SOAKED IN DASHI-BASED SAUCE.
OH.
THESE KOBACHI...
...ALL HAVE THE SAME SHAPE,
BUT THE ILLUSTRATION ON THE BOTTOM IS DIFFERENT.
THAT'S RIGHT.
CLACK
CLACK
WE USED TO PUT PLATES LIKE THIS ON THE TABLE...

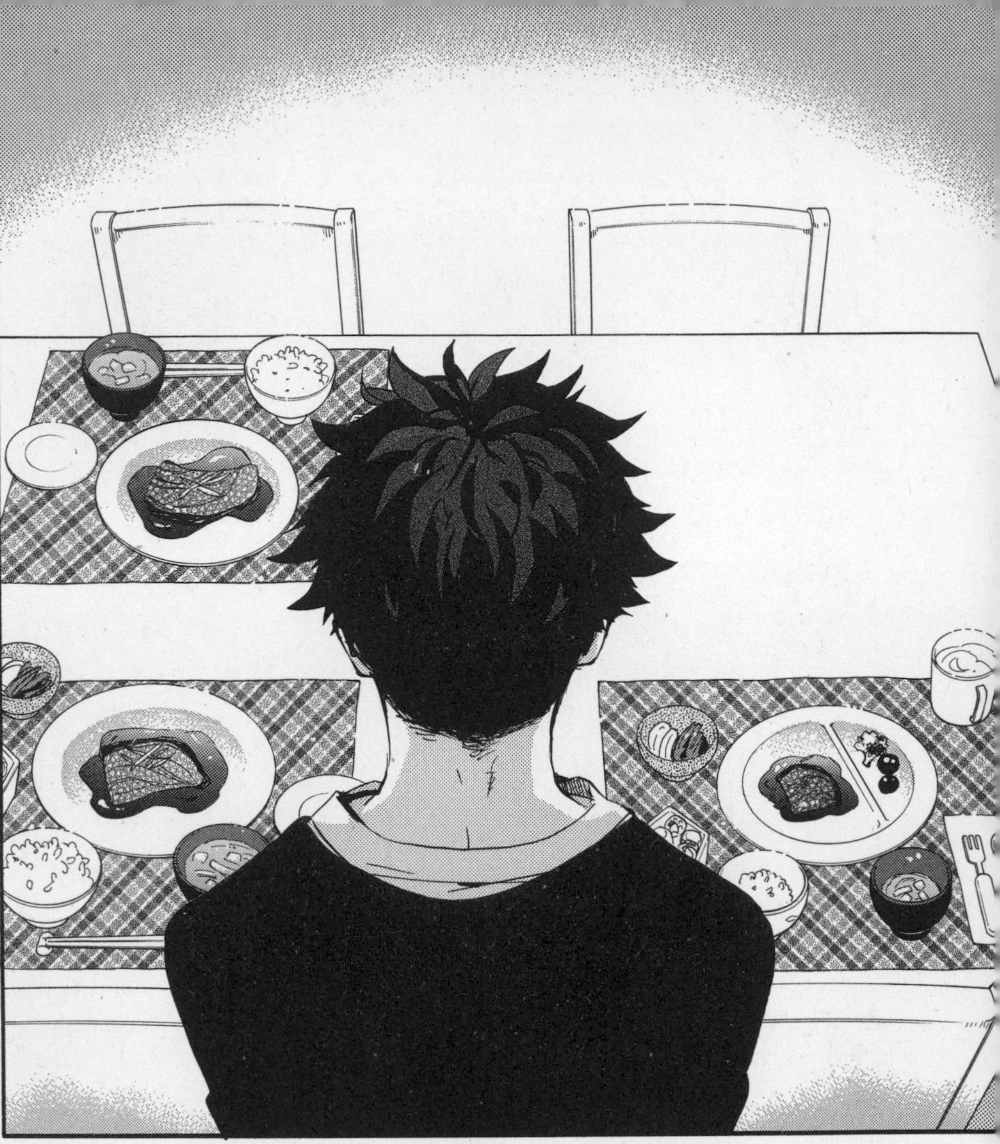

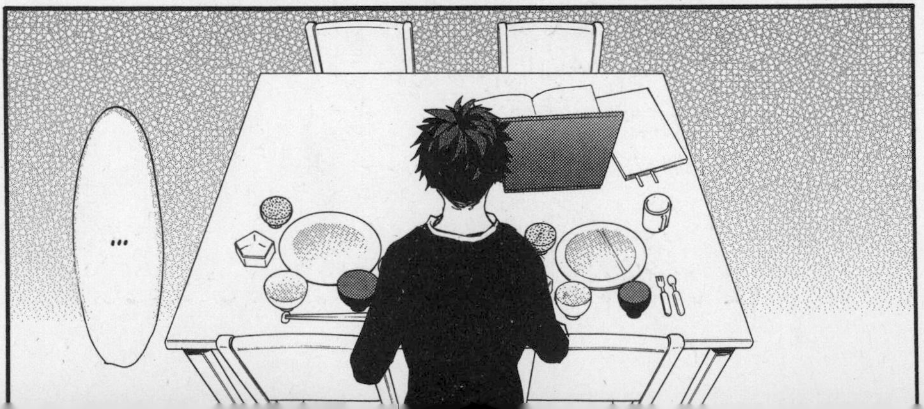
...

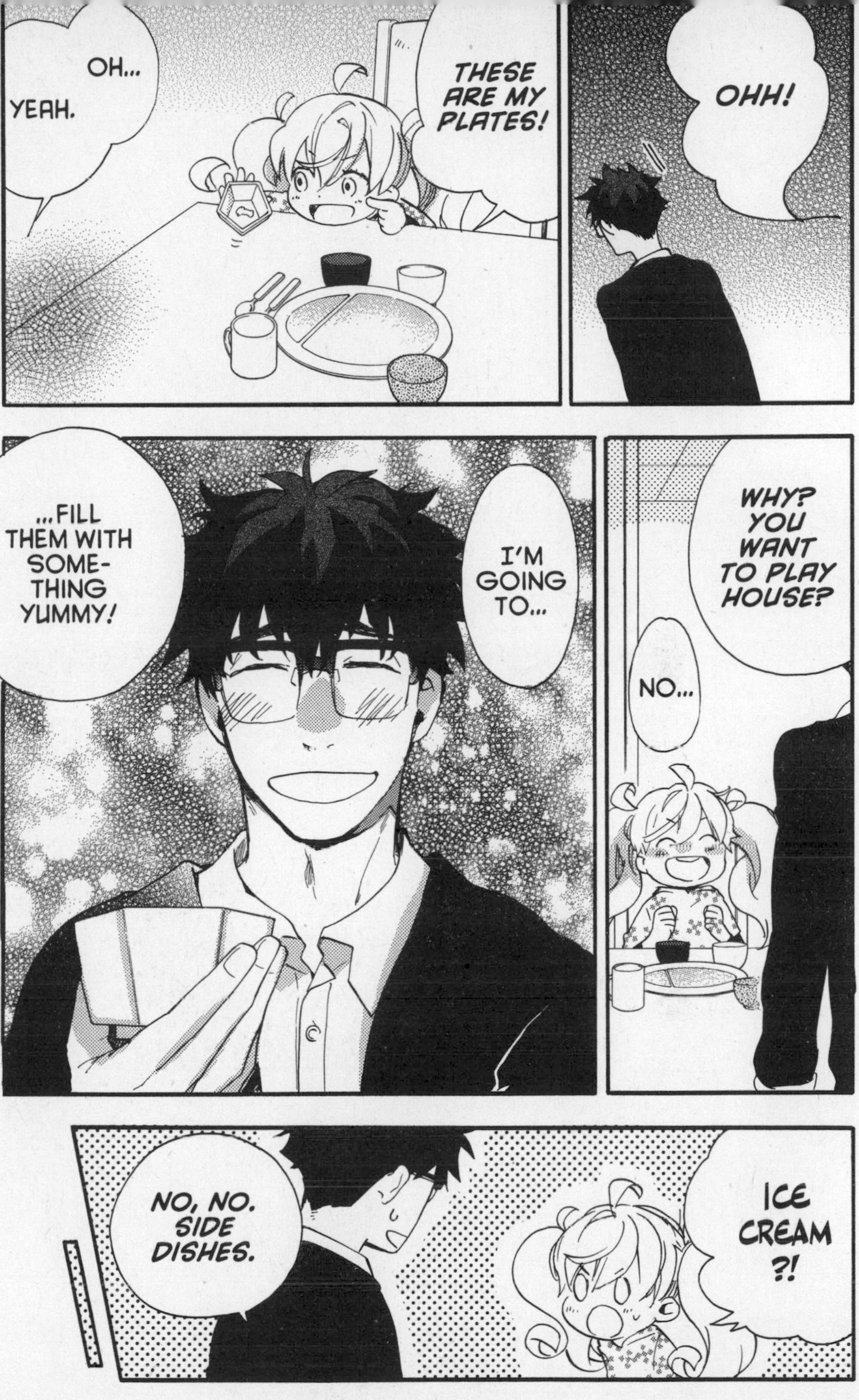
OHH!
THESE ARE MY PLATES!
OH... YEAH.
WHY? YOU WANT TO PLAY HOUSE?
NO...
I'M GOING TO...
...FILL THEM WITH SOME-THING YUMMY!
ICE CREAM?!
NO, NO. SIDE DISHES.

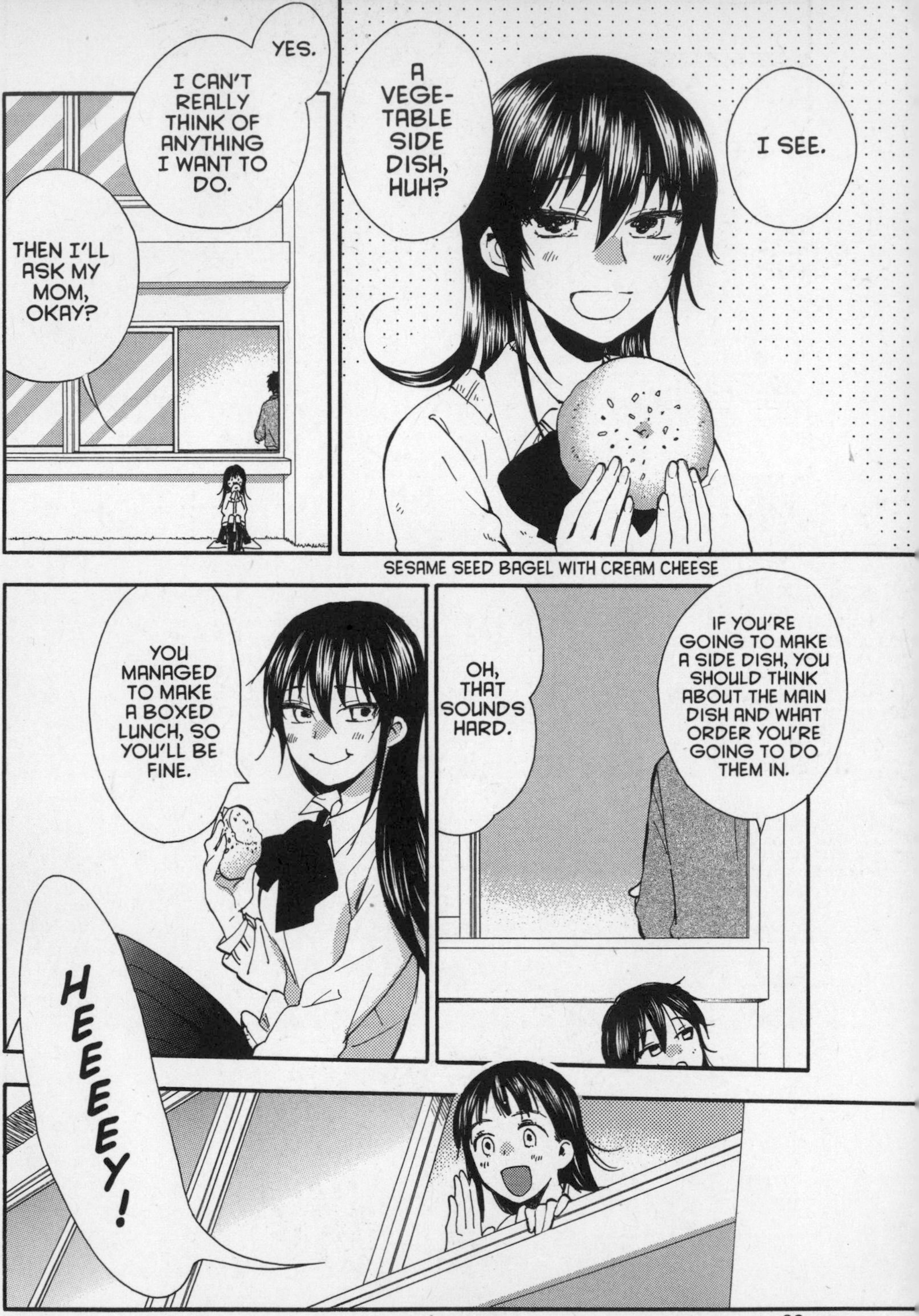
I SEE.
A VEGETABLE SIDE DISH, HUH?
SESAME SEED BAGEL WITH CREAM CHEESE
YES.
I CAN'T REALLY THINK OF ANYTHING I WANT TO DO.
THEN I'LL ASK MY MOM, OKAY?
IF YOU'RE GOING TO MAKE A SIDE DISH, YOU SHOULD THINK ABOUT THE MAIN DISH AND WHAT ORDER YOU'RE GOING TO DO THEM IN.
OH, THAT SOUNDS HARD.
YOU MANAGED TO MAKE A BOXED LUNCH, SO YOU'LL BE FINE.
HEEEEY!

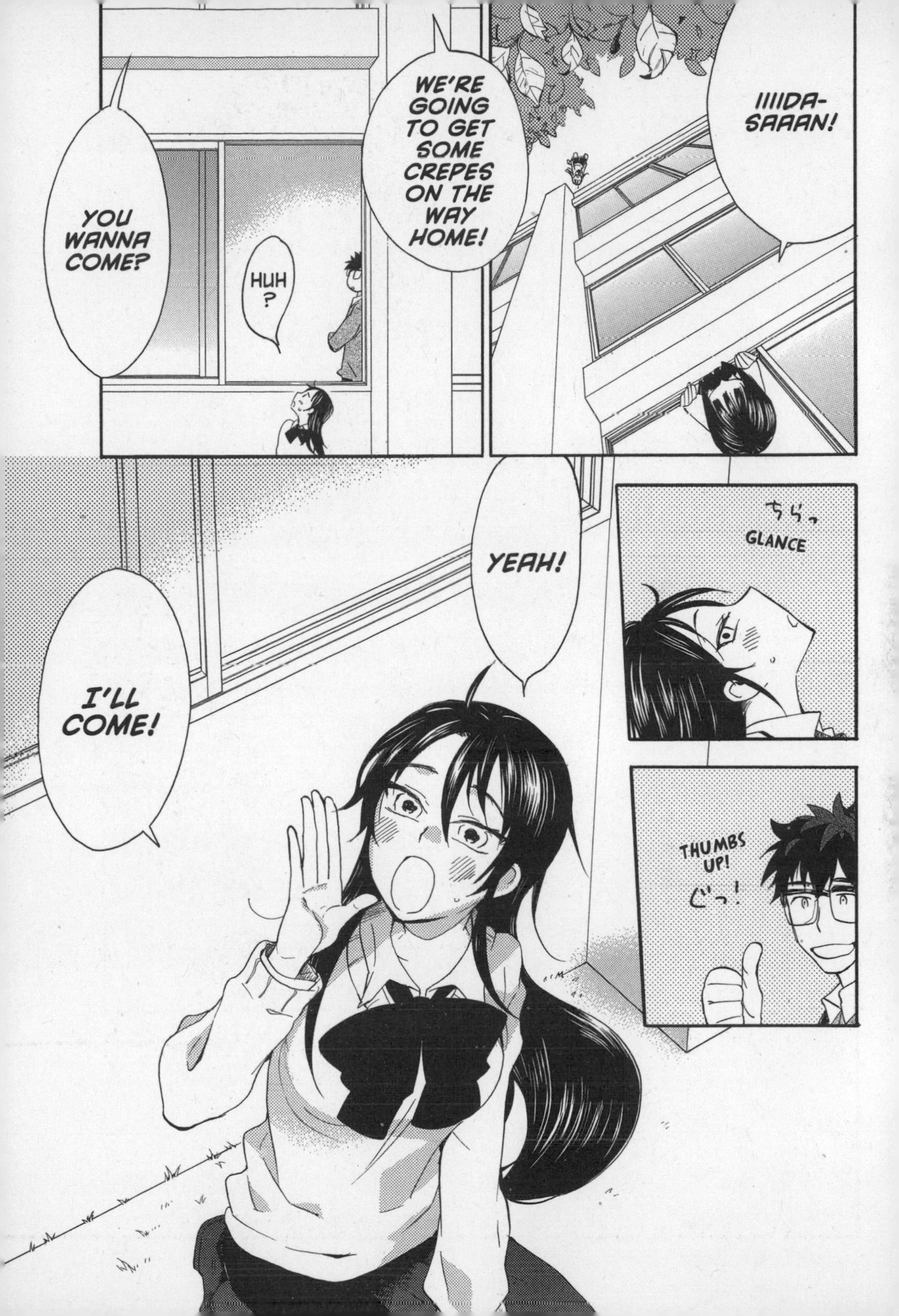
IIIIDA-SAAAN!
WE'RE GOING TO GET SOME CREPES ON THE WAY HOME!
YOU WANNA COME?
HUH?
YEAH!
I'LL COME!
ちらっ
GLANCE
THUMBS UP!
ぐっ!

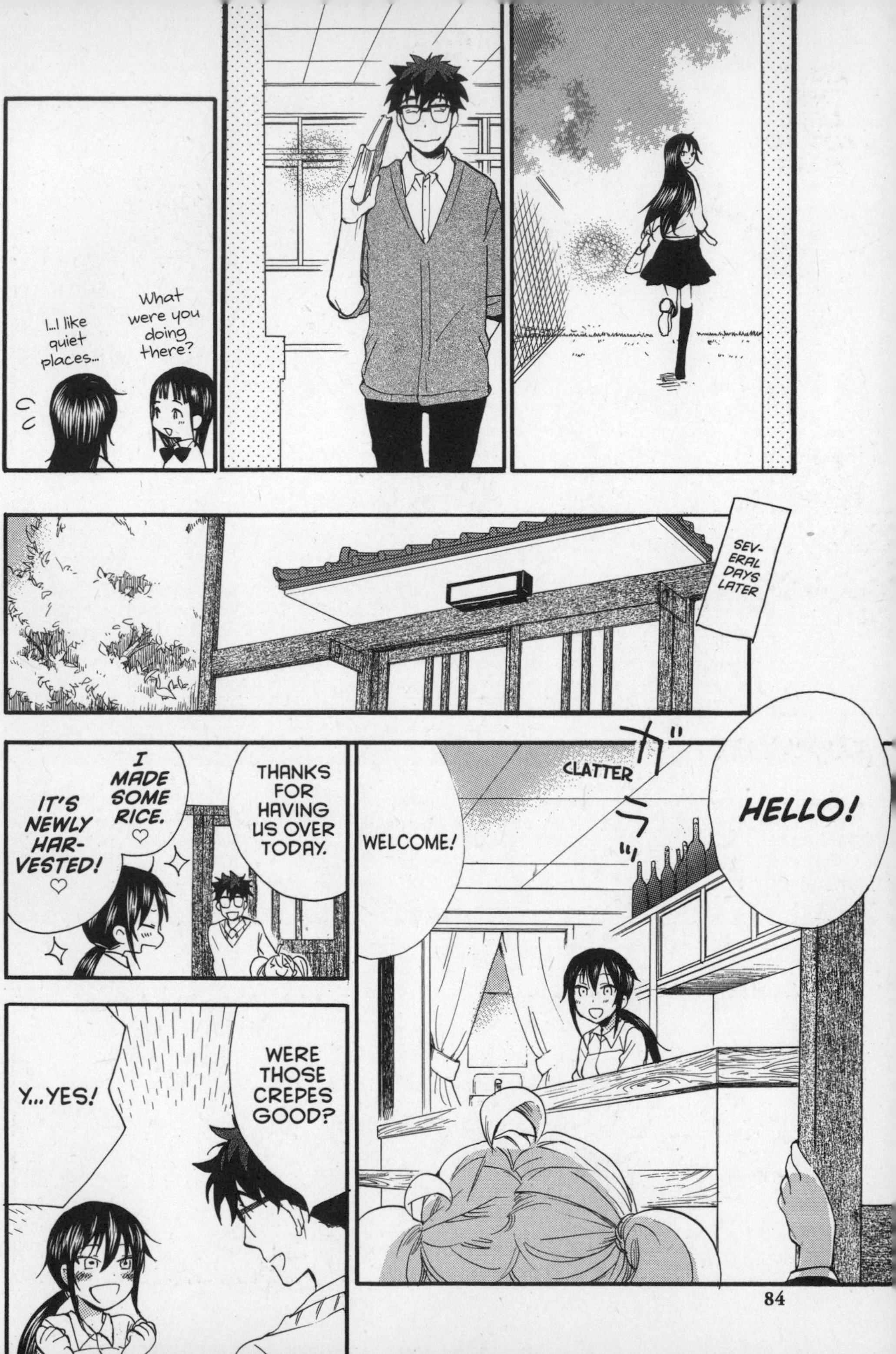
What were you doing there?
I...I like quiet places...
SEV-ERAL DAYS LATER
HELLO!
CLATTER
WELCOME!
THANKS FOR HAVING US OVER TODAY.
I MADE SOME RICE. ♡
IT'S NEWLY HAR-VESTED! ♡
WERE THOSE CREPES GOOD?
Y...YES!

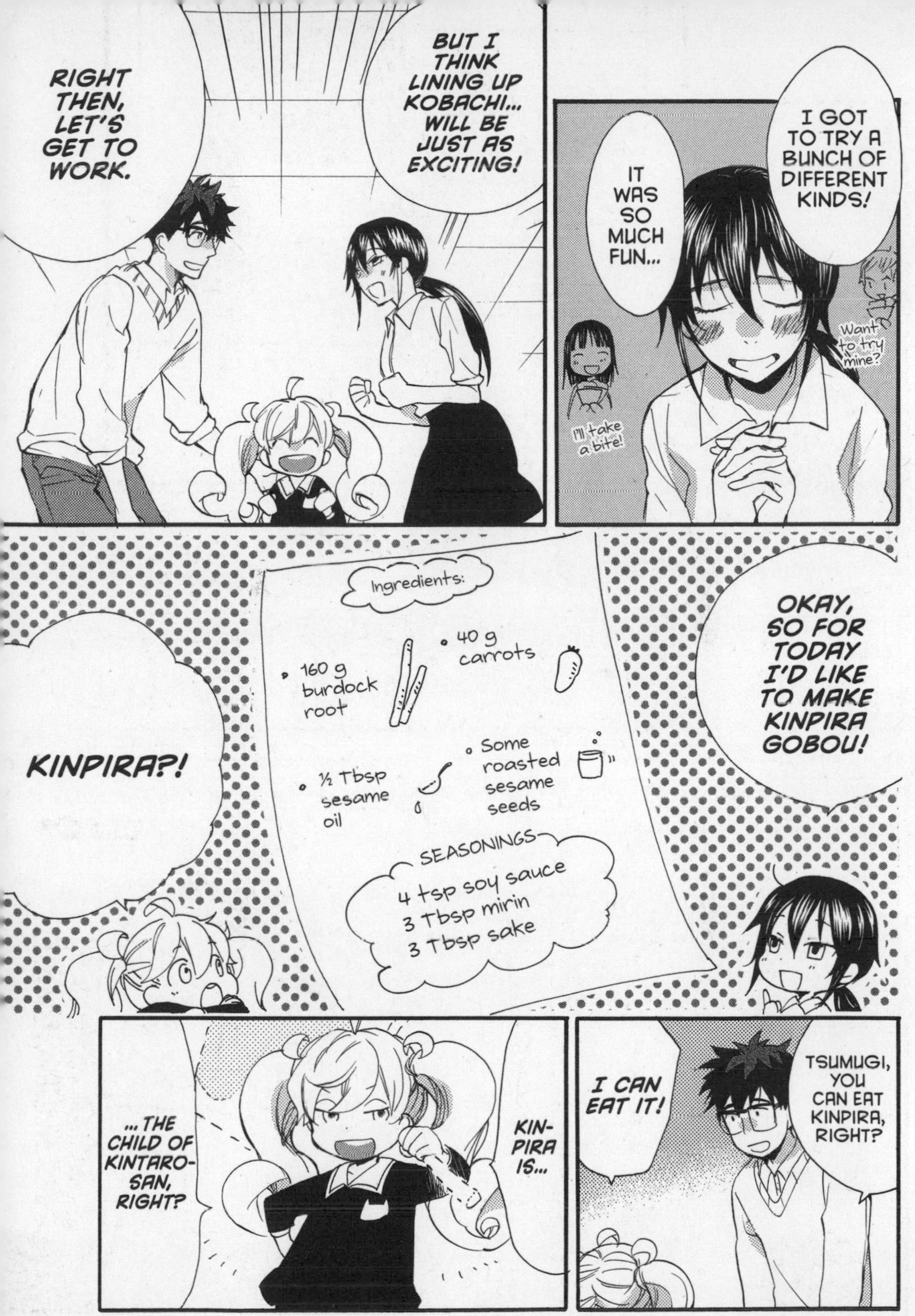
I GOT TO TRY A BUNCH OF DIFFERENT KINDS!
IT WAS SO MUCH FUN...
Want to try mine?
I'll take a bite!
BUT I THINK LINING UP KOBACHI... WILL BE JUST AS EXCITING!
RIGHT THEN, LET'S GET TO WORK.
OKAY, SO FOR TODAY I'D LIKE TO MAKE KINPIRA GOBOU!
Ingredients:
• 160 g burdock root
• 40 g carrots
• ½ Tbsp sesame oil
• Some roasted sesame seeds
SEASONINGS
4 tsp soy sauce
3 Tbsp mirin
3 Tbsp sake
KINPIRA?!
TSUMUGI, YOU CAN EAT KINPIRA, RIGHT?
I CAN EAT IT!
KINPIRA IS...
...THE CHILD OF KINTARO-SAN, RIGHT?

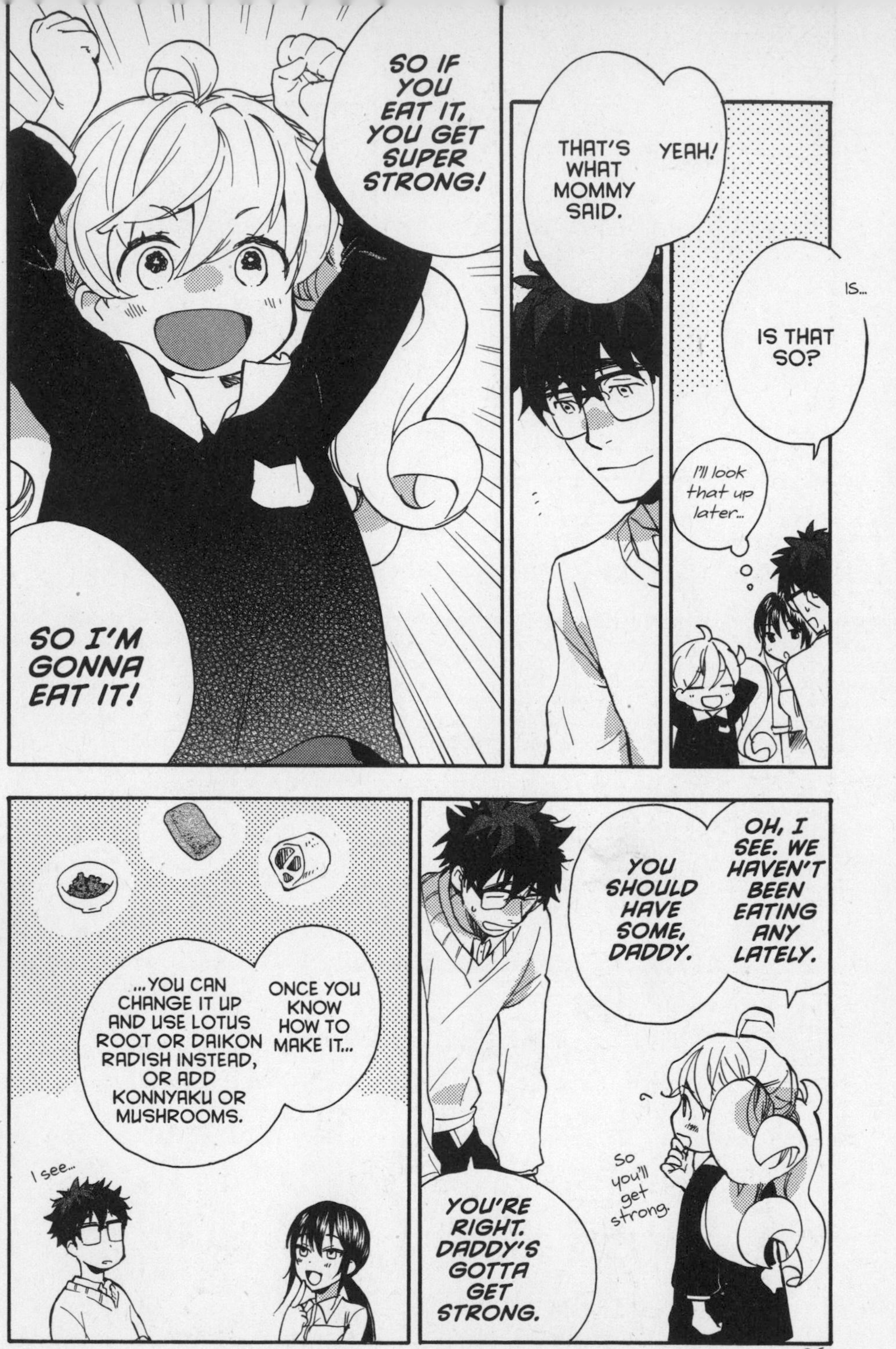
IS...
IS THAT SO?
I'll look that up later...
YEAH!
THAT'S WHAT MOMMY SAID.
SO IF YOU EAT IT, YOU GET SUPER STRONG!
SO I'M GONNA EAT IT!
OH, I SEE. WE HAVEN'T BEEN EATING ANY LATELY.
YOU SHOULD HAVE SOME, DADDY.
So you'll get strong.
YOU'RE RIGHT. DADDY'S GOTTA GET STRONG.
ONCE YOU KNOW HOW TO MAKE IT...
...YOU CAN CHANGE IT UP AND USE LOTUS ROOT OR DAIKON RADISH INSTEAD, OR ADD KONNYAKU OR MUSHROOMS.
I see...

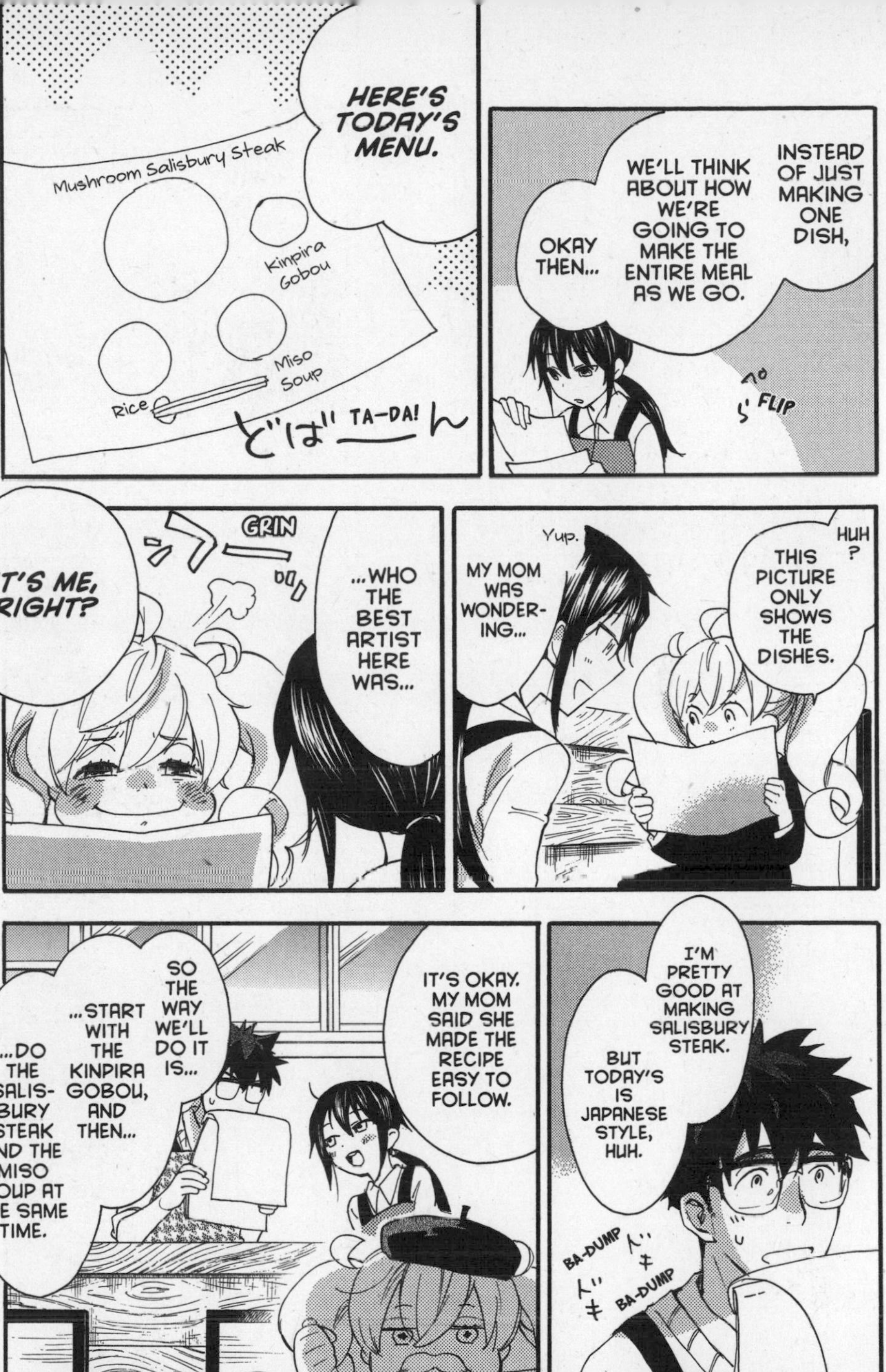
INSTEAD OF JUST MAKING ONE DISH,
WE'LL THINK ABOUT HOW WE'RE GOING TO MAKE THE ENTIRE MEAL AS WE GO.
OKAY THEN...
FLIP
HERE'S TODAY'S MENU.
Mushroom Salisbury Steak
Kinpira Gobou
Miso Soup
Rice
どば——ん TA-DA!
HUH?
THIS PICTURE ONLY SHOWS THE DISHES.
MY MOM WAS WONDERING...
Yup.
...WHO THE BEST ARTIST HERE WAS...
GRIN
IT'S ME, RIGHT?
I'M PRETTY GOOD AT MAKING SALISBURY STEAK.
BUT TODAY'S IS JAPANESE STYLE, HUH.
BA-DUMP
BA-DUMP
IT'S OKAY. MY MOM SAID SHE MADE THE RECIPE EASY TO FOLLOW.
SO THE WAY WE'LL DO IT IS...
...START WITH THE KINPIRA GOBOU, AND THEN...
...DO THE SALISBURY STEAK AND THE MISO SOUP AT THE SAME TIME.

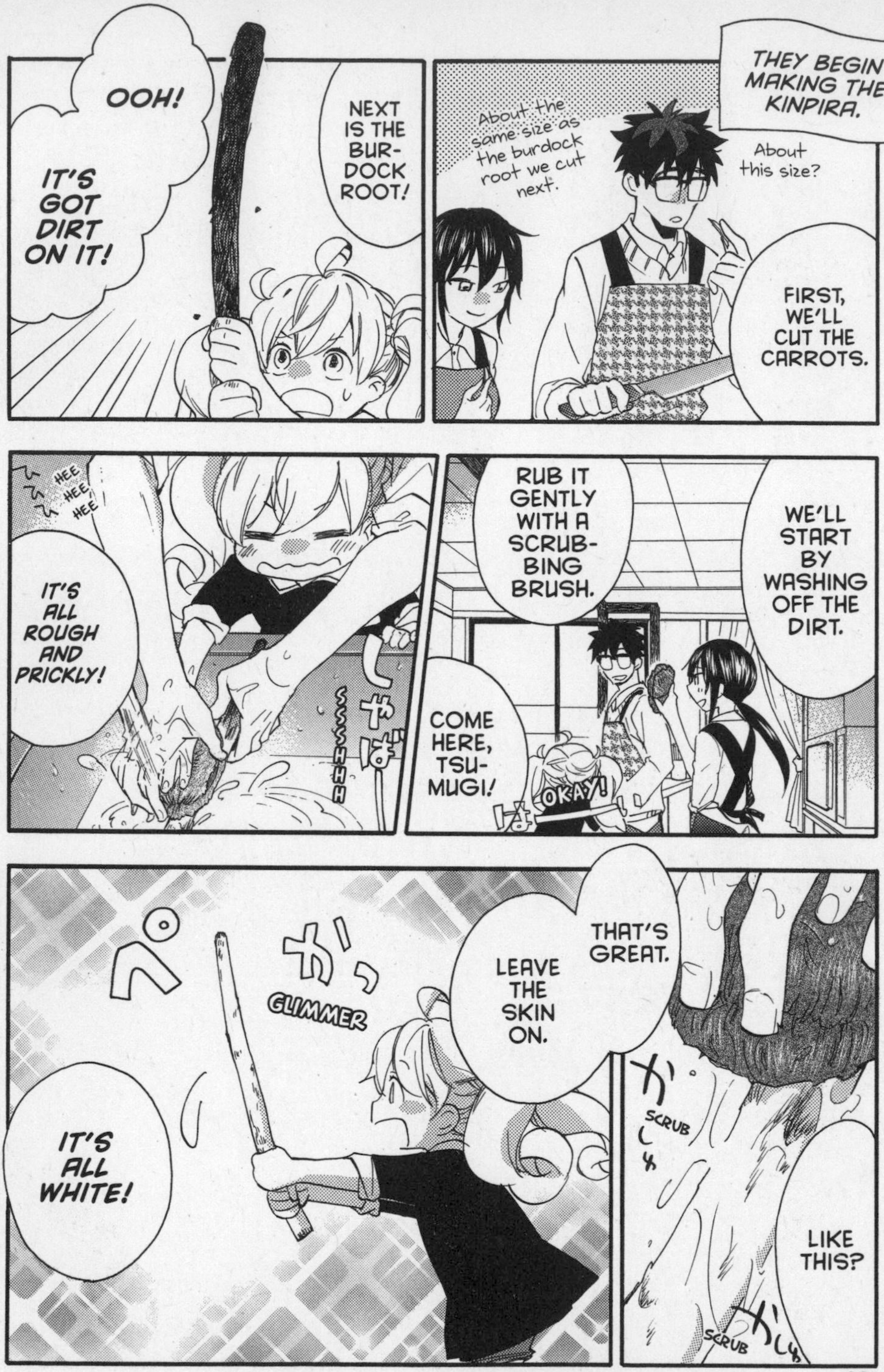
THEY BEGIN MAKING THE KINPIRA.
About this size?
FIRST, WE'LL CUT THE CARROTS.
About the same size as the burdock root we cut next.
NEXT IS THE BUR-DOCK ROOT!
OOH!
IT'S GOT DIRT ON IT!
WE'LL START BY WASHING OFF THE DIRT.
RUB IT GENTLY WITH A SCRUB-BING BRUSH.
COME HERE, TSU-MUGI!
OKAY!
HEE HEE HEE
IT'S ALL ROUGH AND PRICKLY!
SSSHHH
LIKE THIS?
SCRUB
SCRUB
THAT'S GREAT.
LEAVE THE SKIN ON.
GLIMMER
IT'S ALL WHITE!

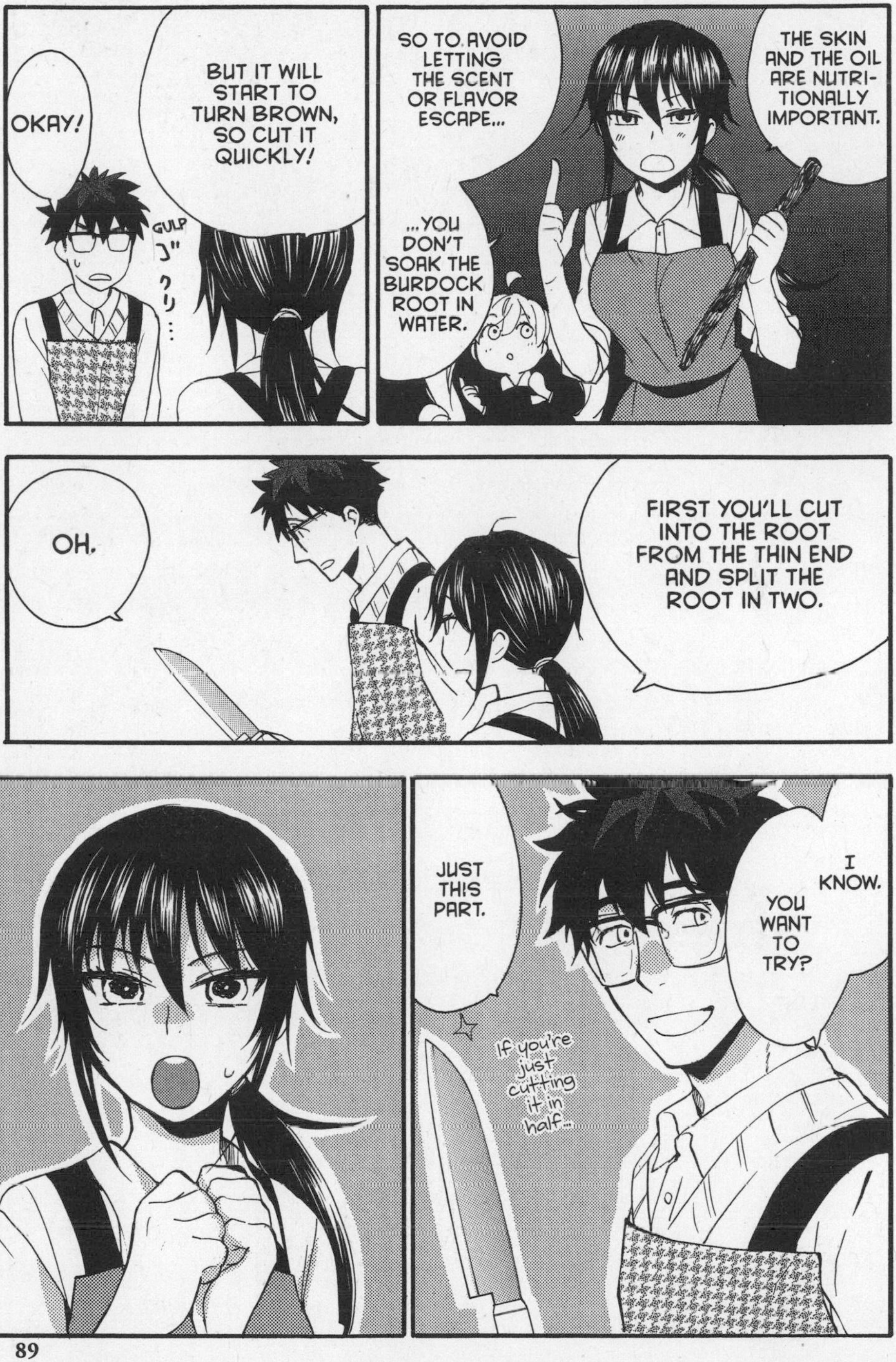
THE SKIN AND THE OIL ARE NUTRITIONALLY IMPORTANT.
SO TO AVOID LETTING THE SCENT OR FLAVOR ESCAPE...
...YOU DON'T SOAK THE BURDOCK ROOT IN WATER.
BUT IT WILL START TO TURN BROWN, SO CUT IT QUICKLY!
OKAY!
GULP
ゴクリ…
FIRST YOU'LL CUT INTO THE ROOT FROM THE THIN END AND SPLIT THE ROOT IN TWO.
OH.
I KNOW. YOU WANT TO TRY?
JUST THIS PART.
If you're just cutting it in half...

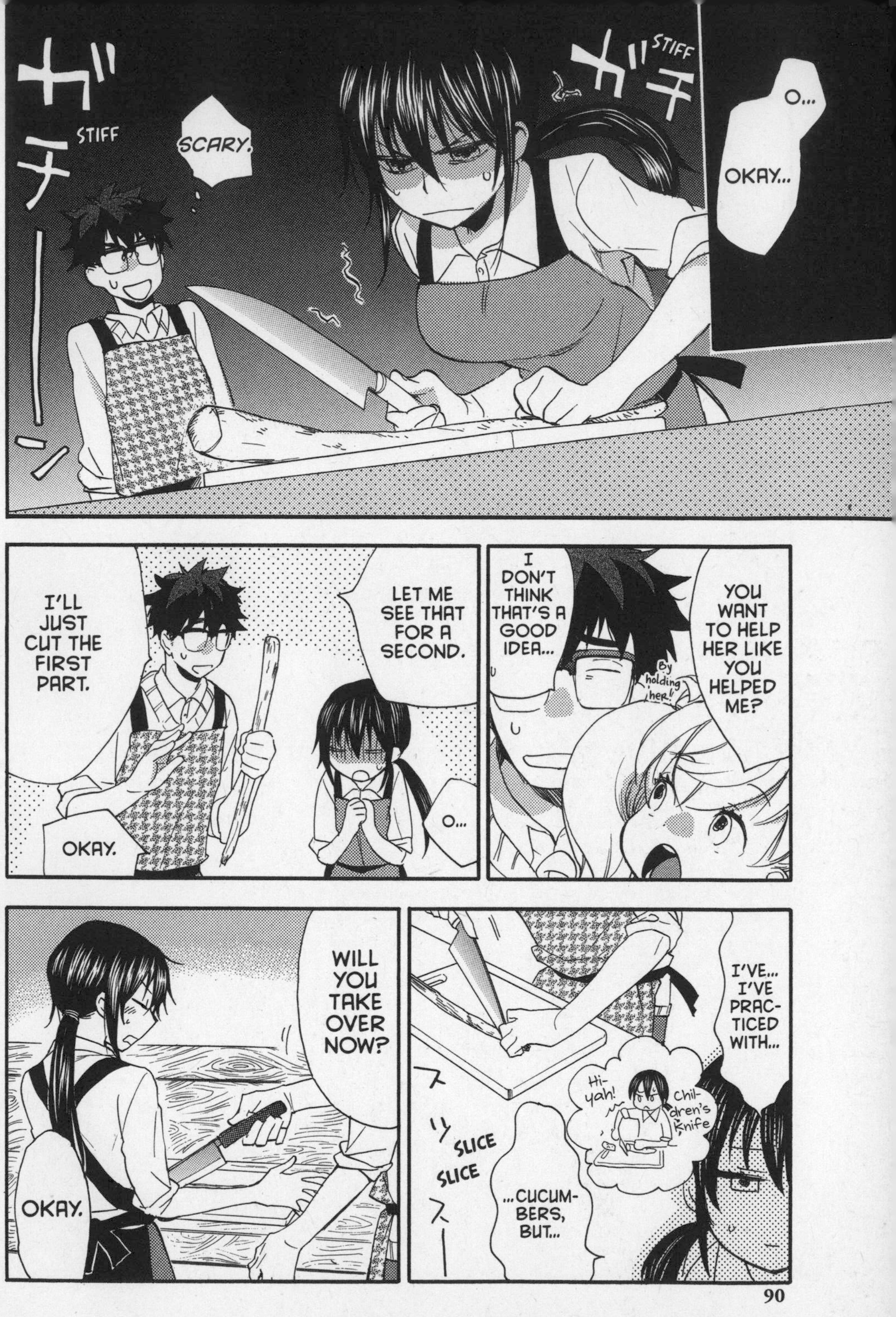
O...
OKAY...
ガチ
STIFF
SCARY.
ガチーン
STIFF
YOU WANT TO HELP HER LIKE YOU HELPED ME?
By holding her!
I DON'T THINK THAT'S A GOOD IDEA...
LET ME SEE THAT FOR A SECOND.
O...
I'LL JUST CUT THE FIRST PART.
OKAY.
I'VE... I'VE PRACTICED WITH...
Chil-dren's Knife
Hi-yah!
...CUCUM-BERS, BUT...
スッ
SLICE
スー
SLICE
WILL YOU TAKE OVER NOW?
OKAY.

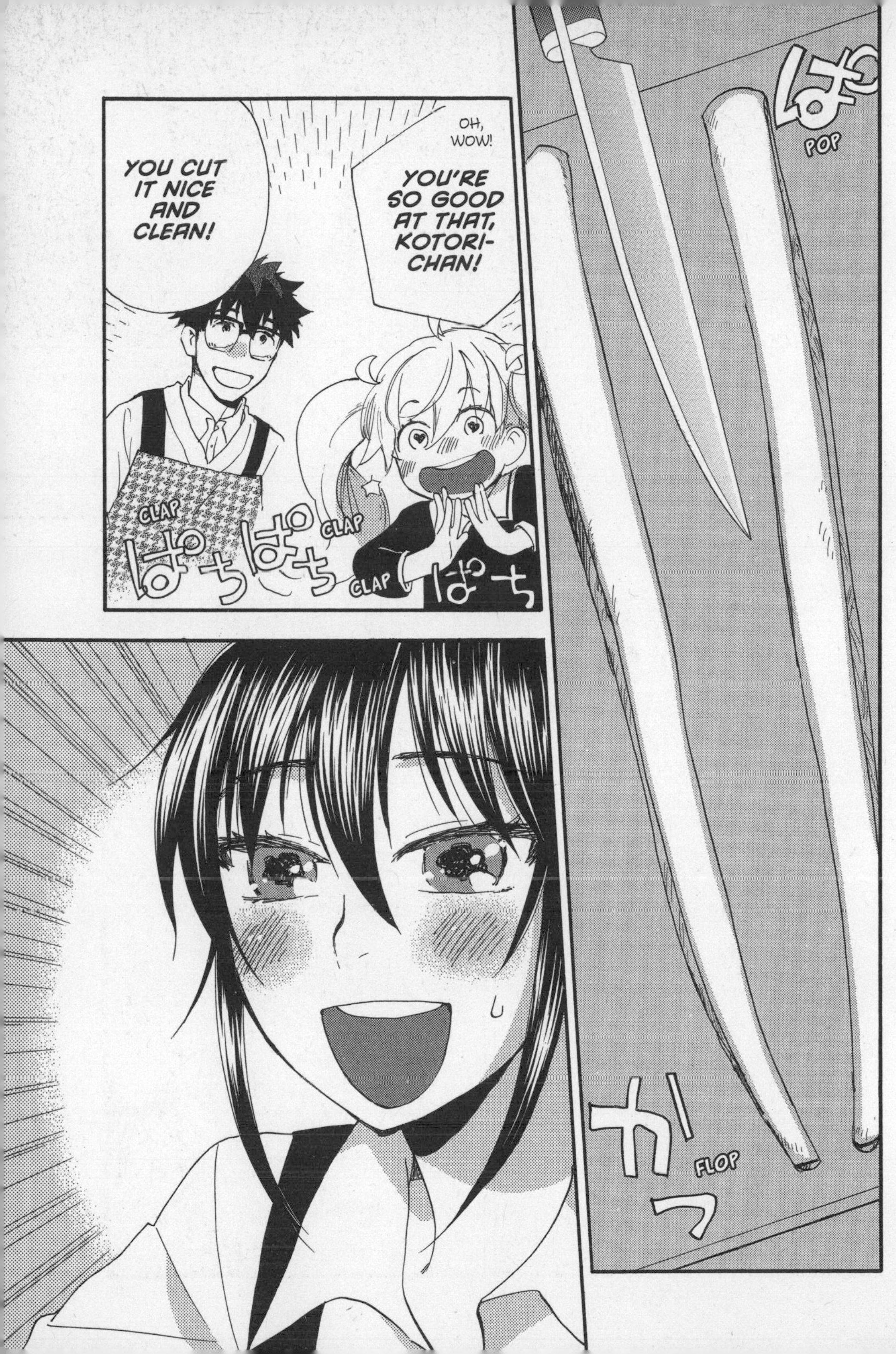
POP
FLOP
OH, WOW!
YOU'RE SO GOOD AT THAT, KOTORI-CHAN!
YOU CUT IT NICE AND CLEAN!
CLAP
CLAP
CLAP
CLAP

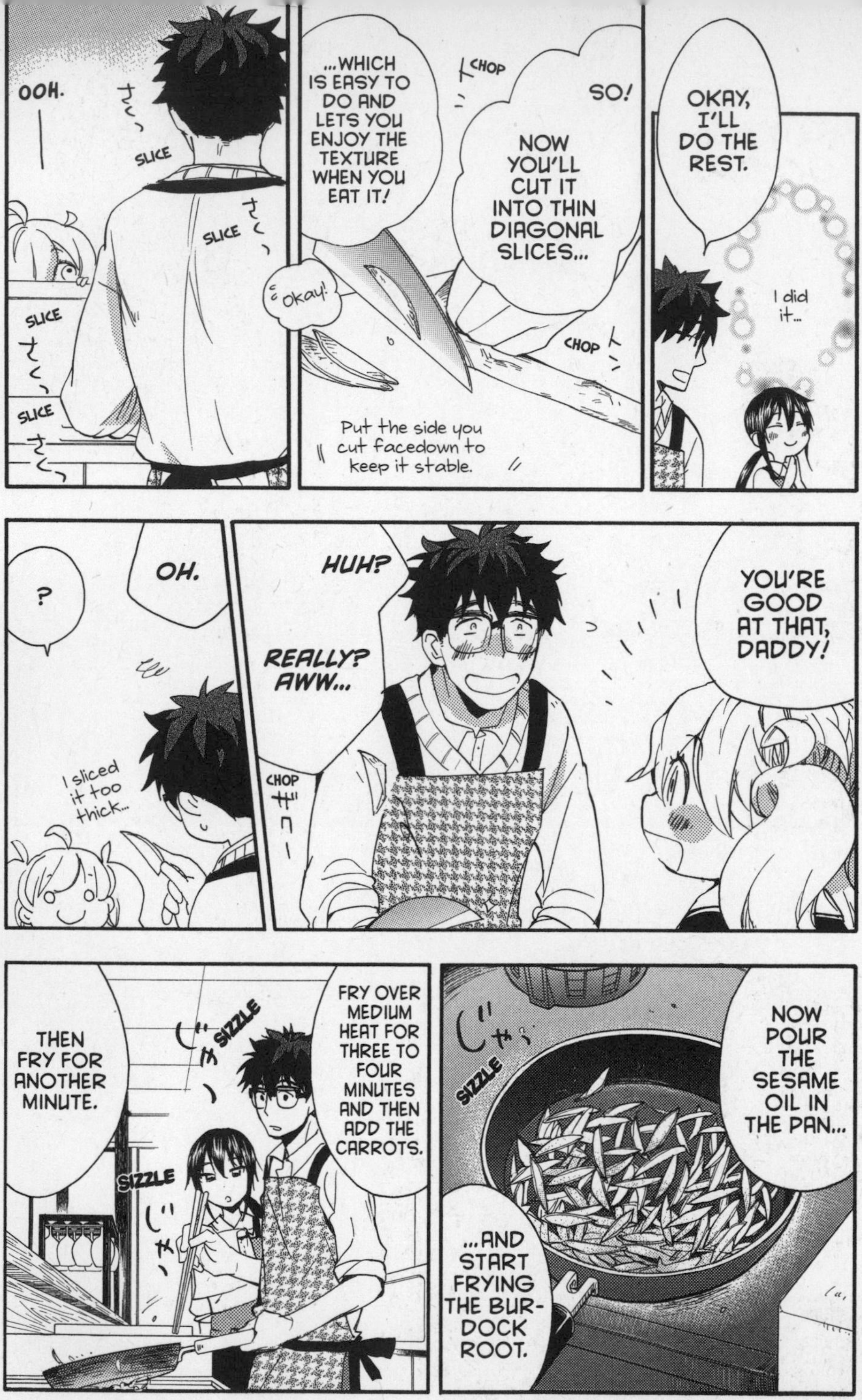
OKAY, I'LL DO THE REST.
I did it...
SO!
NOW YOU'LL CUT IT INTO THIN DIAGONAL SLICES...
CHOP
...WHICH IS EASY TO DO AND LETS YOU ENJOY THE TEXTURE WHEN YOU EAT IT!
Okay!
CHOP
Put the side you cut facedown to keep it stable.
OOH.
SLICE
SLICE
SLICE
SLICE
YOU'RE GOOD AT THAT, DADDY!
HUH?
REALLY? AWW...
CHOP
OH.
?
I sliced it too thick...
NOW POUR THE SESAME OIL IN THE PAN...
SIZZLE
...AND START FRYING THE BURDOCK ROOT.
FRY OVER MEDIUM HEAT FOR THREE TO FOUR MINUTES AND THEN ADD THE CARROTS.
SIZZLE
THEN FRY FOR ANOTHER MINUTE.
SIZZLE

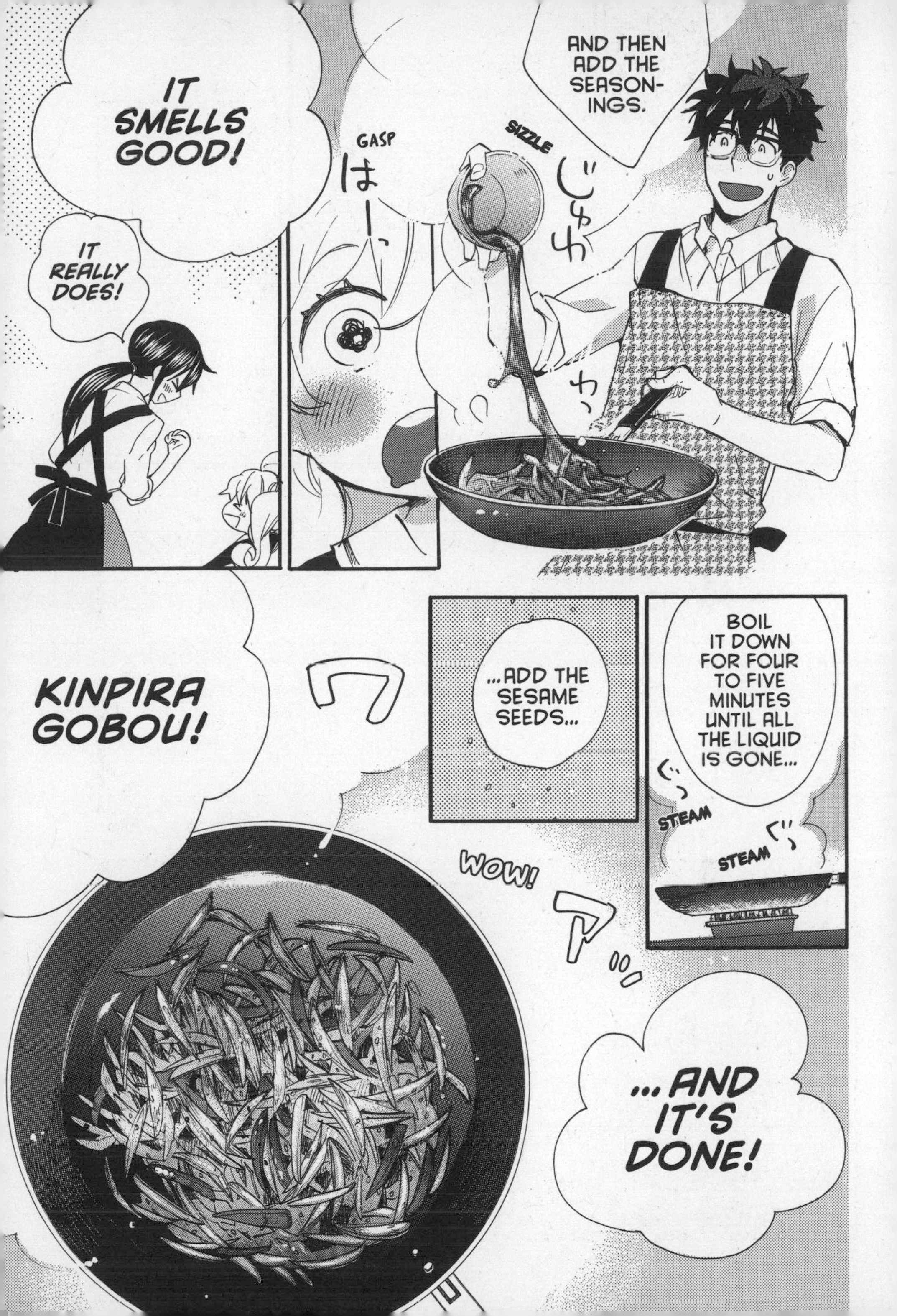
AND THEN ADD THE SEASON-INGS.
SIZZLE
GASP
IT SMELLS GOOD!
IT REALLY DOES!
BOIL IT DOWN FOR FOUR TO FIVE MINUTES UNTIL ALL THE LIQUID IS GONE...
STEAM
STEAM
...ADD THE SESAME SEEDS...
...AND IT'S DONE!
WOW!
KINPIRA GOBOU!

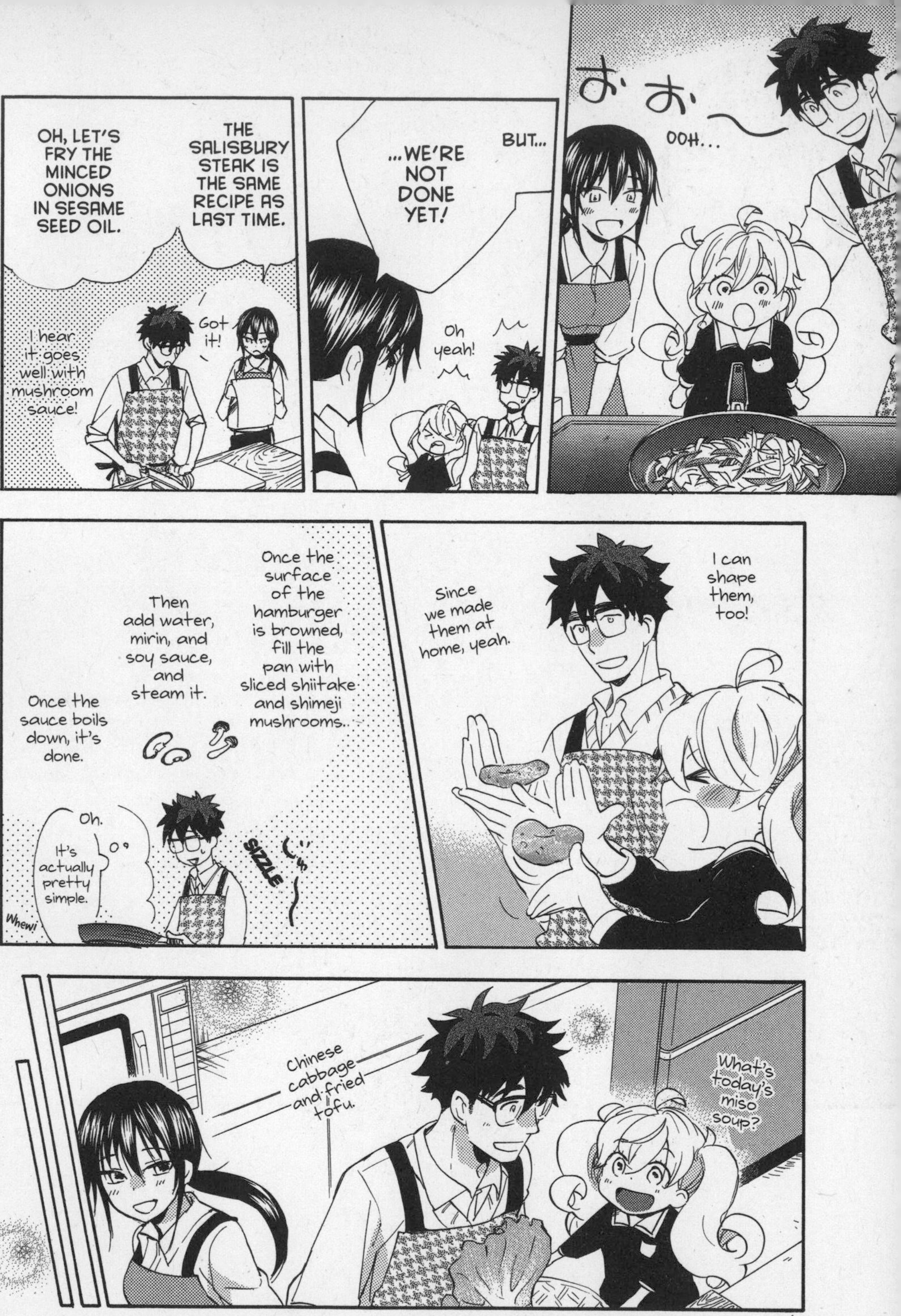
おお〜
OOH...
BUT...
...WE'RE NOT DONE YET!
Oh yeah!
THE SALISBURY STEAK IS THE SAME RECIPE AS LAST TIME.
OH, LET'S FRY THE MINCED ONIONS IN SESAME SEED OIL.
Got it!
I hear it goes well with mushroom sauce!
I can shape them, too!
Since we made them at home, yeah.
Once the surface of the hamburger is browned, fill the pan with sliced shiitake and shimeji mushrooms..
Then add water, mirin, and soy sauce, and steam it.
Once the sauce boils down, it's done.
SIZZLE
Oh.
It's actually pretty simple.
Whew!
What's today's miso soup?
Chinese cabbage and fried tofu.

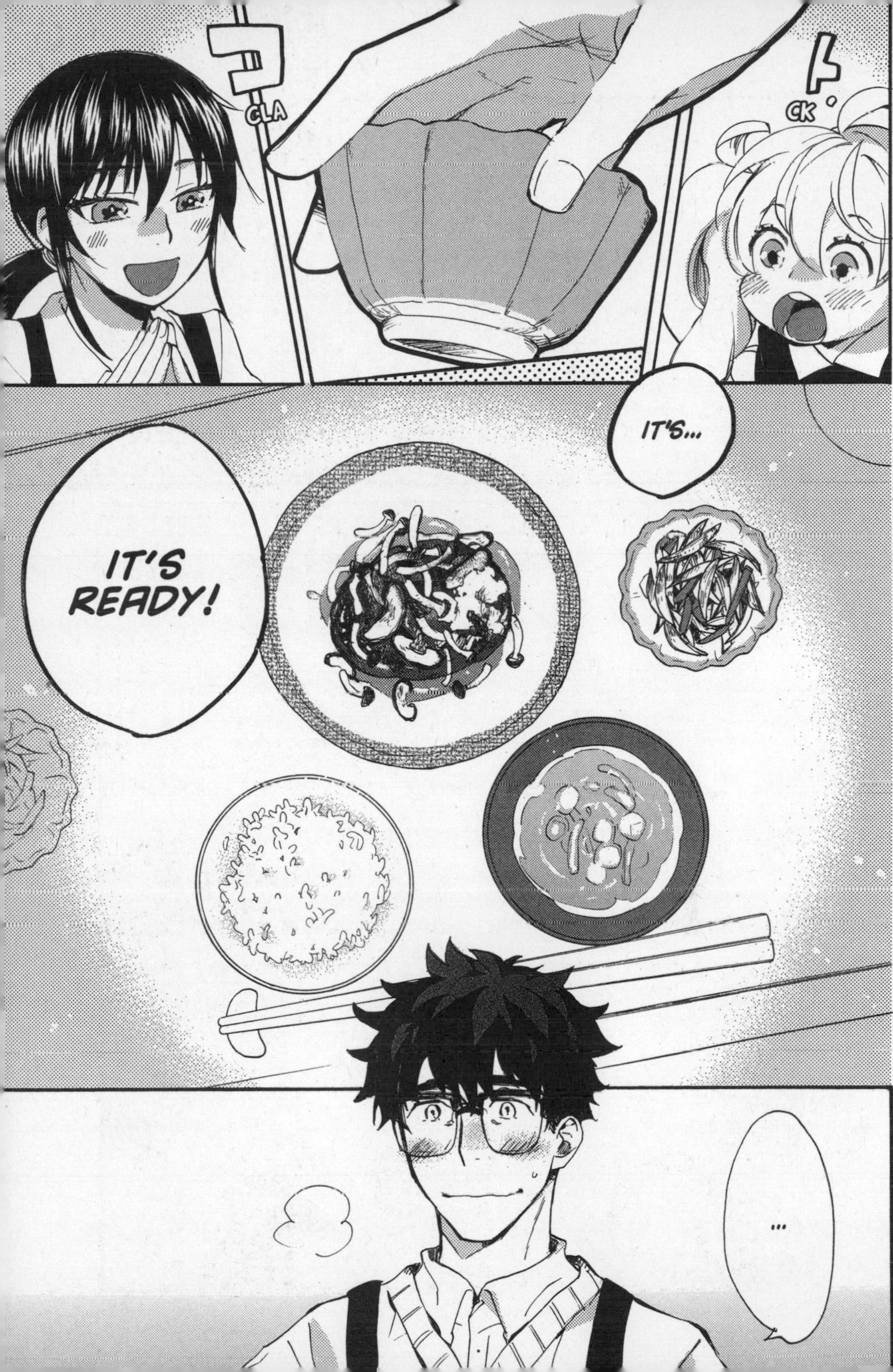

コ
CLA
ト
CK
IT'S...
IT'S READY!
...

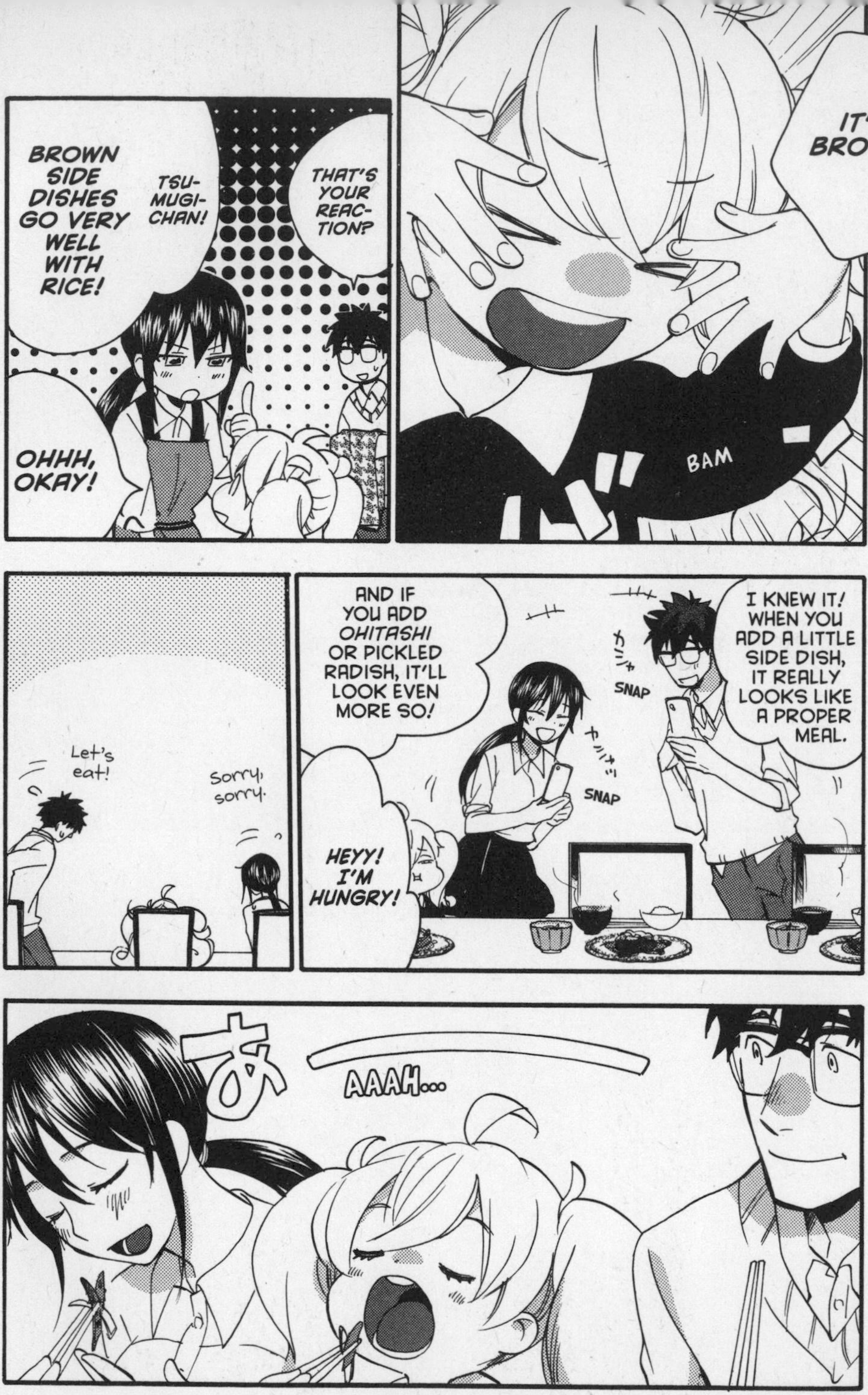
IT'S BROWN!
BAM
THAT'S YOUR REACTION?
TSU-MUGI-CHAN!
BROWN SIDE DISHES GO VERY WELL WITH RICE!
OHHH, OKAY!
I KNEW IT! WHEN YOU ADD A LITTLE SIDE DISH, IT REALLY LOOKS LIKE A PROPER MEAL.
SNAP
AND IF YOU ADD OHITASHI OR PICKLED RADISH, IT'LL LOOK EVEN MORE SO!
SNAP
HEYY! I'M HUNGRY!
Sorry, sorry.
Let's eat!
あ
AAAH...

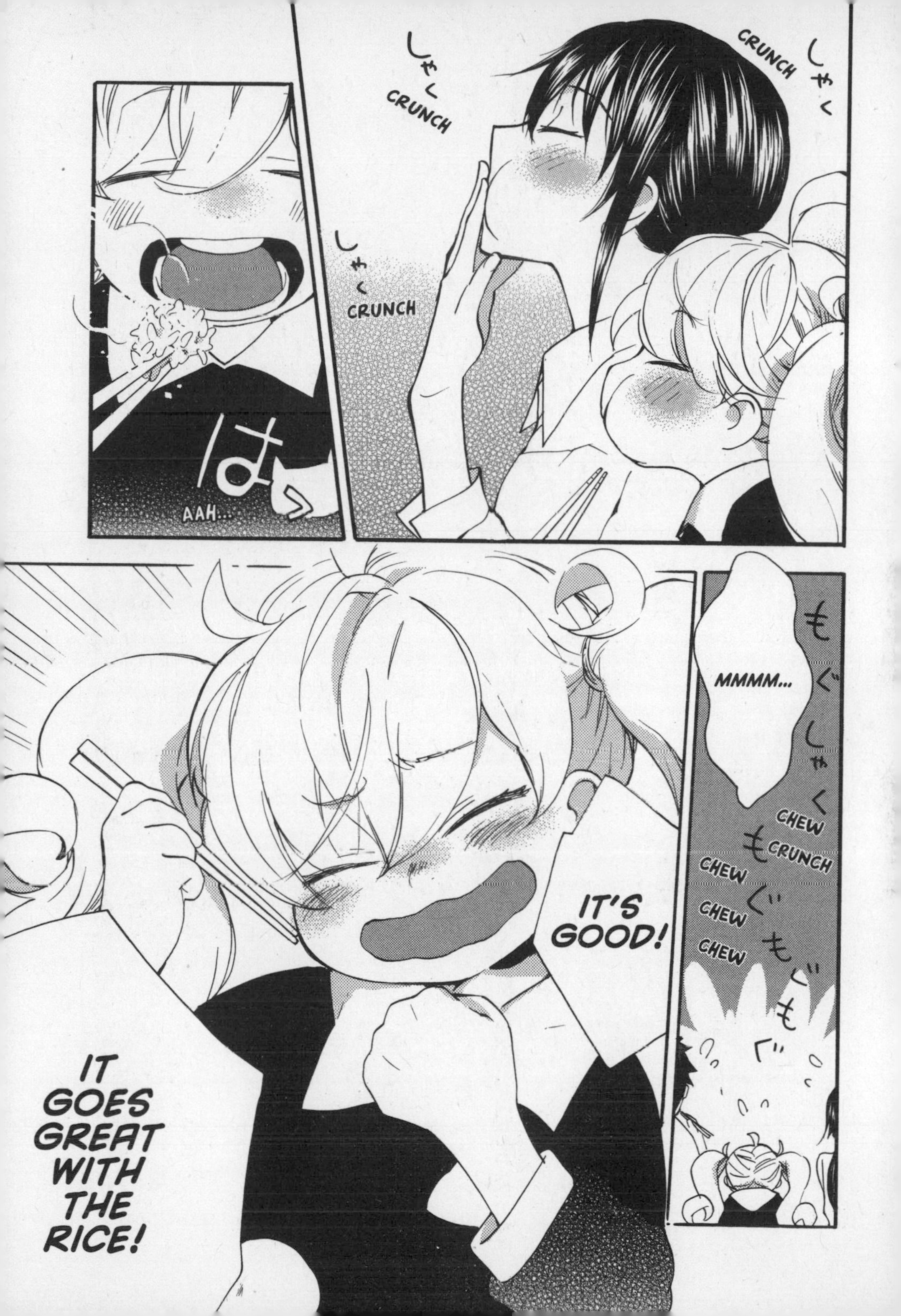
しゃく
CRUNCH
しゃく
CRUNCH
しゃく
CRUNCH
はっ
AAH...
MMMM...
もぐ
しゃく
CHEW
CRUNCH
もぐ
もぐ
もぐ
CHEW
CHEW
CHEW
IT'S GOOD!
IT GOES GREAT WITH THE RICE!

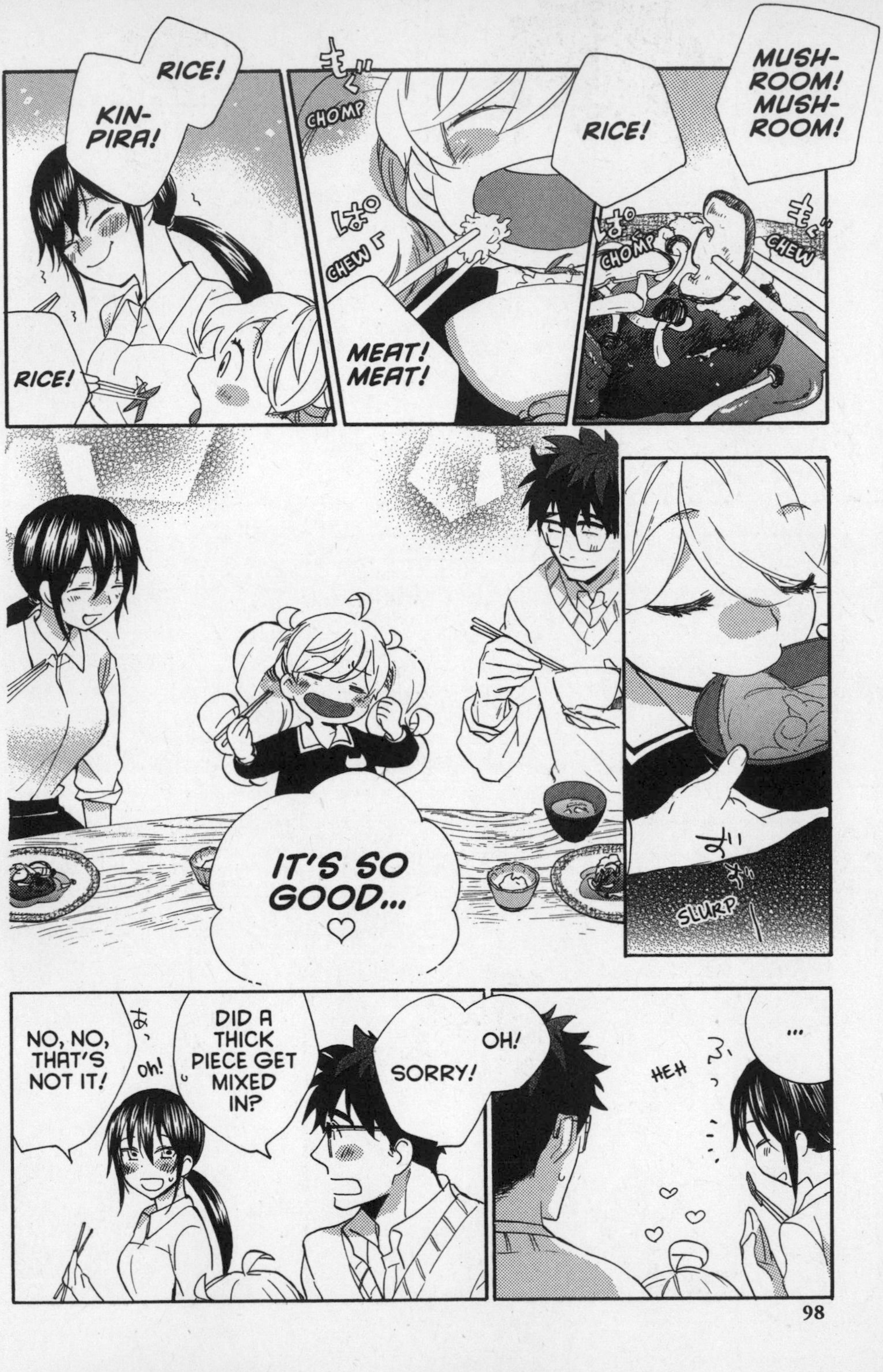

MUSH-ROOM! MUSH-ROOM!
RICE!
もぐ
CHEW
CHOMP
もぐ
CHOMP
CHEW
MEAT! MEAT!
RICE!
KIN-PIRA!
RICE!
SLURP
IT'S SO GOOD... ♡
...
ふっ
HEH
OH!
SORRY!
DID A THICK PIECE GET MIXED IN?
あ、
Oh!
NO, NO, THAT'S NOT IT!

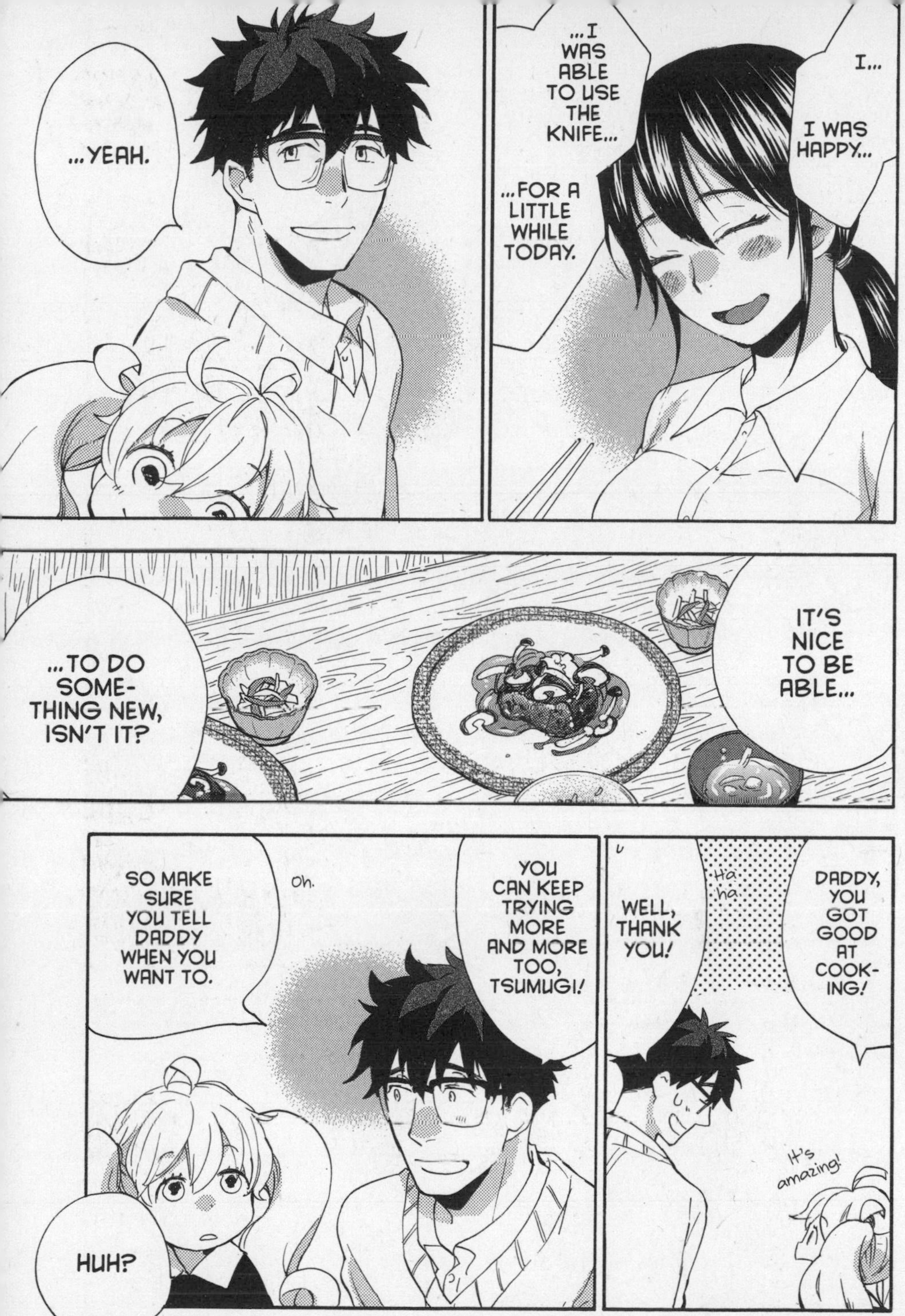
I...
I WAS HAPPY...
...I WAS ABLE TO USE THE KNIFE...
...FOR A LITTLE WHILE TODAY.
...YEAH.
IT'S NICE TO BE ABLE...
...TO DO SOME-THING NEW, ISN'T IT?
DADDY, YOU GOT GOOD AT COOK-ING!
Ha ha
WELL, THANK YOU!
It's amazing!
YOU CAN KEEP TRYING MORE AND MORE TOO, TSUMUGI!
Oh.
SO MAKE SURE YOU TELL DADDY WHEN YOU WANT TO.
HUH?

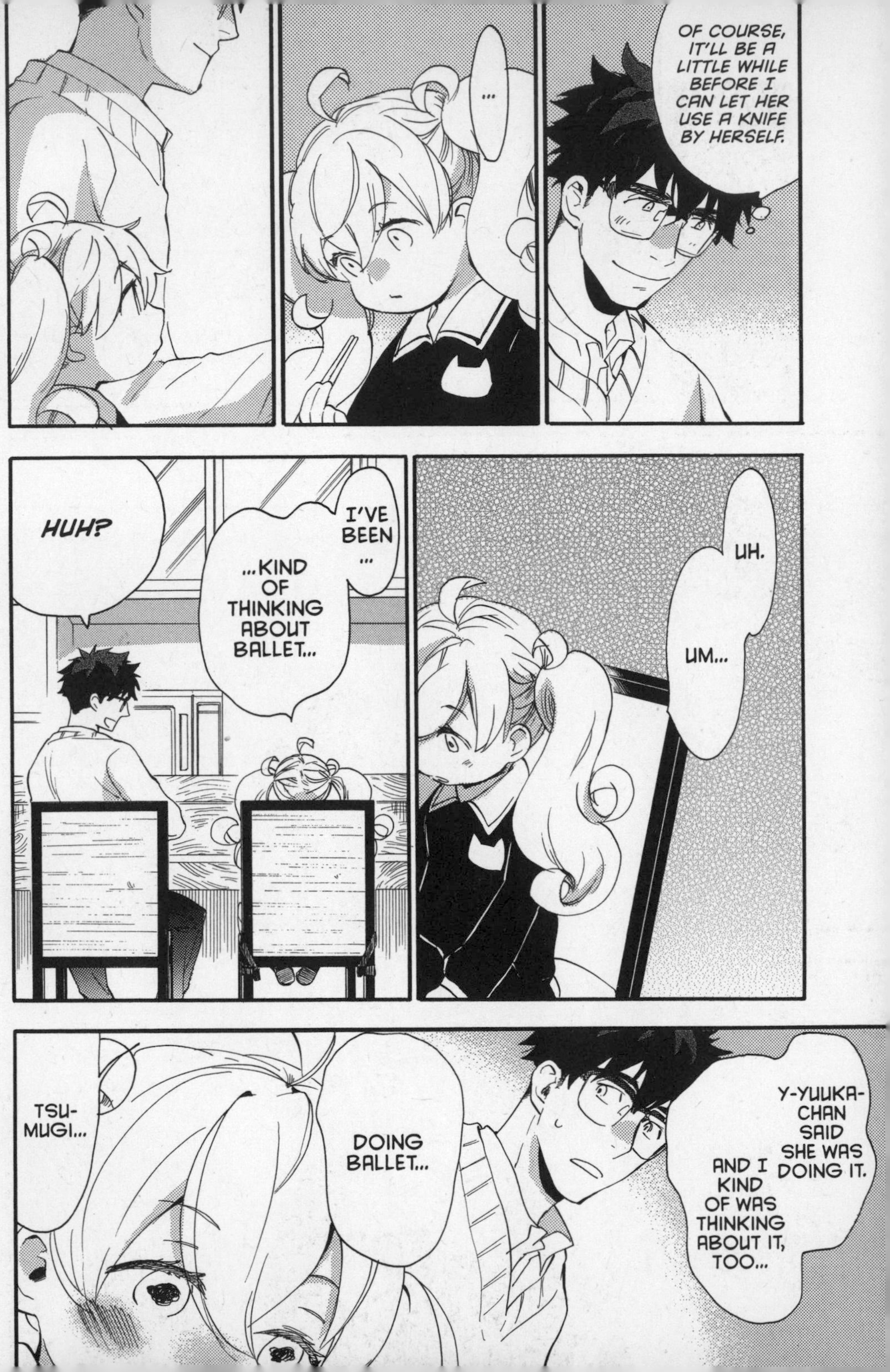
OF COURSE, IT'LL BE A LITTLE WHILE BEFORE I CAN LET HER USE A KNIFE BY HERSELF.
...
UH.
UM...
I'VE BEEN ...
...KIND OF THINKING ABOUT BALLET...
HUH?
Y-YUUKA-CHAN SAID SHE WAS DOING IT.
AND I KIND OF WAS THINKING ABOUT IT, TOO...
DOING BALLET...
TSU-MUGI...

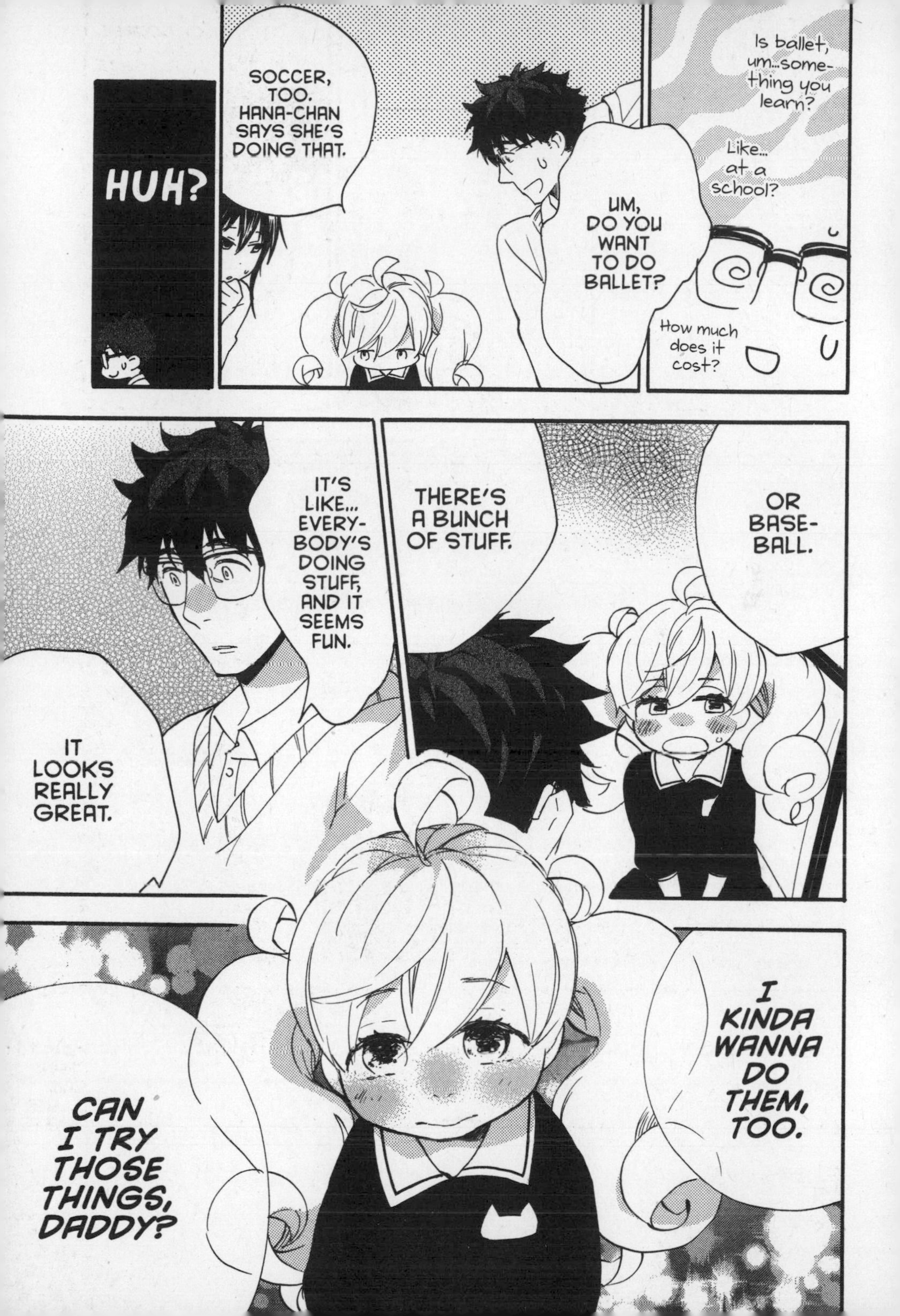
Is ballet, um...something you learn?
Like... at a school?
How much does it cost?
UM, DO YOU WANT TO DO BALLET?
SOCCER, TOO. HANA-CHAN SAYS SHE'S DOING THAT.
HUH?
OR BASEBALL.
THERE'S A BUNCH OF STUFF.
IT'S LIKE... EVERYBODY'S DOING STUFF, AND IT SEEMS FUN.
IT LOOKS REALLY GREAT.
I KINDA WANNA DO THEM, TOO.
CAN I TRY THOSE THINGS, DADDY?

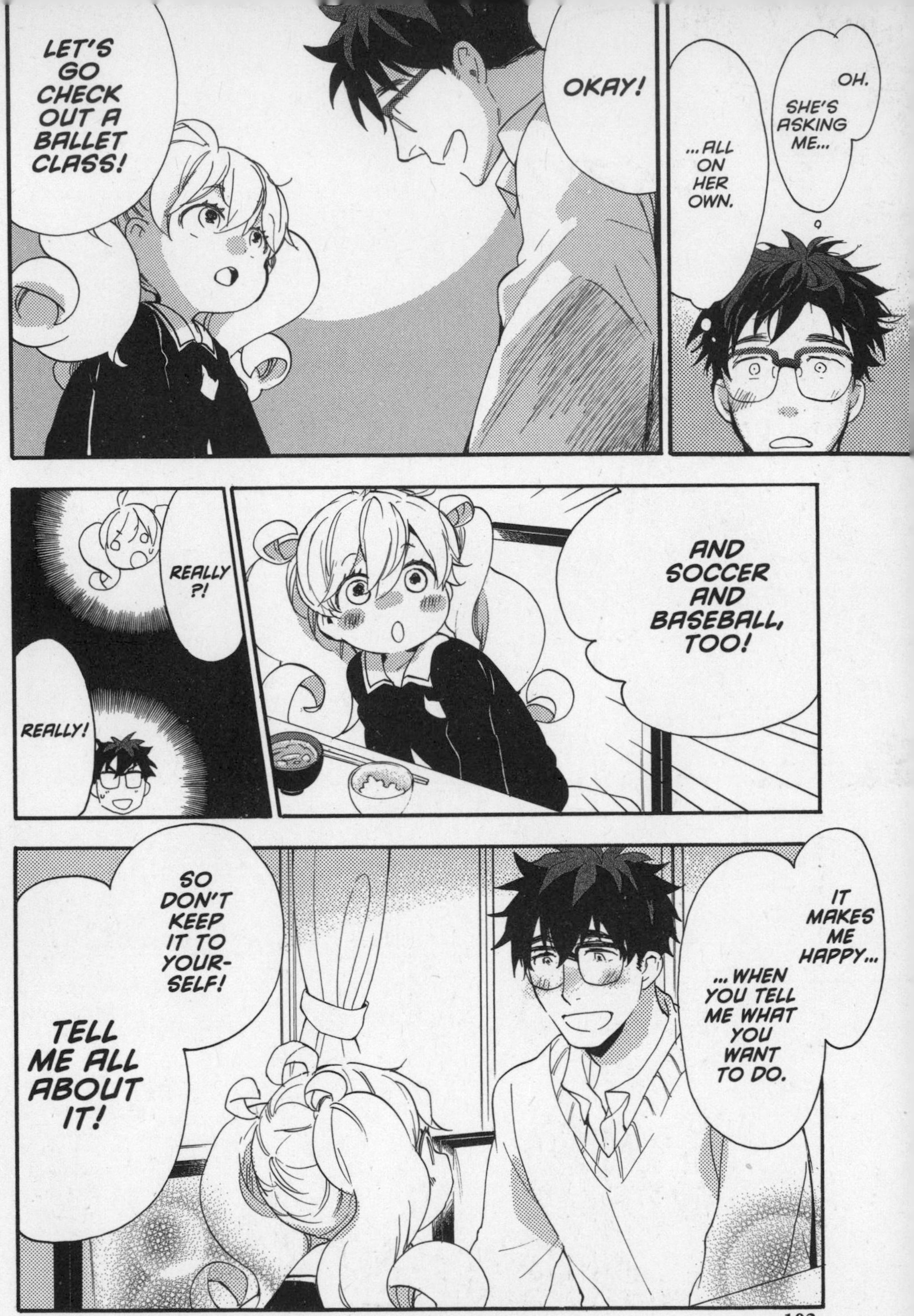
OH. SHE'S ASKING ME...
...ALL ON HER OWN.
OKAY!
LET'S GO CHECK OUT A BALLET CLASS!
AND SOCCER AND BASEBALL, TOO!
REALLY?!
REALLY!
IT MAKES ME HAPPY...
...WHEN YOU TELL ME WHAT YOU WANT TO DO.
SO DON'T KEEP IT TO YOURSELF!
TELL ME ALL ABOUT IT!

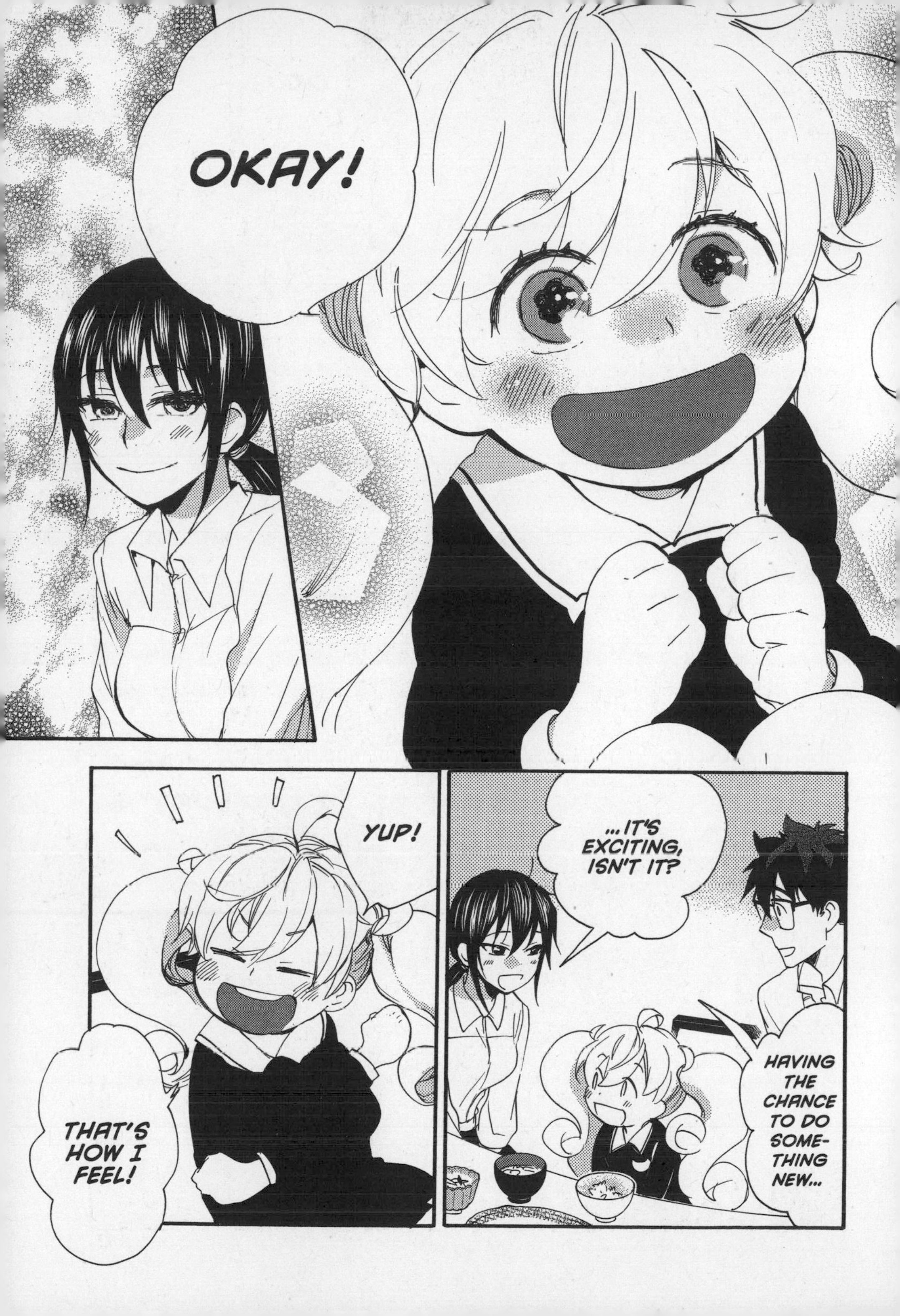
OKAY!
...IT'S EXCITING, ISN'T IT?
HAVING THE CHANCE TO DO SOME-THING NEW...
YUP!
THAT'S HOW I FEEL!

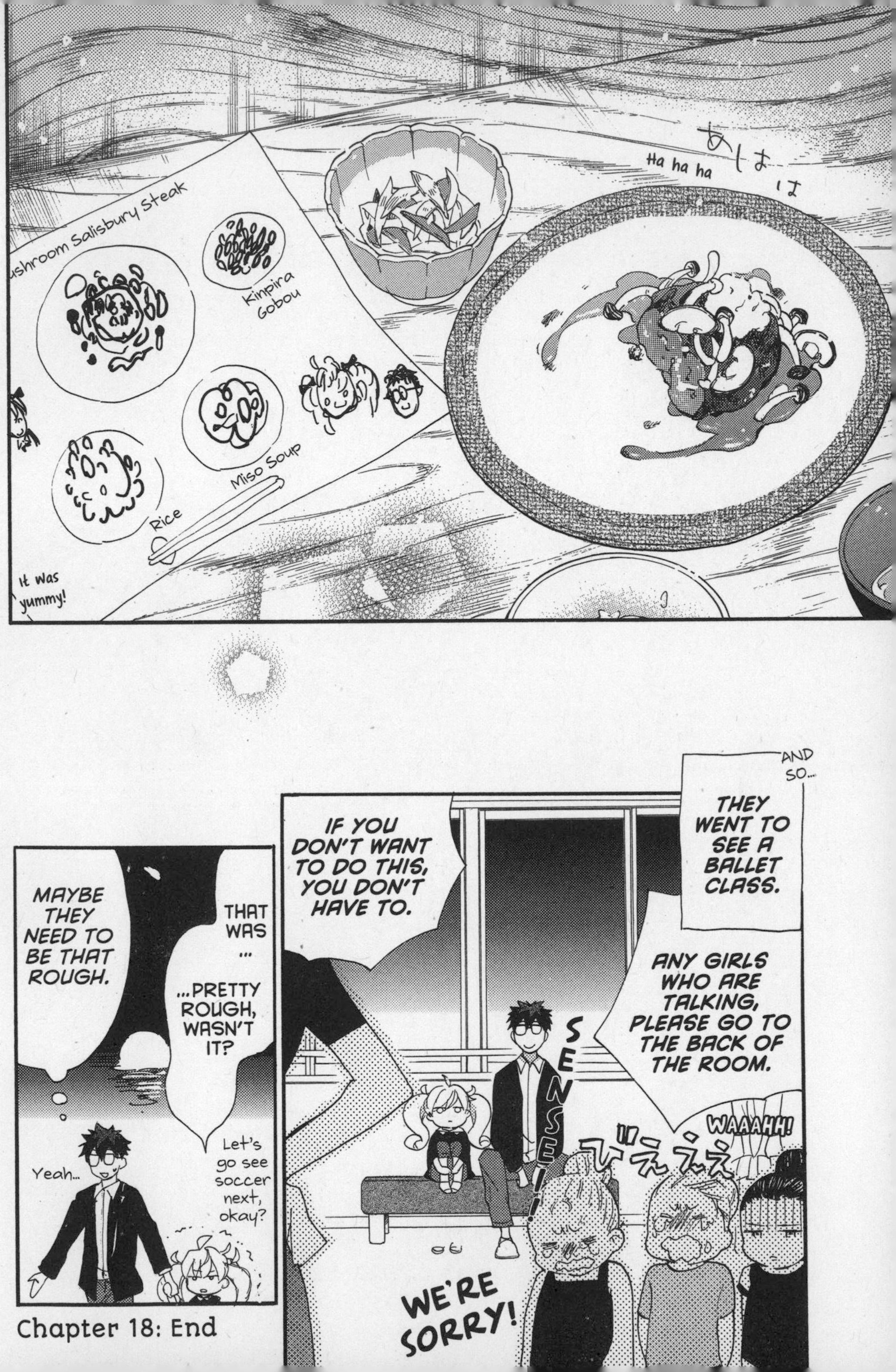
あははは
Ha ha ha
ushroom Salisbury Steak
Kinpira Gobou
Miso Soup
Rice
It was yummy!
AND SO...
THEY WENT TO SEE A BALLET CLASS.
IF YOU DON'T WANT TO DO THIS, YOU DON'T HAVE TO.
ANY GIRLS WHO ARE TALKING, PLEASE GO TO THE BACK OF THE ROOM.
WAAAHH!
びえええ
SENSEI!!
WE'RE SORRY!
THAT WAS ...
...PRETTY ROUGH, WASN'T IT?
MAYBE THEY NEED TO BE THAT ROUGH.
Let's go see soccer next, okay?
Yeah...

Chapter 18: End

KINPIRA GOBOU

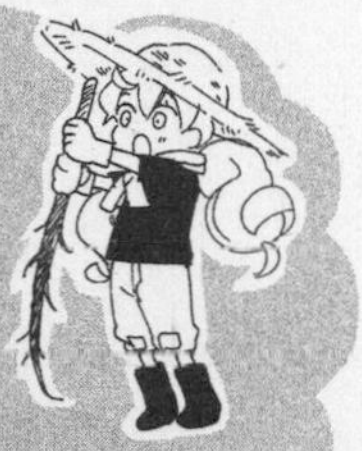

☆ Ingredients ☆ (serves 4)

40 g carrot (You'll use 3-4 cm of the thickest part of the carrot.)
160 g burdock root ½ Tbsp sesame oil
Some roasted sesame seeds (white)

Ⓐ 4 tsp soy sauce 3 Tbsp each of mirin, sake
Note! Don't use cast-iron frying pans or knives.
The burdock root will turn black.

STEPS

1. Peel the carrot and slice off about 1 cm from each side to make square edges... Slice thinly into pieces about the same size as you will cut the burdock root.

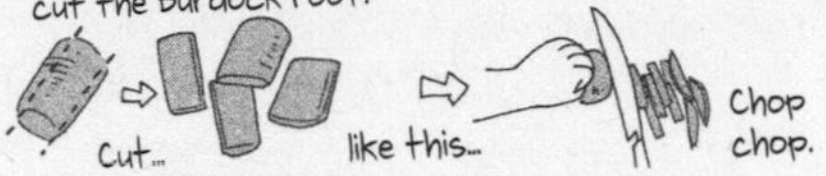

Cut...
like this...
Chop chop.

2. Wash the dirt off the burdock root and scrub lightly with a scrub brush.

POINT A lot of the flavor of the burdock root is in its skin, so don't scrub that part off.

Just get the mud off!

Cut into the root from the thin end and pull it towards you to split it down the middle. Put the side you cut facedown to keep it stable.

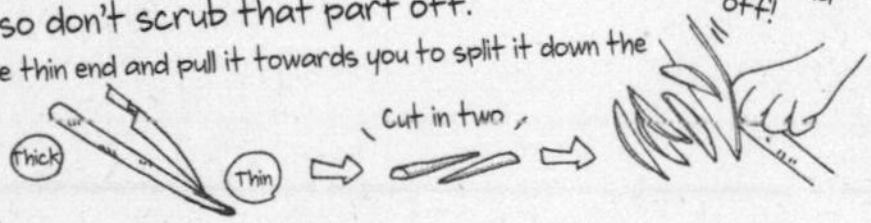

Thick
Thin
Cut in two

POINT Don't soak it in water because you'll lose the scent and flavor. Be ready to fry as soon as you cut it!

3. Put the sesame oil into the frying pan and fry the burdock root from step 2. Fry on medium heat for 3-4 minutes, and then add the carrot from step 1. Fry for an additional minute and then add the ingredients from Group A.

4. Boil it down for 4-5 minutes until the liquid is gone, then add roasted sesame seeds and you're done. ♡

CONVERSION NOTES: 160 G BURDOCK ROOT = JUST OVER 1 CUP

We're sumo wrestling.
Okay, come at me!
YAH!
SLAM
Give up?!
GYAAAH...

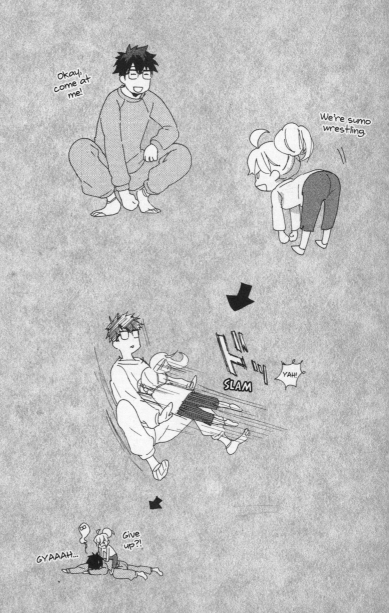

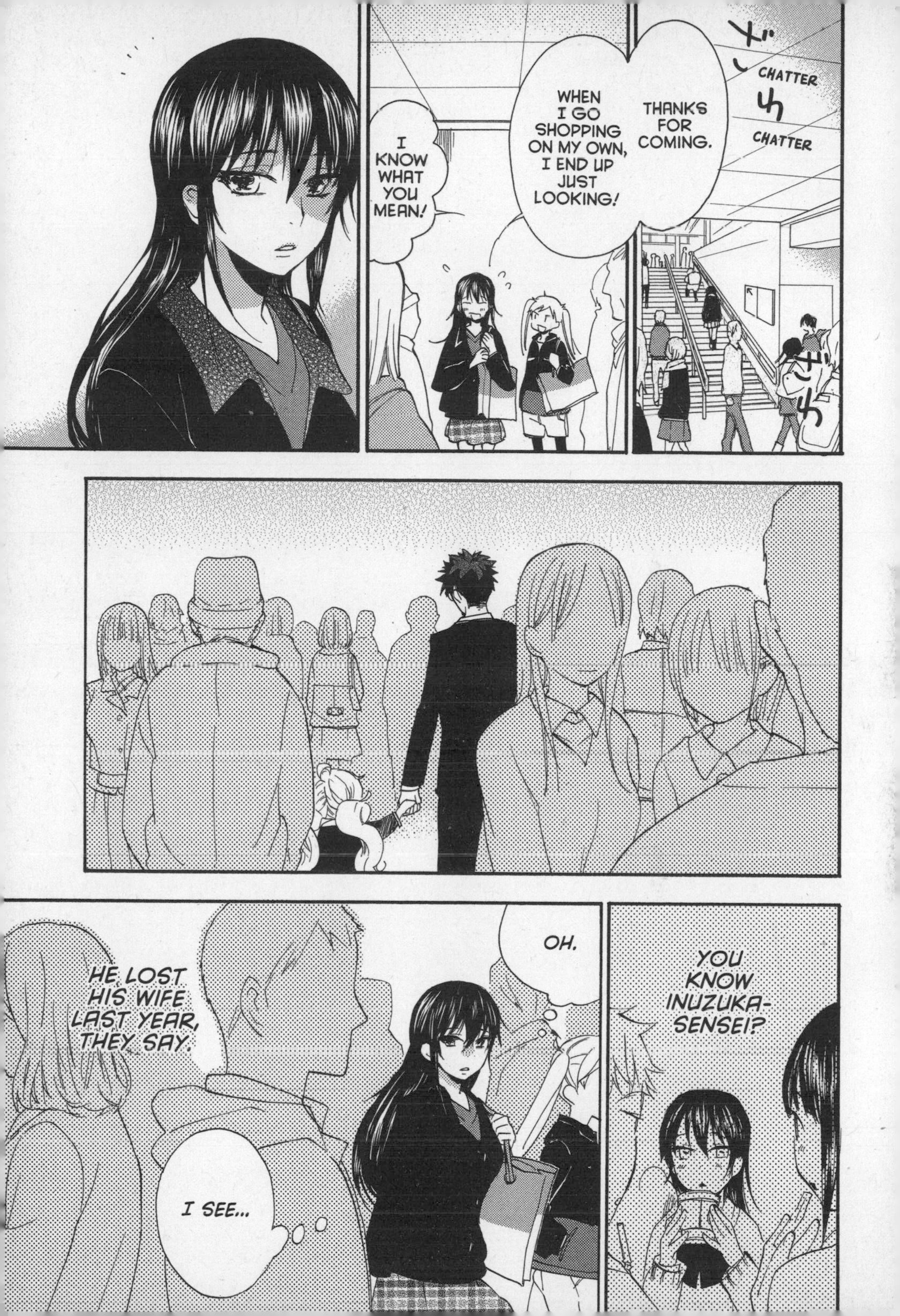
CHATTER
CHATTER
THANKS FOR COMING.
WHEN I GO SHOPPING ON MY OWN, I END UP JUST LOOKING!
I KNOW WHAT YOU MEAN!
YOU KNOW INUZUKA-SENSEI?
OH.
HE LOST HIS WIFE LAST YEAR, THEY SAY.
I SEE...

Chapter 19 | Okonomiyaki Filled With Love

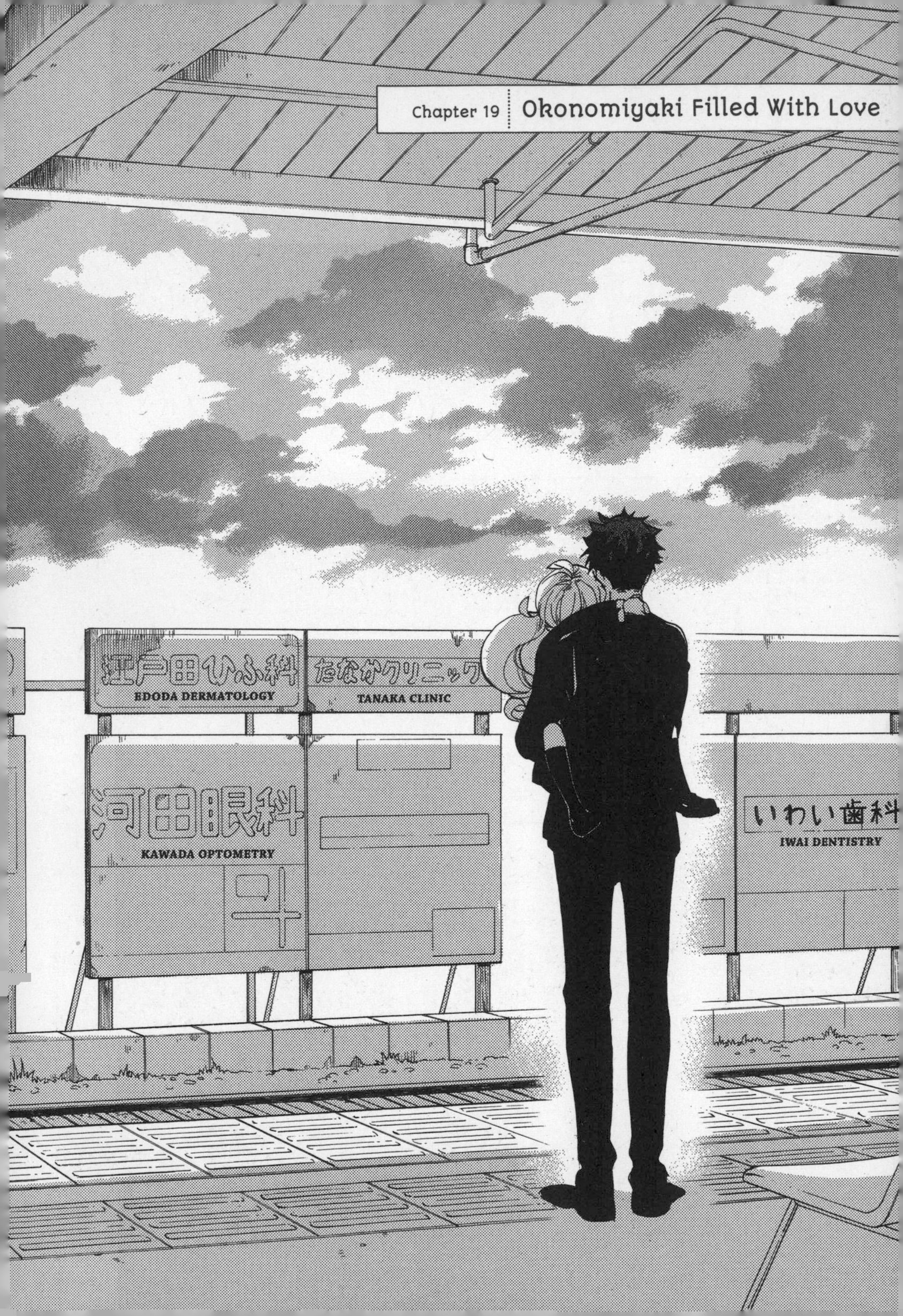
たなかクリニック
TANAKA CLINIC
江戸田ひふ科
EDODA DERMATOLOGY
いわい歯科
IWAI DENTISTRY
河田眼科
KAWADA OPTOMETRY

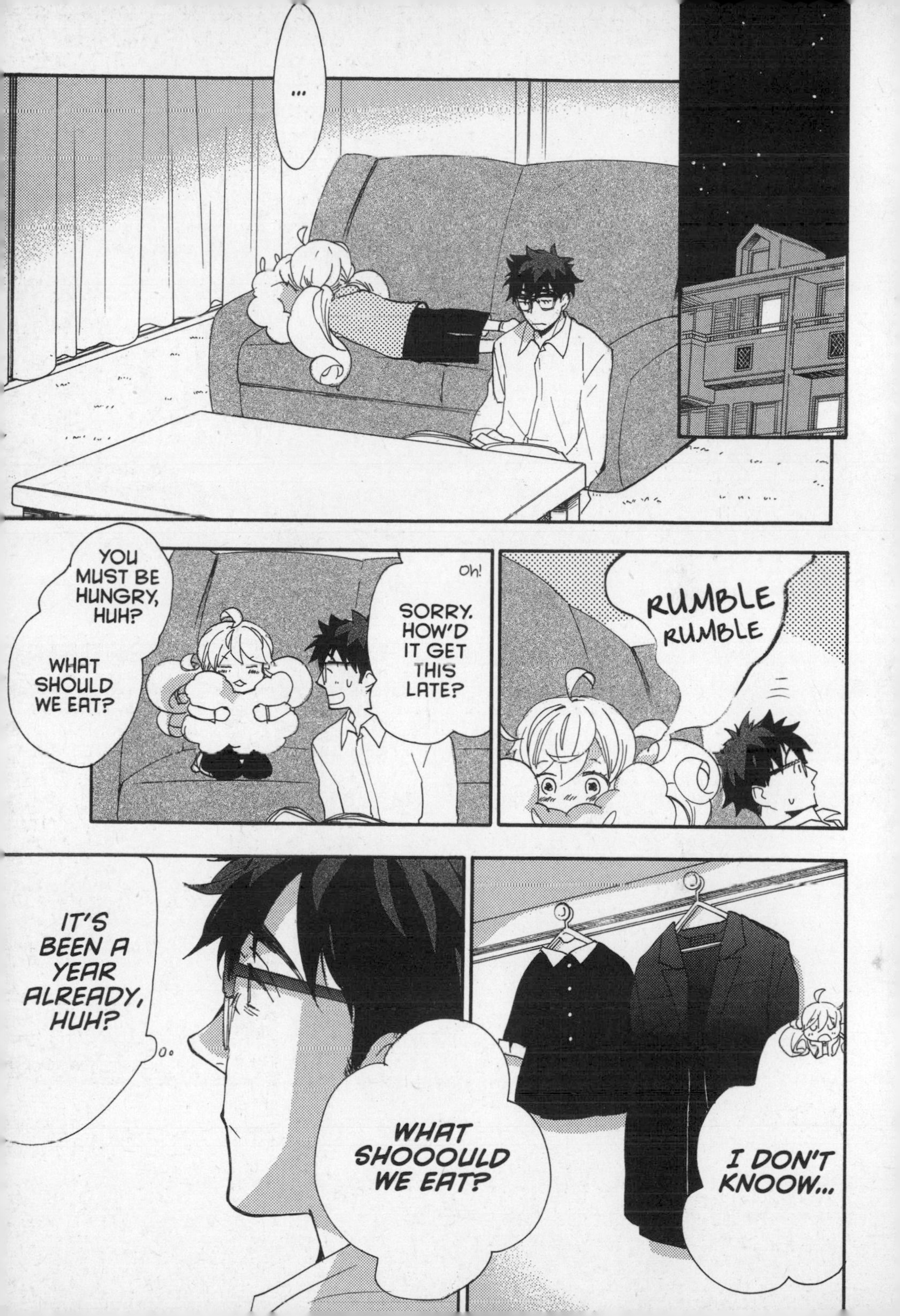
...
RUMBLE RUMBLE
Oh!
SORRY. HOW'D IT GET THIS LATE?
YOU MUST BE HUNGRY, HUH?
WHAT SHOULD WE EAT?
I DON'T KNOOW...
WHAT SHOOOULD WE EAT?
IT'S BEEN A YEAR ALREADY, HUH?

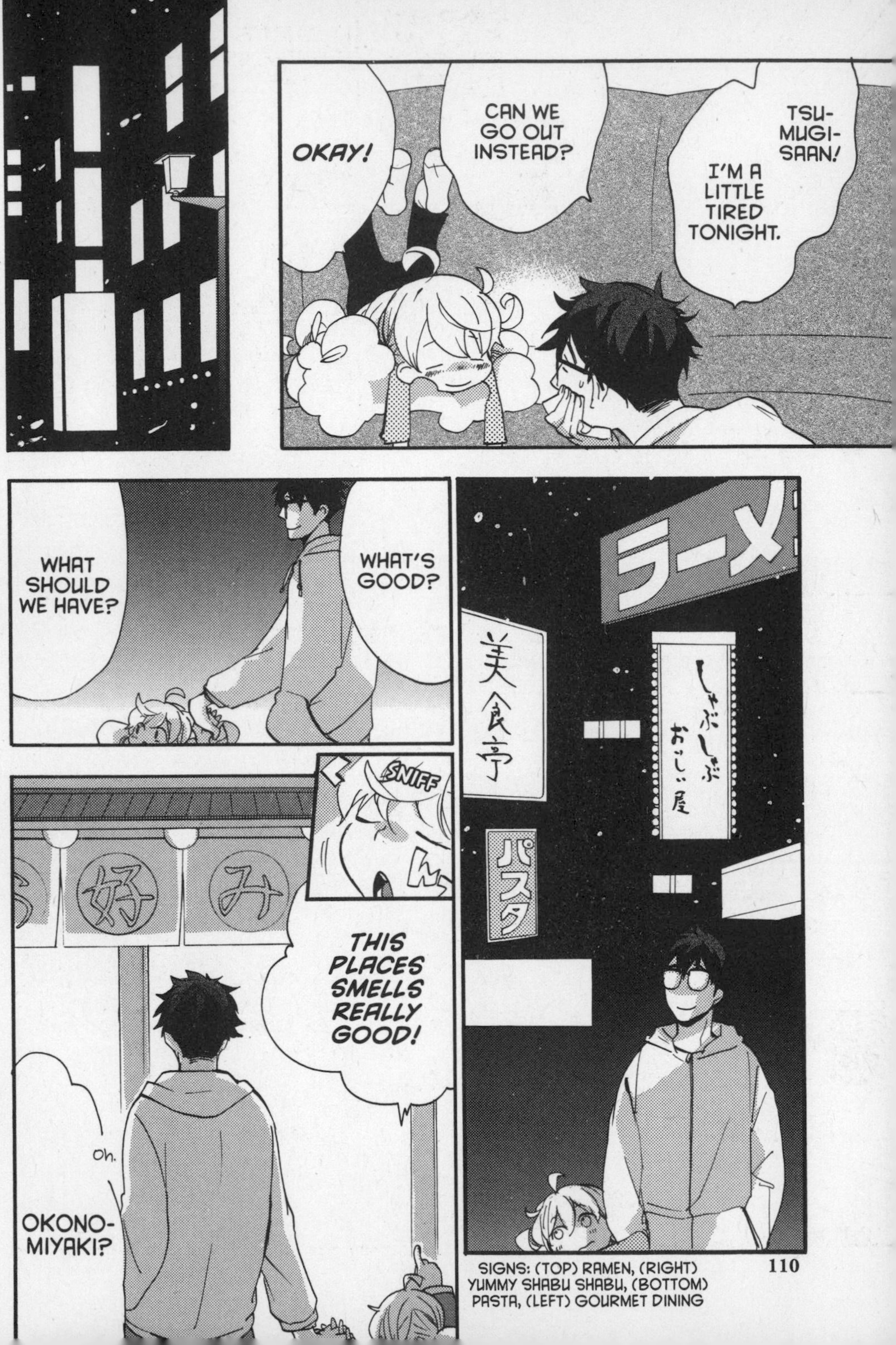
TSU-MUGI-SAAN!
I'M A LITTLE TIRED TONIGHT.
CAN WE GO OUT INSTEAD?
OKAY!
ラーメ
しゃぶしゃぶ おいしい屋
美食亭
パスタ
WHAT'S GOOD?
WHAT SHOULD WE HAVE?
SNIFF
好
み
THIS PLACES SMELLS REALLY GOOD!
Oh.
OKONO-MIYAKI?

SIGNS: (TOP) RAMEN, (RIGHT) YUMMY SHABU SHABU, (BOTTOM) PASTA, (LEFT) GOURMET DINING

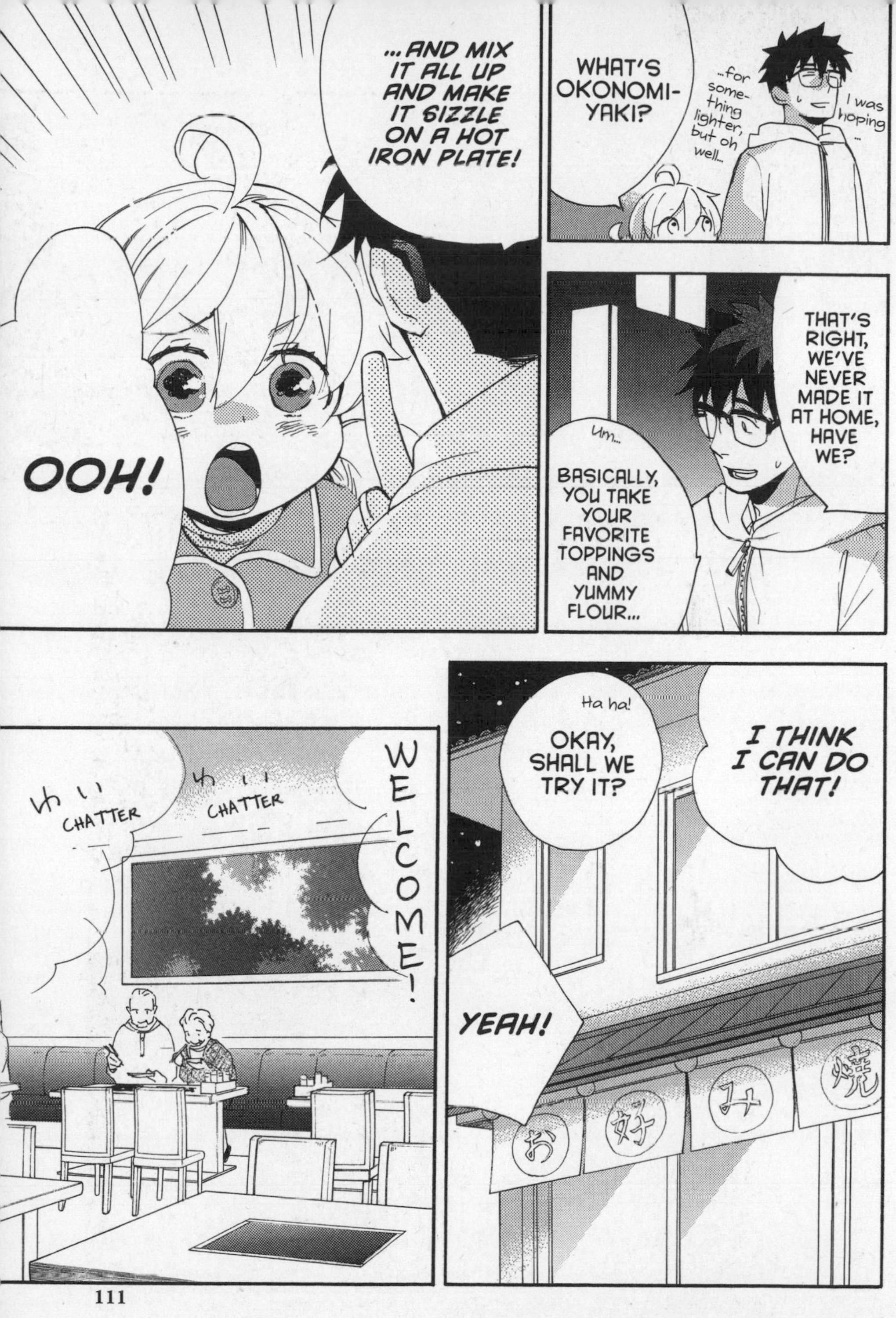
WHAT'S OKONOMI-YAKI?
I was hoping...
...for something lighter, but oh well...
THAT'S RIGHT, WE'VE NEVER MADE IT AT HOME, HAVE WE?
Um...
BASICALLY, YOU TAKE YOUR FAVORITE TOPPINGS AND YUMMY FLOUR...
...AND MIX IT ALL UP AND MAKE IT SIZZLE ON A HOT IRON PLATE!
OOH!
I THINK I CAN DO THAT!
Ha ha!
OKAY, SHALL WE TRY IT?
YEAH!
お好み焼
WELCOME!
わい CHATTER
わい CHATTER

SO HERE'S WHERE YOU MAKE IT SIZZLE, HUH?

THAT'S RIGHT.

I CAN'T WAIT!

HERE YOU ARE!

OOH!

FWOOF

PORK AND SQUID OKONOMI-YAKI.

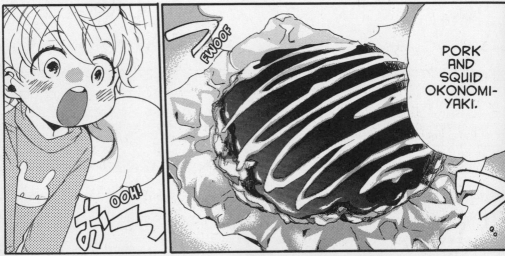

IT'S THE TYPE OF RESTAURANT WHERE IT COMES PRE-MADE!

OH NO!

MIX IT?

...?

HMM...

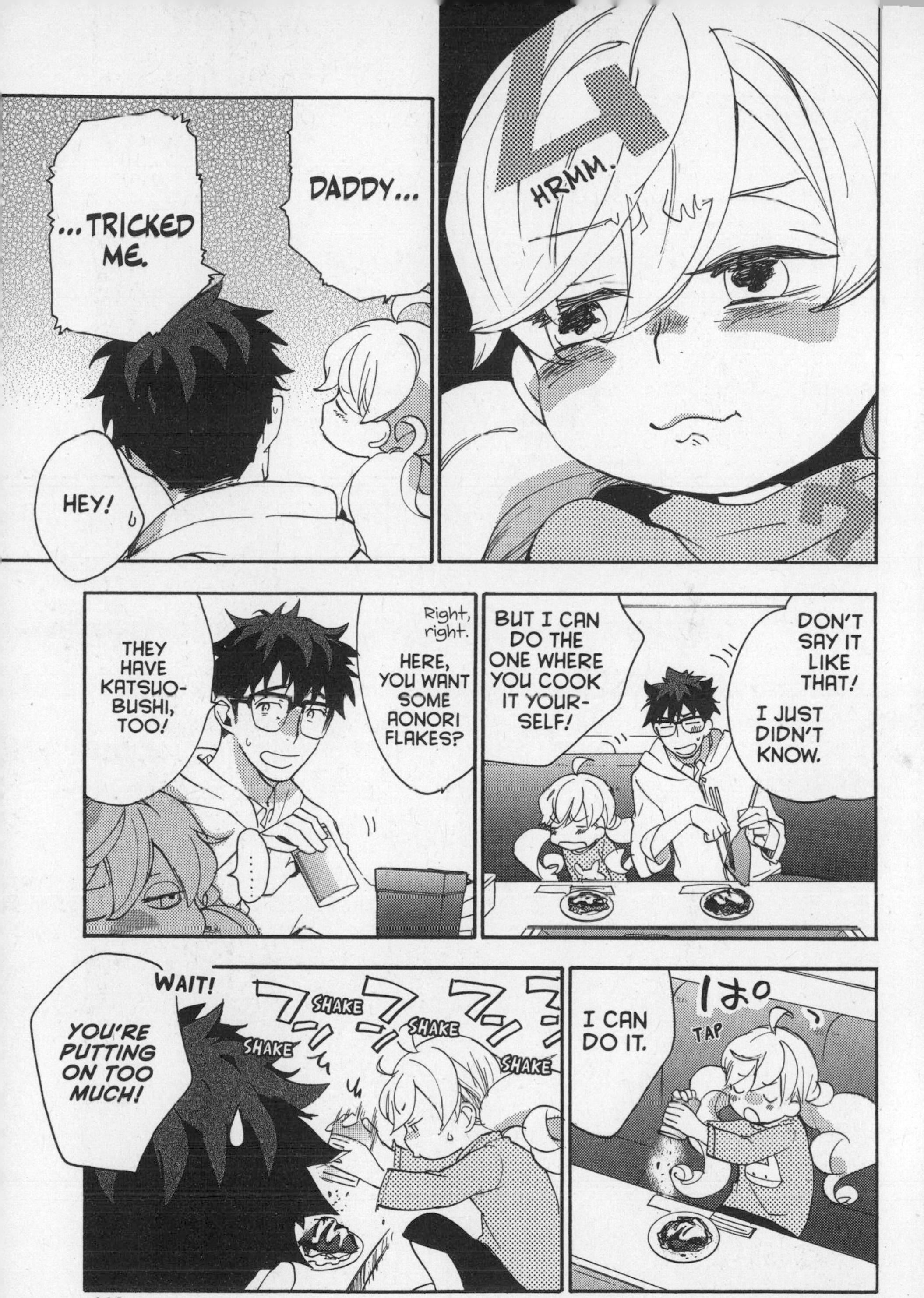
HRMM.
DADDY...
...TRICKED ME.
HEY!
DON'T SAY IT LIKE THAT!
I JUST DIDN'T KNOW.
BUT I CAN DO THE ONE WHERE YOU COOK IT YOURSELF!
Right, right.
HERE, YOU WANT SOME AONORI FLAKES?
THEY HAVE KATSUOBUSHI, TOO!
......
TAP
I CAN DO IT.
SHAKE
SHAKE
SHAKE
SHAKE
WAIT!
YOU'RE PUTTING ON TOO MUCH!

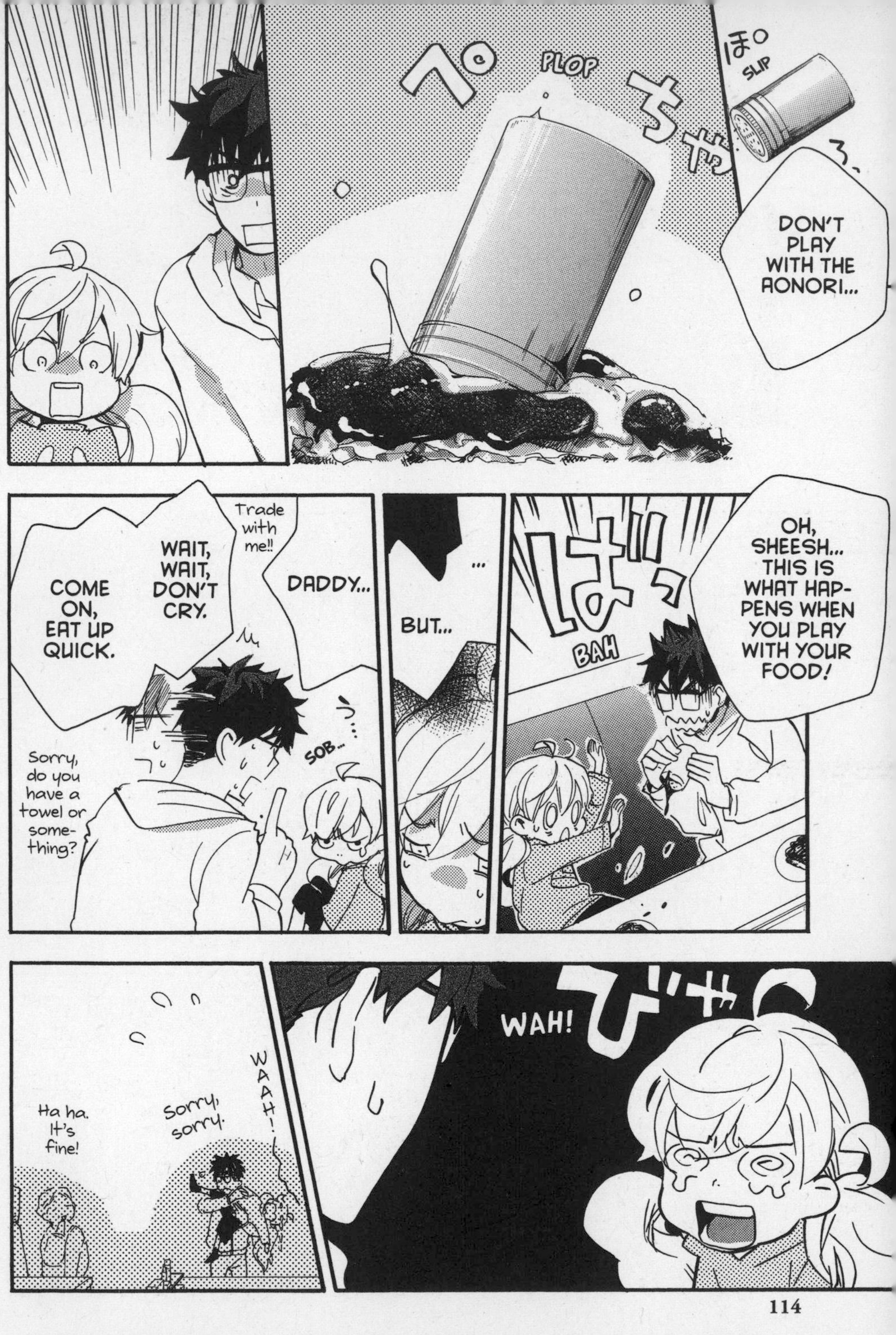
ほ°
SLIP
DON'T PLAY WITH THE AONORI...
ちゃ
へ°
PLOP
OH, SHEESH... THIS IS WHAT HAPPENS WHEN YOU PLAY WITH YOUR FOOD!
ぱっ
BAH
...
BUT...
Trade with me!!
DADDY...
WAIT, WAIT, DON'T CRY.
COME ON, EAT UP QUICK.
SOB...
Sorry, do you have a towel or something?
WAH!
WAAH!
Sorry, sorry.
Ha ha. It's fine!

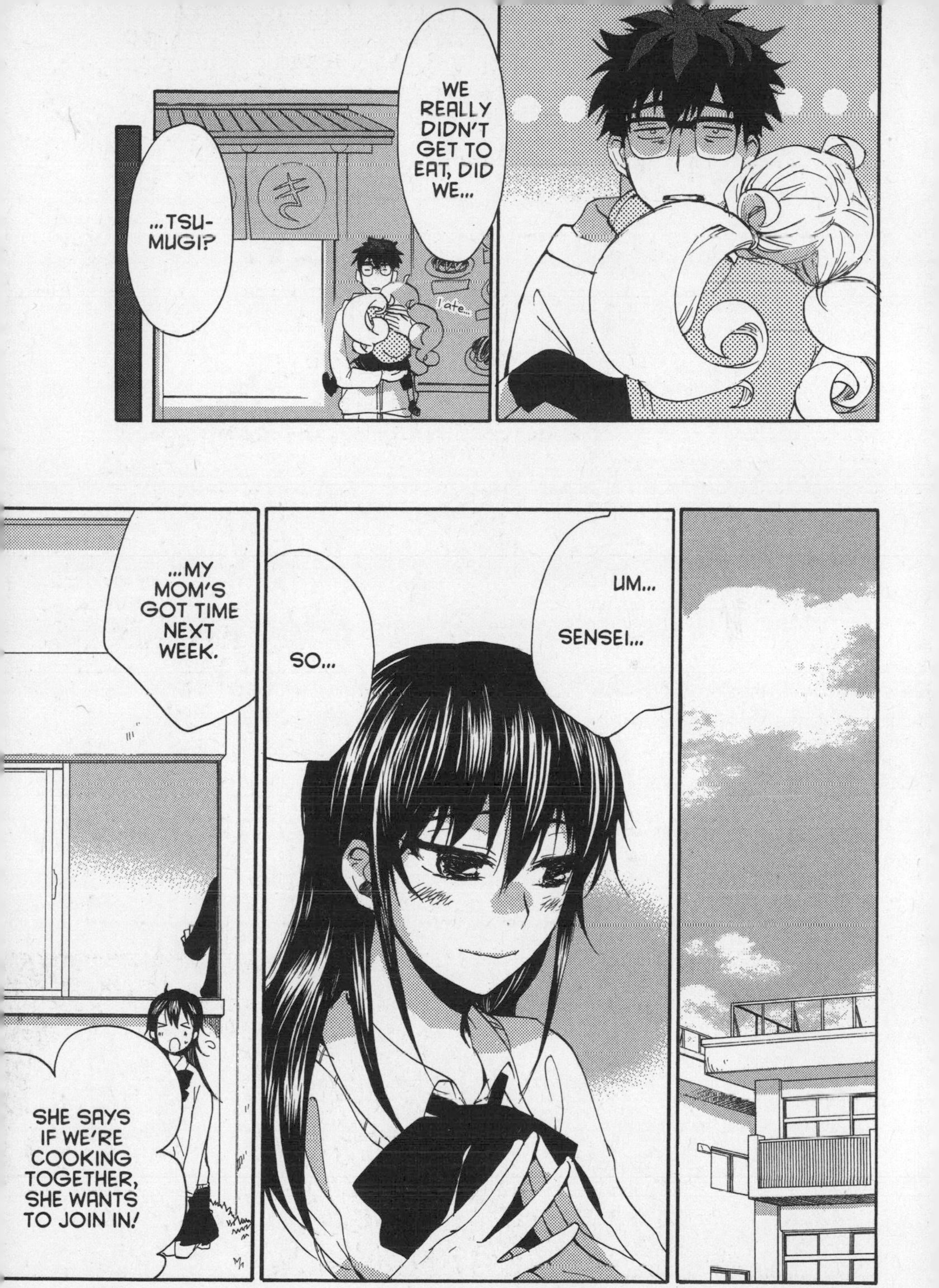
WE REALLY DIDN'T GET TO EAT, DID WE...
...TSU-MUGI?
I ate...
UM... SENSEI...
SO...
...MY MOM'S GOT TIME NEXT WEEK.
SHE SAYS IF WE'RE COOKING TOGETHER, SHE WANTS TO JOIN IN!

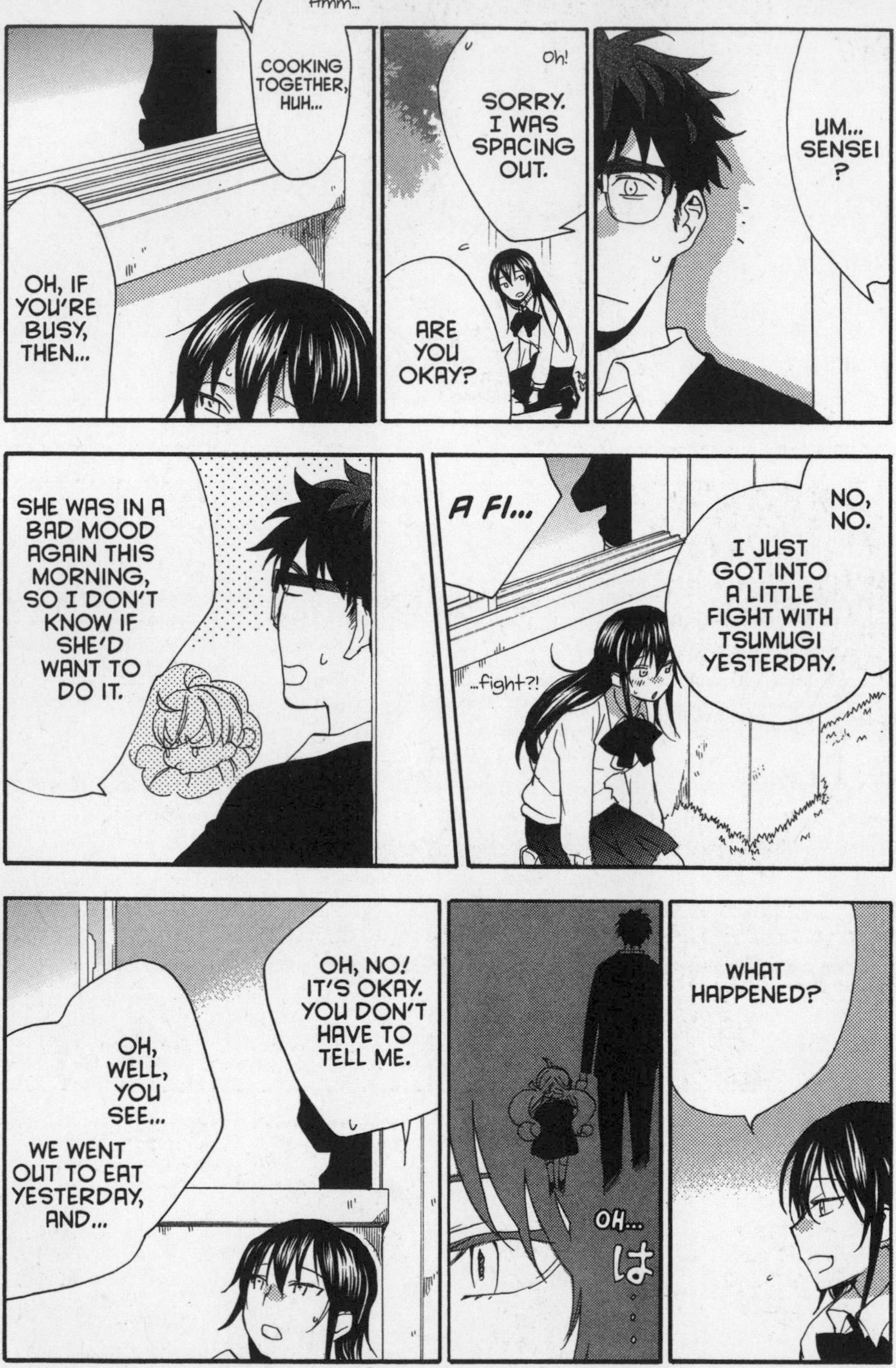
UM... SENSEI ?
Oh!
SORRY. I WAS SPACING OUT.
ARE YOU OKAY?
Hmm...
COOKING TOGETHER, HUH...
OH, IF YOU'RE BUSY, THEN...
NO, NO.
I JUST GOT INTO A LITTLE FIGHT WITH TSUMUGI YESTERDAY.
A FI...
...fight?!
SHE WAS IN A BAD MOOD AGAIN THIS MORNING, SO I DON'T KNOW IF SHE'D WANT TO DO IT.
WHAT HAPPENED?
OH...
は
OH, NO! IT'S OKAY. YOU DON'T HAVE TO TELL ME.
OH, WELL, YOU SEE...
WE WENT OUT TO EAT YESTERDAY, AND...

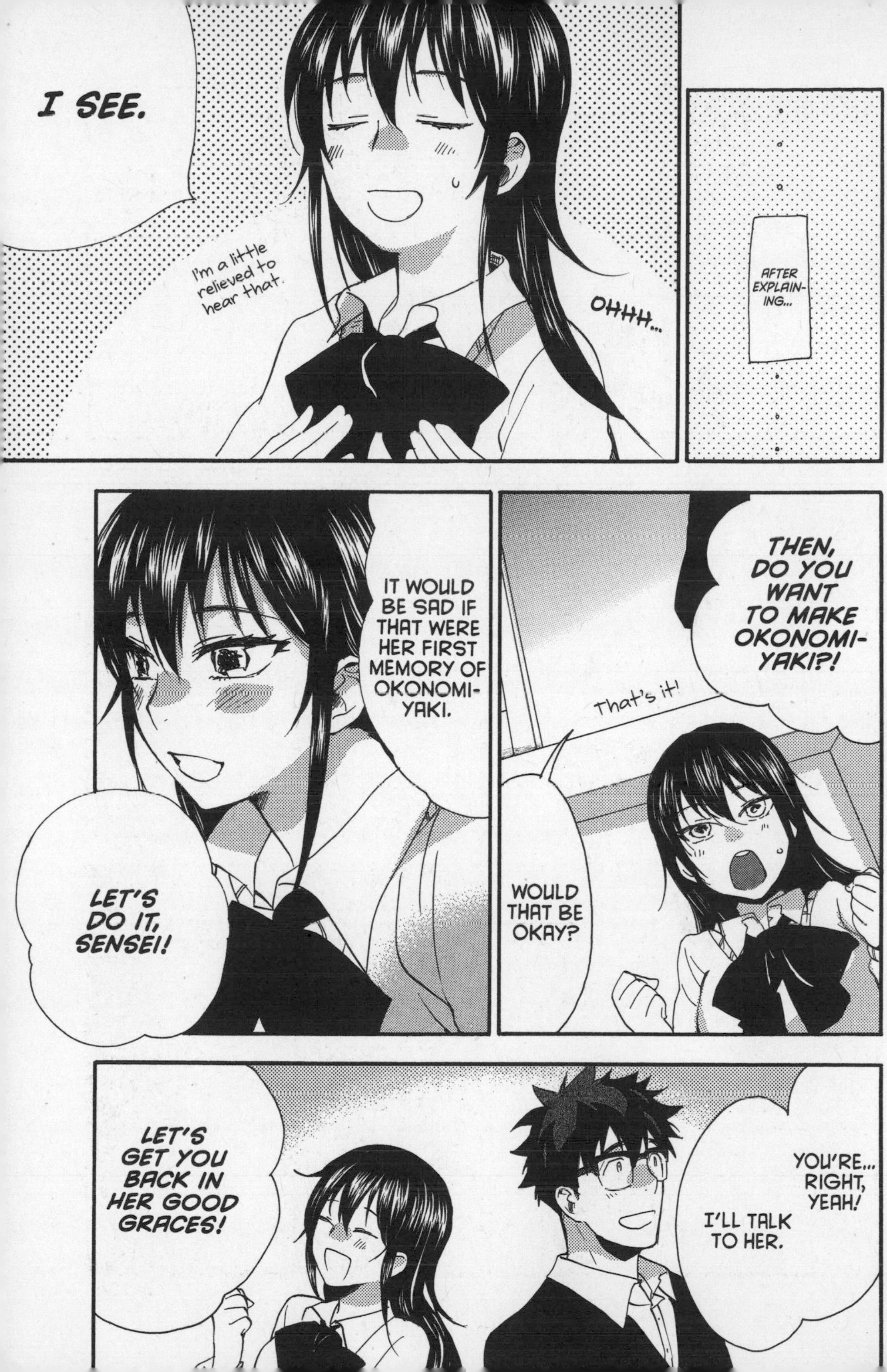
AFTER EXPLAINING...
OHHH...
I SEE.
I'm a little relieved to hear that.
THEN, DO YOU WANT TO MAKE OKONOMIYAKI?!
That's it!
WOULD THAT BE OKAY?
IT WOULD BE SAD IF THAT WERE HER FIRST MEMORY OF OKONOMIYAKI.
LET'S DO IT, SENSEI!
YOU'RE... RIGHT, YEAH!
I'LL TALK TO HER.
LET'S GET YOU BACK IN HER GOOD GRACES!

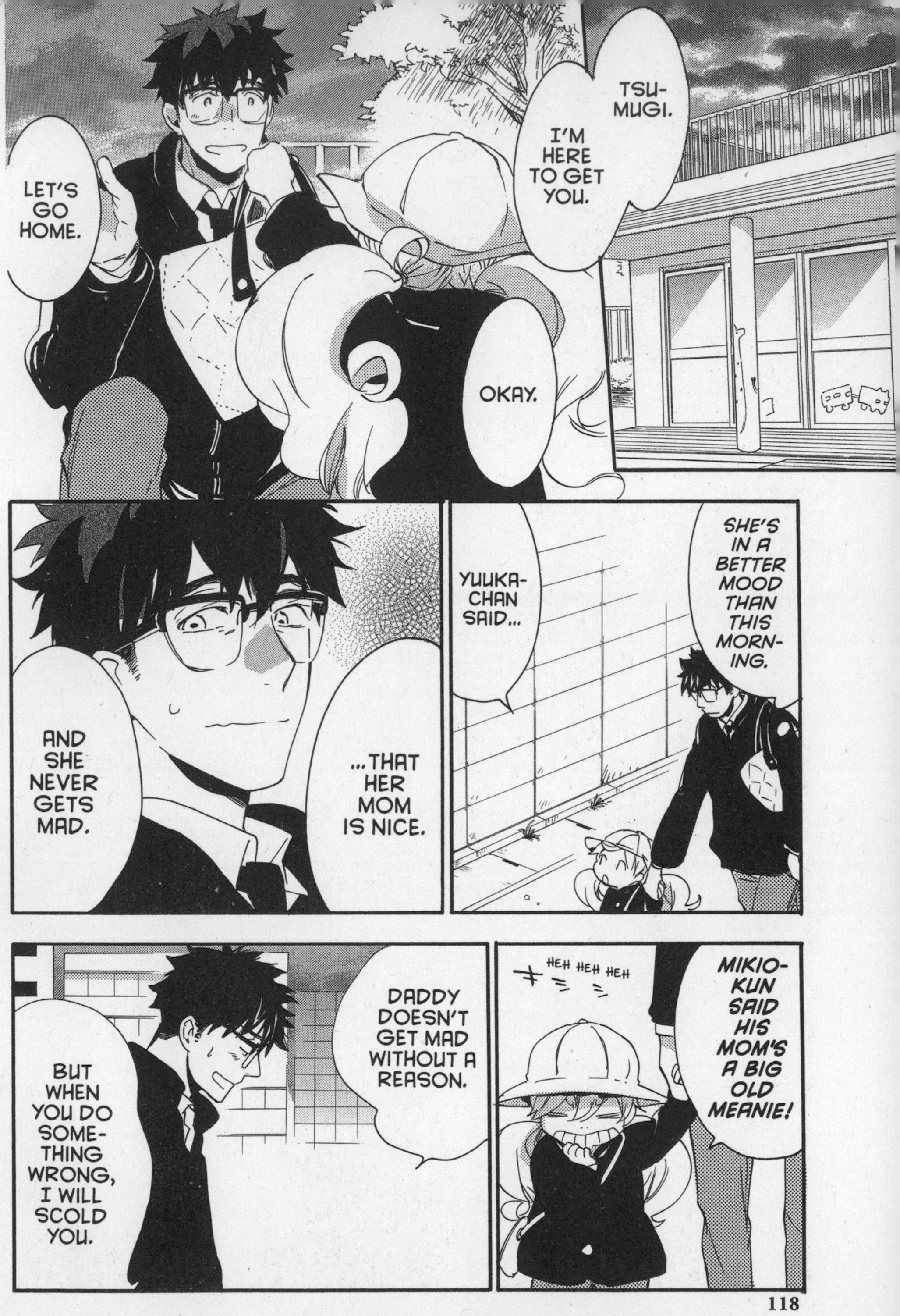

TSU-MUGI.
I'M HERE TO GET YOU.
LET'S GO HOME.
OKAY.
SHE'S IN A BETTER MOOD THAN THIS MORNING.
YUUKA-CHAN SAID...
...THAT HER MOM IS NICE.
AND SHE NEVER GETS MAD.
HEH HEH HEH
MIKIO-KUN SAID HIS MOM'S A BIG OLD MEANIE!
DADDY DOESN'T GET MAD WITHOUT A REASON.
BUT WHEN YOU DO SOME-THING WRONG, I WILL SCOLD YOU.

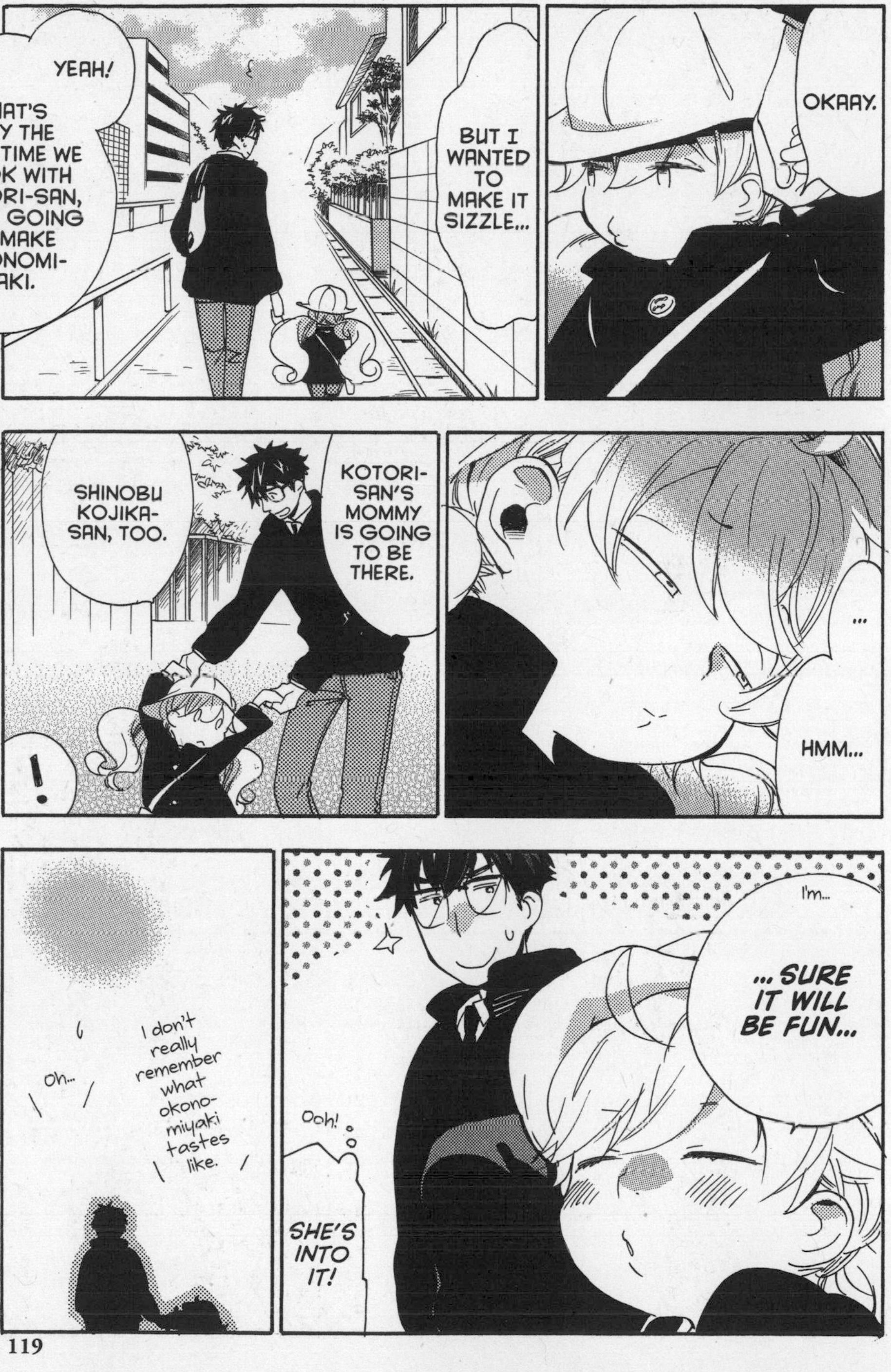
OKAAY.
BUT I WANTED TO MAKE IT SIZZLE...
YEAH!
THAT'S WHY THE NEXT TIME WE COOK WITH KOTORI-SAN, WE'RE GOING TO MAKE OKONOMIYAKI.
...
HMM...
KOTORI-SAN'S MOMMY IS GOING TO BE THERE.
SHINOBU KOJIKA-SAN, TOO.
!
I'm...
... SURE IT WILL BE FUN...
Ooh!
SHE'S INTO IT!
I don't really remember what okonomiyaki tastes like.
Oh...

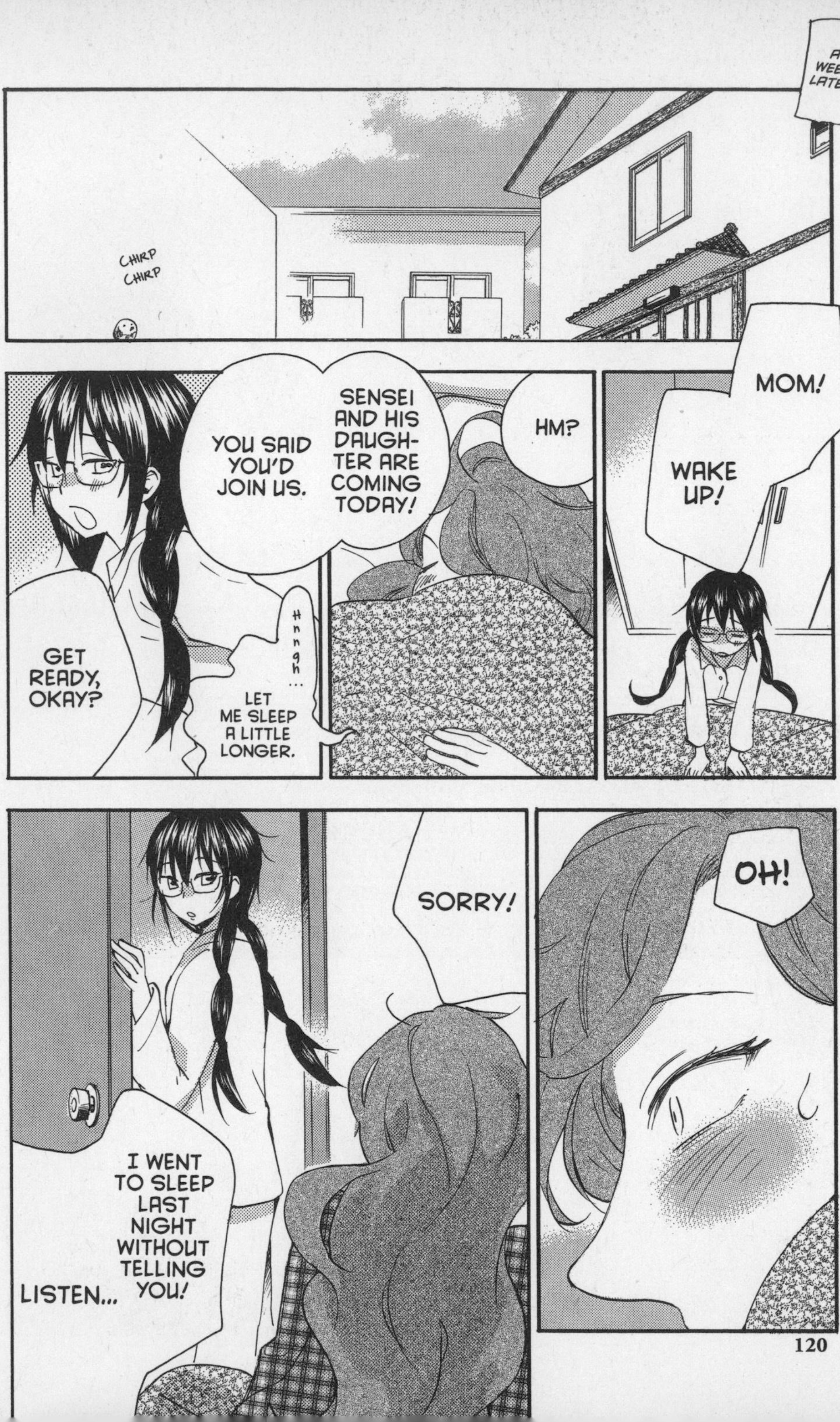
A WEEK LATER
CHIRP CHIRP
MOM!
WAKE UP!
HM?
SENSEI AND HIS DAUGHTER ARE COMING TODAY!
YOU SAID YOU'D JOIN US.
GET READY, OKAY?
Hnngh...
LET ME SLEEP A LITTLE LONGER.
OH!
SORRY!
I WENT TO SLEEP LAST NIGHT WITHOUT TELLING YOU!
LISTEN...

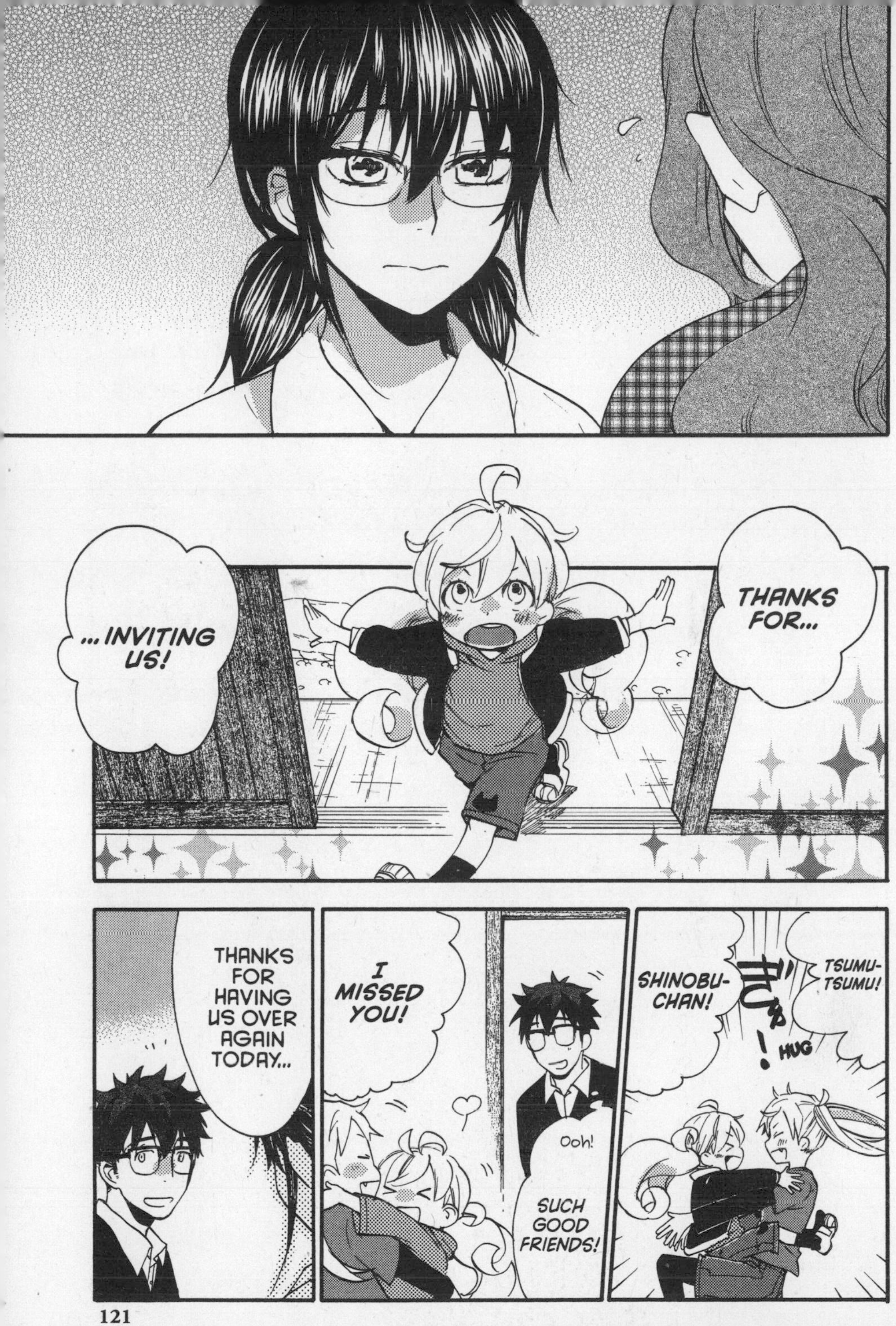
THANKS FOR...
...INVITING US!
TSUMU-TSUMU!
SHINOBU-CHAN!
ぎゅ!
HUG
I MISSED YOU!
Ooh!
SUCH GOOD FRIENDS!
THANKS FOR HAVING US OVER AGAIN TODAY...

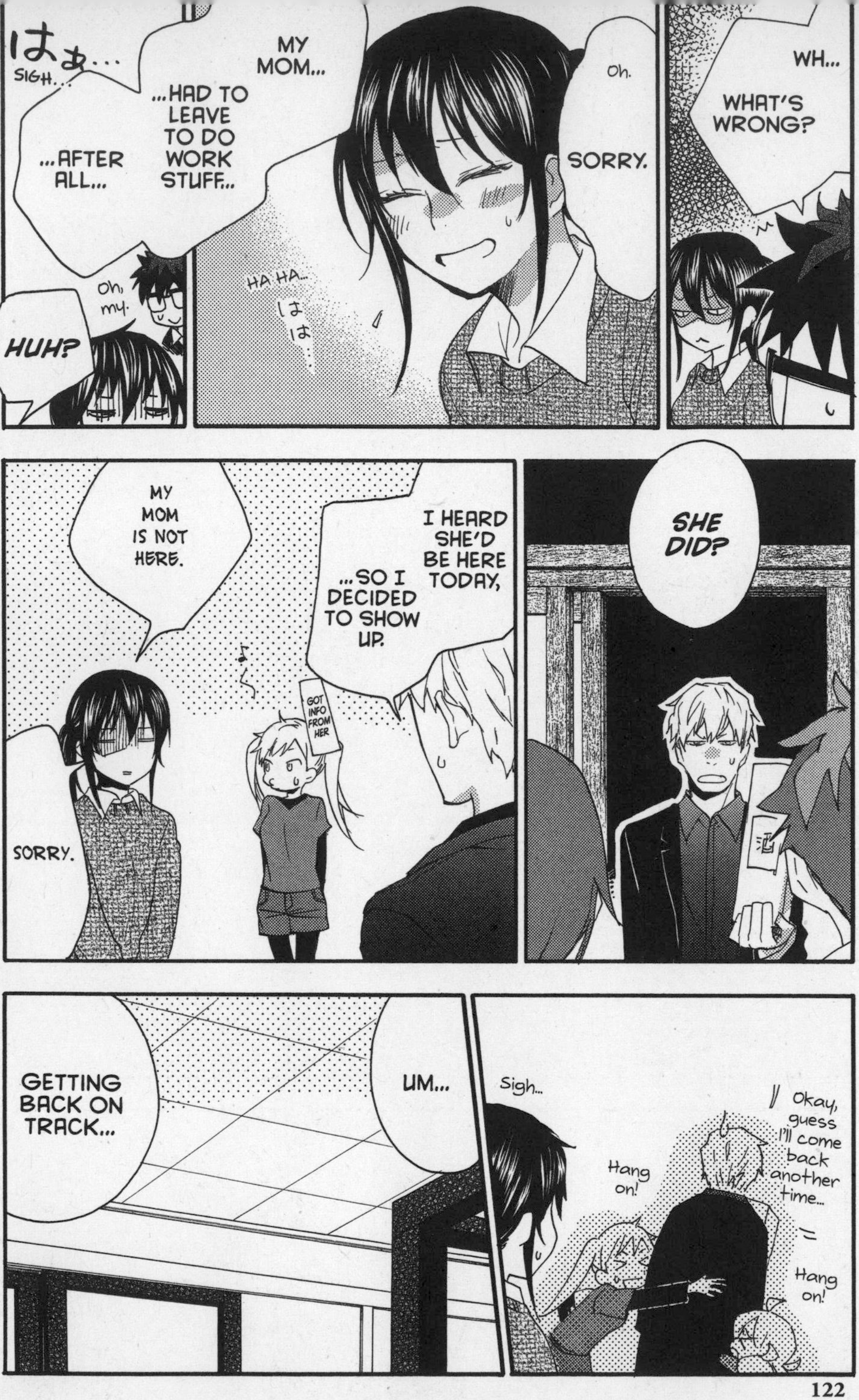
WH...
WHAT'S WRONG?
Oh.
SORRY.
MY MOM...
...HAD TO LEAVE TO DO WORK STUFF...
...AFTER ALL...
HA HA...
はは…
はぁ…
SIGH...
Oh, my.
HUH?
SHE DID?
I HEARD SHE'D BE HERE TODAY,
...SO I DECIDED TO SHOW UP.
GOT INFO FROM HER
MY MOM IS NOT HERE.
SORRY.
Sigh...
Okay, guess I'll come back another time...
Hang on!
Hang on!
UM...
GETTING BACK ON TRACK...

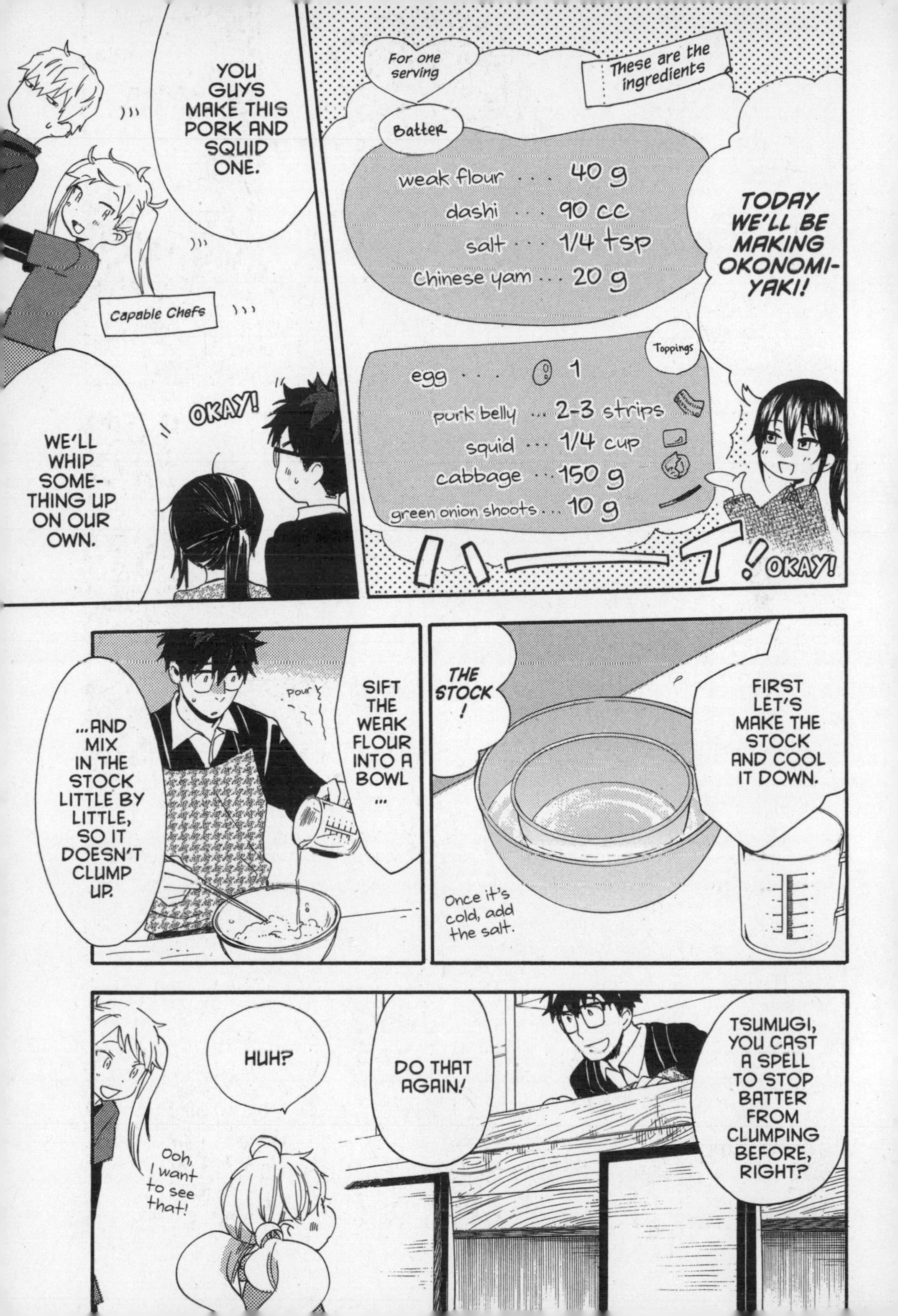
These are the ingredients
For one serving
TODAY WE'LL BE MAKING OKONOMIYAKI!
Batter
weak flour ... 40 g
dashi ... 90 cc
salt ... 1/4 tsp
Chinese yam ... 20 g
Toppings
egg ... 1
pork belly ... 2-3 strips
squid ... 1/4 cup
cabbage ... 150 g
green onion shoots ... 10 g
OKAY!
YOU GUYS MAKE THIS PORK AND SQUID ONE.
Capable Chefs
OKAY!
WE'LL WHIP SOMETHING UP ON OUR OWN.
FIRST LET'S MAKE THE STOCK AND COOL IT DOWN.
THE STOCK!
Once it's cold, add the salt.
SIFT THE WEAK FLOUR INTO A BOWL...
Pour
...AND MIX IN THE STOCK LITTLE BY LITTLE, SO IT DOESN'T CLUMP UP.
TSUMUGI, YOU CAST A SPELL TO STOP BATTER FROM CLUMPING BEFORE, RIGHT?
DO THAT AGAIN!
HUH?
Ooh, I want to see that!

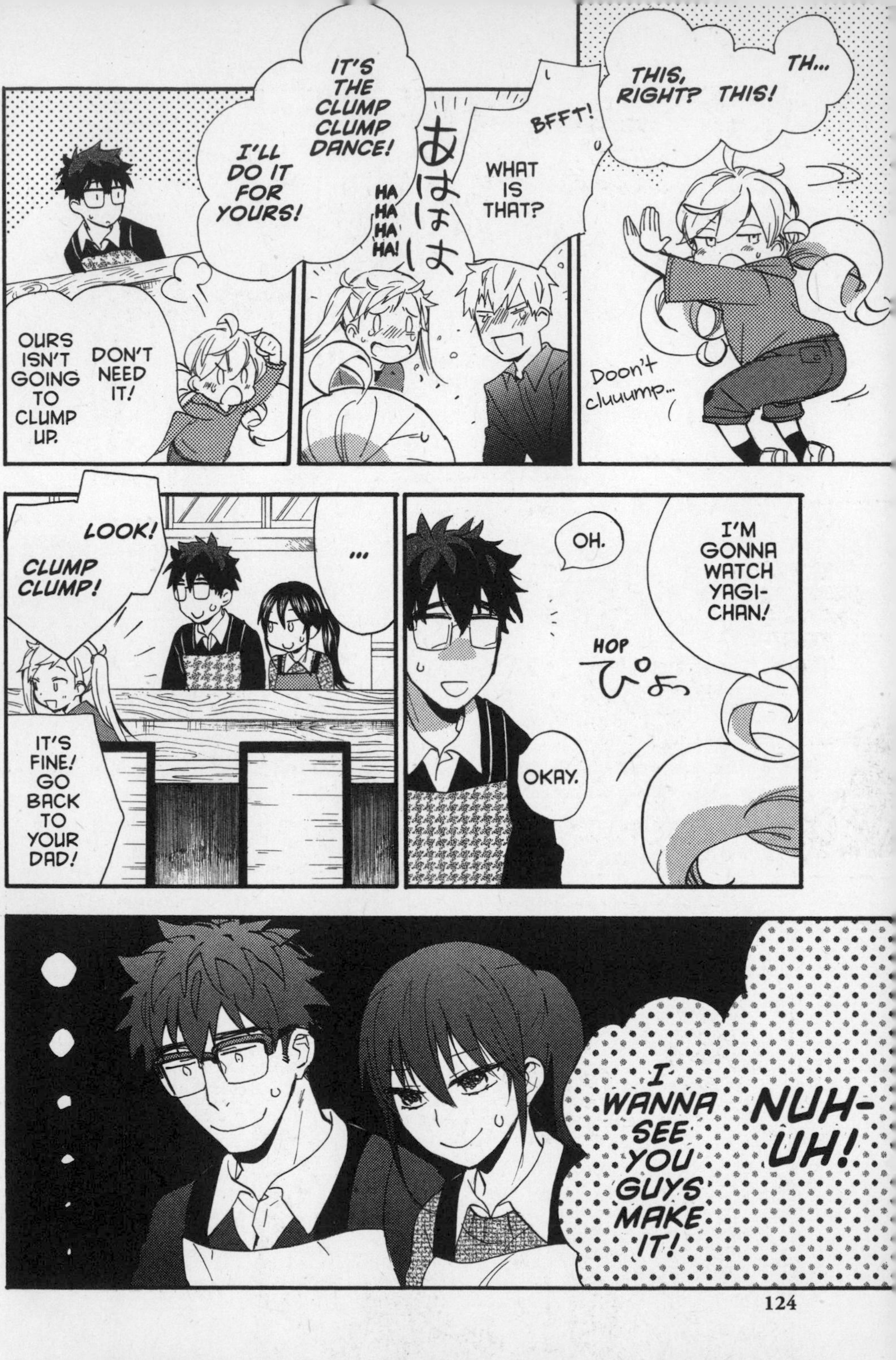
TH... THIS!
THIS, RIGHT?
Doon't cluuump...
BFFT!
WHAT IS THAT?
あはは
HA HA HA HA!
IT'S THE CLUMP CLUMP DANCE!
I'LL DO IT FOR YOURS!
DON'T NEED IT!
OURS ISN'T GOING TO CLUMP UP.
I'M GONNA WATCH YAGI-CHAN!
OH.
HOP
ぴょ
OKAY.
...
LOOK!
CLUMP CLUMP!
IT'S FINE! GO BACK TO YOUR DAD!
NUH-UH!
I WANNA SEE YOU GUYS MAKE IT!

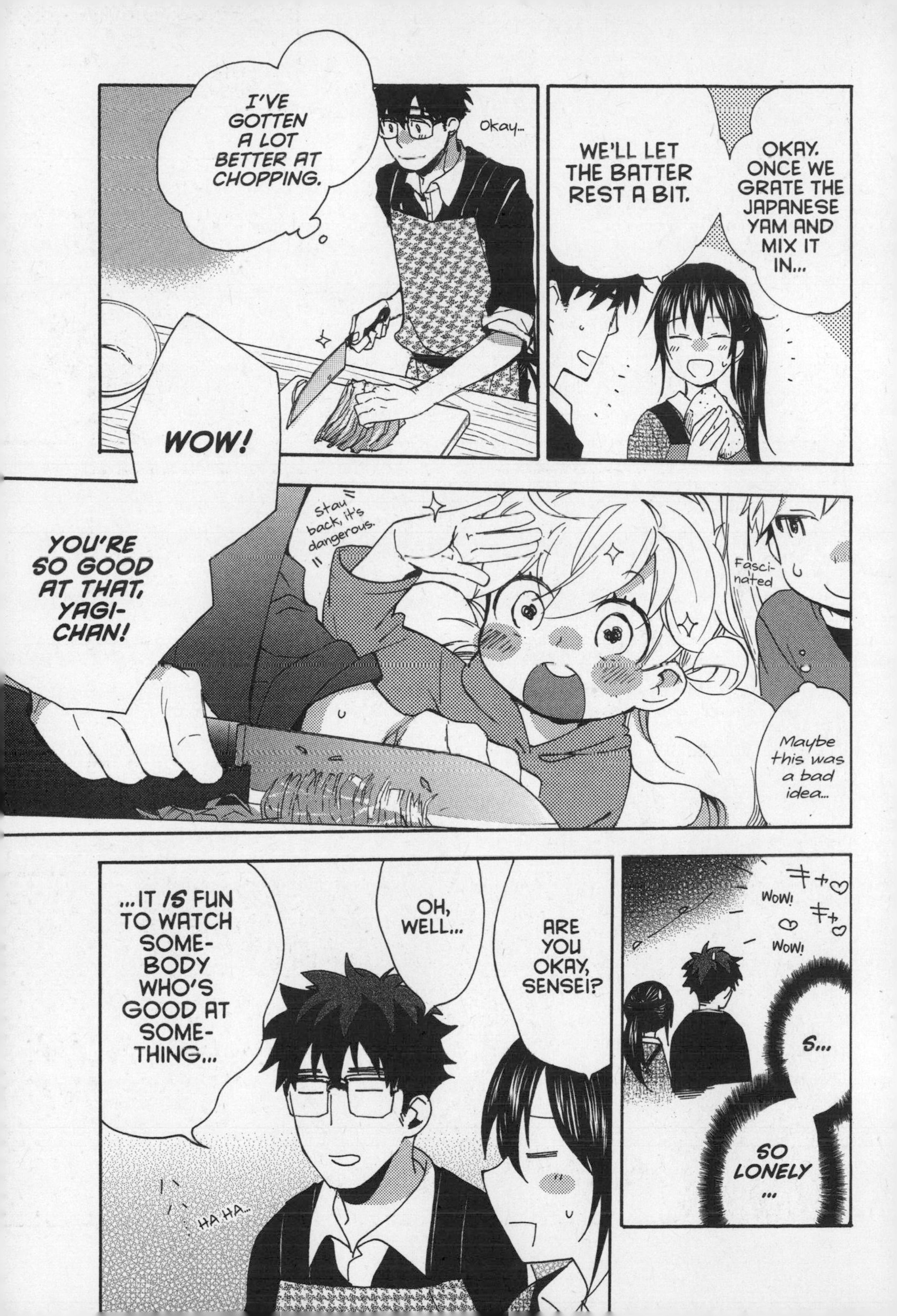
OKAY. ONCE WE GRATE THE JAPANESE YAM AND MIX IT IN...
WE'LL LET THE BATTER REST A BIT.
Okay...
I'VE GOTTEN A LOT BETTER AT CHOPPING.
WOW!
Fascinated
Stay back, it's dangerous.
YOU'RE SO GOOD AT THAT, YAGI-CHAN!
Maybe this was a bad idea...
WOW!
WOW!
S...
SO LONELY ...
ARE YOU OKAY, SENSEI?
OH, WELL...
...IT IS FUN TO WATCH SOMEBODY WHO'S GOOD AT SOMETHING...
HA HA...

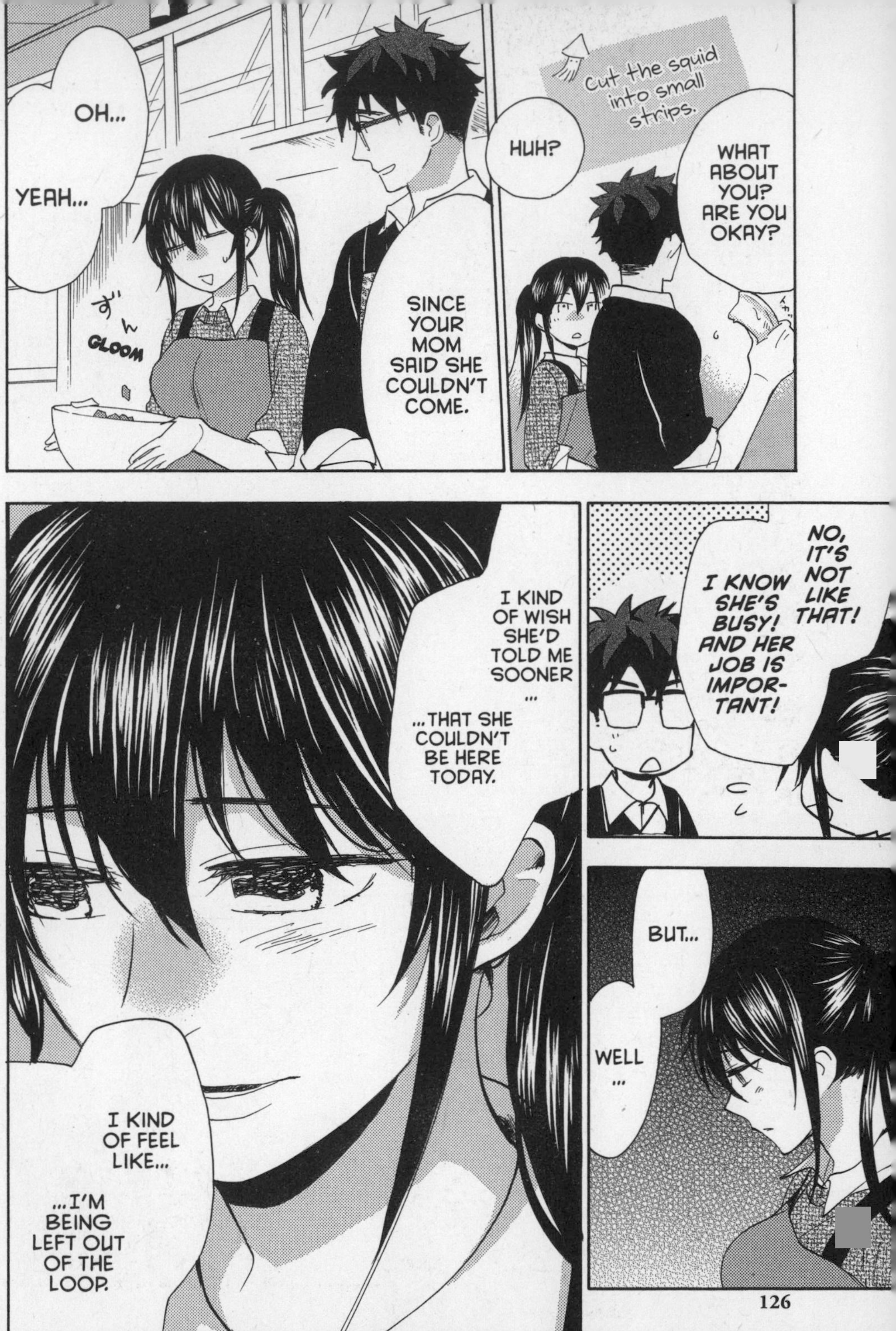
Cut the squid into small strips.
WHAT ABOUT YOU? ARE YOU OKAY?
HUH?
SINCE YOUR MOM SAID SHE COULDN'T COME.
OH...
YEAH...
ずん
GLOOM
NO, IT'S NOT LIKE THAT!
I KNOW SHE'S BUSY! AND HER JOB IS IMPORTANT!
BUT...
WELL...
I KIND OF WISH SHE'D TOLD ME SOONER...
...THAT SHE COULDN'T BE HERE TODAY.
I KIND OF FEEL LIKE...
...I'M BEING LEFT OUT OF THE LOOP.

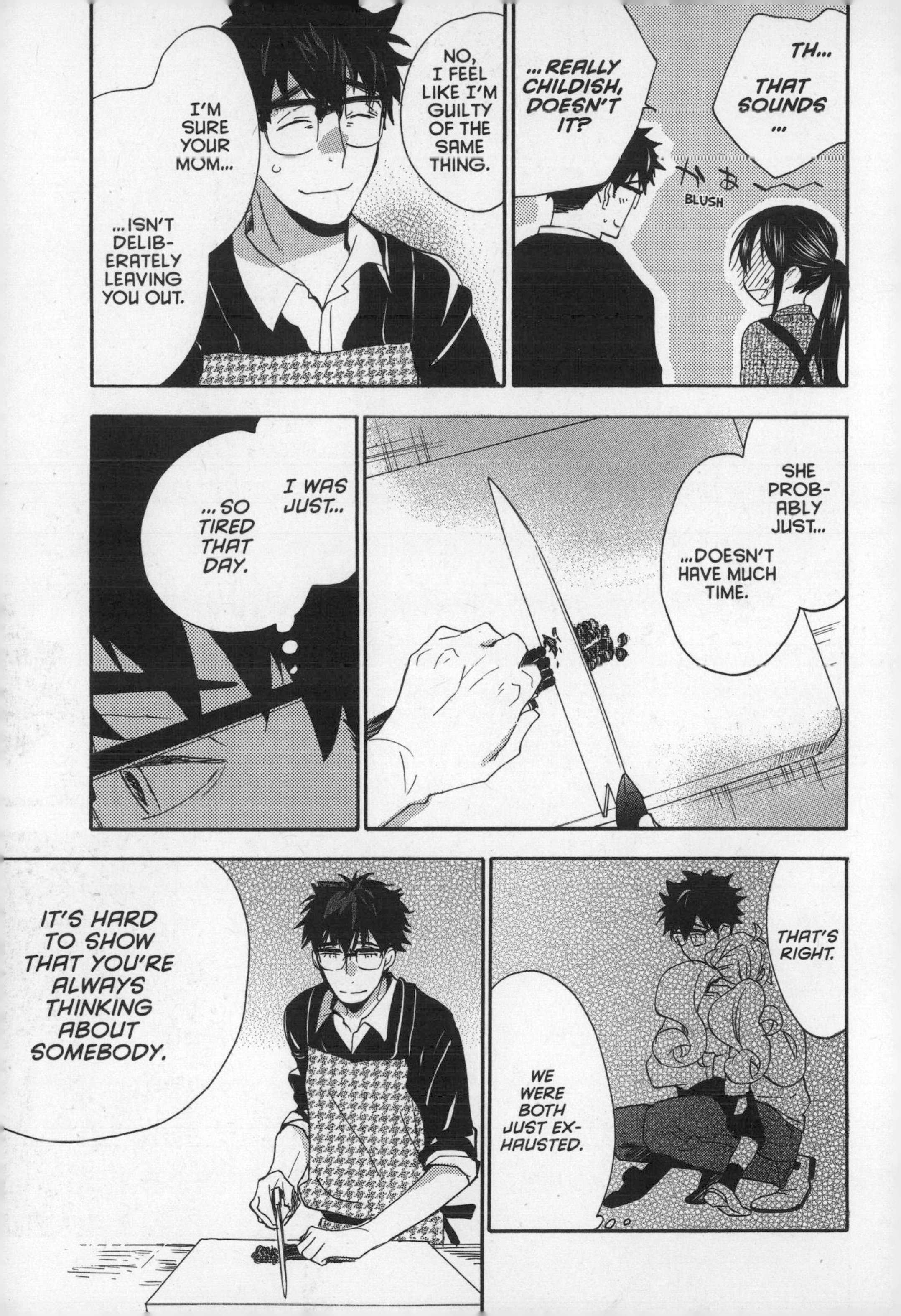
TH... THAT SOUNDS ...
...REALLY CHILDISH, DOESN'T IT?
BLUSH
NO, I FEEL LIKE I'M GUILTY OF THE SAME THING.
I'M SURE YOUR MOM...
...ISN'T DELIBERATELY LEAVING YOU OUT.
SHE PROBABLY JUST...
...DOESN'T HAVE MUCH TIME.
I WAS JUST...
...SO TIRED THAT DAY.
THAT'S RIGHT.
WE WERE BOTH JUST EXHAUSTED.
IT'S HARD TO SHOW THAT YOU'RE ALWAYS THINKING ABOUT SOMEBODY.

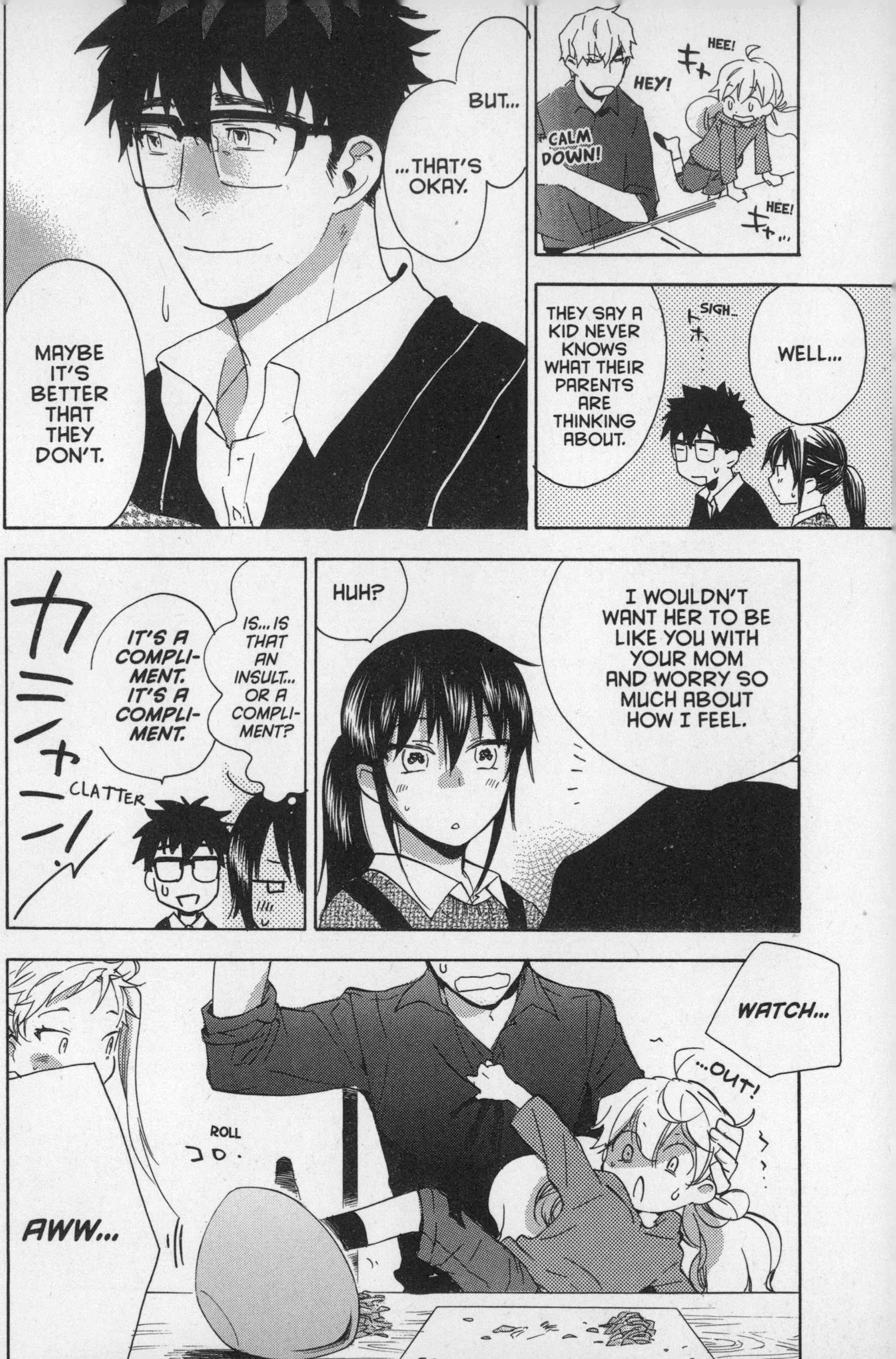
HEE!
HEY!
CALM DOWN!
HEE!
WELL...
SIGH..
THEY SAY A KID NEVER KNOWS WHAT THEIR PARENTS ARE THINKING ABOUT.
BUT...
...THAT'S OKAY.
MAYBE IT'S BETTER THAT THEY DON'T.
I WOULDN'T WANT HER TO BE LIKE YOU WITH YOUR MOM AND WORRY SO MUCH ABOUT HOW I FEEL.
HUH?
IS... IS THAT AN INSULT... OR A COMPLIMENT?
IT'S A COMPLIMENT. IT'S A COMPLIMENT.
CLATTER
WATCH...
...OUT!
ROLL
AWW...

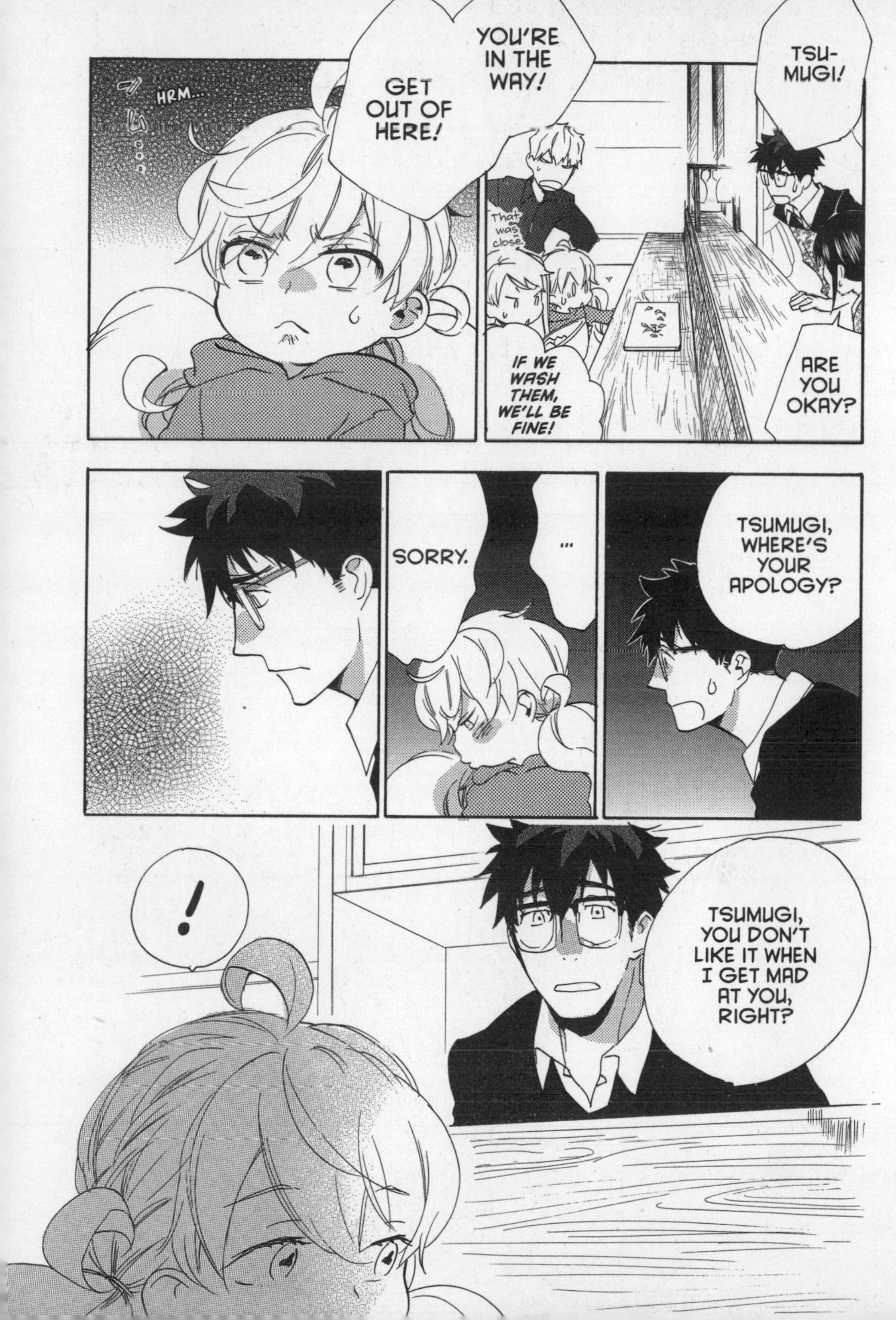
TSU-MUGI!
ARE YOU OKAY?
That was close.
IF WE WASH THEM, WE'LL BE FINE!
YOU'RE IN THE WAY!
GET OUT OF HERE!
HRM...
TSUMUGI, WHERE'S YOUR APOLOGY?
...
SORRY.
TSUMUGI, YOU DON'T LIKE IT WHEN I GET MAD AT YOU, RIGHT?
!

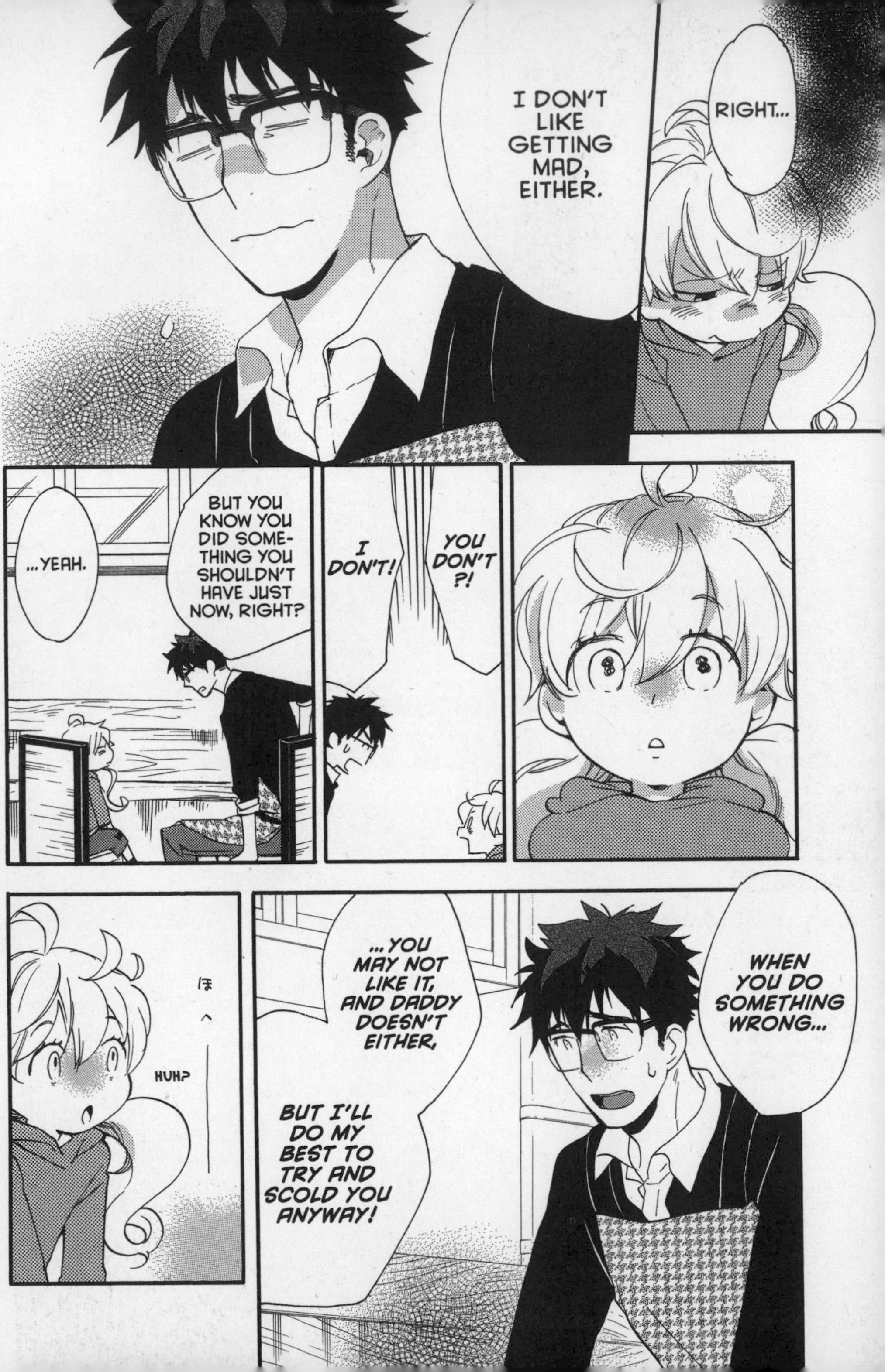
RIGHT...
I DON'T LIKE GETTING MAD, EITHER.
YOU DON'T ?!
I DON'T!
BUT YOU KNOW YOU DID SOME-THING YOU SHOULDN'T HAVE JUST NOW, RIGHT?
...YEAH.
WHEN YOU DO SOMETHING WRONG...
...YOU MAY NOT LIKE IT, AND DADDY DOESN'T EITHER,
BUT I'LL DO MY BEST TO TRY AND SCOLD YOU ANYWAY!
ほへ
HUH?

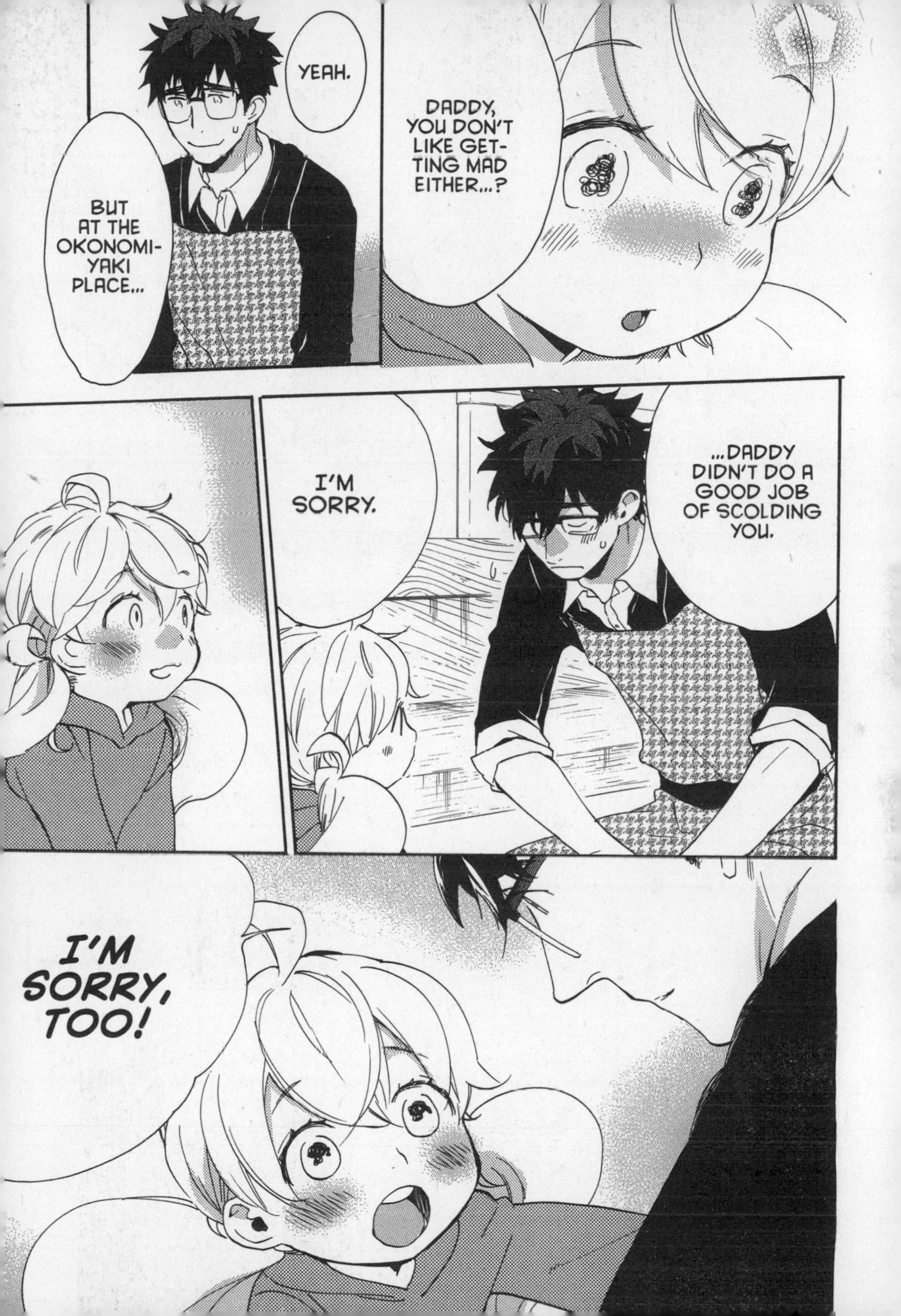
DADDY, YOU DON'T LIKE GETTING MAD EITHER...?
YEAH.
BUT AT THE OKONOMIYAKI PLACE...
...DADDY DIDN'T DO A GOOD JOB OF SCOLDING YOU.
I'M SORRY.
I'M SORRY, TOO!

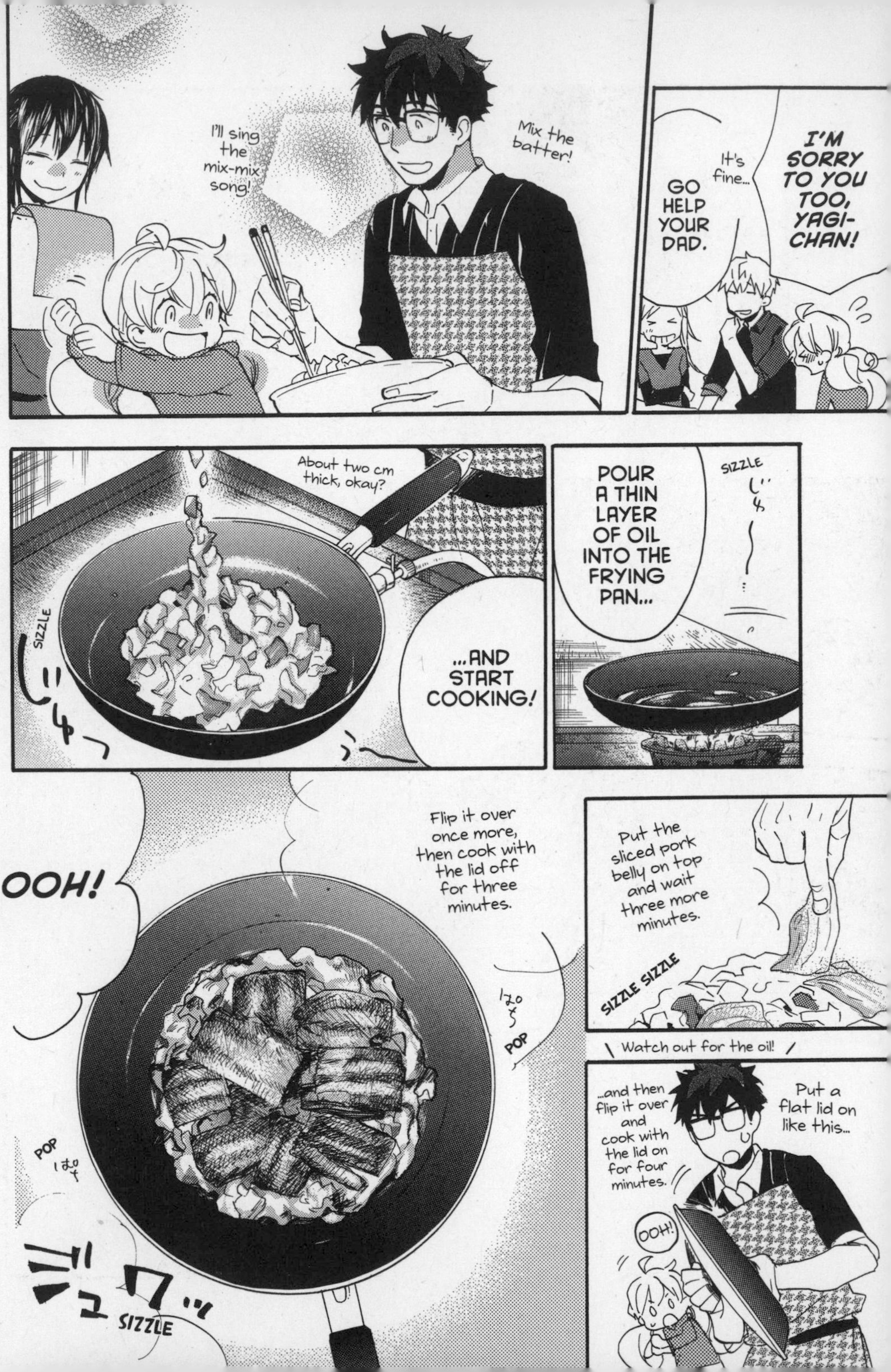
I'M SORRY TO YOU TOO, YAGI-CHAN!
It's fine...
GO HELP YOUR DAD.
Mix the batter!
I'll sing the mix-mix song!
SIZZLE
POUR A THIN LAYER OF OIL INTO THE FRYING PAN...
About two cm thick, okay?
...AND START COOKING!
SIZZLE
Put the sliced pork belly on top and wait three more minutes.
SIZZLE SIZZLE
Watch out for the oil!
Put a flat lid on like this...
...and then flip it over and cook with the lid on for four minutes.
OOH!
Flip it over once more, then cook with the lid off for three minutes.
OOH!
POP
POP
SIZZLE

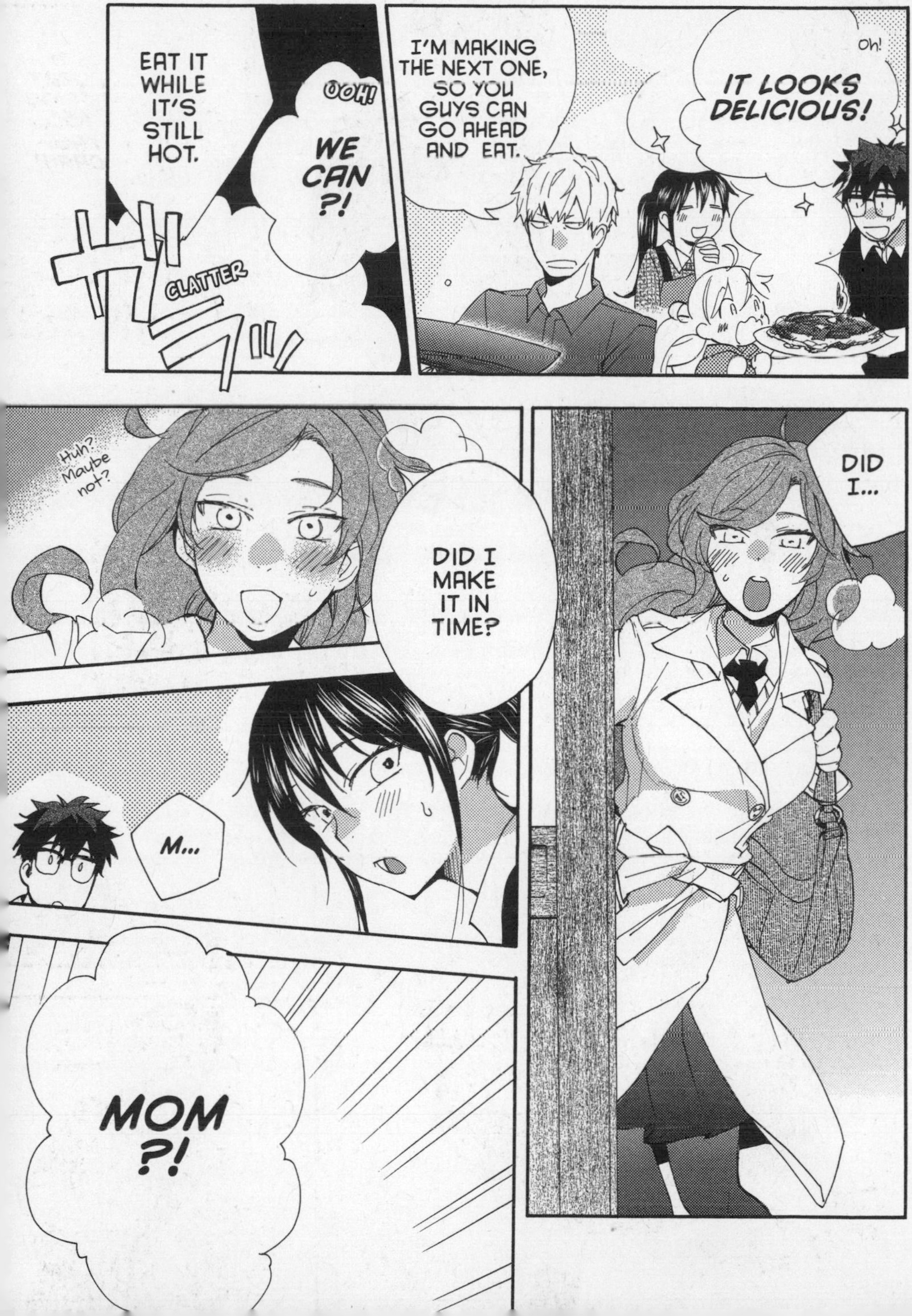
Oh!
IT LOOKS DELICIOUS!
I'M MAKING THE NEXT ONE, SO YOU GUYS CAN GO AHEAD AND EAT.
OOH!
WE CAN?!
EAT IT WHILE IT'S STILL HOT.
CLATTER
DID I...
DID I MAKE IT IN TIME?
Huh? Maybe not?
M...
MOM?!

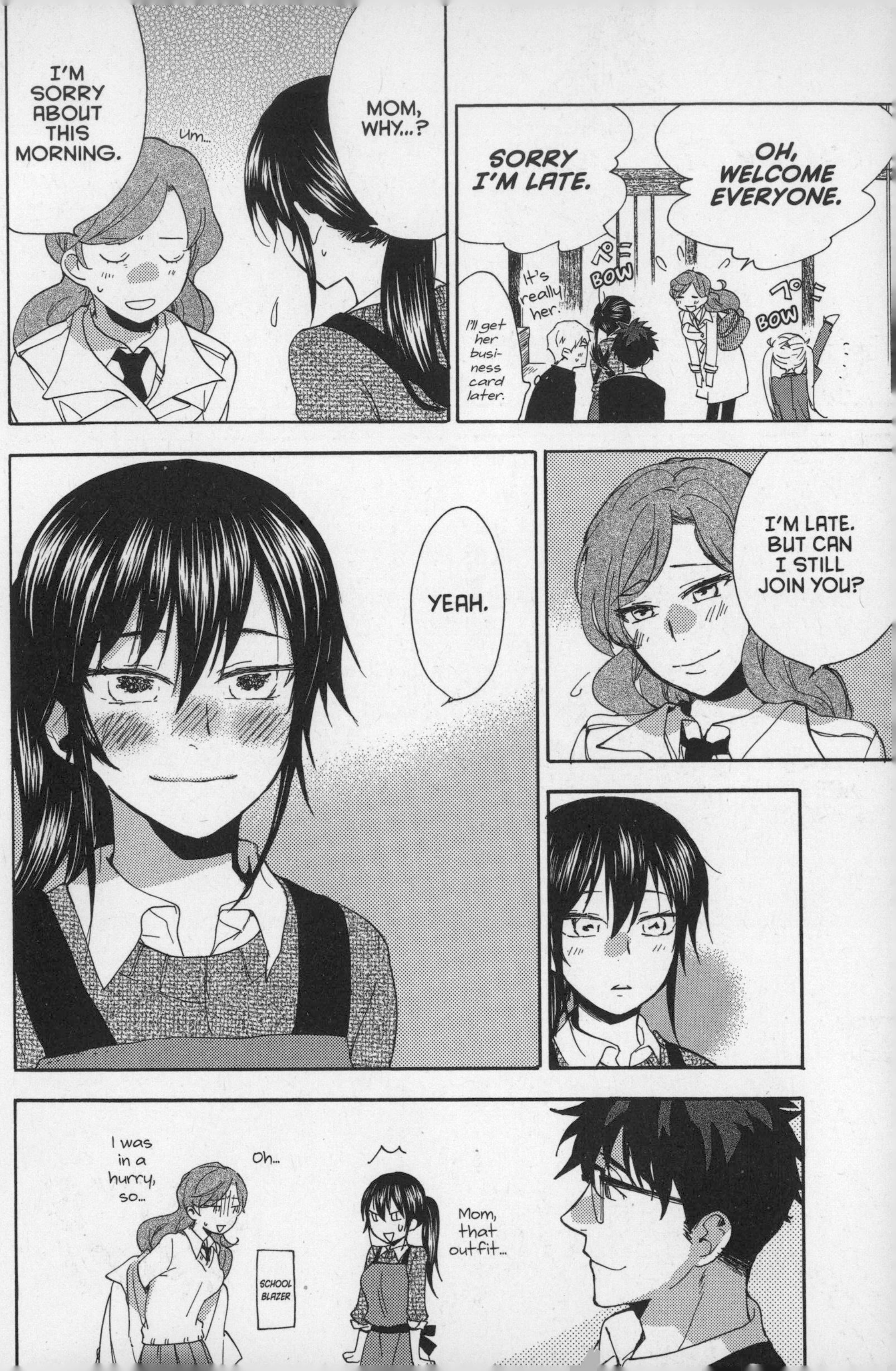
OH, WELCOME EVERYONE.
BOW
BOW
SORRY I'M LATE.
It's really her.
I'll get her business card later.
MOM, WHY...?
Um...
I'M SORRY ABOUT THIS MORNING.
I'M LATE. BUT CAN I STILL JOIN YOU?
YEAH.
Mom, that outfit...
Oh...
I was in a hurry, so...
SCHOOL BLAZER

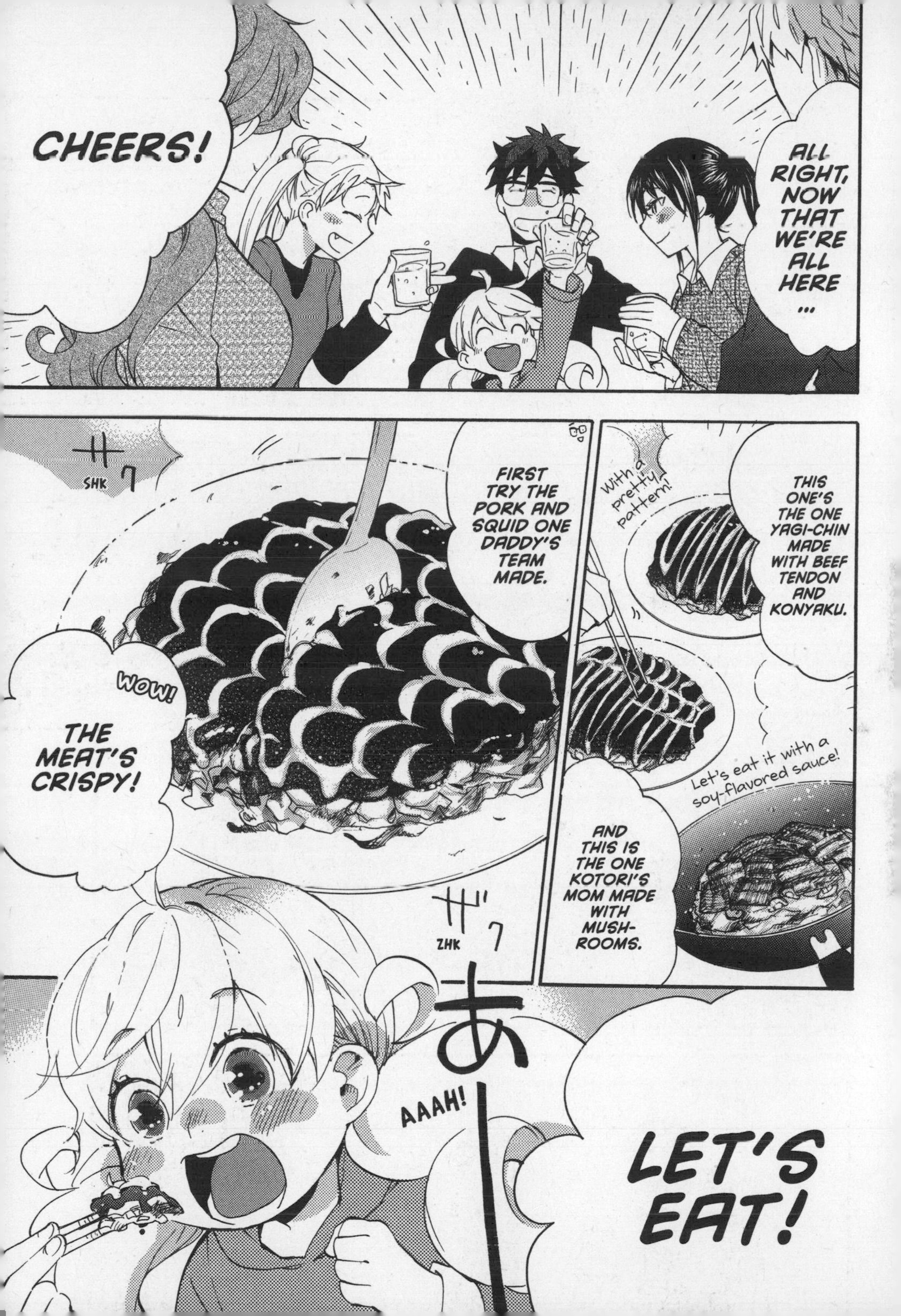
ALL RIGHT, NOW THAT WE'RE ALL HERE...
CHEERS!
THIS ONE'S THE ONE YAGI-CHIN MADE WITH BEEF TENDON AND KONYAKU.
With a pretty pattern!
Let's eat it with a soy-flavored sauce!
AND THIS IS THE ONE KOTORI'S MOM MADE WITH MUSH-ROOMS.
FIRST TRY THE PORK AND SQUID ONE DADDY'S TEAM MADE.
SHK
WOW!
THE MEAT'S CRISPY!
ZHK
LET'S EAT!
あー
AAAH!

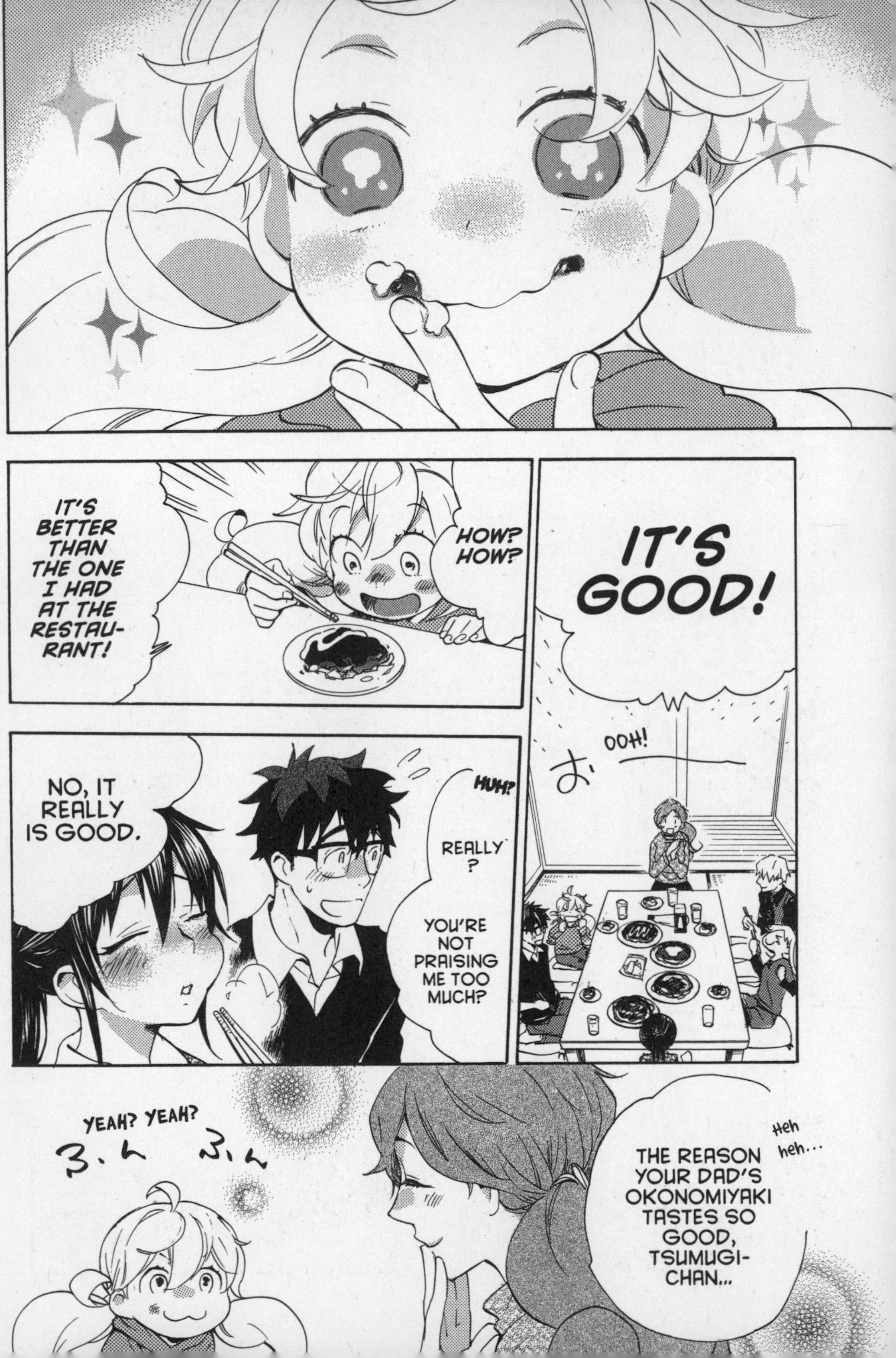
IT'S GOOD!
OOH!
お
HOW? HOW?
IT'S BETTER THAN THE ONE I HAD AT THE RESTAU-RANT!
HUH?
REALLY?
YOU'RE NOT PRAISING ME TOO MUCH?
NO, IT REALLY IS GOOD.
Heh heh...
THE REASON YOUR DAD'S OKONOMIYAKI TASTES SO GOOD, TSUMUGI-CHAN...
YEAH? YEAH?
ふん ふん

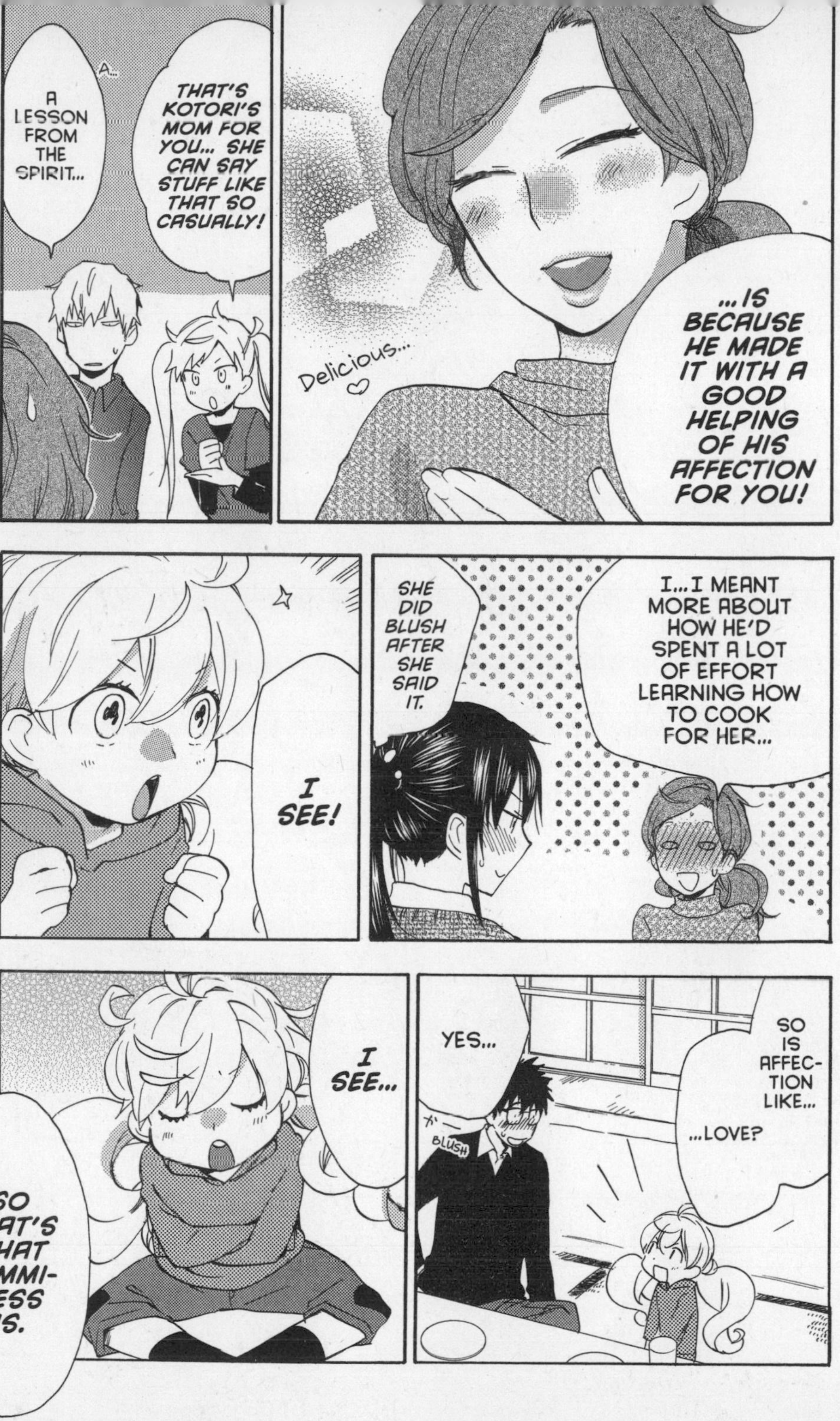
...IS BECAUSE HE MADE IT WITH A GOOD HELPING OF HIS AFFECTION FOR YOU!
Delicious...
THAT'S KOTORI'S MOM FOR YOU... SHE CAN SAY STUFF LIKE THAT SO CASUALLY!
A... A LESSON FROM THE SPIRIT...
I...I MEANT MORE ABOUT HOW HE'D SPENT A LOT OF EFFORT LEARNING HOW TO COOK FOR HER...
SHE DID BLUSH AFTER SHE SAID IT.
I SEE!
SO IS AFFECTION LIKE...
...LOVE?
YES...
BLUSH
I SEE...
SO THAT'S WHAT YUMMINESS IS.

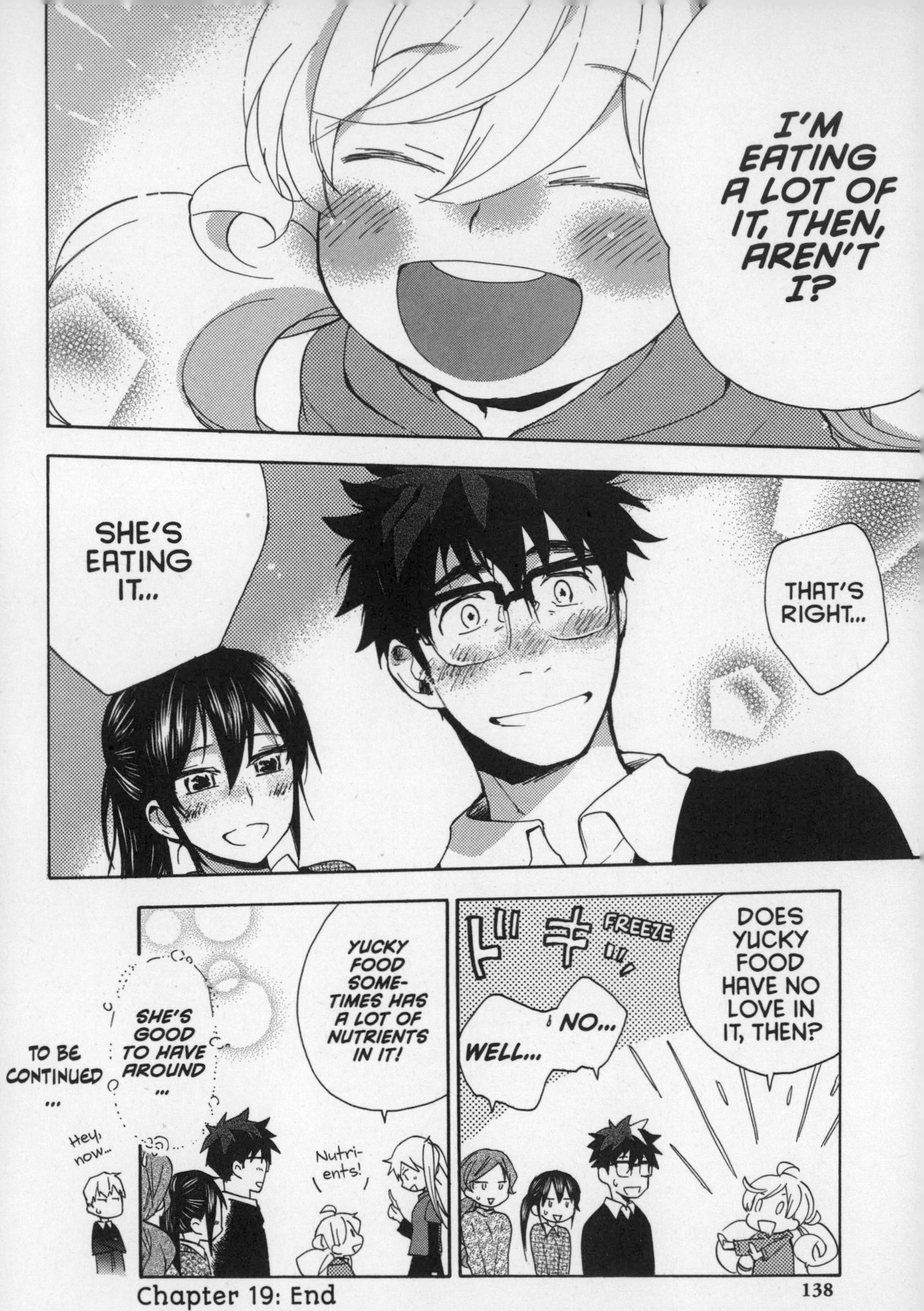
I'M EATING A LOT OF IT, THEN, AREN'T I?
THAT'S RIGHT...
SHE'S EATING IT...
DOES YUCKY FOOD HAVE NO LOVE IN IT, THEN?
ドキ
FREEZE
NO... WELL...
YUCKY FOOD SOME-TIMES HAS A LOT OF NUTRIENTS IN IT!
Nutri-ents!
SHE'S GOOD TO HAVE AROUND ...
Hey, now...
TO BE CONTINUED ...

Chapter 19: End

HOORAY! **OKONOMIYAKI**

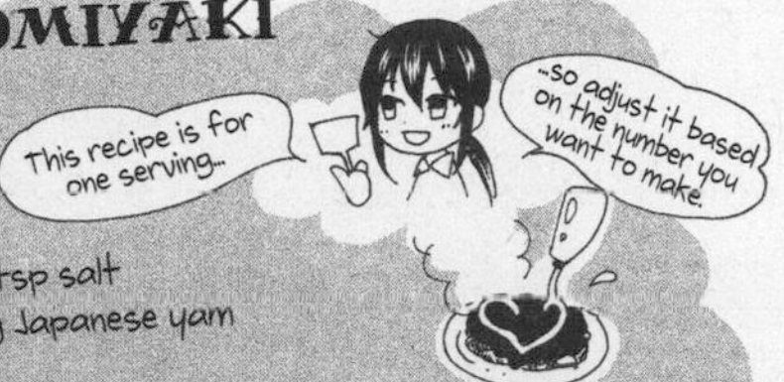

This recipe is for one serving...
...so adjust it based on the number you want to make.

☆ Ingredients ☆ (makes 1 serving)

● Batter

90 cc bonito stock 1/4 tsp salt
40 g weak flour 20 g Japanese yam

◆ toppings

150 g cabbage 1/4 Japanese squid 10 g green onion shoots
2-3 strips pork belly 1 egg

POINT Add whatever ingredients you want, like tempura flakes, pickled ginger, konnyaku, shiitake mushrooms, or cheese!

Some vegetable oil
Some sauce, mayonnaise, katsuobushi, aonori, etc.

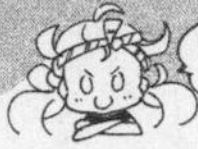

Steps

1. Make the stock, cool it, and add salt.
2. Sift the weak flour into a bowl and mix in the ingredients from step 1 slowly so it doesn't clump.
3. Grate the Japanese yam and mix it in. Then let the mix rest for a while.
4. Cut the cabbage into 1 cm squares and make sure it's dry. Cut the squid into small strips. Chop the green onion shoots into slightly large pieces. Cut each pork belly strip into 4-5 pieces.

   Squares

5. Put the cabbage, squid, and green onion from step 4 into a bowl and add the ingredients from Step 3. Crack the egg in and give everything a mixing.

   POINT Warning Mix the filling for each okonomiyaki just before you fry it. If you mix several at once, by the time you're done cooking, the moisture will be gone and it might not be good.

6. Pour a thin layer of oil into the frying pan and add the ingredients from step 5, spreading the batter out across the pan so that it's about 2 cm thick. Shape the edges with a spatula. Line up the pork belly from step 4 on top of the batter.
7. Fry for 3 minutes and then flip. Cover with a lid and fry for 4 minutes. Flip again and cook for 3 minutes with the lid off.
8. Transfer to a plate and add the sauce and mayonnaise, katsuobushi, aonori, or other toppings, and it's done.

Sweetness & Lightning | Recipe — 19

CONVERSION NOTES: 90 CC DASHI STOCK = ABOUT 1/3 CUP, 40 G WEAK FLOUR = ABOUT 1/3 CUP, 20 G CHINESE YAM = 2 TBSP, 150 G CABBAGE = ABOUT 1 CUP, 10 G GREEN ONION SHOOTS = 1 TBSP

The katsuo-bushi is alive!

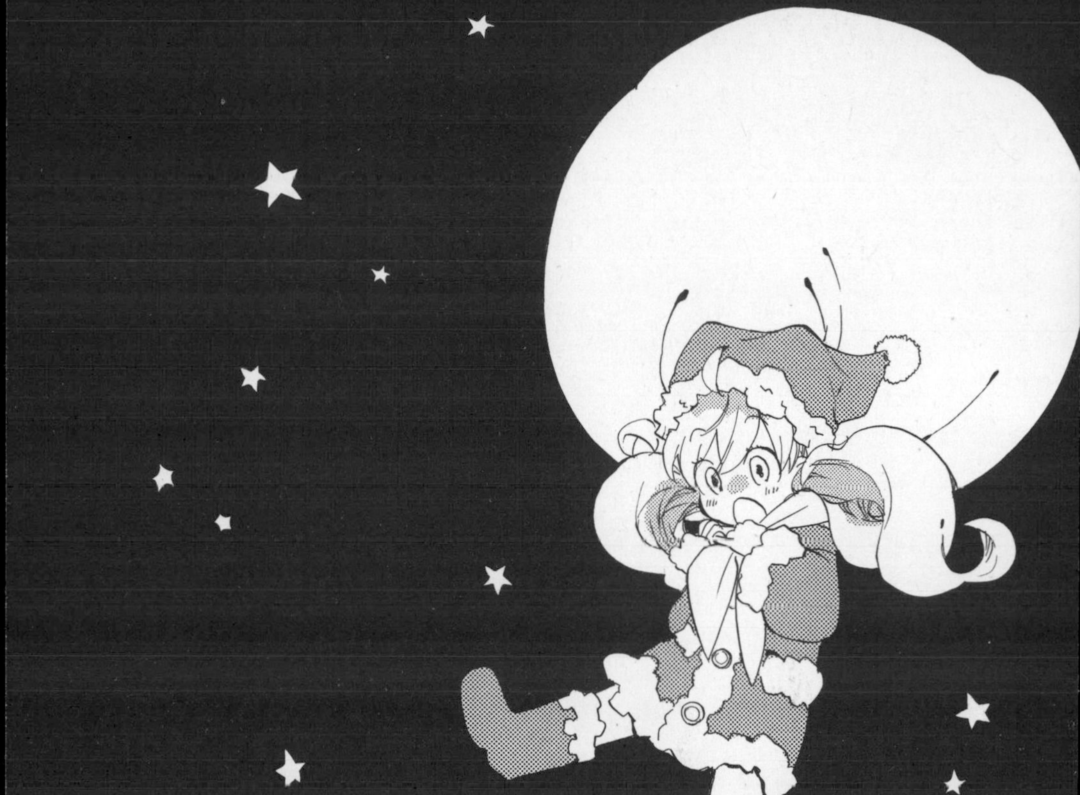

Chapter 20 Christmas and Beef Stew

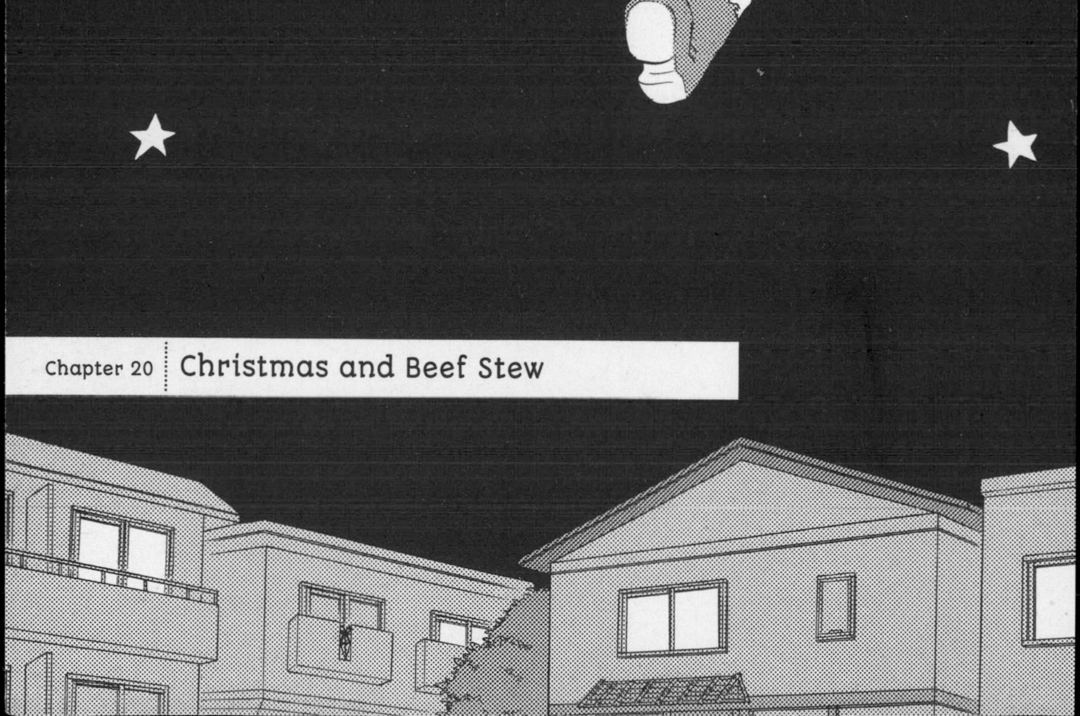

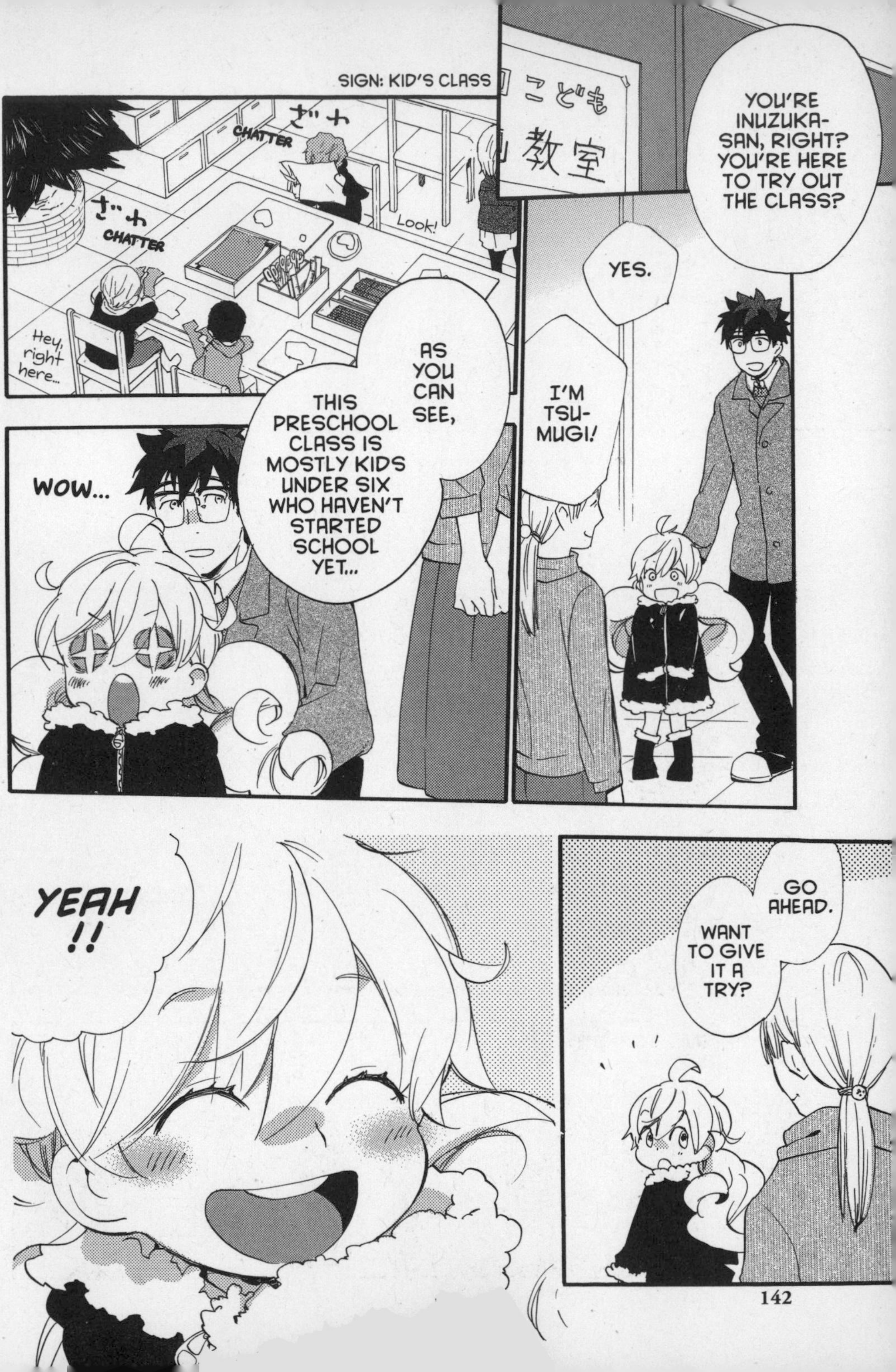
こども教室
SIGN: KID'S CLASS
YOU'RE INUZUKA-SAN, RIGHT? YOU'RE HERE TO TRY OUT THE CLASS?
YES.
I'M TSUMUGI!
ざわ CHATTER
ざわ CHATTER
Look!
Hey, right here...
AS YOU CAN SEE, THIS PRESCHOOL CLASS IS MOSTLY KIDS UNDER SIX WHO HAVEN'T STARTED SCHOOL YET...
WOW...
GO AHEAD. WANT TO GIVE IT A TRY?
YEAH!!

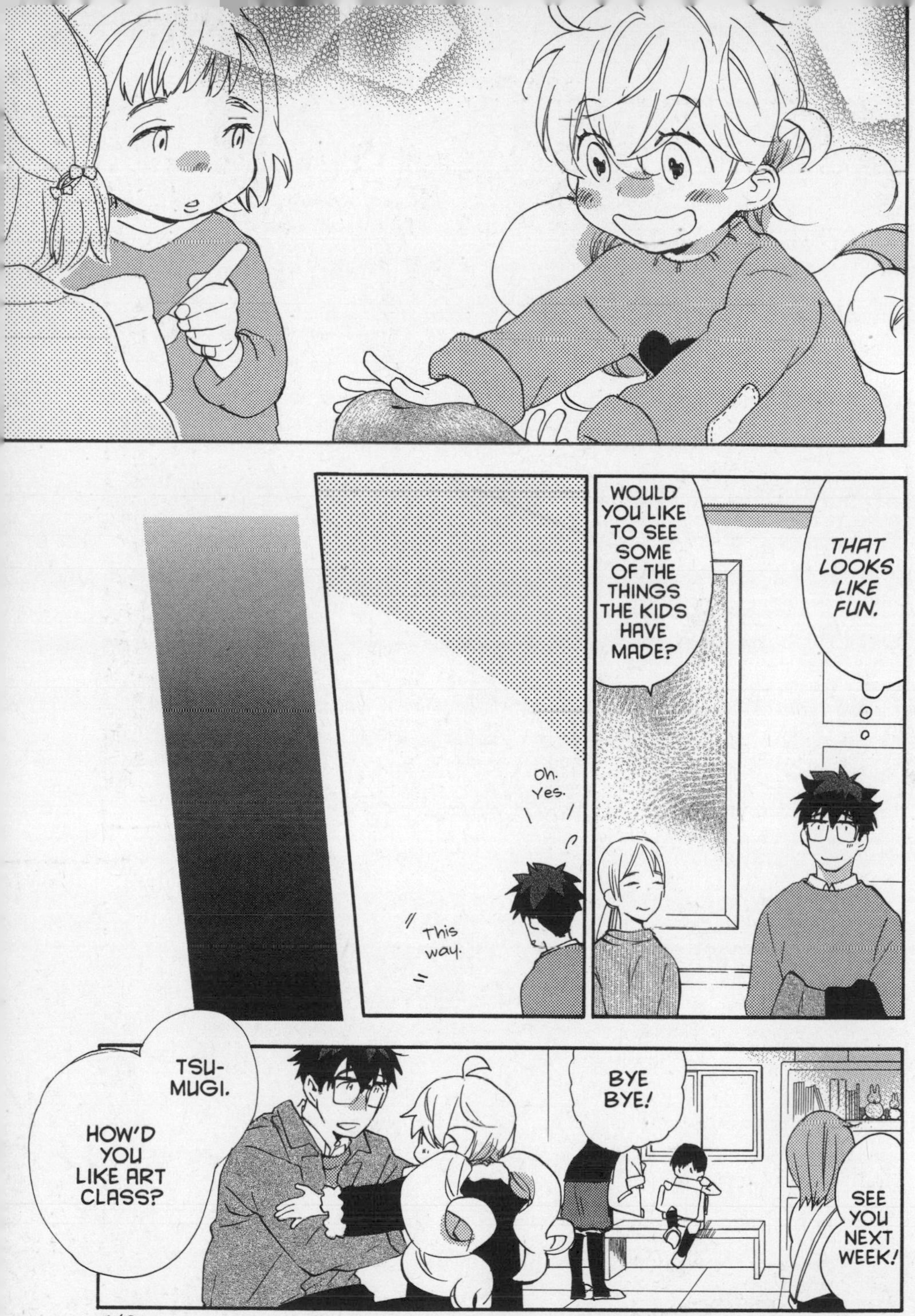
THAT LOOKS LIKE FUN.
WOULD YOU LIKE TO SEE SOME OF THE THINGS THE KIDS HAVE MADE?
Oh. Yes.
This way.
SEE YOU NEXT WEEK!
BYE BYE!
TSU-MUGI.
HOW'D YOU LIKE ART CLASS?

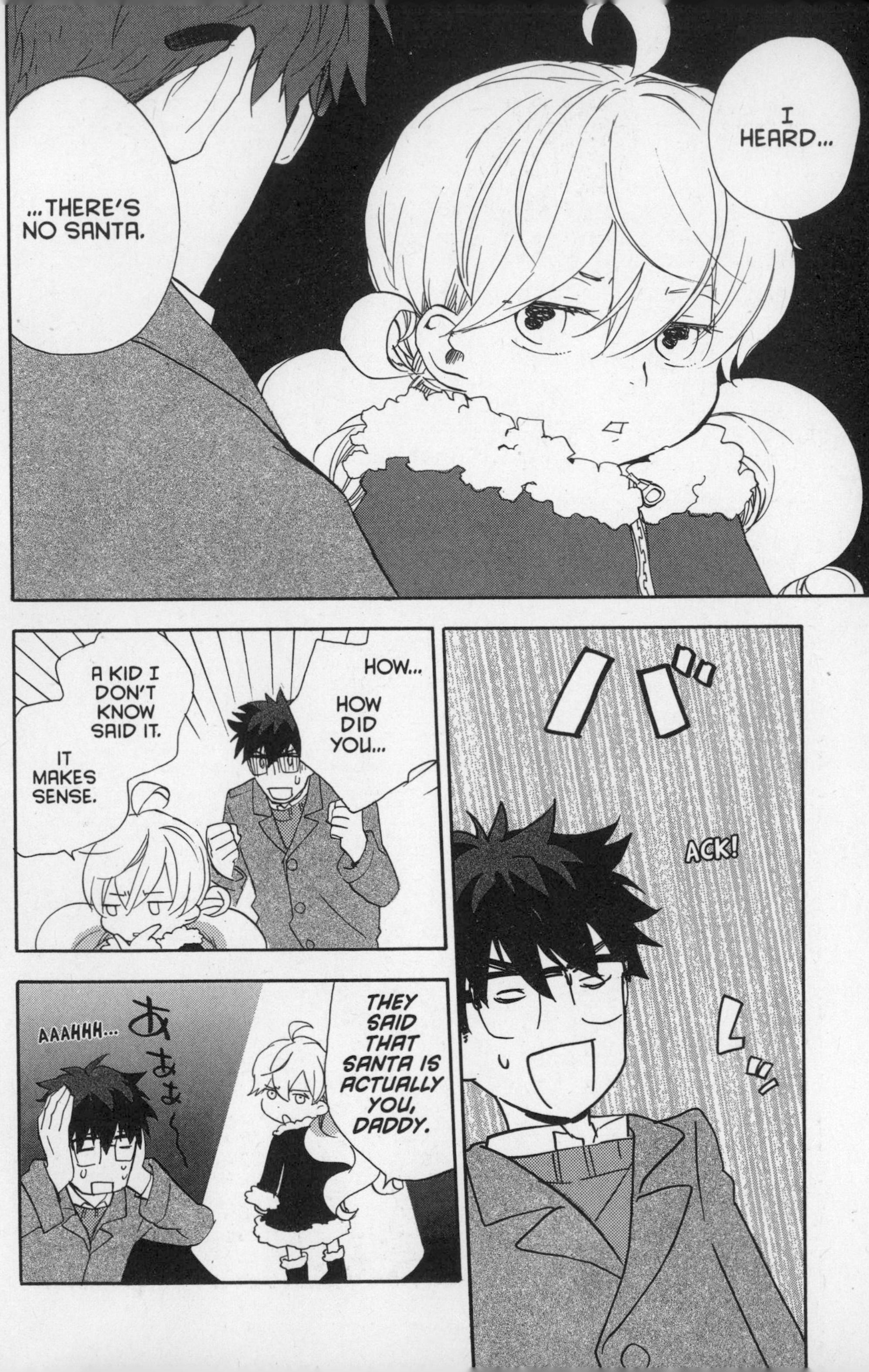
I HEARD...
...THERE'S NO SANTA.
ACK!
HOW...
HOW DID YOU...
A KID I DON'T KNOW SAID IT.
IT MAKES SENSE.
THEY SAID THAT SANTA IS ACTUALLY YOU, DADDY.
AAAHHH...

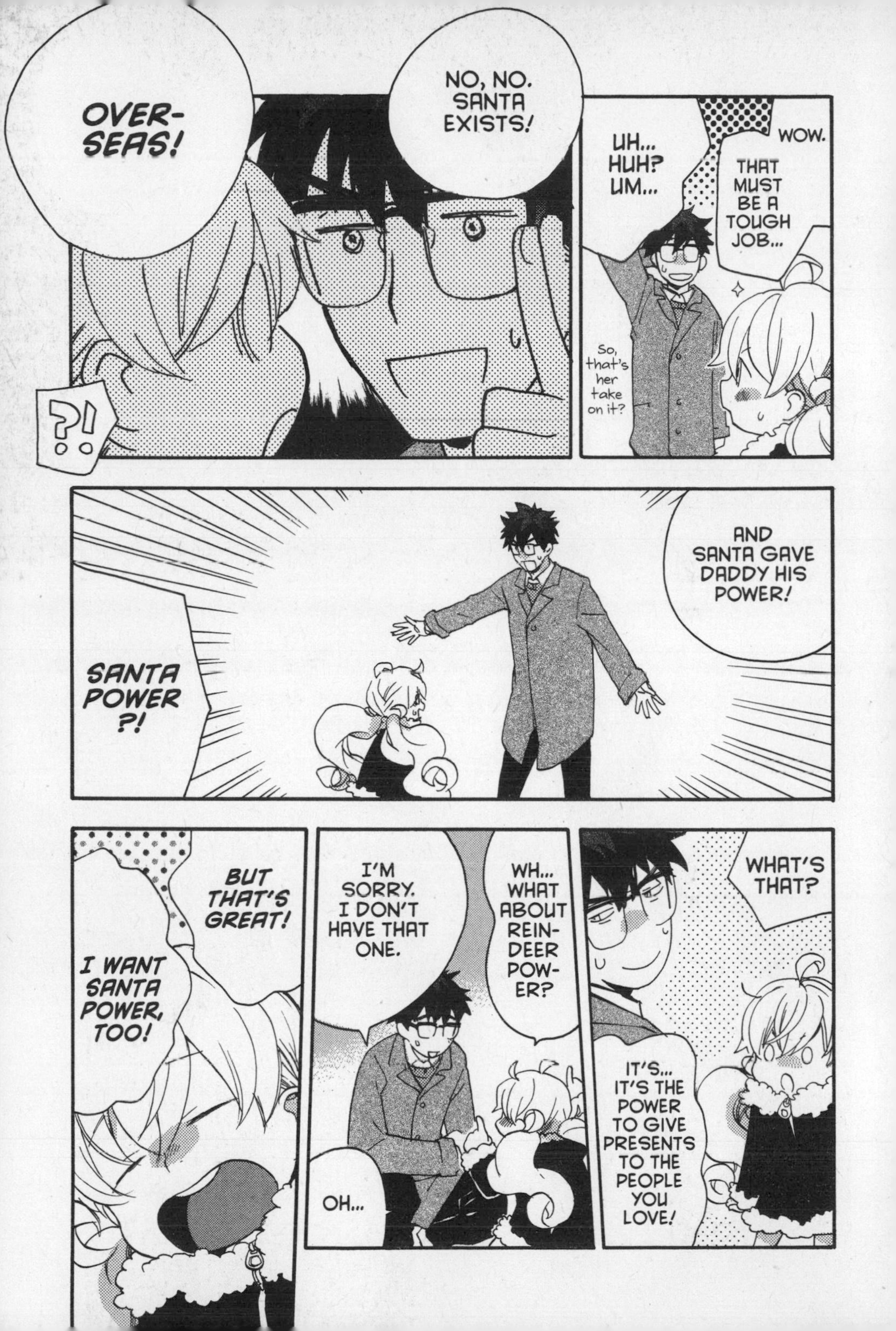
WOW.
THAT MUST BE A TOUGH JOB...
UH... HUH? UM...
So, that's her take on it?
NO, NO. SANTA EXISTS!
OVER-SEAS!
?!
AND SANTA GAVE DADDY HIS POWER!
SANTA POWER ?!
WHAT'S THAT?
IT'S... IT'S THE POWER TO GIVE PRESENTS TO THE PEOPLE YOU LOVE!
WH... WHAT ABOUT REIN-DEER POW-ER?
I'M SORRY. I DON'T HAVE THAT ONE.
OH...
BUT THAT'S GREAT!
I WANT SANTA POWER, TOO!

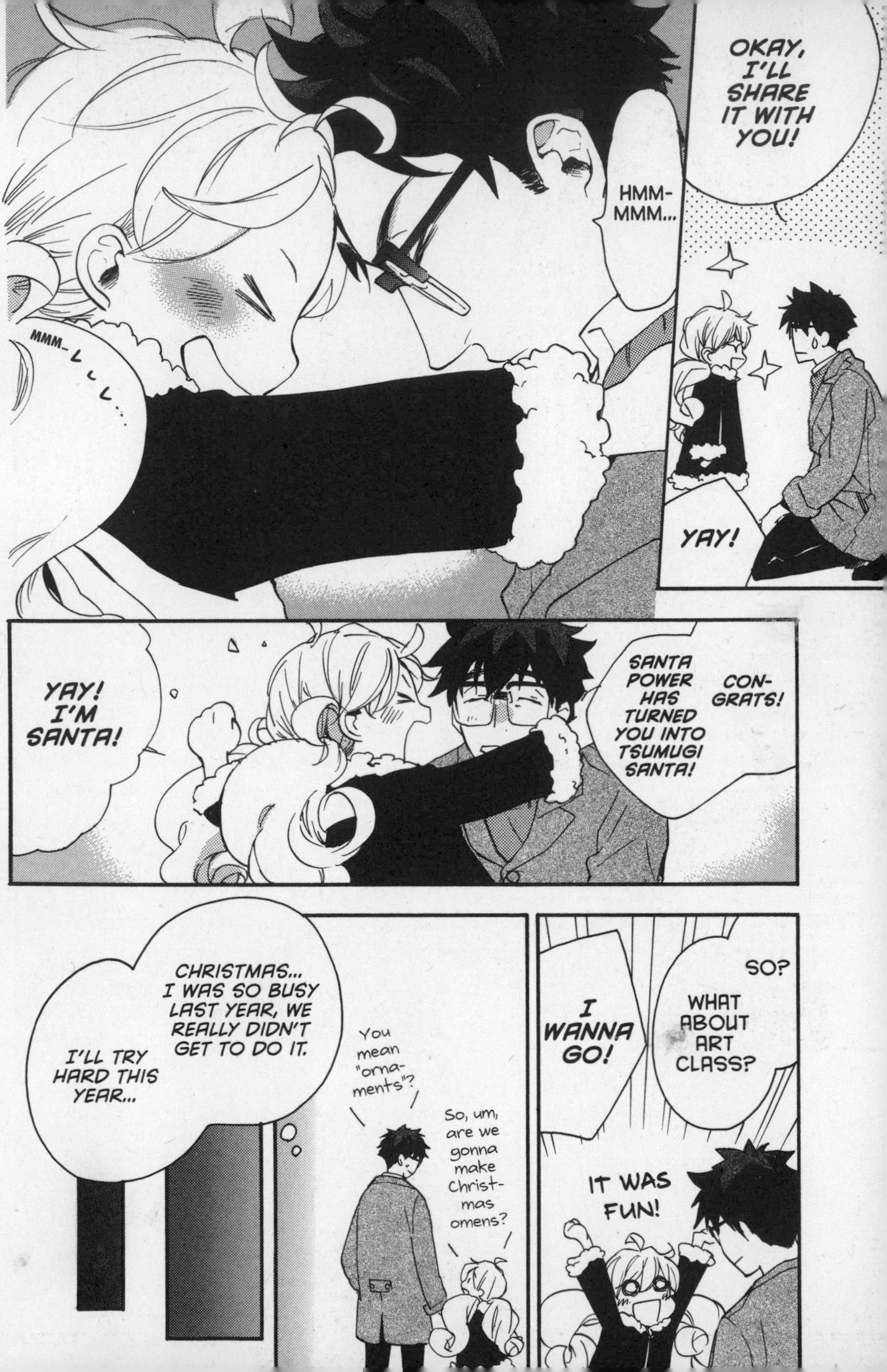
OKAY, I'LL SHARE IT WITH YOU!
YAY!
HMM-MMM...
MMM...
CON-GRATS!
SANTA POWER HAS TURNED YOU INTO TSUMUGI SANTA!
YAY! I'M SANTA!
SO?
WHAT ABOUT ART CLASS?
I WANNA GO!
IT WAS FUN!
CHRISTMAS... I WAS SO BUSY LAST YEAR, WE REALLY DIDN'T GET TO DO IT.
I'LL TRY HARD THIS YEAR...
So, um, are we gonna make Christ-mas omens?
You mean "orna-ments"?

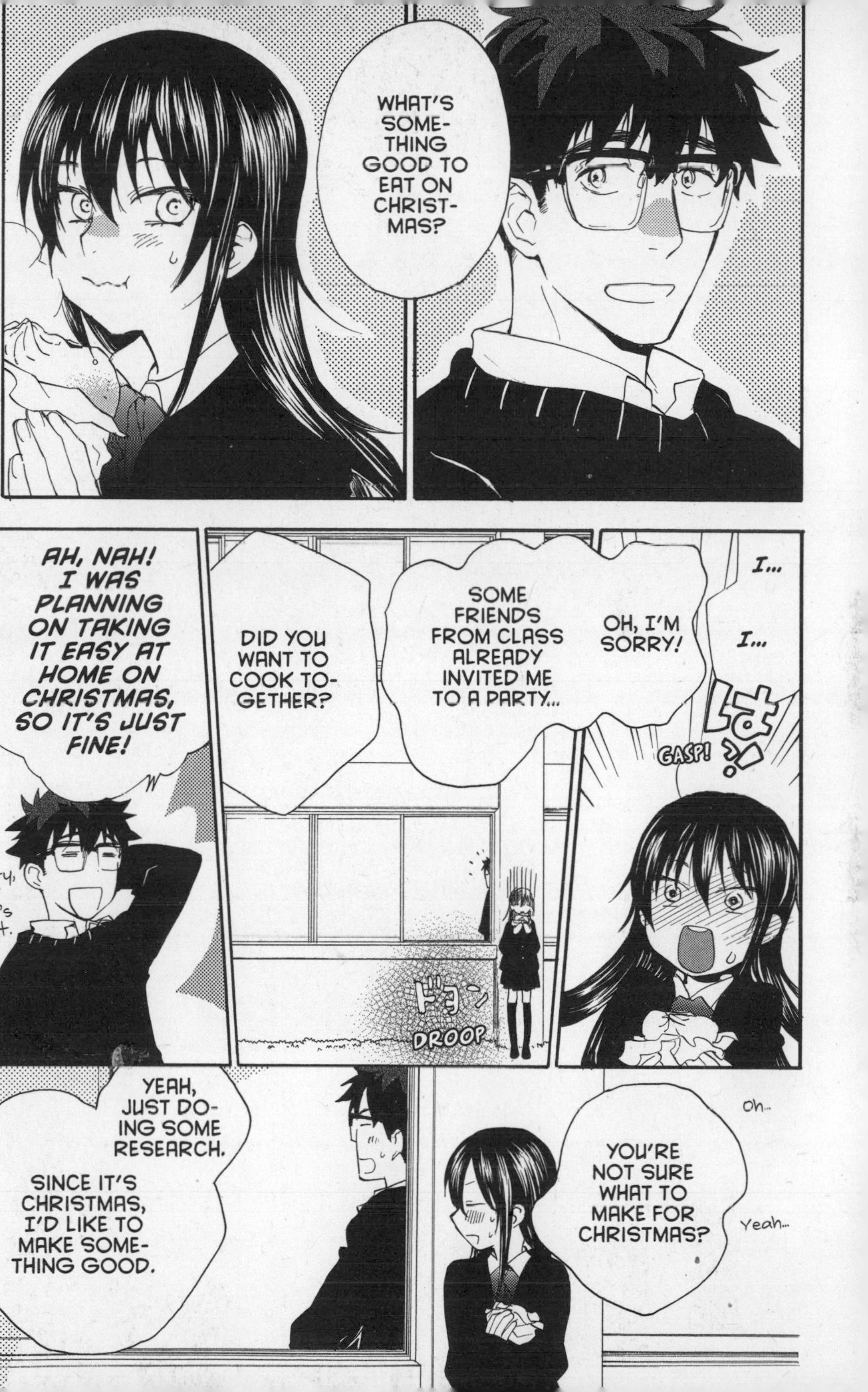

WHAT'S SOME-THING GOOD TO EAT ON CHRIST-MAS?
I...
I...
は
GASP!
OH, I'M SORRY!
SOME FRIENDS FROM CLASS ALREADY INVITED ME TO A PARTY...
DID YOU WANT TO COOK TO-GETHER?
ドヨーン
DROOP
AH, NAH! I WAS PLANNING ON TAKING IT EASY AT HOME ON CHRISTMAS, SO IT'S JUST FINE!
A party, huh? That's great.
Oh...
YOU'RE NOT SURE WHAT TO MAKE FOR CHRISTMAS?
Yeah...
YEAH, JUST DO-ING SOME RESEARCH.
SINCE IT'S CHRISTMAS, I'D LIKE TO MAKE SOME-THING GOOD.

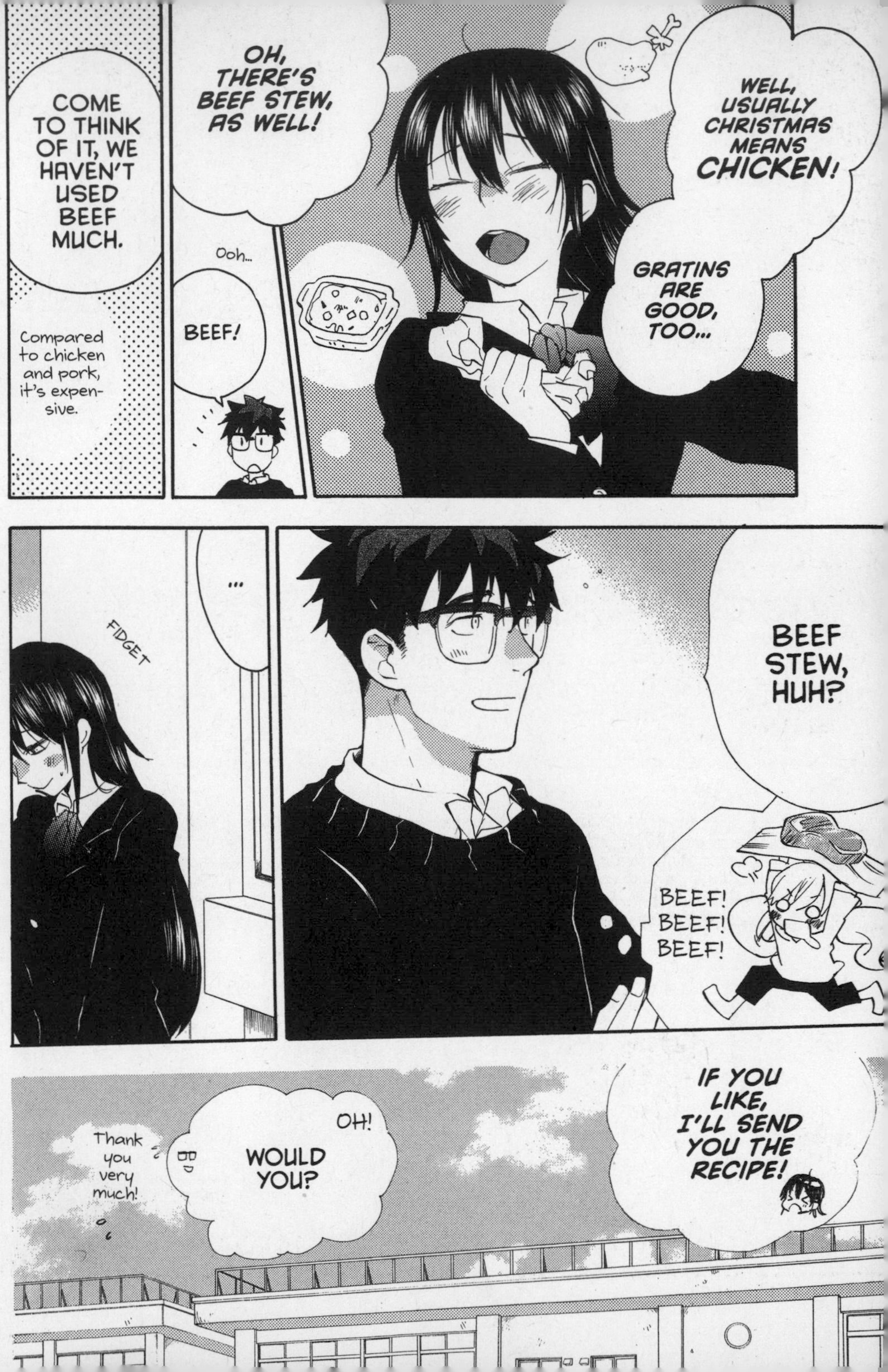
WELL, USUALLY CHRISTMAS MEANS CHICKEN!
GRATINS ARE GOOD, TOO...
OH, THERE'S BEEF STEW, AS WELL!
Ooh...
BEEF!
COME TO THINK OF IT, WE HAVEN'T USED BEEF MUCH.
Compared to chicken and pork, it's expensive.
BEEF STEW, HUH?
BEEF! BEEF! BEEF!
...
FIDGET
IF YOU LIKE, I'LL SEND YOU THE RECIPE!
OH!
WOULD YOU?
Thank you very much!

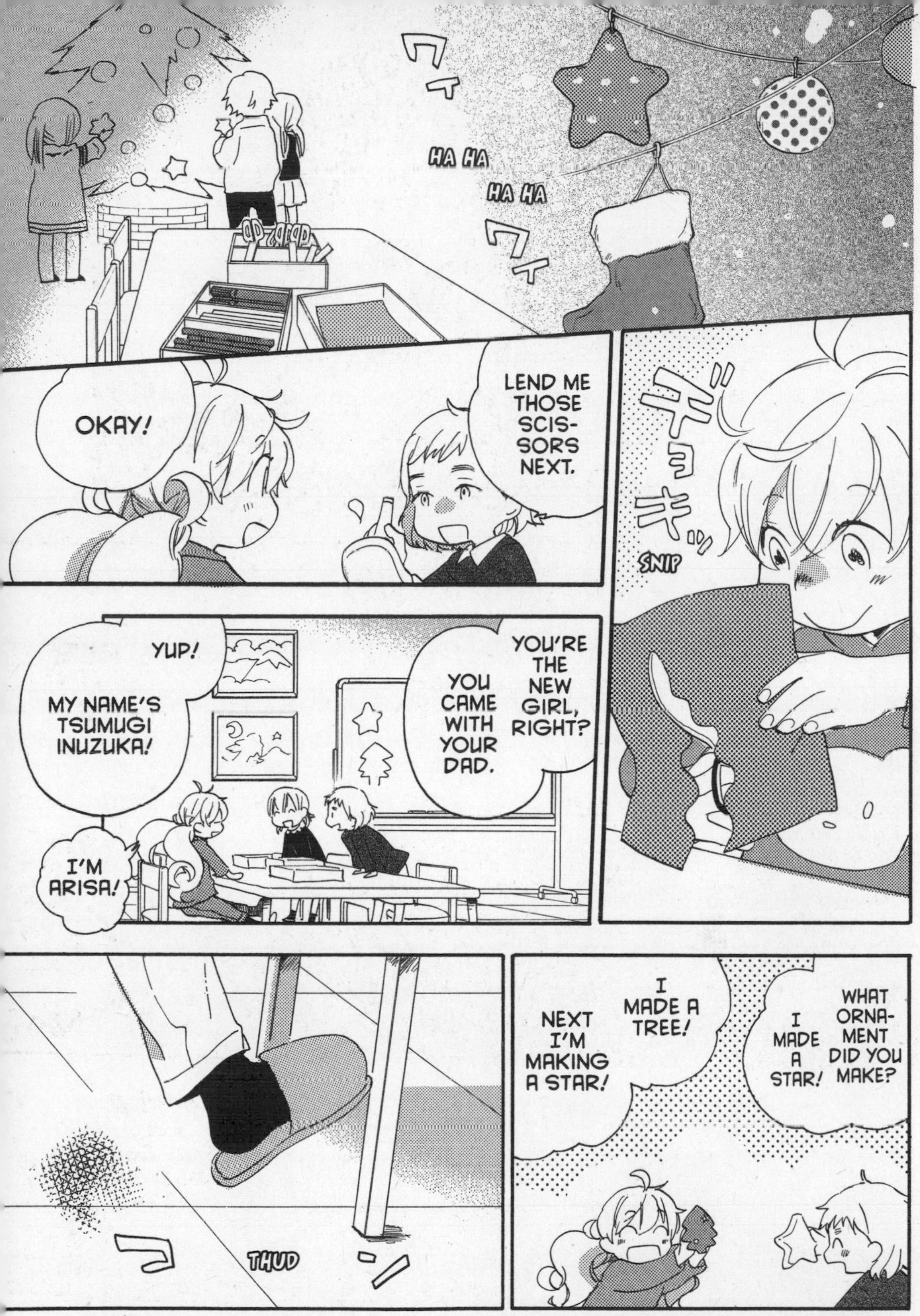
ワイ
HA HA
HA HA
ワイ
ギョキッ
SNIP
LEND ME THOSE SCISSORS NEXT.
OKAY!
YOU'RE THE NEW GIRL, RIGHT?
YOU CAME WITH YOUR DAD.
YUP!
MY NAME'S TSUMUGI INUZUKA!
I'M ARISA!
WHAT ORNAMENT DID YOU MAKE?
I MADE A STAR!
I MADE A TREE!
NEXT I'M MAKING A STAR!
コ
THUD
ン

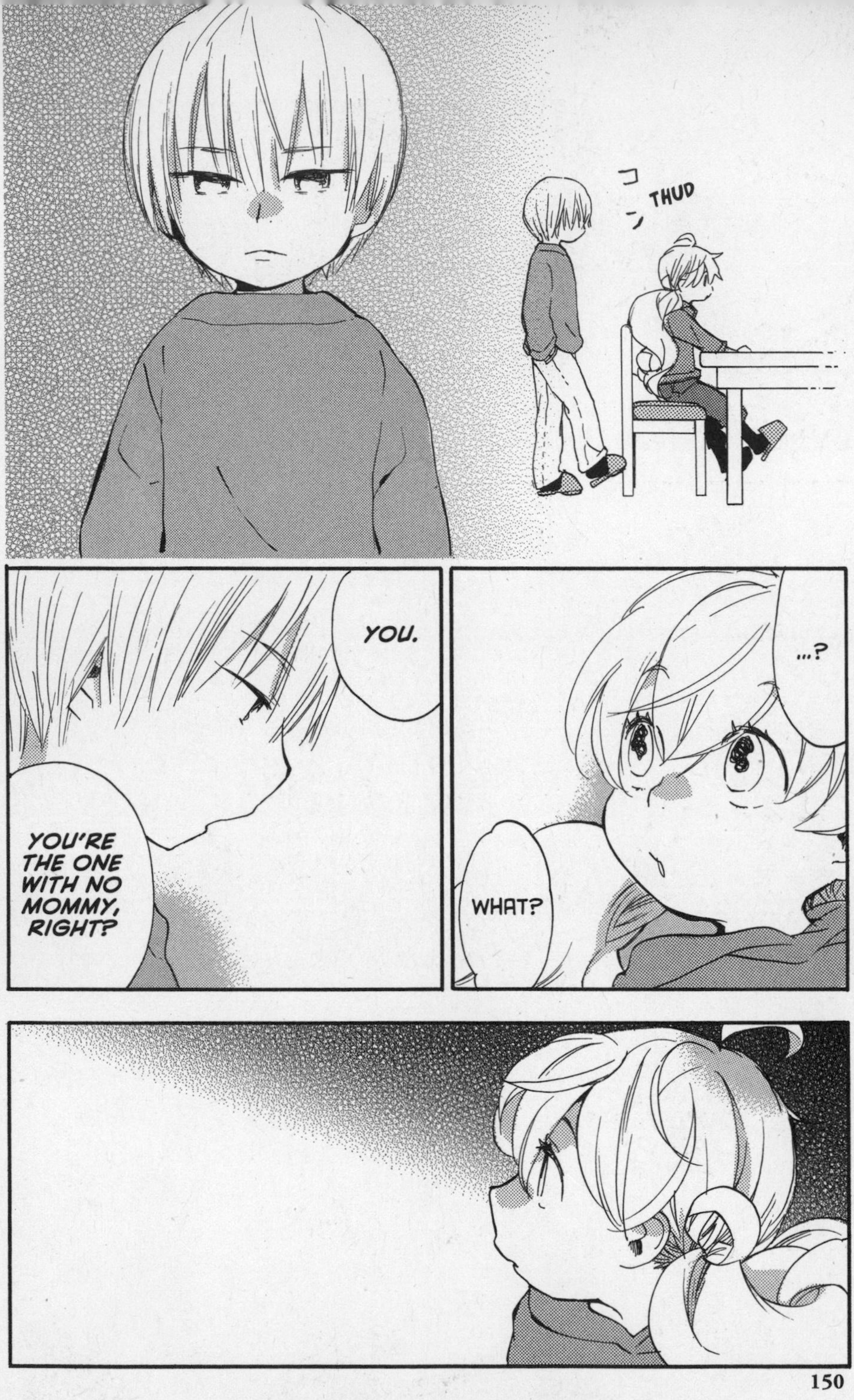
コン
THUD
...?
WHAT?
YOU.
YOU'RE THE ONE WITH NO MOMMY, RIGHT?

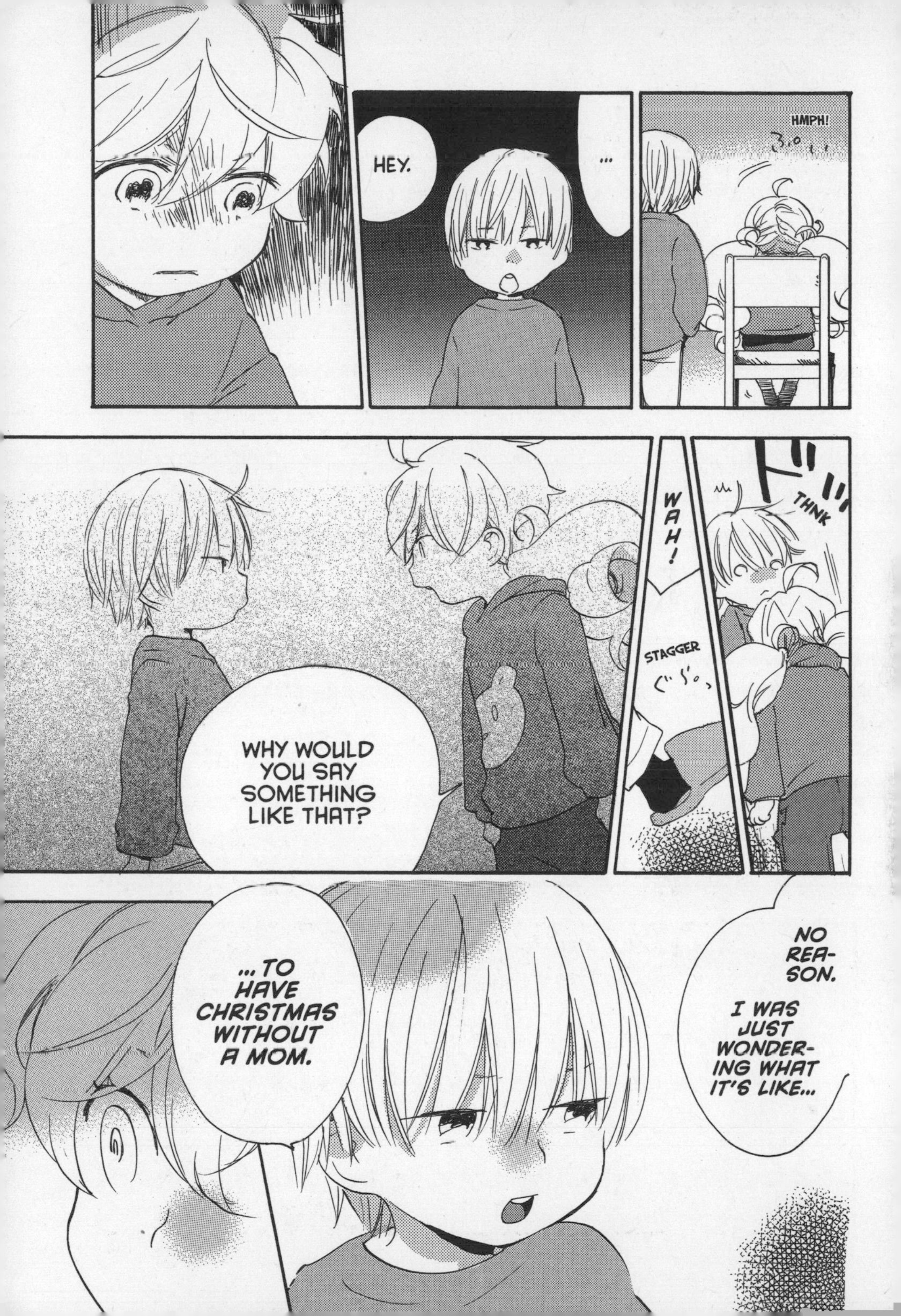
HMPH!
...
HEY.
THNK
WAH!
STAGGER
WHY WOULD YOU SAY SOMETHING LIKE THAT?
NO REA-SON.
I WAS JUST WONDER-ING WHAT IT'S LIKE...
...TO HAVE CHRISTMAS WITHOUT A MOM.

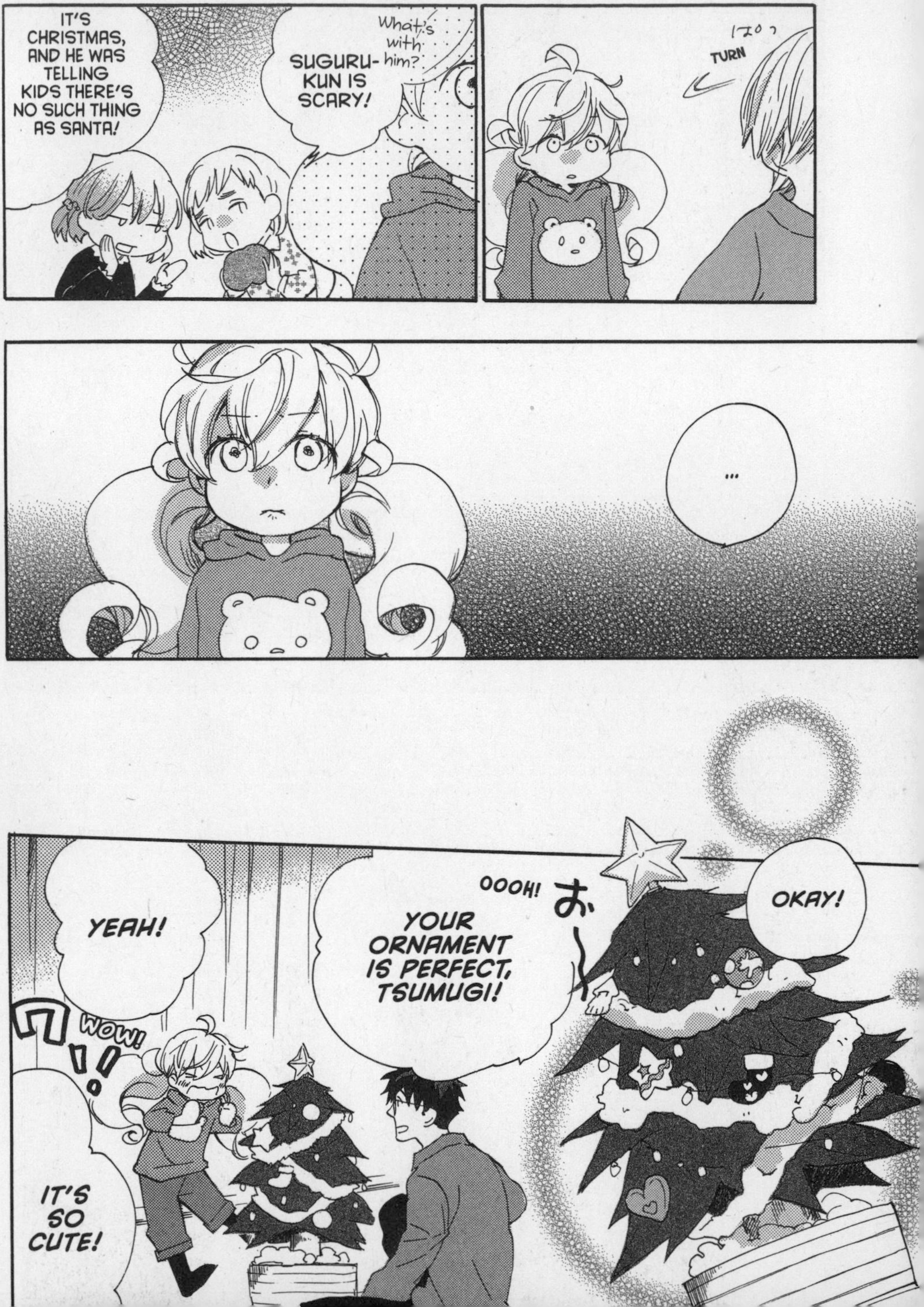
TURN
What's with him?
SUGURU-KUN IS SCARY!
IT'S CHRISTMAS, AND HE WAS TELLING KIDS THERE'S NO SUCH THING AS SANTA!
...
OKAY!
OOOH!
お〜
YOUR ORNAMENT IS PERFECT, TSUMUGI!
YEAH!
WOW!
IT'S SO CUTE!

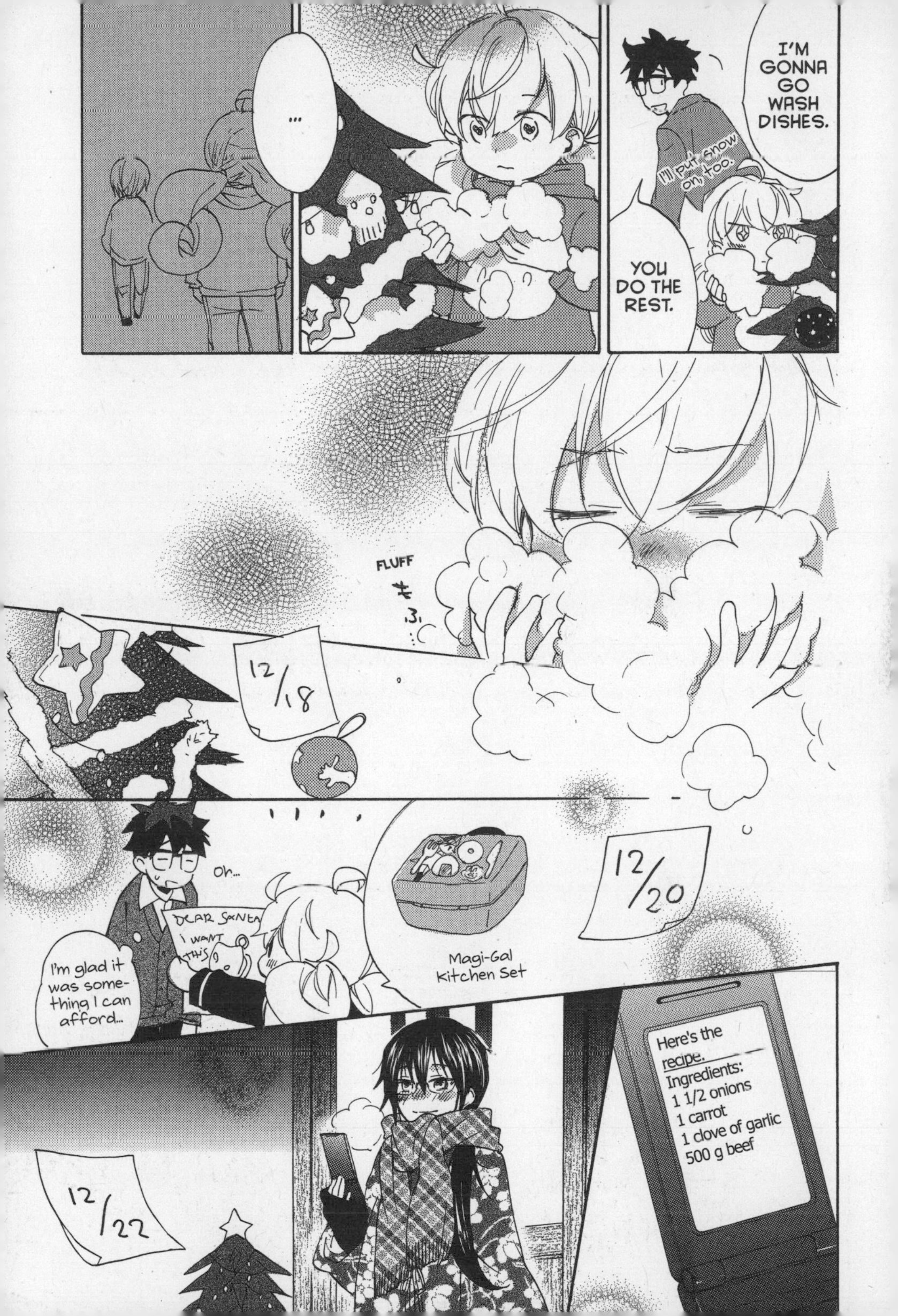
I'M GONNA GO WASH DISHES.
I'll put snow on, too.
YOU DO THE REST.
...
FLUFF
もふ
12/18
12/20
Magi-Gal Kitchen Set
Oh...
DEAR SANTA
I WANT THIS
I'm glad it was something I can afford...
Here's the recipe.
Ingredients:
1 1/2 onions
1 carrot
1 clove of garlic
500 g beef
12/22

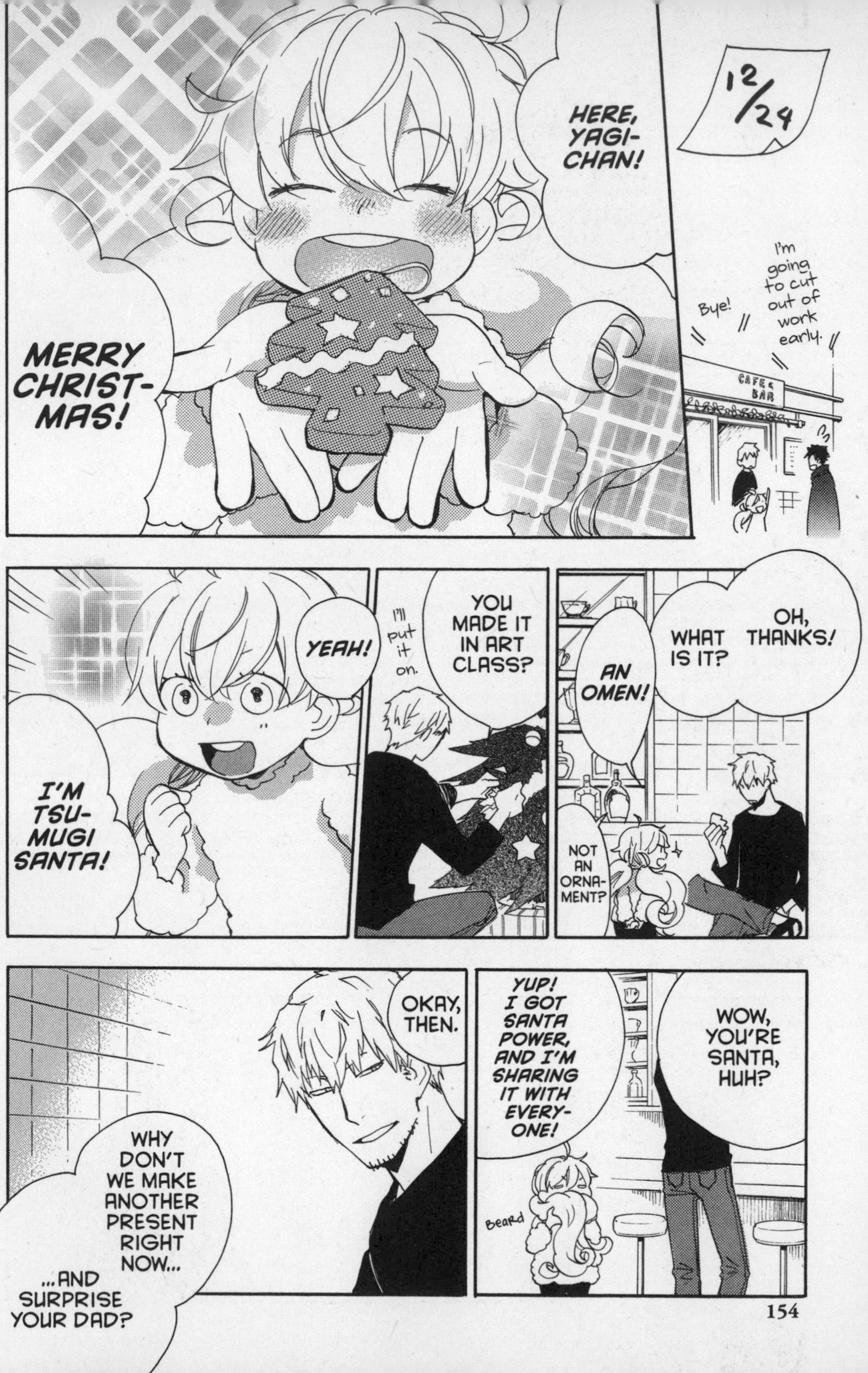
12/24
I'm going to cut out of work early.
Bye!
CAFE & BAR
HERE, YAGI-CHAN!
MERRY CHRISTMAS!
OH, THANKS!
WHAT IS IT?
AN OMEN!
NOT AN ORNAMENT?
YOU MADE IT IN ART CLASS?
I'll put it on.
YEAH!
I'M TSUMUGI SANTA!
WOW, YOU'RE SANTA, HUH?
YUP! I GOT SANTA POWER, AND I'M SHARING IT WITH EVERYONE!
Beard
OKAY, THEN.
WHY DON'T WE MAKE ANOTHER PRESENT RIGHT NOW...
...AND SURPRISE YOUR DAD?

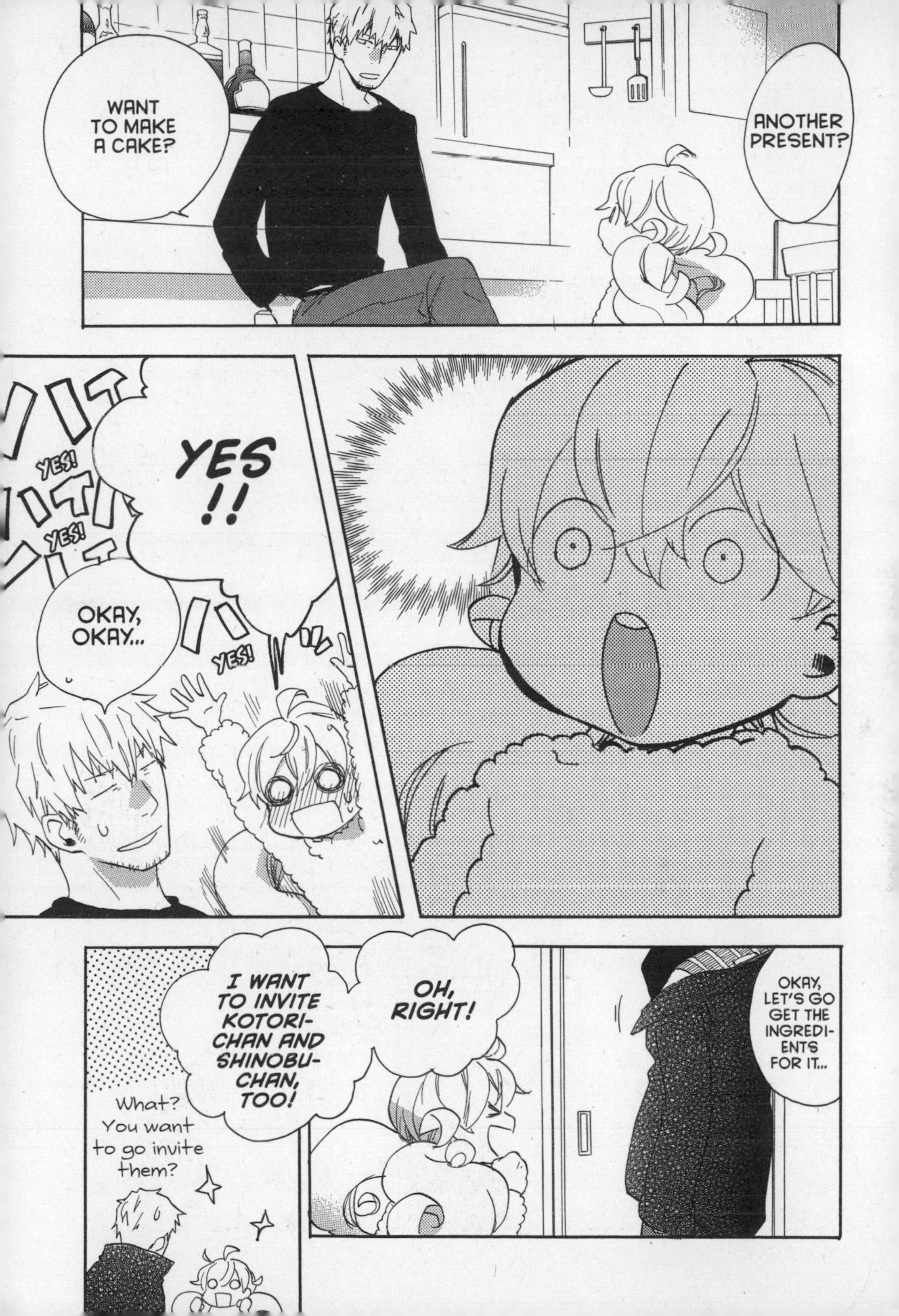
ANOTHER PRESENT?
WANT TO MAKE A CAKE?
YES !!
YES!
YES!
YES!
OKAY, OKAY...
OKAY, LET'S GO GET THE INGREDI- ENTS FOR IT...
OH, RIGHT!
I WANT TO INVITE KOTORI- CHAN AND SHINOBU- CHAN, TOO!
What? You want to go invite them?

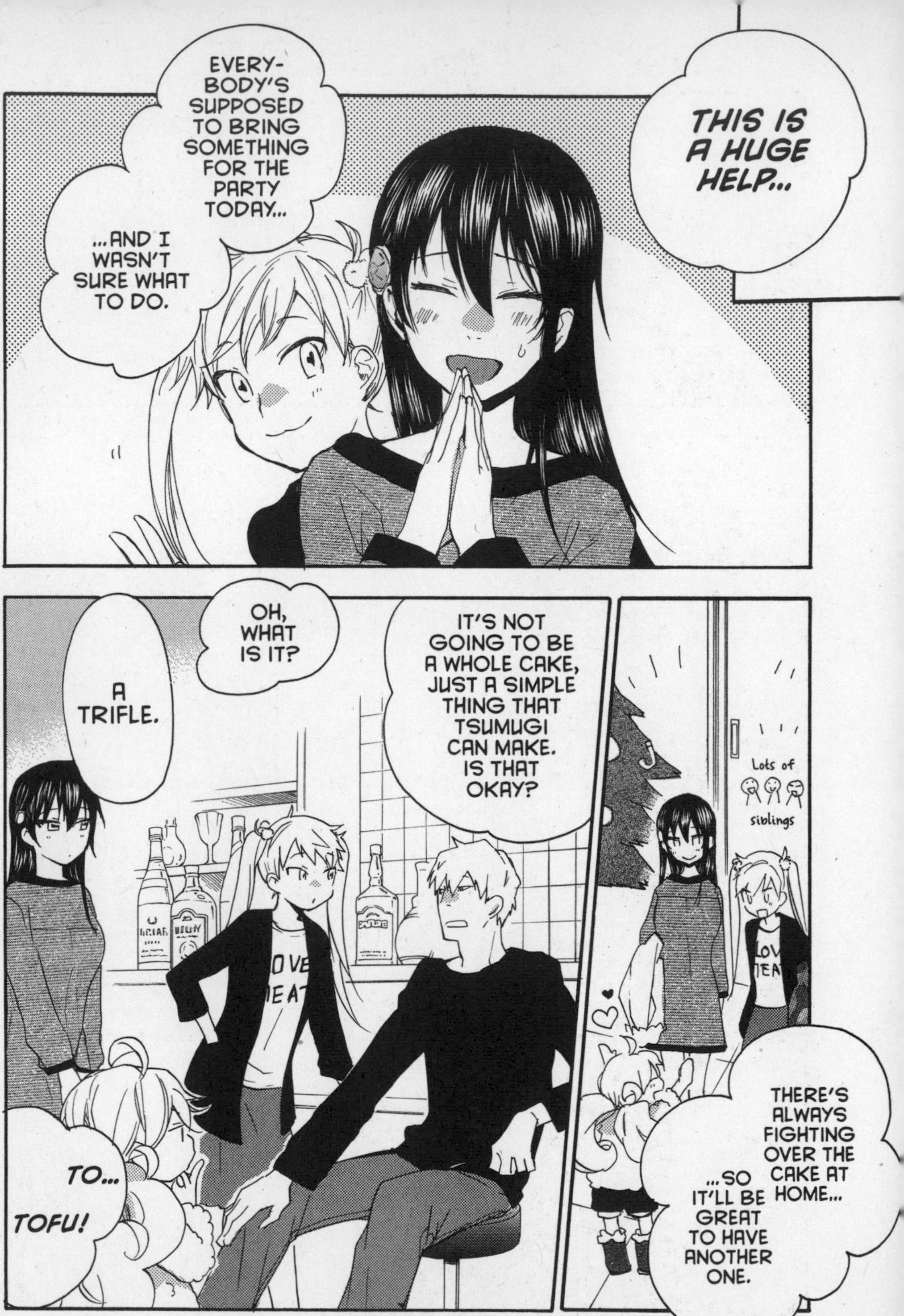
THIS IS A HUGE HELP...
EVERYBODY'S SUPPOSED TO BRING SOMETHING FOR THE PARTY TODAY...
...AND I WASN'T SURE WHAT TO DO.
Lots of siblings
THERE'S ALWAYS FIGHTING OVER THE CAKE AT HOME...
...SO IT'LL BE GREAT TO HAVE ANOTHER ONE.
IT'S NOT GOING TO BE A WHOLE CAKE, JUST A SIMPLE THING THAT TSUMUGI CAN MAKE. IS THAT OKAY?
OH, WHAT IS IT?
A TRIFLE.
TO... TOFU!

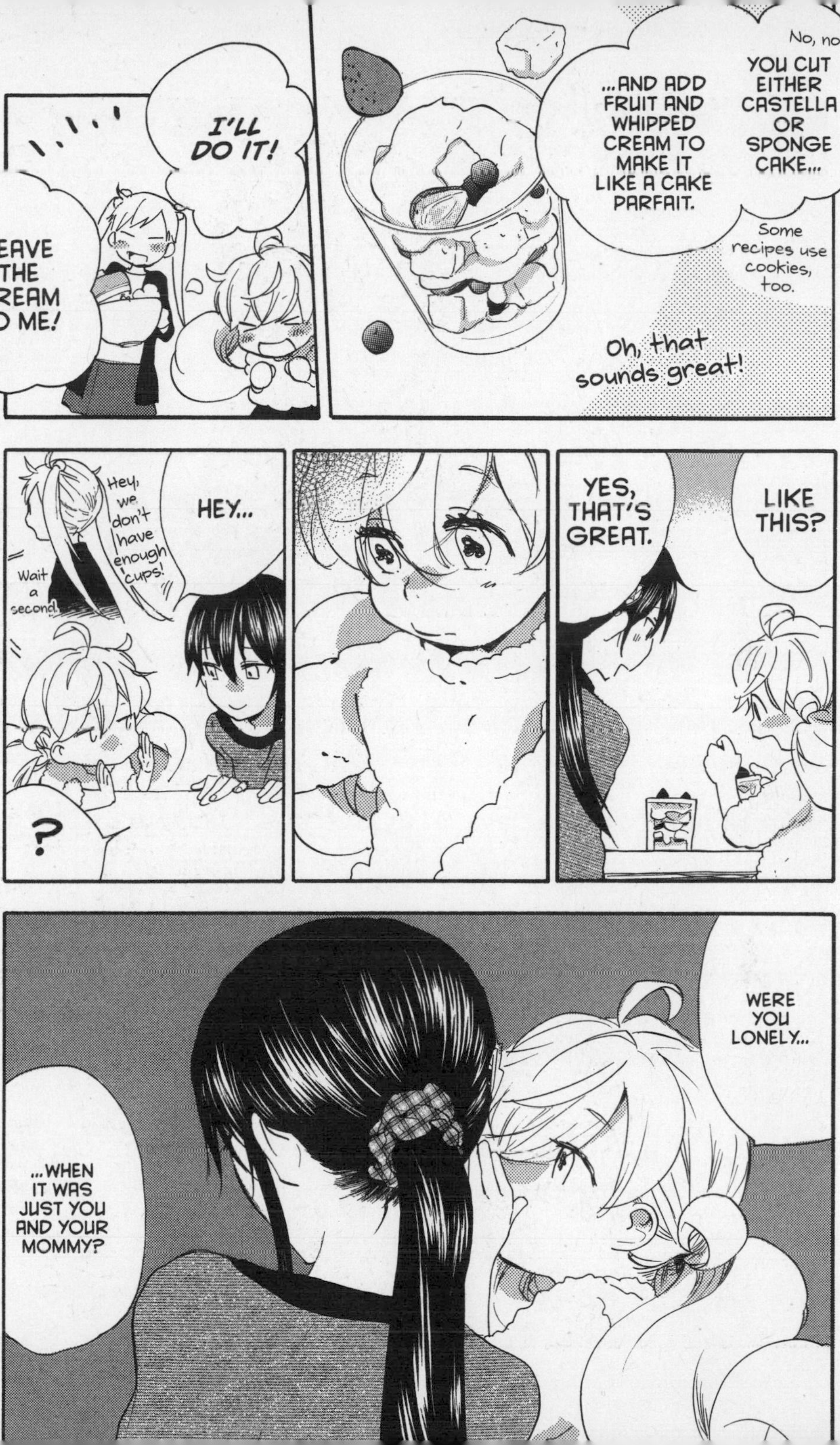
No, no.
YOU CUT EITHER CASTELLA OR SPONGE CAKE...
...AND ADD FRUIT AND WHIPPED CREAM TO MAKE IT LIKE A CAKE PARFAIT.
Some recipes use cookies, too.
Oh, that sounds great!
I'LL DO IT!
LEAVE THE CREAM TO ME!
LIKE THIS?
YES, THAT'S GREAT.
HEY...
Hey, we don't have enough cups!
Wait a second.
?
WERE YOU LONELY...
...WHEN IT WAS JUST YOU AND YOUR MOMMY?

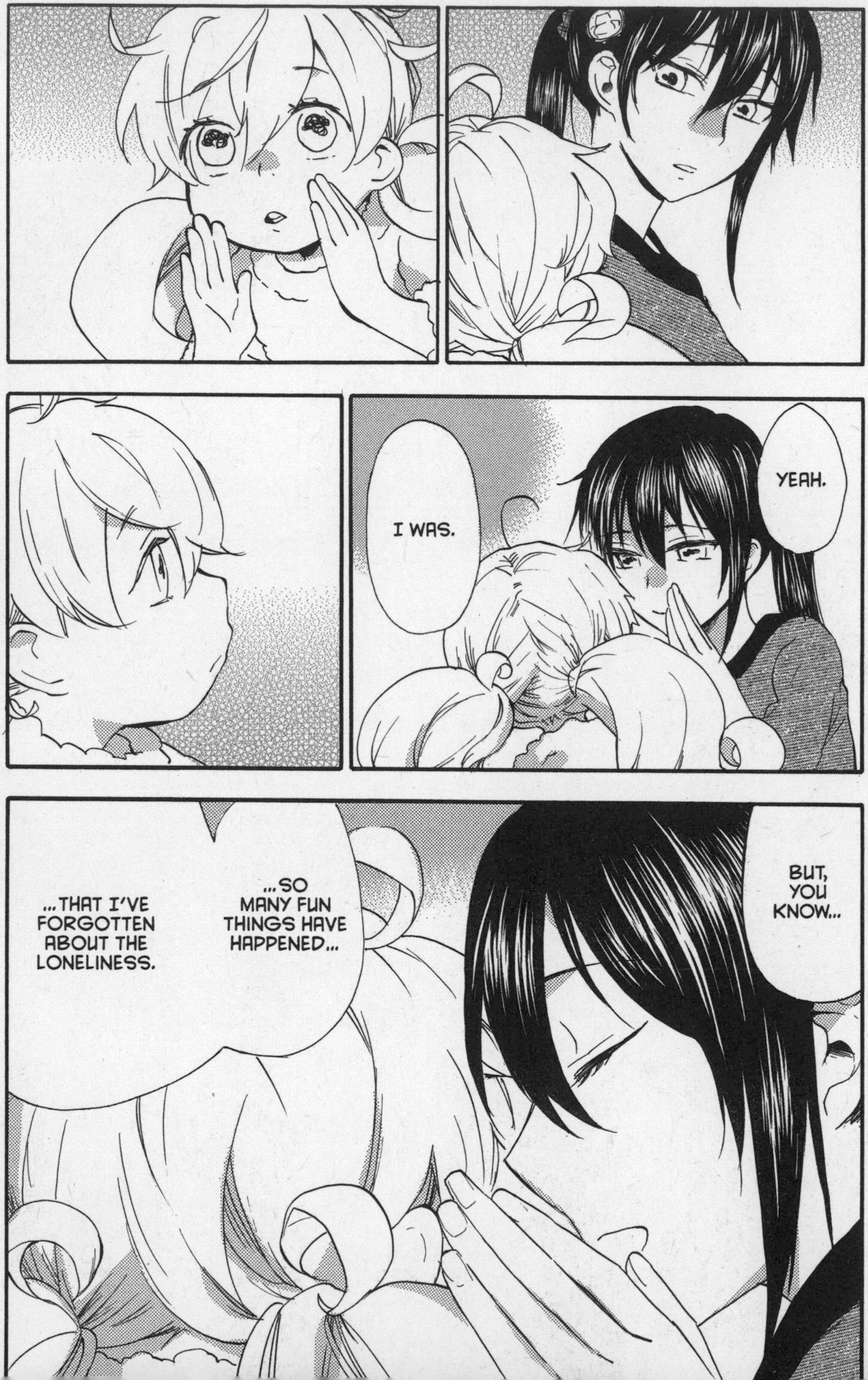
YEAH.
I WAS.
BUT, YOU KNOW...
...SO MANY FUN THINGS HAVE HAPPENED...
...THAT I'VE FORGOTTEN ABOUT THE LONELINESS.

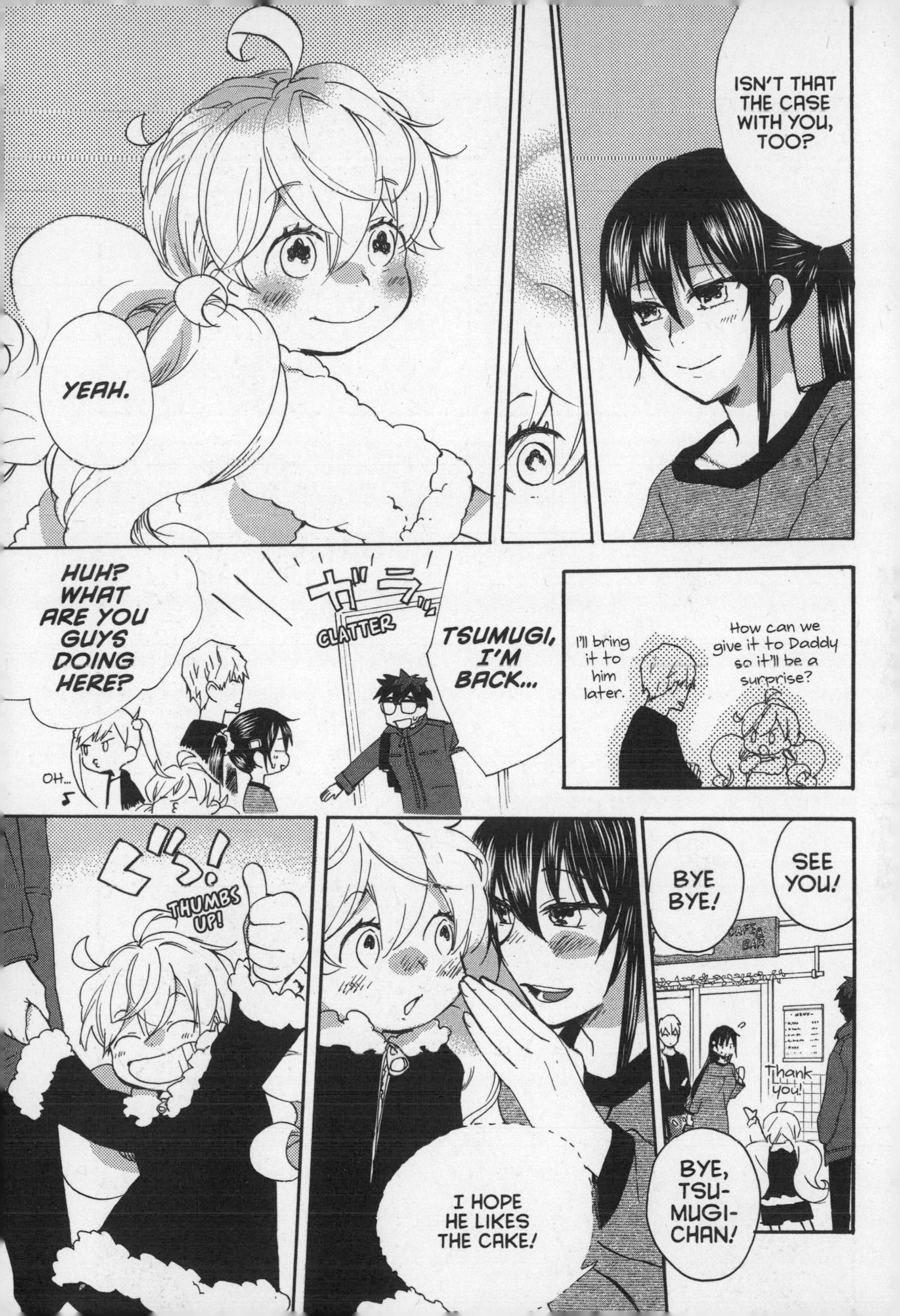
ISN'T THAT THE CASE WITH YOU, TOO?
YEAH.
How can we give it to Daddy so it'll be a surprise?
I'll bring it to him later.
TSUMUGI, I'M BACK...
CLATTER
HUH? WHAT ARE YOU GUYS DOING HERE?
OH...
SEE YOU!
BYE BYE!
CAFE & BAR
Thank you!
BYE, TSU-MUGI-CHAN!
I HOPE HE LIKES THE CAKE!
THUMBS UP!

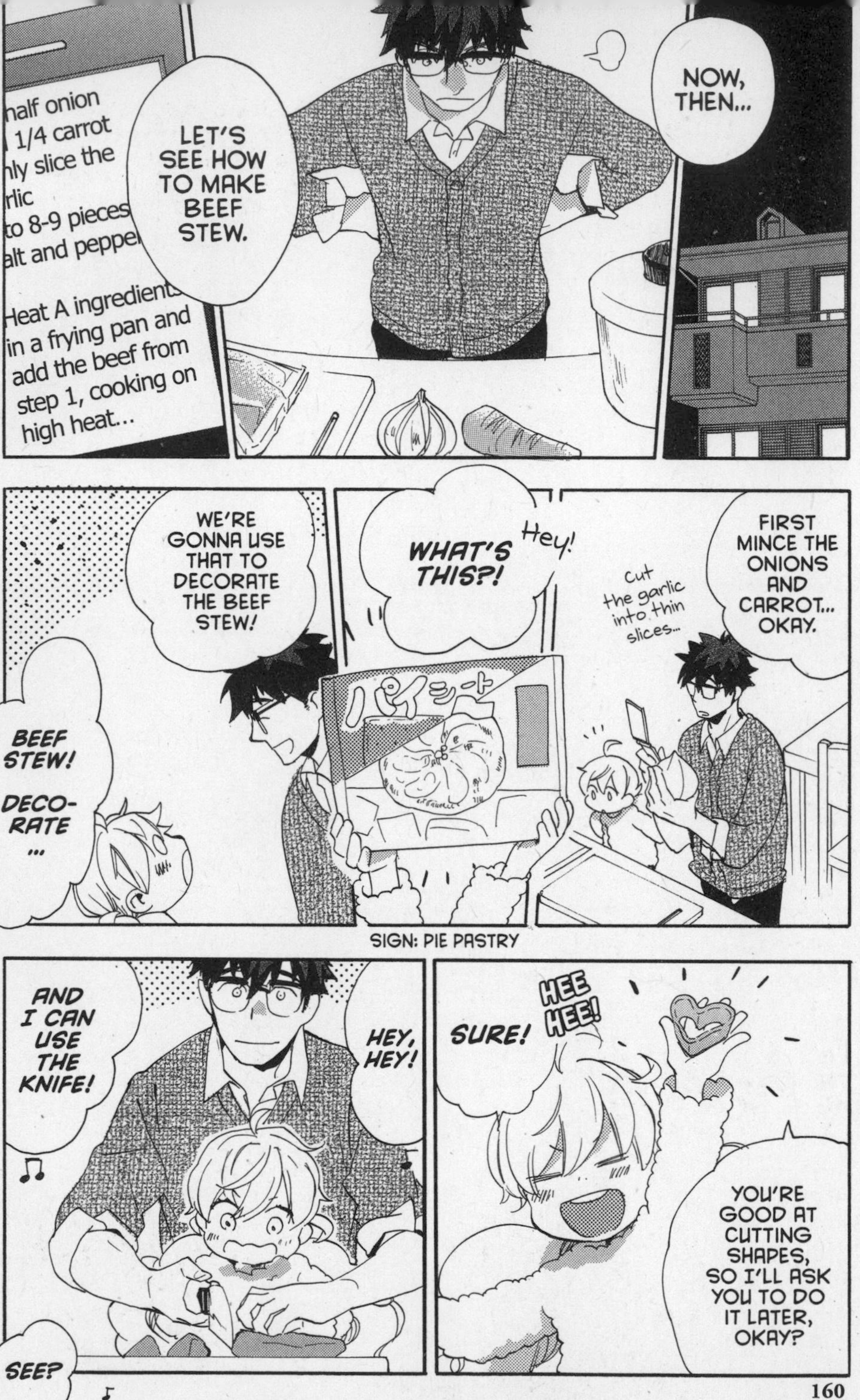
NOW, THEN...
LET'S SEE HOW TO MAKE BEEF STEW.
half onion
1/4 carrot
nly slice the
rlic
to 8-9 pieces
alt and peppe
Heat A ingredients
in a frying pan and
add the beef from
step 1, cooking on
high heat...
FIRST MINCE THE ONIONS AND CARROT... OKAY.
Cut the garlic into thin slices...
WHAT'S THIS?!
Hey!
パイシート
WE'RE GONNA USE THAT TO DECORATE THE BEEF STEW!
BEEF STEW!
DECO-RATE ...
SURE!
HEE HEE!
YOU'RE GOOD AT CUTTING SHAPES, SO I'LL ASK YOU TO DO IT LATER, OKAY?
HEY, HEY!
AND I CAN USE THE KNIFE!
SEE?

SIGN: PIE PASTRY

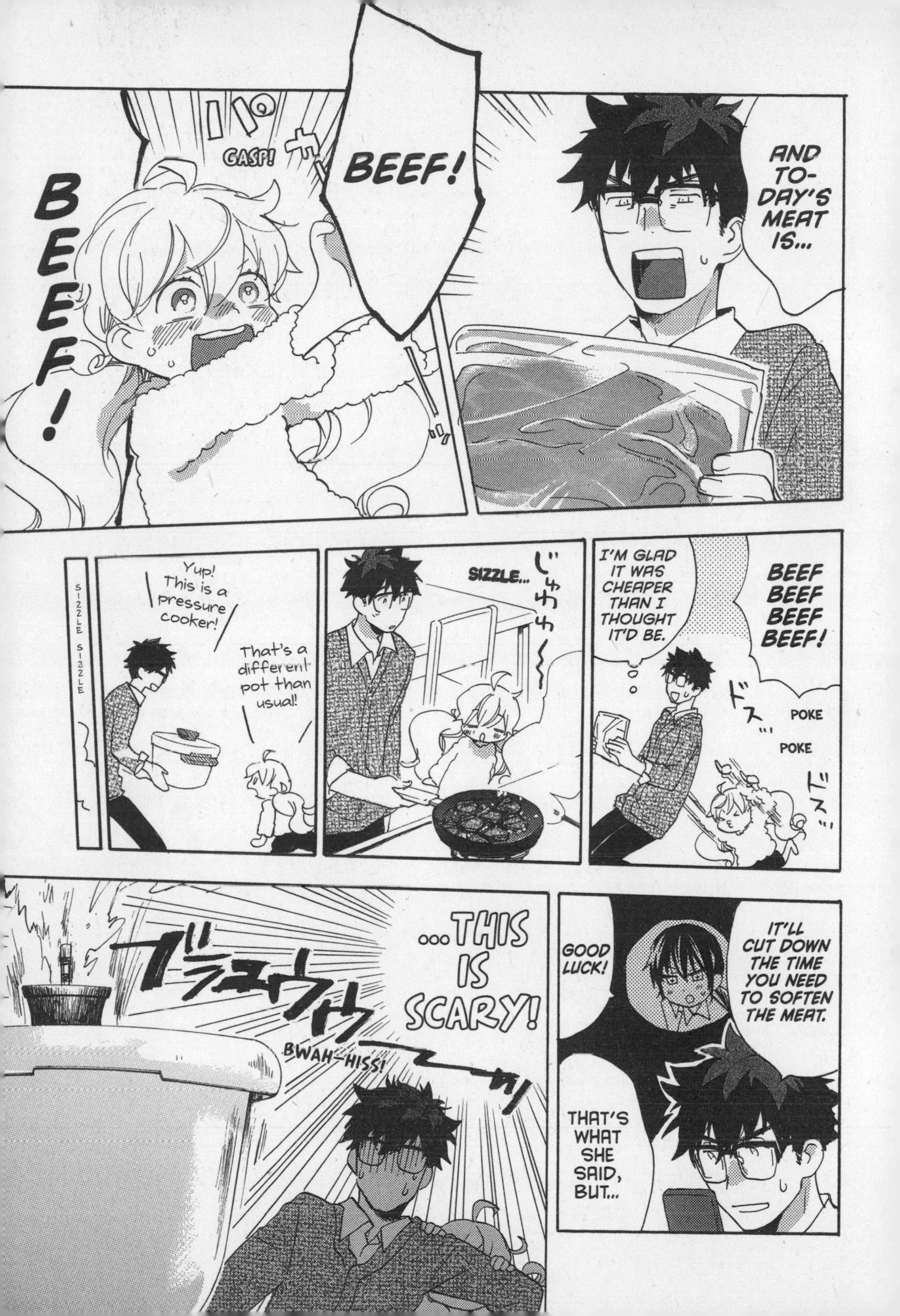
AND TO-DAY'S MEAT IS...
BEEF!
GASP!
BEEF!
I'M GLAD IT WAS CHEAPER THAN I THOUGHT IT'D BE.
BEEF BEEF BEEF BEEF!
POKE
POKE
SIZZLE...
SIZZLE SIZZLE
Yup! This is a pressure cooker!
That's a different pot than usual!
IT'LL CUT DOWN THE TIME YOU NEED TO SOFTEN THE MEAT.
GOOD LUCK!
THAT'S WHAT SHE SAID, BUT...
...THIS IS SCARY!
BWAH-HISS!

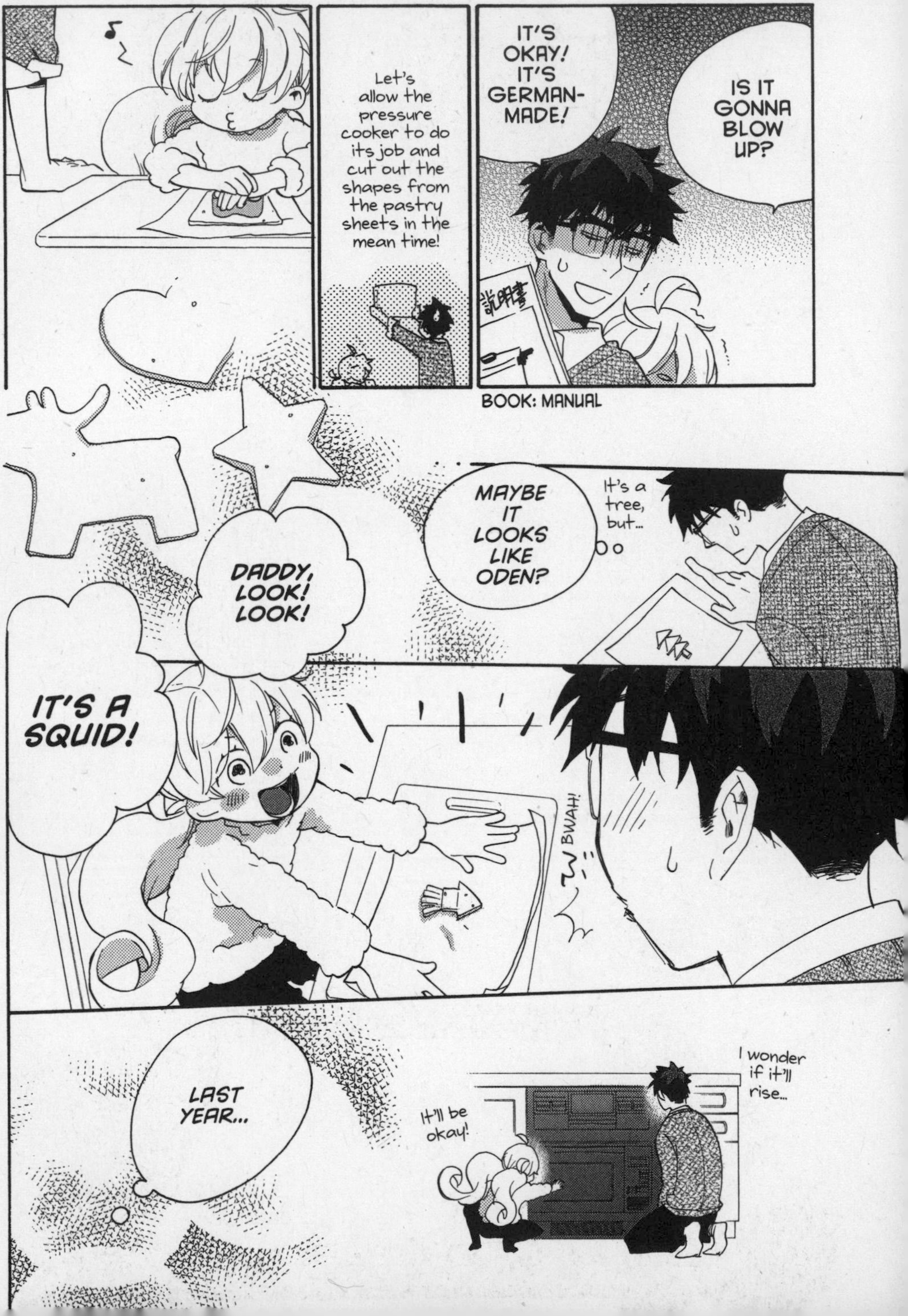
IS IT GONNA BLOW UP?
IT'S OKAY! IT'S GERMAN-MADE!
説明書
BOOK: MANUAL
Let's allow the pressure cooker to do its job and cut out the shapes from the pastry sheets in the mean time!
It's a tree, but...
MAYBE IT LOOKS LIKE ODEN?
DADDY, LOOK! LOOK!
IT'S A SQUID!
BWAH!
I wonder if it'll rise...
It'll be okay!
LAST YEAR...

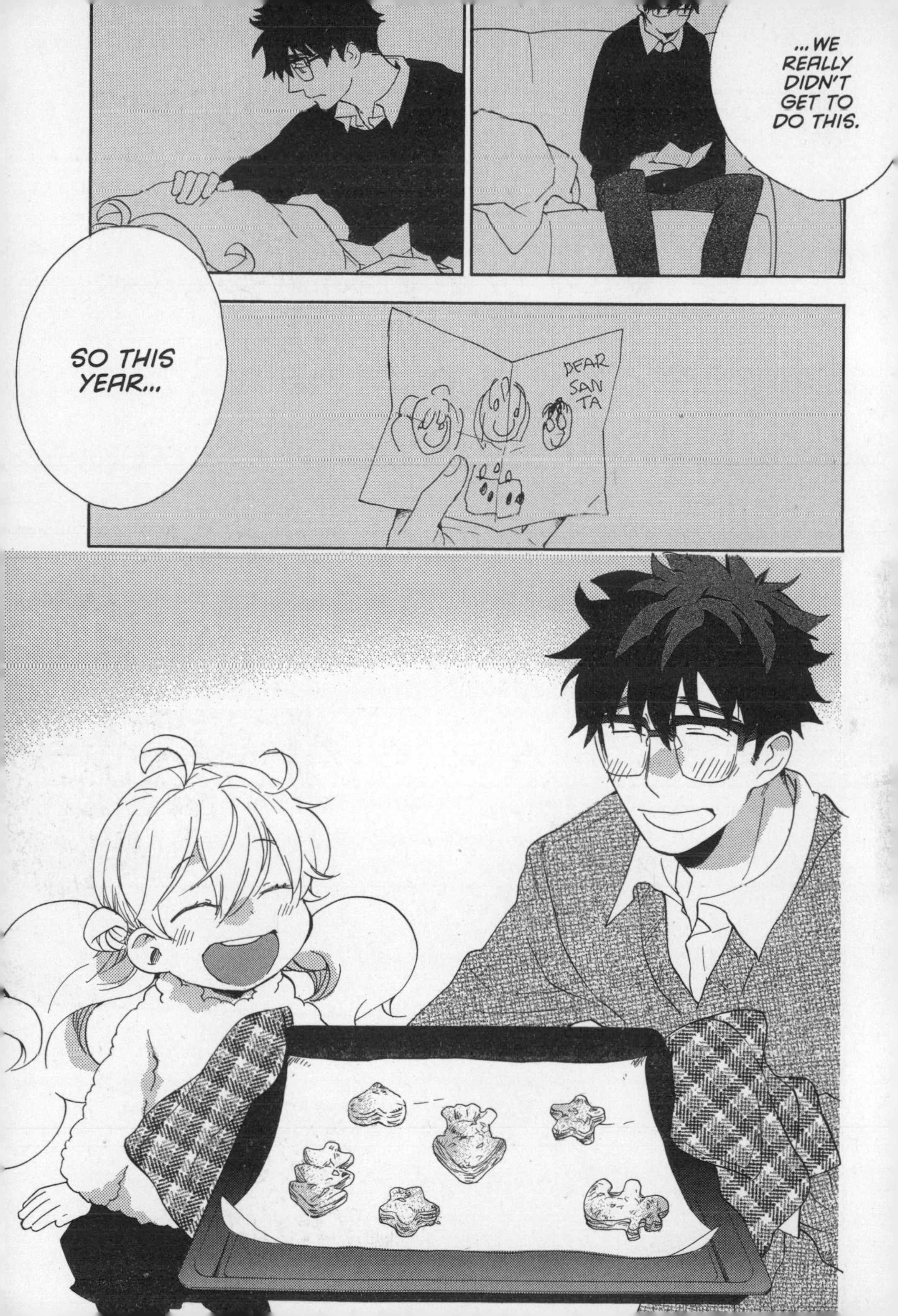
...WE REALLY DIDN'T GET TO DO THIS.
SO THIS YEAR...
DEAR SAN TA

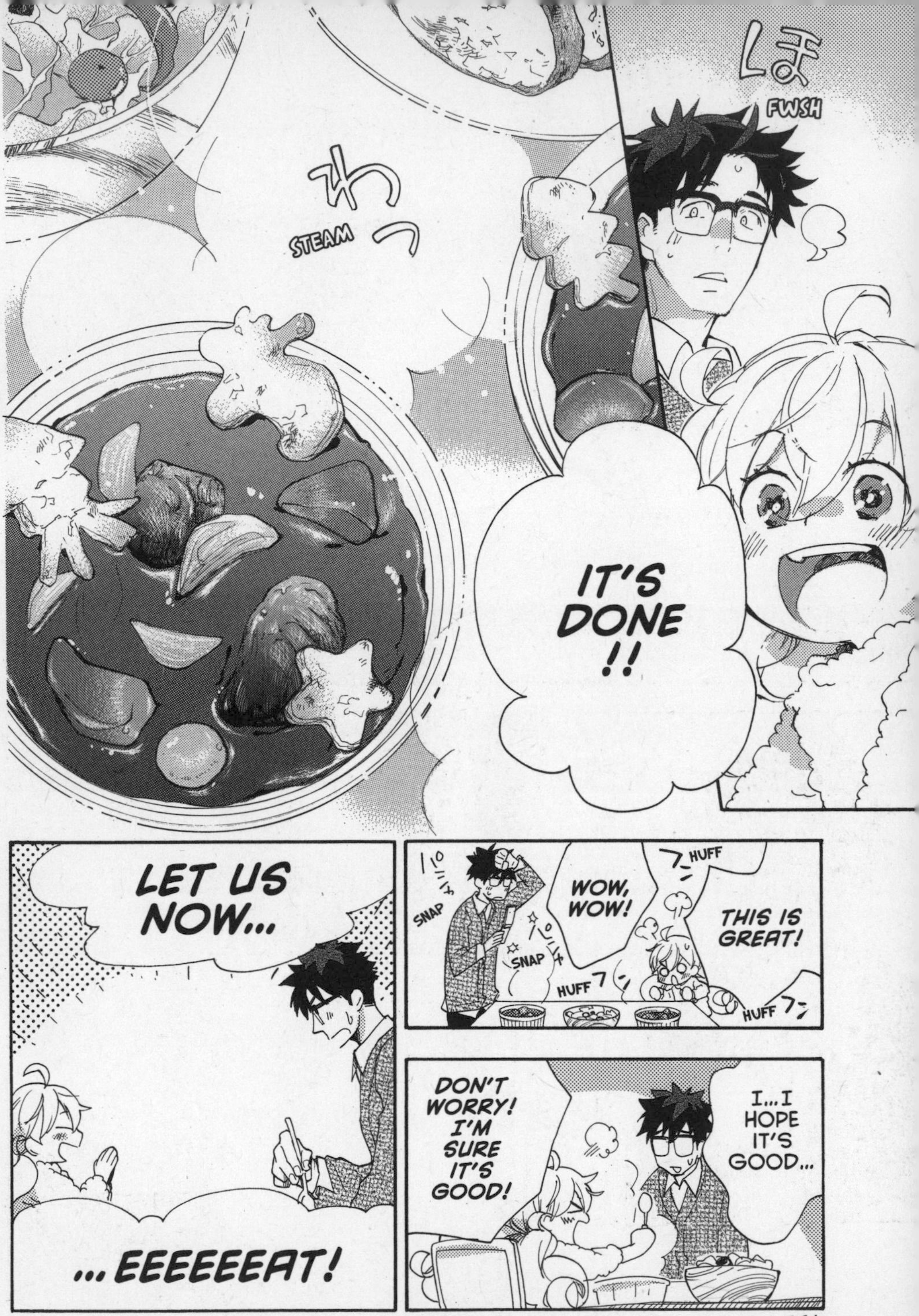
しま
FWSH
わっ
STEAM
IT'S DONE!!
HUFF
WOW, WOW!
THIS IS GREAT!
SNAP
SNAP
HUFF
HUFF
I...I HOPE IT'S GOOD...
DON'T WORRY! I'M SURE IT'S GOOD!
LET US NOW...
...EEEEEEAT!

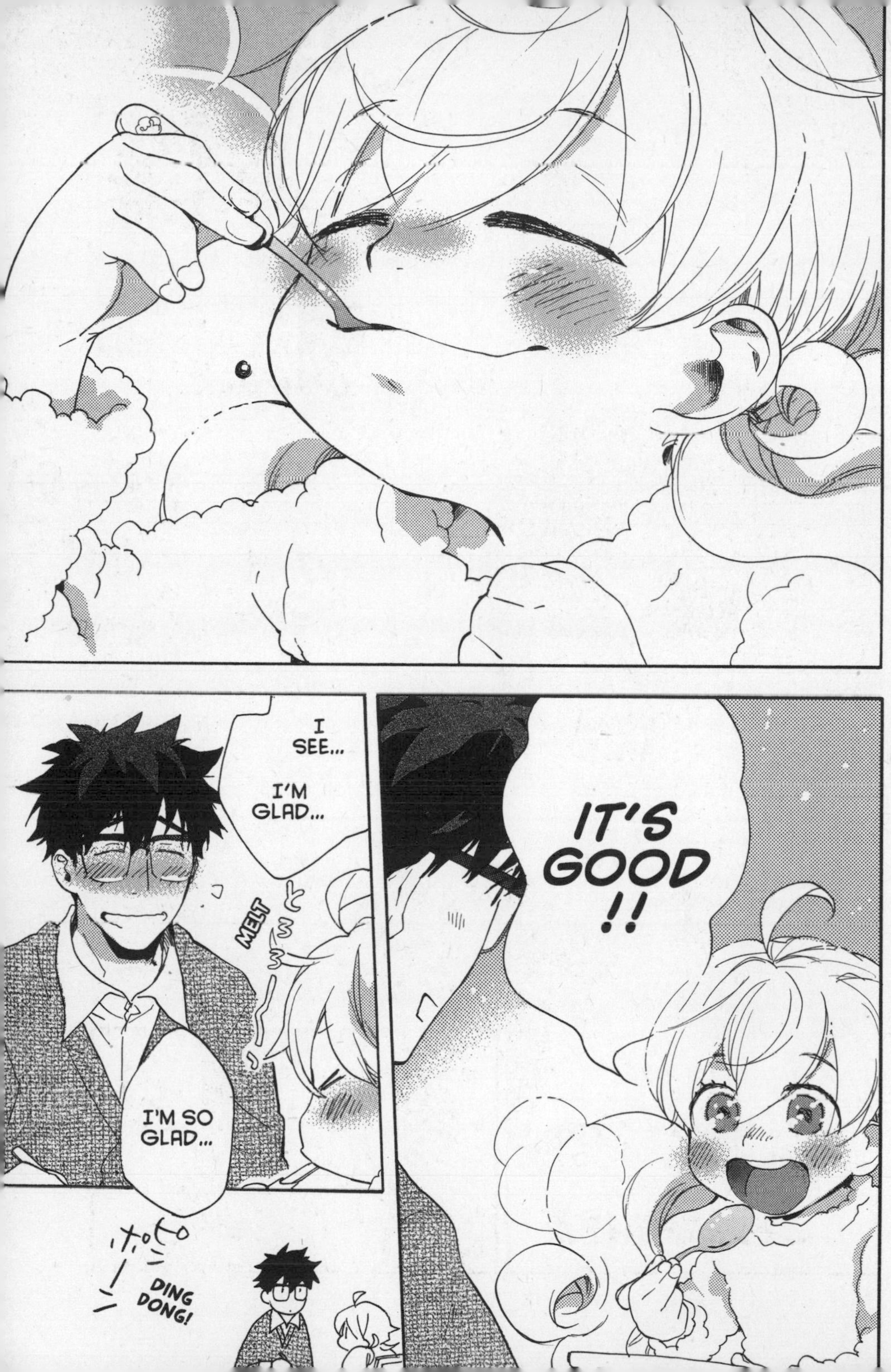
IT'S GOOD!!
I SEE...
I'M GLAD...
MELT
I'M SO GLAD...
DING DONG!

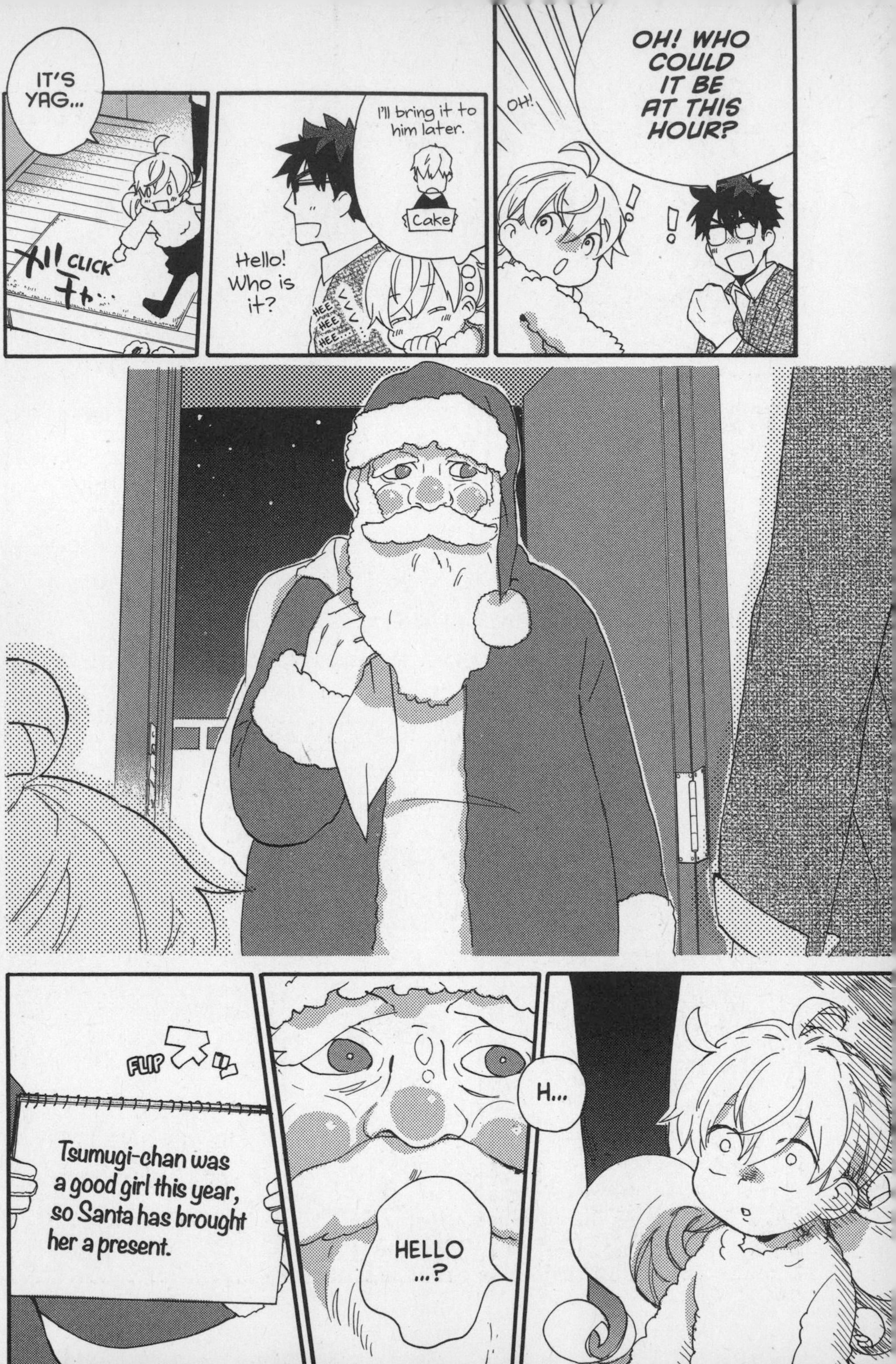
OH! WHO COULD IT BE AT THIS HOUR?
OH!
!
!
I'll bring it to him later.
Cake
Hello! Who is it?
HEE HEE HEE...
IT'S YAG...
CLICK
H...
HELLO ...?
FLIP
Tsumugi-chan was a good girl this year, so Santa has brought her a present.

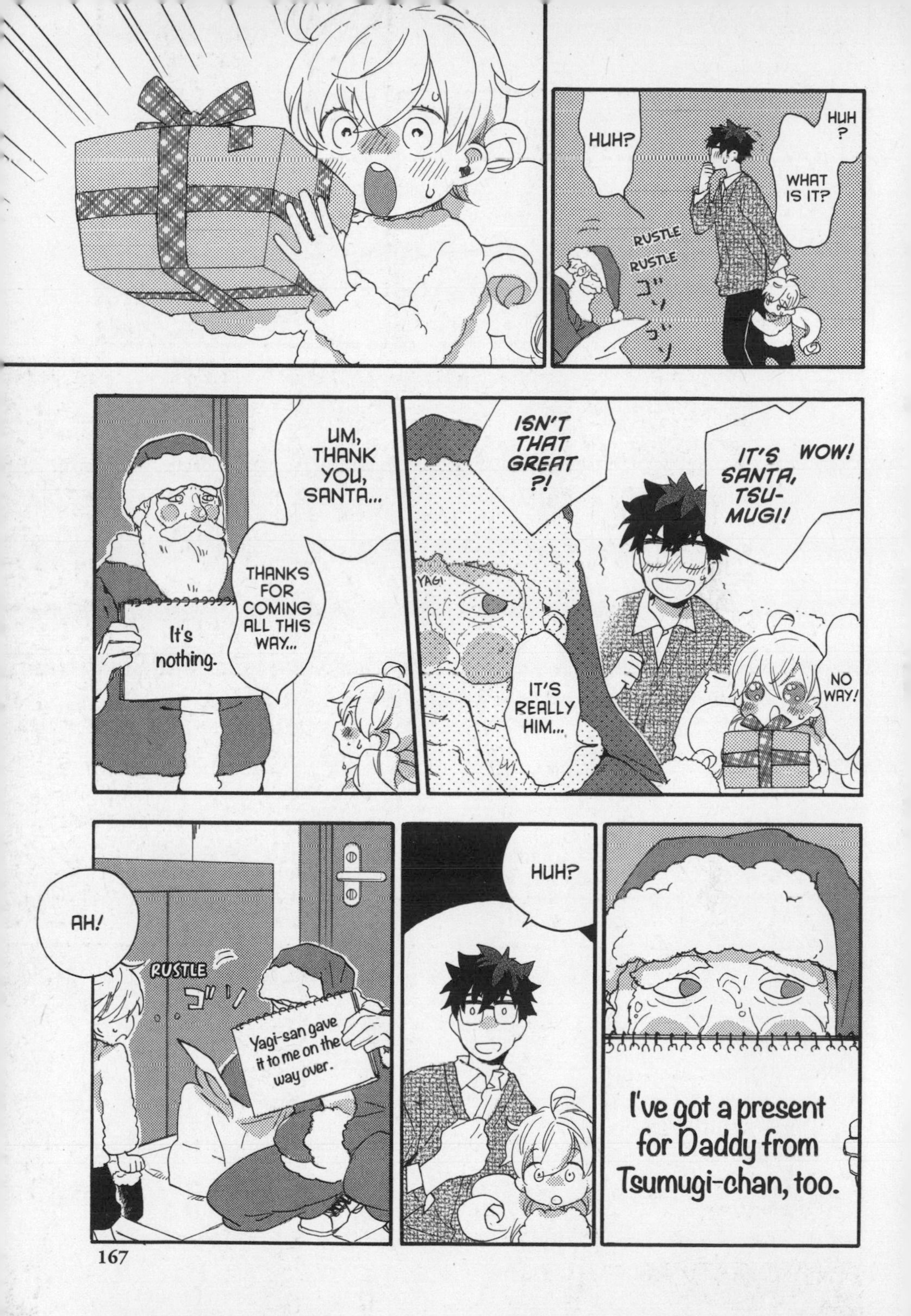
HUH ?
WHAT IS IT?
HUH?
RUSTLE
RUSTLE
ゴソゴソ
WOW!
IT'S SANTA, TSUMUGI!
ISN'T THAT GREAT ?!
NO WAY!
IT'S REALLY HIM...
YAGI
UM, THANK YOU, SANTA...
THANKS FOR COMING ALL THIS WAY...
It's nothing.
I've got a present for Daddy from Tsumugi-chan, too.
HUH?
AH!
RUSTLE
ゴソ
Yagi-san gave it to me on the way over.

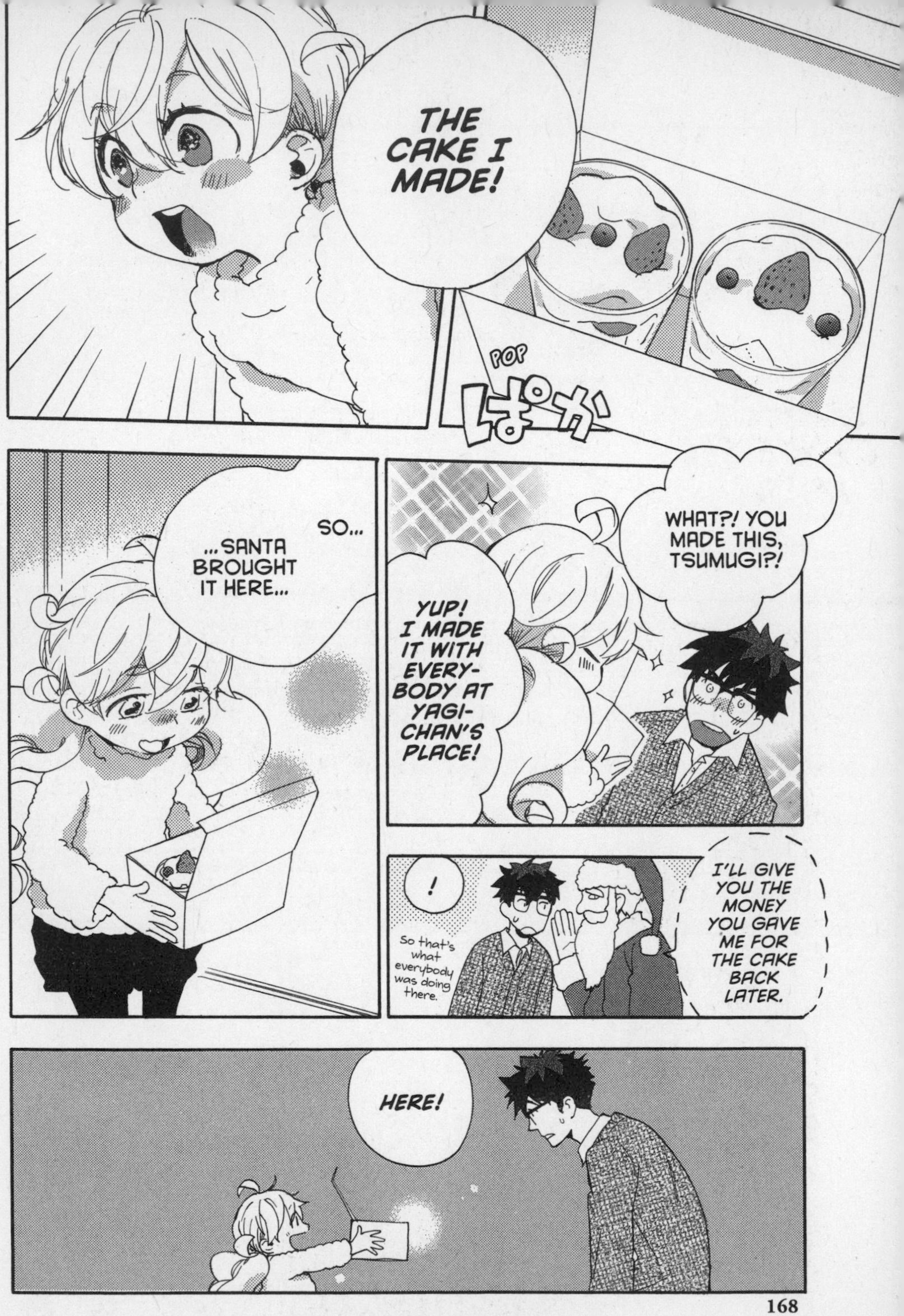
POP
ぱか
THE CAKE I MADE!
WHAT?! YOU MADE THIS, TSUMUGI?!
YUP! I MADE IT WITH EVERY-BODY AT YAGI-CHAN'S PLACE!
I'LL GIVE YOU THE MONEY YOU GAVE ME FOR THE CAKE BACK LATER.
!
So that's what everybody was doing there.
SO...
...SANTA BROUGHT IT HERE...
HERE!

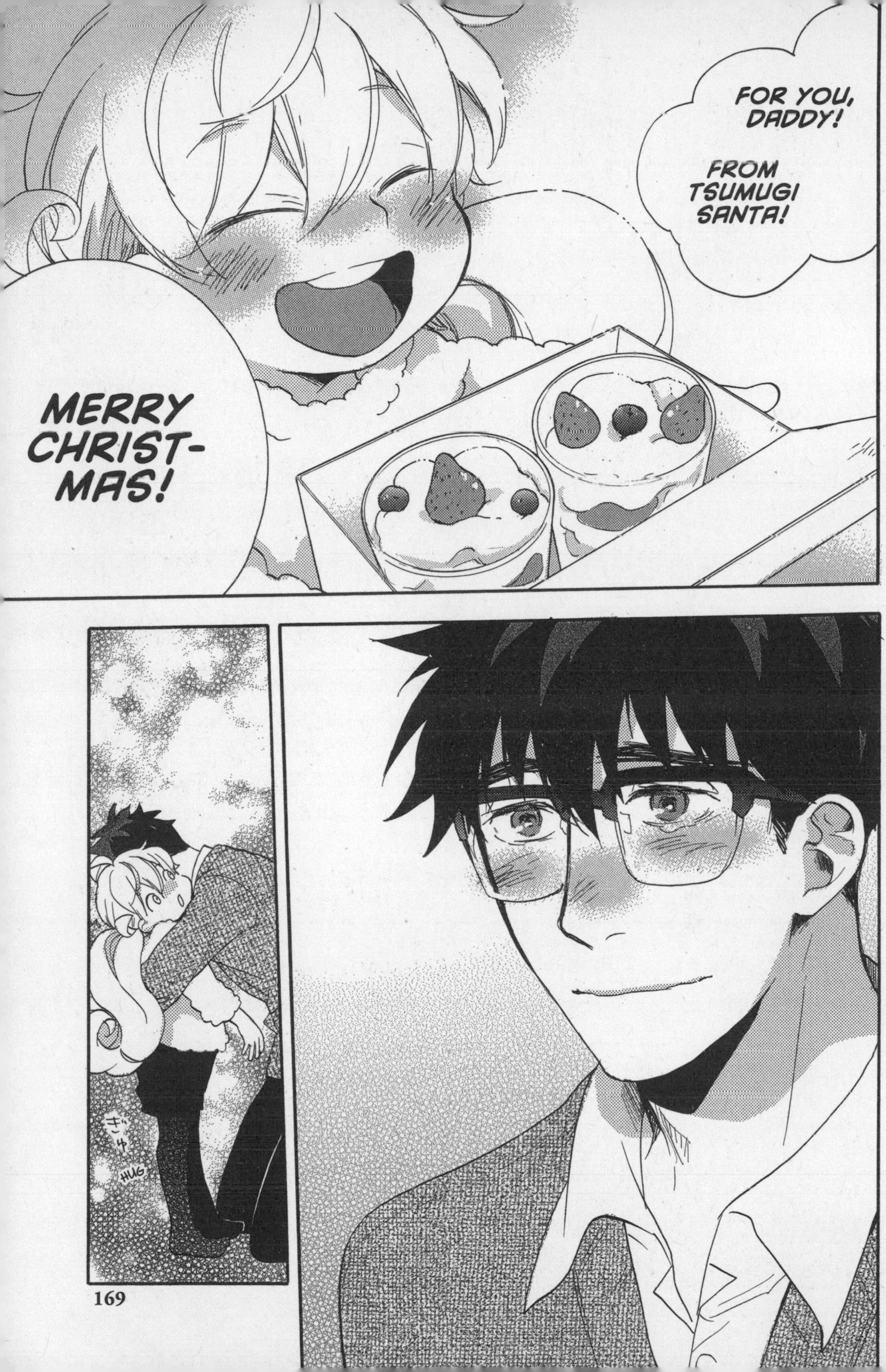
FOR YOU, DADDY!
FROM TSUMUGI SANTA!
MERRY CHRIST-MAS!
ぎゅ
HUG

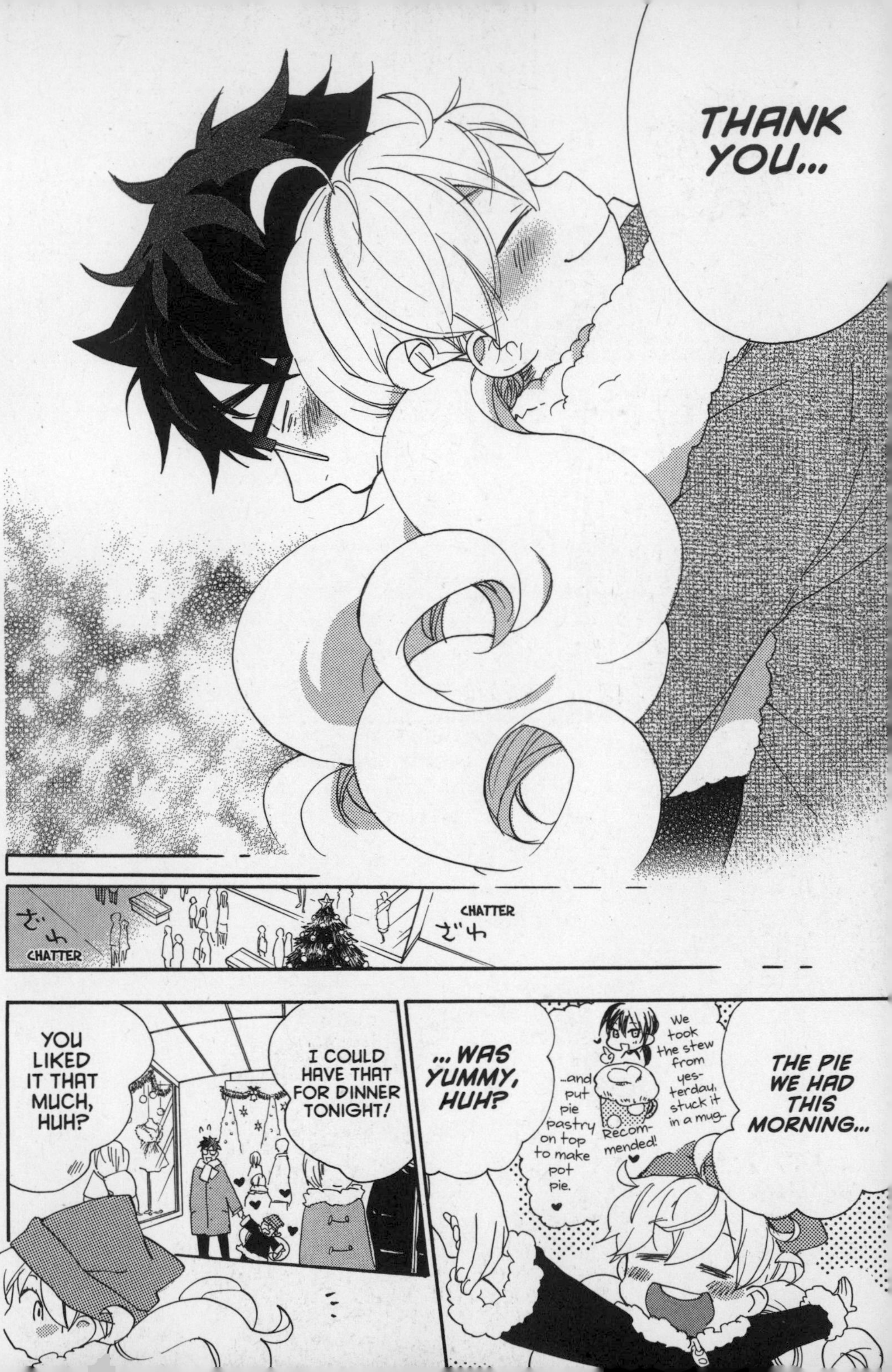
THANK YOU...
CHATTER
ざわ
ざわ
CHATTER
THE PIE WE HAD THIS MORNING...
We took the stew from yes-terday, stuck it in a mug...
...and put pie pastry on top to make pot pie.
Recom-mended!
...WAS YUMMY, HUH?
I COULD HAVE THAT FOR DINNER TONIGHT!
YOU LIKED IT THAT MUCH, HUH?

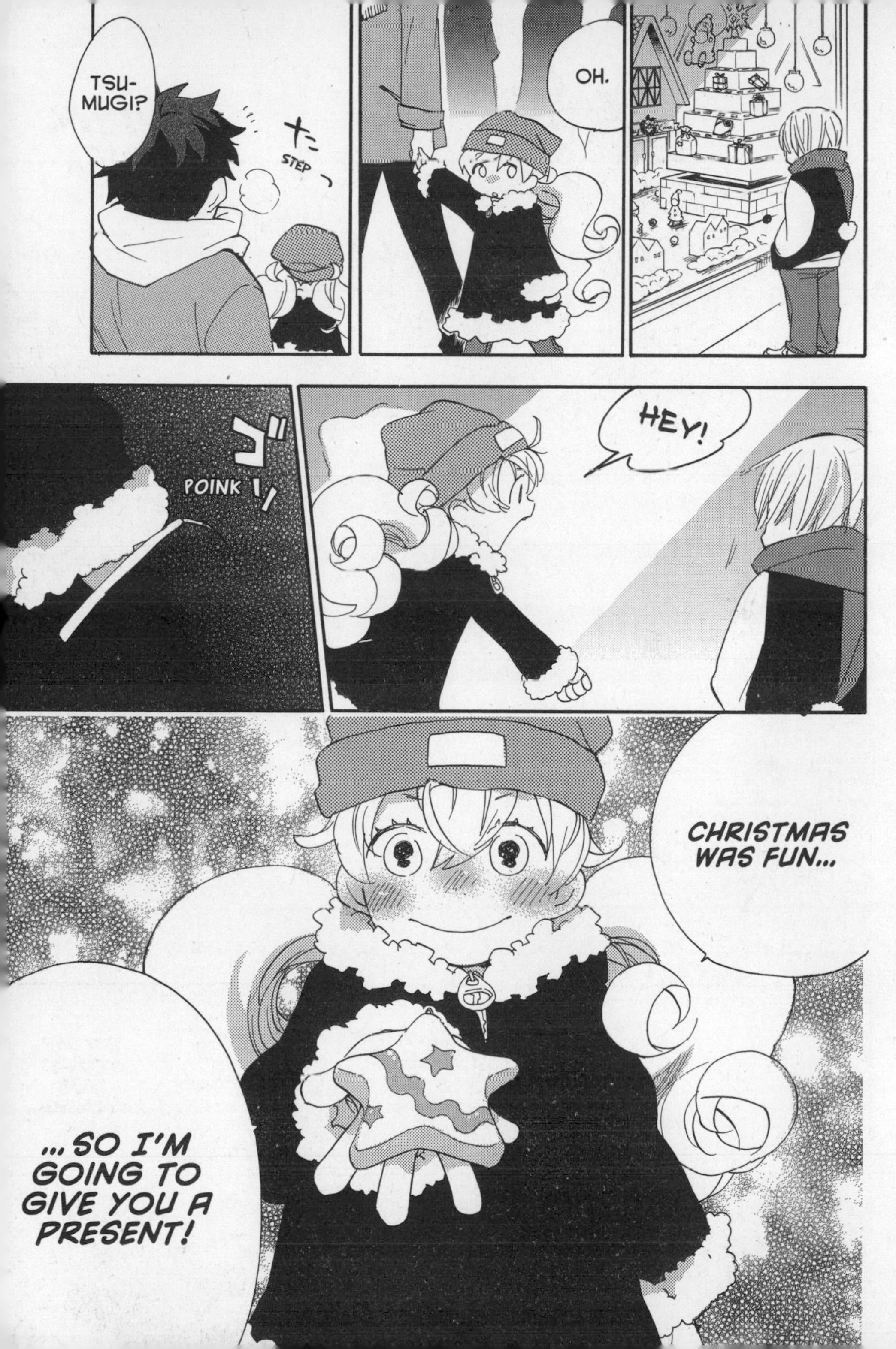
OH.
TSU-MUGI?
STEP
HEY!
POINK
CHRISTMAS WAS FUN...
...SO I'M GOING TO GIVE YOU A PRESENT!

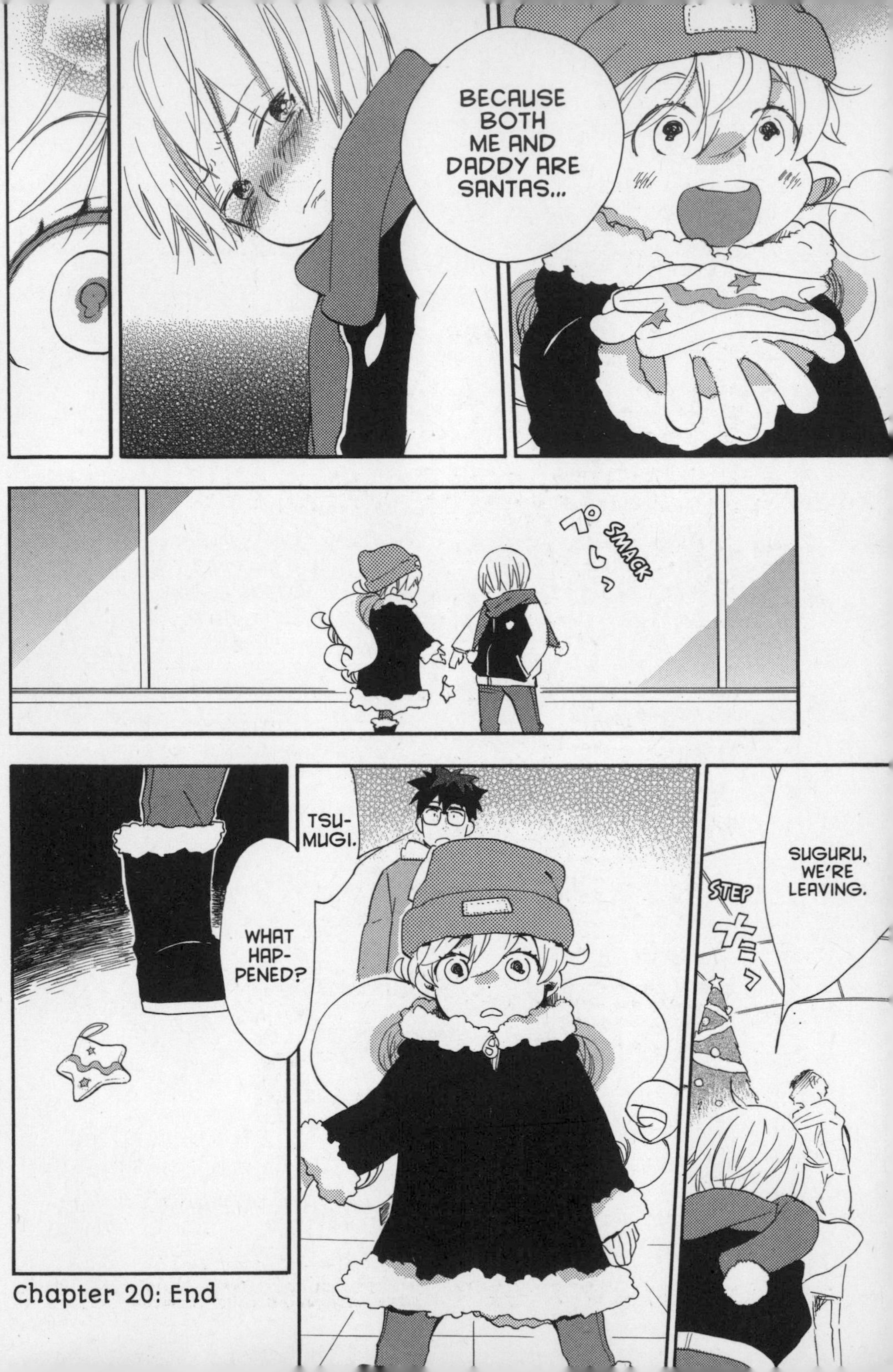
BECAUSE BOTH ME AND DADDY ARE SANTAS...
SMACK
STEP
SUGURU, WE'RE LEAVING.
TSU-MUGI.
WHAT HAP-PENED?

Chapter 20: End

BA-DUM BA-DUM ドキドキ!

BEEF STEW

☆ Ingredients ☆ (serves 3)

1½ onions 1 carrot 1 clove garlic 500 g beef flank (steak)

Some salt and pepper 200 cc red wine 6 mushrooms

Ⓐ 10 g butter ½ Tbsp vegetable oil

Ⓑ 200 cc water 150 g canned tomatoes 1 can demi-glace sauce ½ tsp salt
Bouquet garni (one piece each of celery and parsley, and one bay leaf tied with a string)

Ⓒ 10 g butter ½ Tbsp vegetable oil

Steps

1. Mince 1/2 of an onion and 1/4 of the carrot. Thinly slice the garlic. Cut the beef into 8 or 9 even portions and season with salt and pepper.
2. Heat A ingredients in a frying pan and add the beef from step 1. Sear the meat on high heat. Once all sides are browned, take it out and transfer to a pressure cooker.
3. Use the oil remaining in the frying pan from step 2 to fry the onion, carrot, and garlic from step 1. Once the onion is caramelized, add the red wine. Scrape any burnt parts off the pan and add them and the soup to the pressure cooker mentioned in step 2.
4. Turn on the pressure cooker and, once the soup comes to a boil, turn to low heat and simmer 3-4 minutes. Add the ingredients from Group B and cover with the lid.
5. Once you start to clearly hear noises from the pressure cooker, turn to medium heat and pressure cook for 15 minutes. Turn off the heat and let it sit for 15 minutes. Once that time is up, release the pressure and open the lid.
6. Cut the whole onion into wedges and chop up the remaining carrot into chunks. Wipe any dirt off the mushrooms and remove the stems.
7. Heat C ingredients in a frying pan. Add the ingredients from step 6 (first carrots, then onions) and slowly fry on low heat. Finally, add the mushrooms, and fry them as well.
8. Add ingredients from step 7 to the pressure cooker from step 5 and boil for 20-30 minutes. Season to taste and...

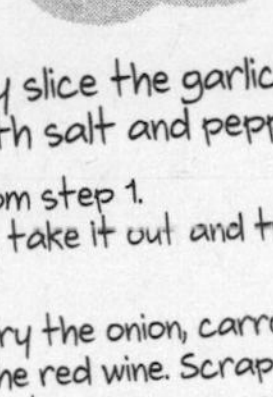
Done!

POINT Once the stew thickens up, the bottom of the pressure cooker has a tendency to burn, so stir with a spatula once in a while. Also, note that the meat will fall apart easily!

CONVERSION NOTES: 500 G BEEF FLANK = ABOUT 1.1 POUNDS, 200 CC RED WINE = JUST UNDER 1 CUP, 10 G BUTTER = JUST OVER 2 TSP, 200 CC WATER = JUST UNDER 1 CUP, 150 G CANNED TOMATOES = ABOUT 2/3 CUP OR 5.3 OZ

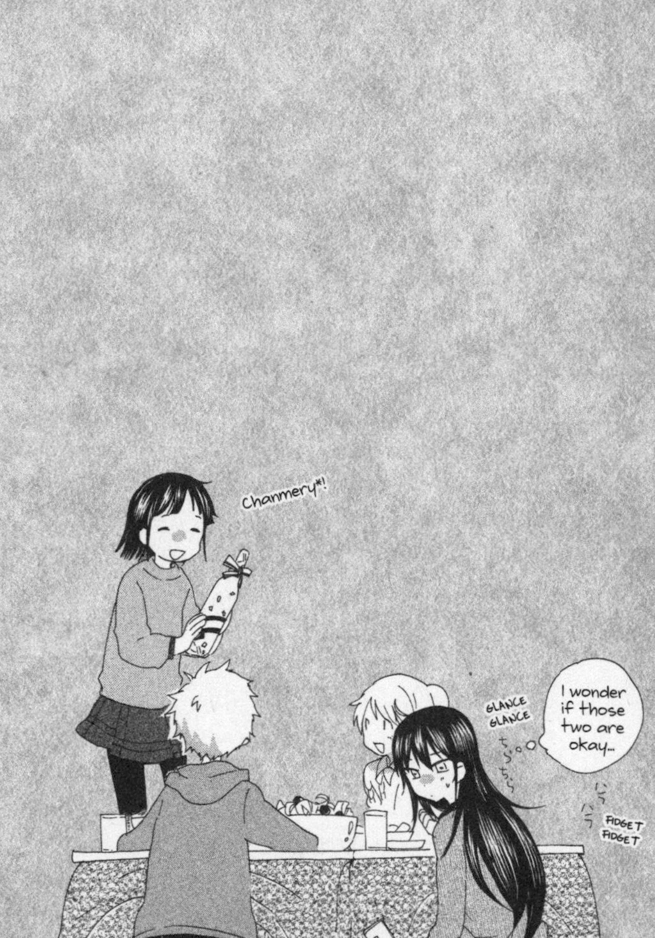
Chanmery*!
I wonder if those two are okay...
GLANCE GLANCE
FIDGET FIDGET

* A NON-ALCOHOLIC CHILDREN'S CHAMPAGNE SERVED AT CHRISTMAS.

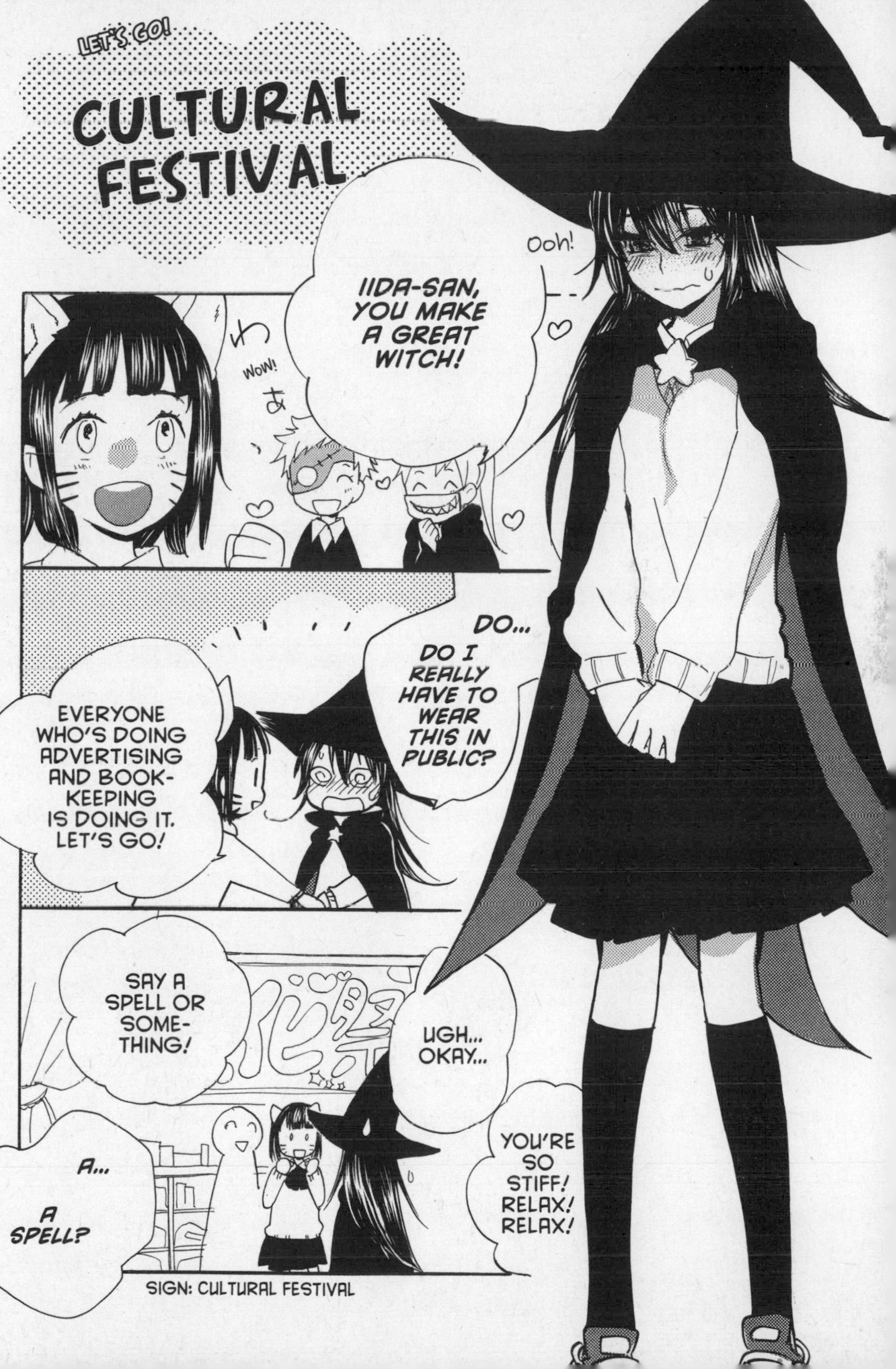
LET'S GO!
CULTURAL FESTIVAL
Ooh!
IIDA-SAN, YOU MAKE A GREAT WITCH!
わ WOW! あ
DO... DO I REALLY HAVE TO WEAR THIS IN PUBLIC?
EVERYONE WHO'S DOING ADVERTISING AND BOOK-KEEPING IS DOING IT. LET'S GO!
UGH... OKAY...
SAY A SPELL OR SOME-THING!
YOU'RE SO STIFF! RELAX! RELAX!
A... A SPELL?
SIGN: CULTURAL FESTIVAL

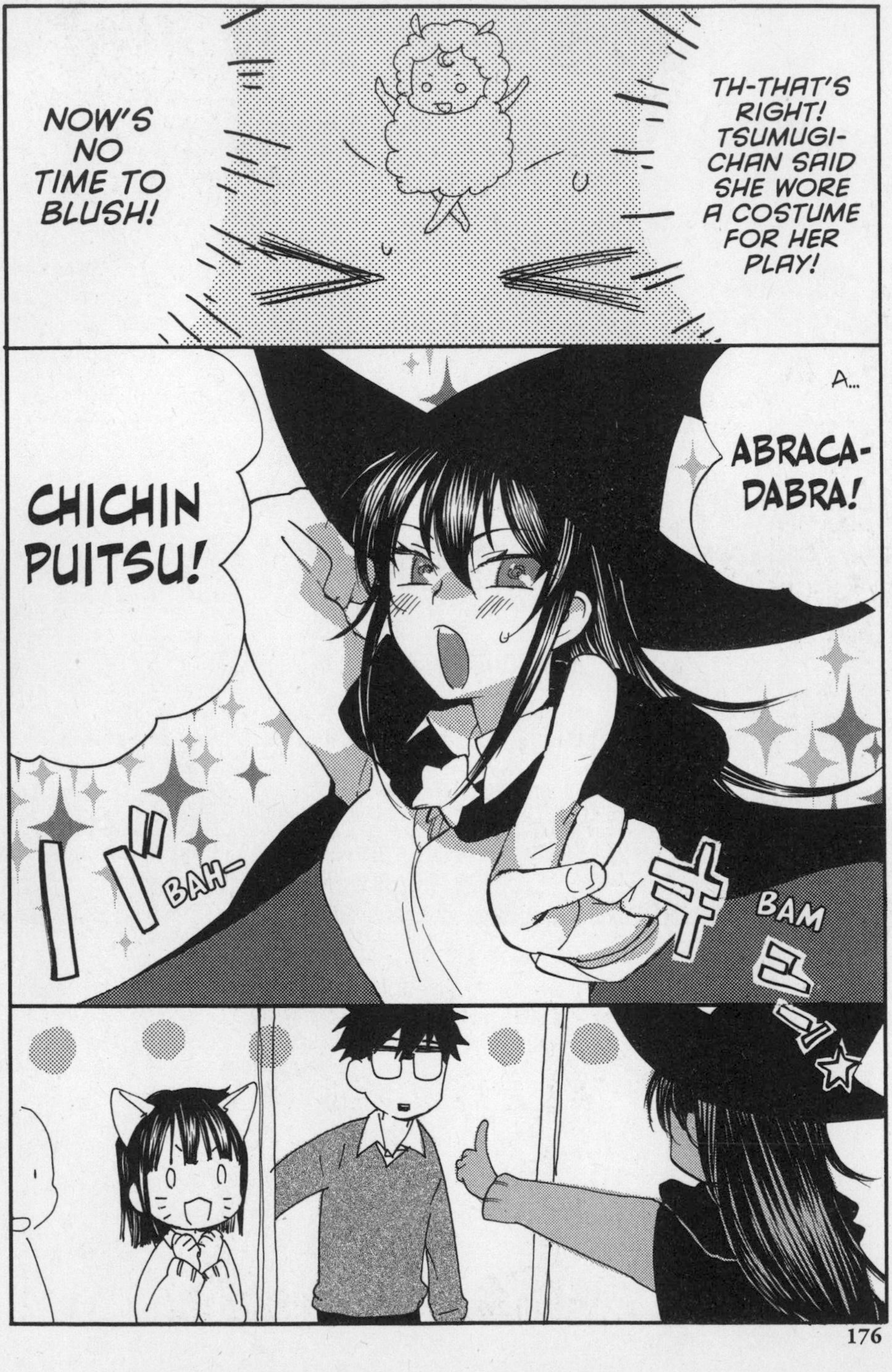
TH-THAT'S RIGHT! TSUMUGI-CHAN SAID SHE WORE A COSTUME FOR HER PLAY!
NOW'S NO TIME TO BLUSH!
A...
ABRACA-DABRA!
CHICHIN PUITSU!
BAM
BAH-

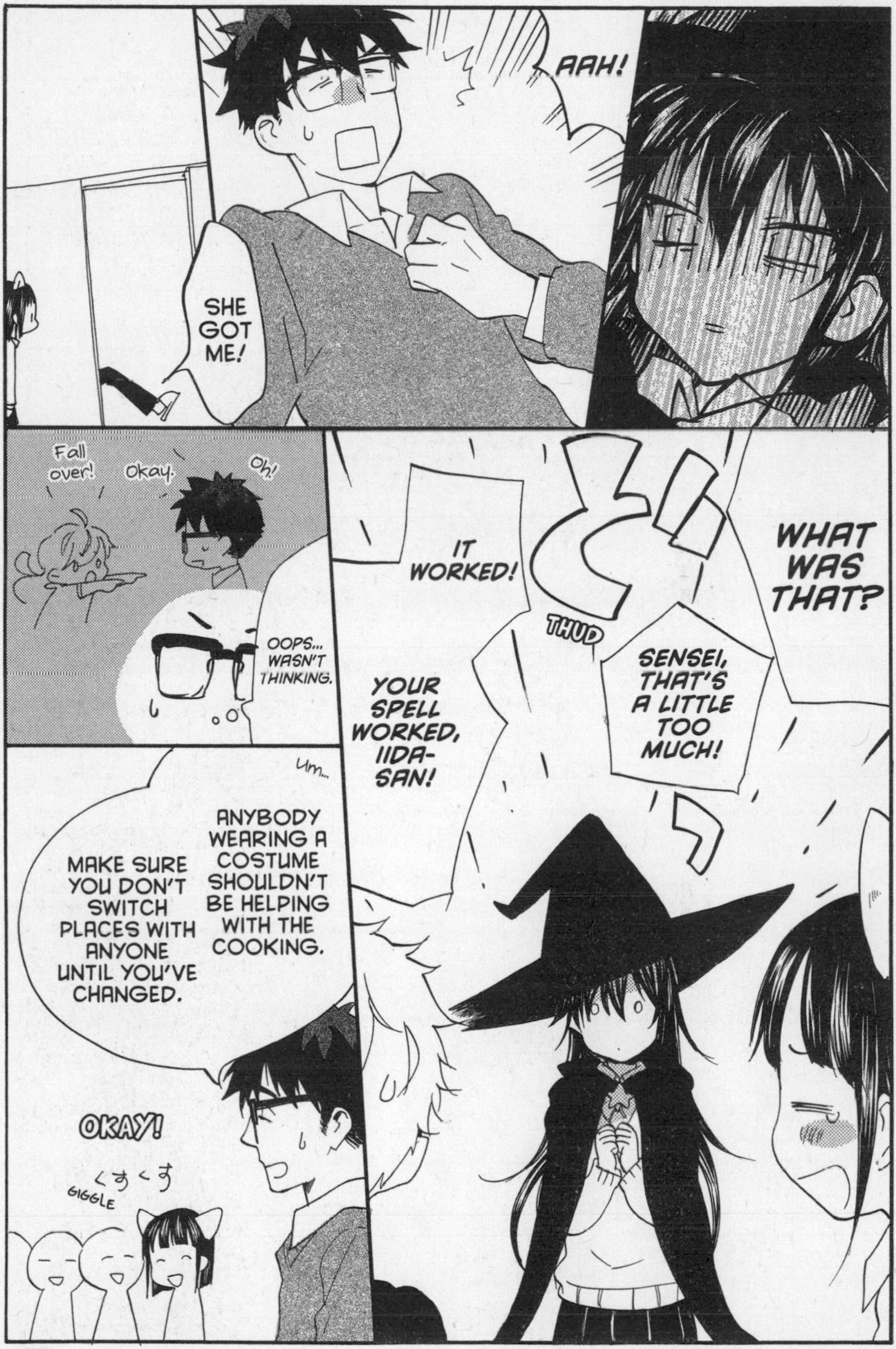
AAH!
SHE GOT ME!
WHAT WAS THAT?
SENSEI, THAT'S A LITTLE TOO MUCH!
IT WORKED!
THUD
YOUR SPELL WORKED, IIDA-SAN!
Oh!
Okay.
Fall over!
OOPS... WASN'T THINKING.
Um...
ANYBODY WEARING A COSTUME SHOULDN'T BE HELPING WITH THE COOKING.
MAKE SURE YOU DON'T SWITCH PLACES WITH ANYONE UNTIL YOU'VE CHANGED.
OKAY!
くすくす
GIGGLE

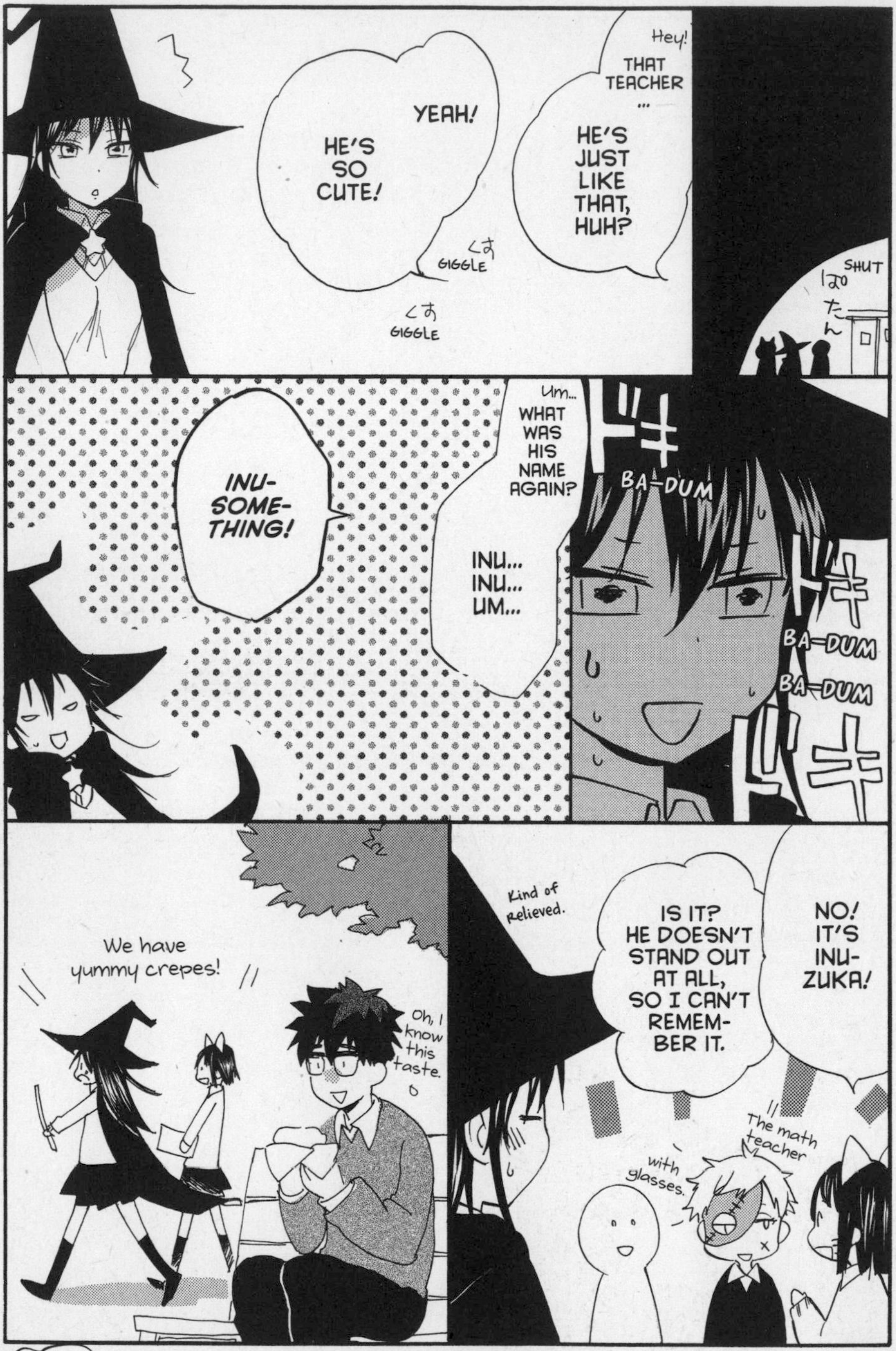
ぱたん
SHUT
Hey! THAT TEACHER ... HE'S JUST LIKE THAT, HUH?
YEAH! HE'S SO CUTE!
くす GIGGLE
くす GIGGLE
ドキ BA-DUM
ドキ BA-DUM
ドキ BA-DUM
Um... WHAT WAS HIS NAME AGAIN?
INU... INU... UM...
INU-SOMETHING!
NO! IT'S INU-ZUKA!
IS IT? HE DOESN'T STAND OUT AT ALL, SO I CAN'T REMEMBER IT.
Kind of relieved.
The math teacher with glasses.
Oh, I know this taste.
We have yummy crepes!

The End

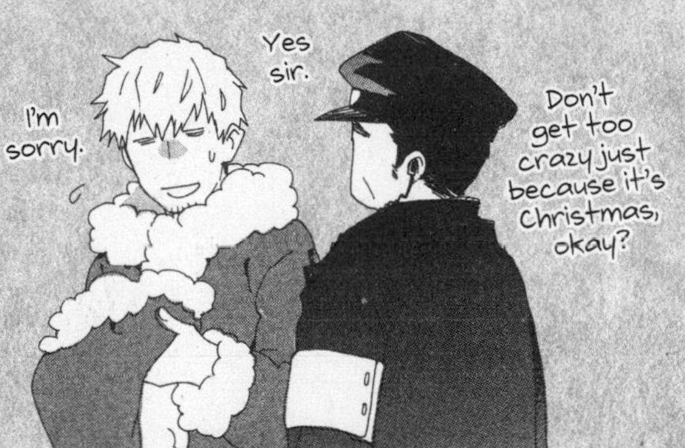
Don't get too crazy just because it's Christmas, okay?
Yes sir.
I'm sorry.

AFTERWORD

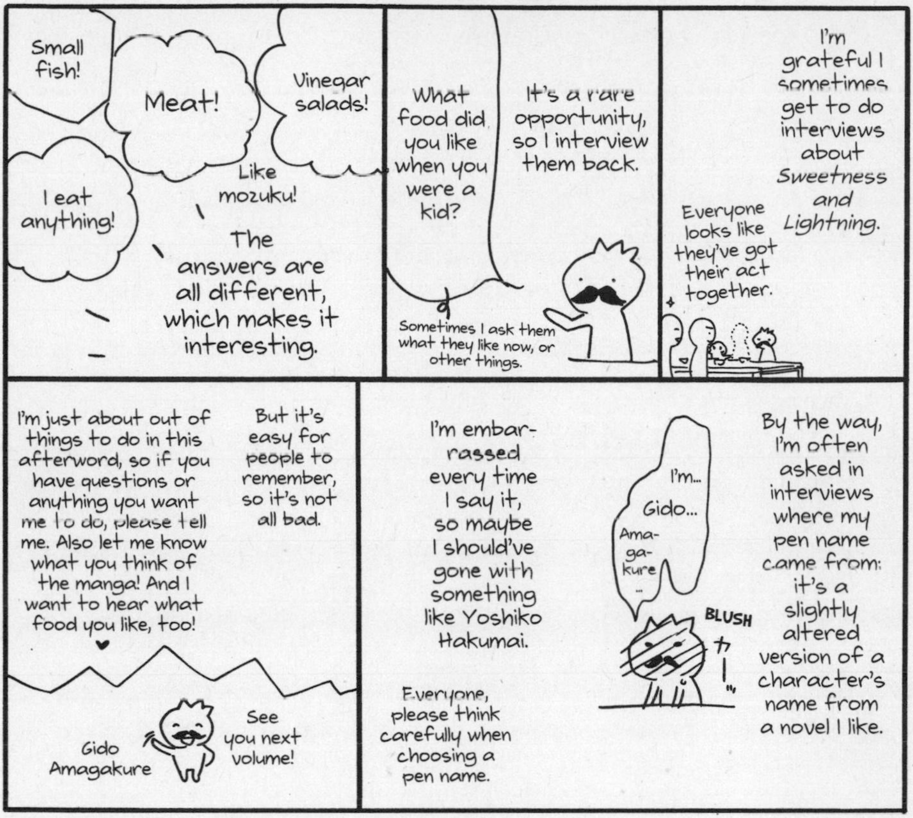
I'm grateful I sometimes get to do interviews about Sweetness and Lightning.
Everyone looks like they've got their act together.
It's a rare opportunity, so I interview them back.
What food did you like when you were a kid?
Sometimes I ask them what they like now, or other things.
Vinegar salads!
Meat!
Small fish!
I eat anything!
Like mozuku!
The answers are all different, which makes it interesting.
By the way, I'm often asked in interviews where my pen name came from: it's a slightly altered version of a character's name from a novel I like.
I'm... Gido... Amagakure...
BLUSH
I'm embarrassed every time I say it, so maybe I should've gone with something like Yoshiko Hakumai.
Everyone, please think carefully when choosing a pen name.
But it's easy for people to remember, so it's not all bad.
I'm just about out of things to do in this afterword, so if you have questions or anything you want me to do, please tell me. Also let me know what you think of the manga! And I want to hear what food you like, too! ♥
See you next volume!
Gido Amagakure

★ THANKS TO: ★

KOZ-tan, GON-chan, Tsuru-san, Wakayama-san, M-chan

My Family

T-Shiro-sama, K-Yama-sama, Jun Abe-sama,

Photo and Research Support: Tabegoto-ya, Norabou-sama

Cooking Advisor: Akari Taitou

& everyone else who helped me!!

Translation Notes

Shougayaki, page 4: Also known as Ginger Pork or Ginger-fried Pork. *Shougayaki* literally means "ginger-fried" and may be applied to other meats, but in most cases, pork is the primary meat used.

Cultural festival, page 40: A standard of most schools, the *bunka-sai,* or cultural festival, is a time where students have a fair on school grounds. Each class or various clubs often have displays and performances such as stage plays, dances, mini-restaurants or food stands, and art exhibits.

Kobachi, page 73: Literally, a small plate or planter. This term can refer to both the plate itself, or dishes that are served in small plates.

Kinpira gobou, page 73: Kinpira is a style of cooking that involves sautéing and simmering root vegetable in soy saunce and mirin (cooking saké). Gobou is also known as burdock root, the root of a plant belonging to the sunflower family. It has a taste that can be described as sweet and pungeant, and it is a popular ingredient in East Asian cooking.

Kintaro, page 85: A superhuman child from Japaneses folklore, also known as "Golden Boy."

Okonomiyaki, page 108: Also known as Japanese pizza. A savory pancake that is mixed and topped with a variety of items, usually depending on region and preference. Common toppings include pork belly, squid, cheese, aonori (seaweed flakes), katsuobushi (flakes from dried, fermented skipjack tuna), and mayonnaise.

Traditional Christmas foods in Japan, page 148: As Kotori mentions, chicken is one food that has become customary to eat in Japan for Christmas. Another traditional food is Christmas cake.

Chanmery, page 174: A non-acoholic, sparkling beverage created to allow children to celebrate with their families at Christmas parties. The name is a portmanteau of "Champagne" and "Merry Christmas." It typically comes in flavors such as Red, White, and Rosé.

Tsumugi's brought home a boy!

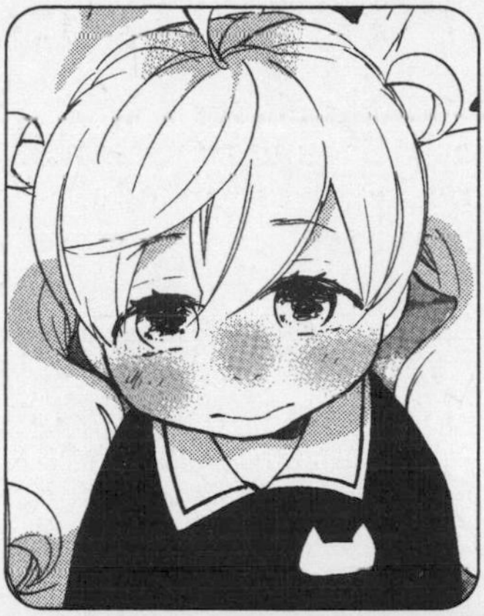

And it's that bratty kid Suguru!

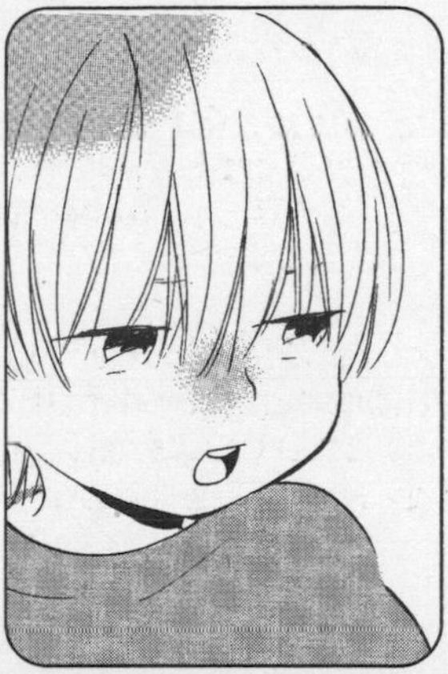

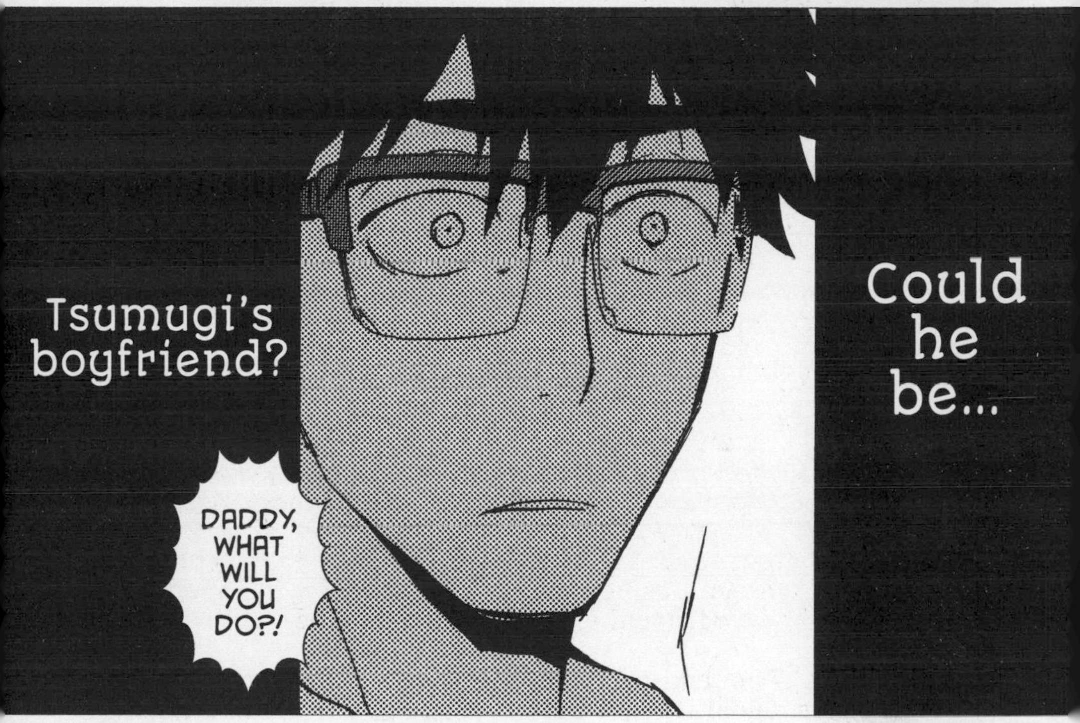
Could he be...
Tsumugi's boyfriend?
DADDY, WHAT WILL YOU DO?!

甘々と稲妻 Sweetness & Lightning 5

On Sale April 2017

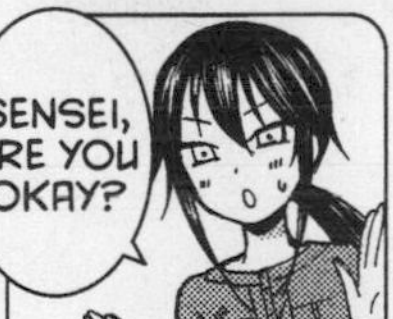
SENSEI, ARE YOU OKAY?

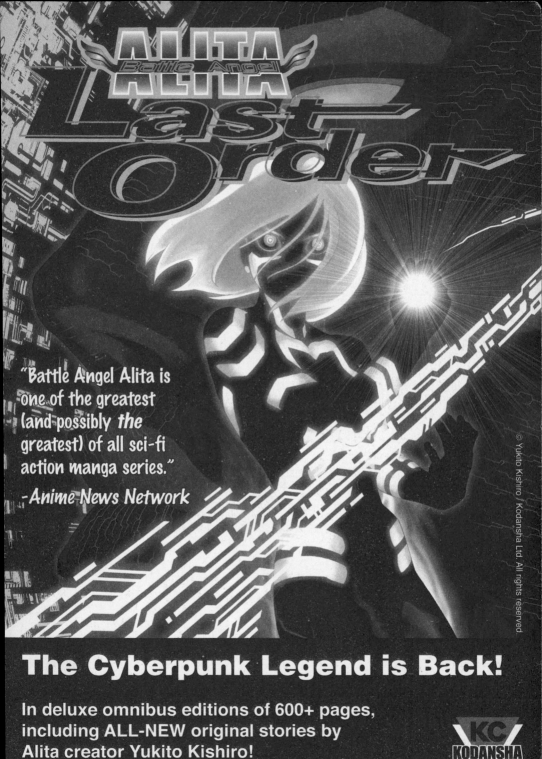

ALITA
Battle Angel
Last Order

"Battle Angel Alita is one of the greatest (and possibly *the* greatest) of all sci-fi action manga series."

-Anime News Network

The Cyberpunk Legend is Back!

In deluxe omnibus editions of 600+ pages, including ALL-NEW original stories by Alita creator Yukito Kishiro!

KC
KODANSHA
COMICS

NO.6

A PERFECT LIFE
IN A PERFECT CITY

For Shion, an elite student in the technologically sophisticated city No. 6, life is carefully choreographed. One fateful day, he takes a misstep, sheltering a fugitive his age from a typhoon. Helping this boy throws Shion's life down a path to discovering the appalling secrets behind the "perfection" of No. 6.

KC/
KODANSHA
COMICS

Say I Love You.

KC KODANSHA COMICS

Mei Tachibana has no friends — and says she doesn't need them!

But everything changes when she accidentally roundhouse kicks the most popular boy in school! However, Yamato Kurosawa isn't angry in the slightest— in fact, he thinks his ordinary life could use an unusual girl like Mei. But winning Mei's trust will be a tough task. How long will she refuse to say, "I love you"?

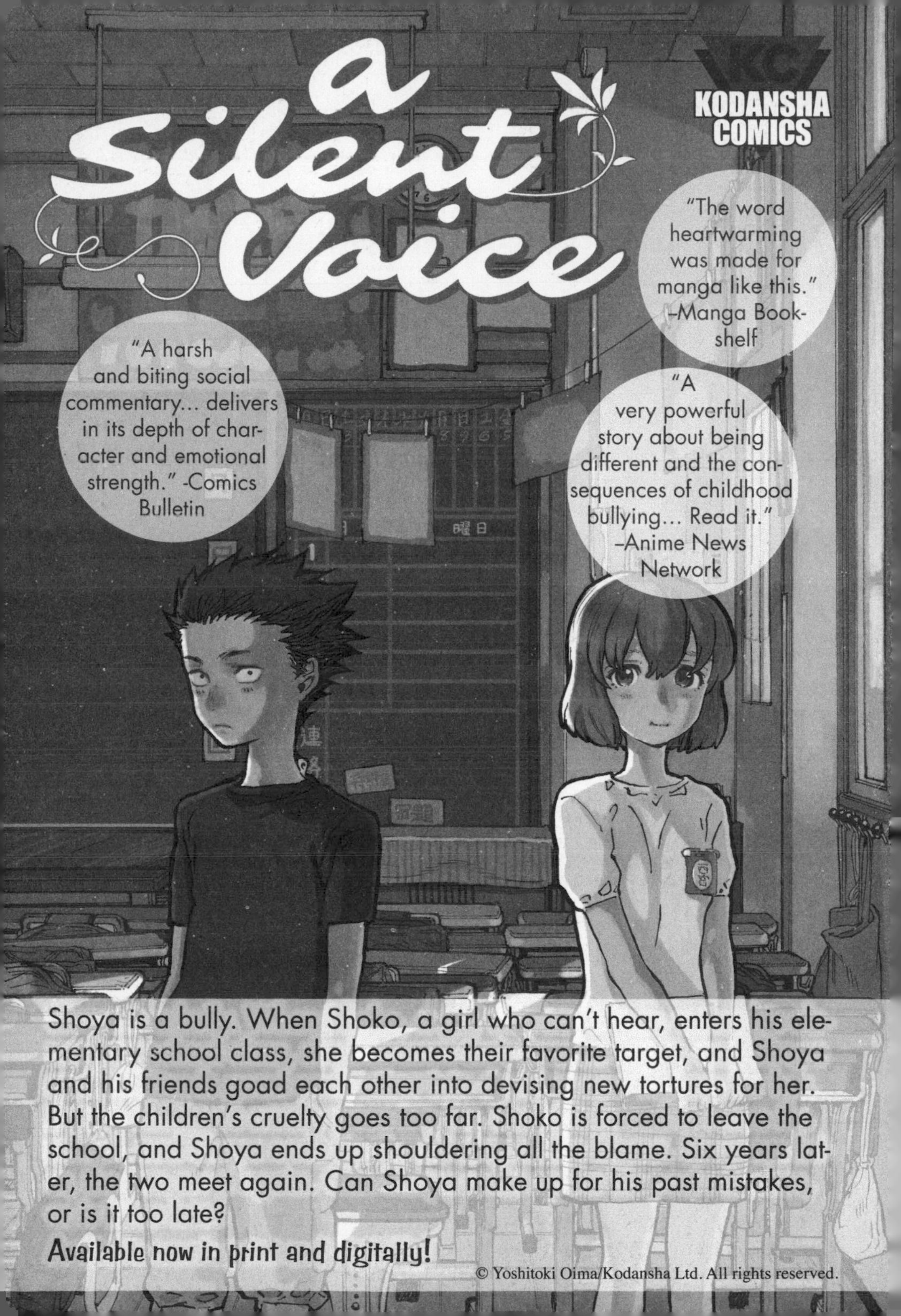
a Silent Voice
KODANSHA COMICS
"The word heartwarming was made for manga like this." –Manga Bookshelf
"A harsh and biting social commentary... delivers in its depth of character and emotional strength." -Comics Bulletin
"A very powerful story about being different and the consequences of childhood bullying... Read it." –Anime News Network
Shoya is a bully. When Shoko, a girl who can't hear, enters his elementary school class, she becomes their favorite target, and Shoya and his friends goad each other into devising new tortures for her. But the children's cruelty goes too far. Shoko is forced to leave the school, and Shoya ends up shouldering all the blame. Six years later, the two meet again. Can Shoya make up for his past mistakes, or is it too late?
Available now in print and digitally!
© Yoshitoki Oima/Kodansha Ltd. All rights reserved.

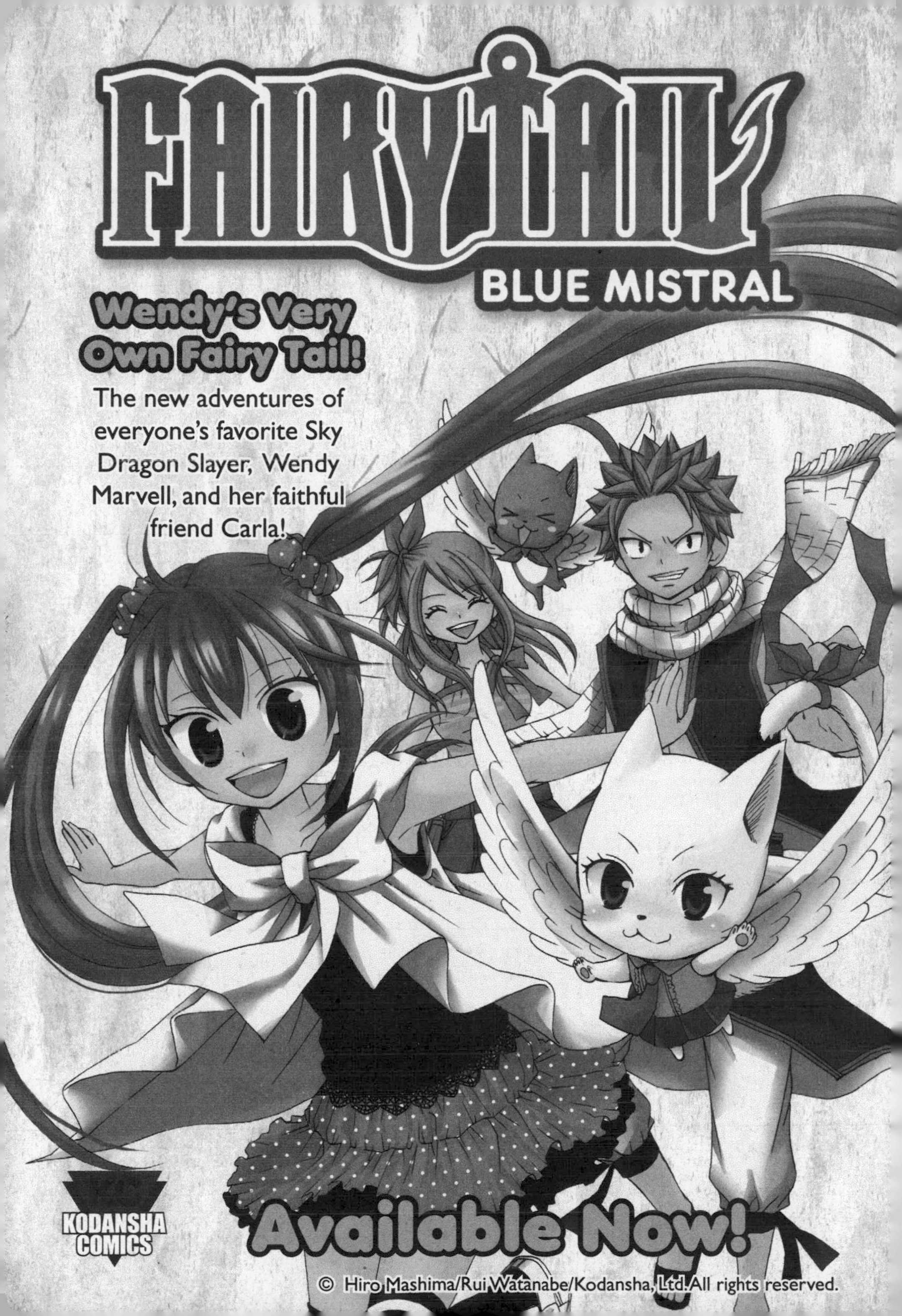
FAIRY TAIL
BLUE MISTRAL
Wendy's Very Own Fairy Tail!
The new adventures of everyone's favorite Sky Dragon Slayer, Wendy Marvell, and her faithful friend Carla!
KODANSHA COMICS
Available Now!
© Hiro Mashima/Rui Watanabe/Kodansha, Ltd. All rights reserved.

Maria
THE VIRGIN WITCH

PURITY AND POWER

As a war to determine the rightful ruler of medieval France ravages the land, the witch Maria decides she will not stand idly by as men kill each other in the name of God and glory. Using her powerful magic, she summons various beasts and demons —even going as far as using a succubus to seduce soldiers into sub-mission under the veil of night— all to stop the needless slaughter. However, after the Arch-angel Michael puts an end to her meddling, he curses her to lose her powers if she ever gives up her virginity. Will she forgo the forbidden fruit of adulthood in order to bring an end to the merciless machine of war?
Available now in print and digitally!

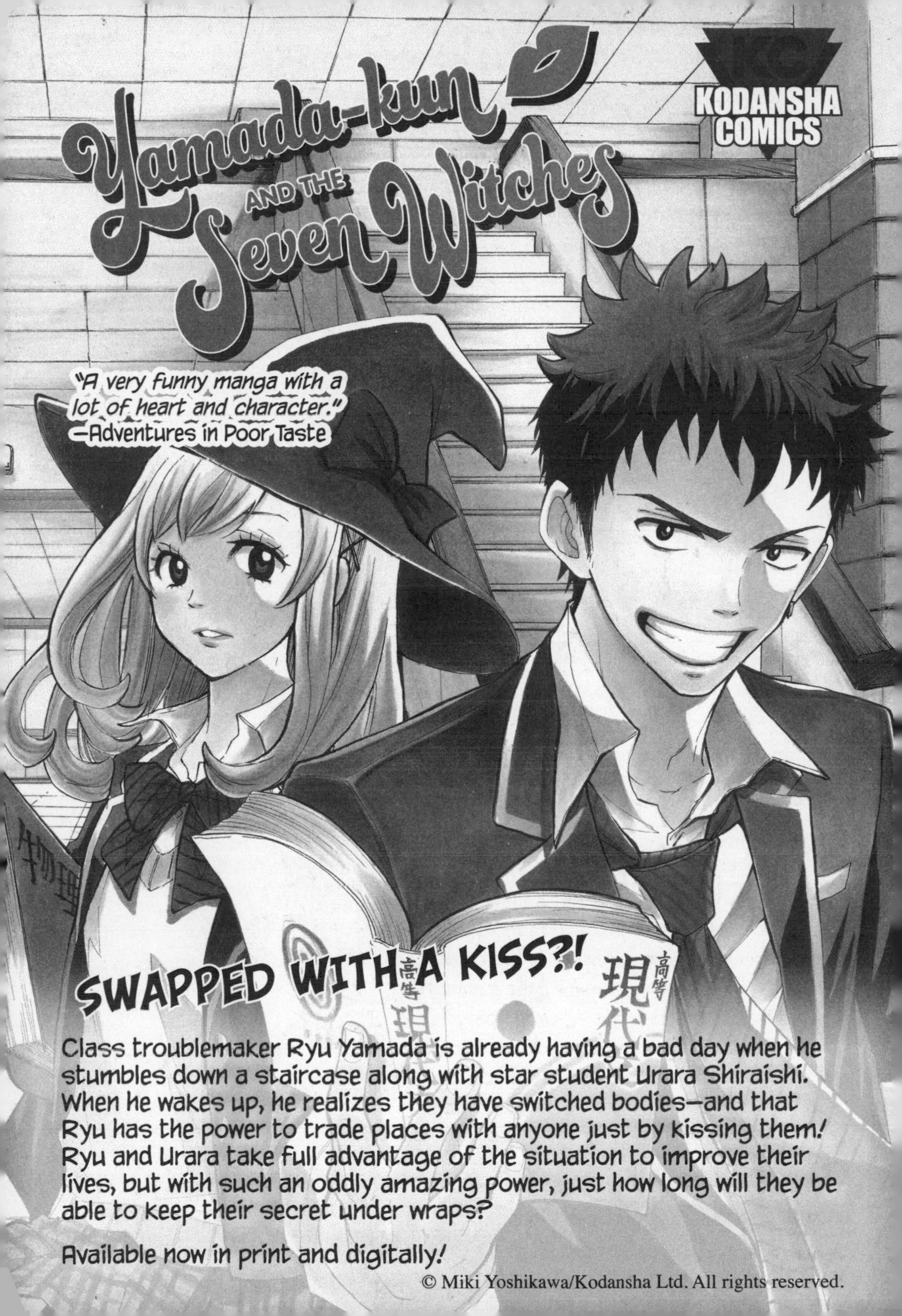
KODANSHA COMICS
Yamada-kun AND THE Seven Witches
"A very funny manga with a lot of heart and character."
—Adventures in Poor Taste
SWAPPED WITH A KISS?!
Class troublemaker Ryu Yamada is already having a bad day when he stumbles down a staircase along with star student Urara Shiraishi. When he wakes up, he realizes they have switched bodies—and that Ryu has the power to trade places with anyone just by kissing them! Ryu and Urara take full advantage of the situation to improve their lives, but with such an oddly amazing power, just how long will they be able to keep their secret under wraps?
Available now in print and digitally!
© Miki Yoshikawa/Kodansha Ltd. All rights reserved.

A Kodansha Comics Trade Paperback Original.

Sweetness & Lightning volume 4 copyright © 2015 Gido Amagakure
English translation copyright © 2017 Gido Amagakure

All rights reserved.

Published in the United States by Kodansha Comics,
an imprint of Kodansha USA Publishing, LLC, New York.

Publication rights for this English edition arranged through Kodansha Ltd.,
Tokyo.

First published in Japan in 2015 by Kodansha Ltd., Tokyo, as *Ama-ama to Inadzuma* volume 4.

ISBN 978-1-63236-400-5

Printed in the United States of America.

www.kodanshacomics.com

9 8 7 6 5 4 3 2 1

Translation: Adam Lensenmayer
Lettering: Lys Blakeslee
Editing: Ajani Oloye
Kodansha Comics edition cover design: Phil Balsman